CIMA

MANAGEMENT

PAPER F2

FINANCIAL MANAGEMENT

PRACTICE & REVISION KIT

This Kit is for exams in 2012.

In this Kit we:

- Discuss the **best strategies** for revising and taking your F2 exam

- Show you how to be well prepared for the **2012 exams**

- Give you **lots of great guidance** on tackling questions

- Demonstrate how you can **build your own exams**

- Provide you with **three** mock exams

FOR EXAMS IN 2012

BPP LEARNING MEDIA

First edition January 2010
Second edition July 2010
Third edition January 2011

Fourth edition January 2012

ISBN 9781 4453 8091 9
eISBN 9781 4453 7647 9
(Previous ISBN 9780 7517 9457 1)

British Library Cataloguing-in-Publication Data
A catalogue record for this book
is available from the British Library

Published by

BPP Learning Media Ltd
BPP House, Aldine Place
London W12 8AA

www.bpp.com/learningmedia

Printed in the United Kingdom

Your learning materials, published by BPP
Learning Media Ltd, are printed on paper sourced
from sustainable, managed forests.

We are grateful to the Chartered Institute of
Management Accountants for permission to
reproduce past examination questions. The
answers to past examination questions have been
prepared by BPP Learning Media Ltd.

Contents

Page

Finding questions and using the Practice and Revision Kit

Question index   iv
Topic index   vii
Using your BPP Learning Media Practice and Revision Kit   ix

Passing F2

Revising F2   x
Passing the F2 exam   xi
The exam paper   xiii
What the examiner means   xvii

Planning your question practice

BPP's question plan   xviii
Build your own exams   xix

Questions and answers

Questions   3
Answers   79

Exam practice

Mock exam 1
- Questions   221
- Plan of attack   231
- Answers   232

Mock exam 2 (September 2011 resit examination)
- Questions   243
- Plan of attack   255
- Answers   256

Mock exam 3 (November 2011 examination)
- Questions   271
- Plan of attack   285
- Answers   286

Mathematical tables   303

Review form

Question index

The headings in this checklist/index indicate the main topics of questions, but questions often cover several different topics.

Preparation questions, listed in italics, provide you with a firm foundation for attempts at exam-standard questions.

Questions set under the old syllabus's *Financial Reporting (FR)* and *Financial Analysis (FA)* are included because their style and content are similar to those that appear in the Paper F2 exam.

	Marks	Time allocation Mins	Page number Question	Answer
Part A: Issues in recognition and measurement				
Substance over form and revenue recognition				
1 ETH (FA 11/09)	10	18	3	79
Financial instruments				
2 AZG (FA 5/08)	10	18	3	79
3 RP (Pilot paper)	10	18	4	80
4 DG (FA 11/09)	10	18	4	81
5 BCL (11/10)	10	18	5	82
6 MNB (3/11)	10	18	5	84
7 QWE (5/11)	10	18	6	85
Employee benefits				
8 *Preparation question: Defined benefit scheme*	–	–	6	86
9 BGA (FA 11/07)	10	18	8	87
10 EAU (5/11)	10	18	8	88
Asset valuation and changing prices				
11 Leisure (FR, 5/01, amended)	25	45	9	89
12 BG (Pilot paper)	10	18	10	90
Share-based payment				
13 JKL (3/11)	10	18	10	91
14 LBP (11/10)	10	18	11	92
Part B: Group financial statements				
Consolidated financial statements				
15 *Preparation question: Simple consolidation*	–	–	12	94
16 ABC and DEF (FA 11/05, amended)	10	18	13	96
17 AAY (FA 5/08)	10	18	14	96
18 DNT (FA 11/08)	10	18	15	98
19 MX (5/10)	10	18	15	99
20 AB Group (11/10)	10	18	16	100
21 ERT (3/11)	25	45	16	102
Associates and joint ventures				
22 *Preparation question: Joint venture*	–	–	18	105
23 JKA (Pilot paper)	10	18	18	106
24 AJ (FA 5/05)	25	45	19	107
25 ST (FA 5/06)	10	18	21	109
26 AB (Pilot paper)	10	18	21	110
27 DF (5/10)	10	18	22	111
28 PQ (11/09, amended)	10	18	23	113

		Time allocation	Page number	
	Marks	Mins	Question	Answer

Part C: More complex group topics

Changes in group structures and more complex group structures

29 Preparation question: Part disposal	–	–	24	114
30 Preparation question: 'D' shaped group statement of financial position	–	–	26	116
31 Preparation question: 'D' shaped group income statement	–	–	27	117
32 Big Group	30	54	28	118
33 AZ (FA 5/06)	25	45	29	121
34 RW (FA 5/05)	10	18	30	123
35 AD (FA 11/06)	25	45	31	125
36 RBE (5/11)	10	18	32	128
37 SOT Group (5/10)	25	45	33	129
38 ROB Group (11/10)	25	45	34	132

Foreign currency translation

39 Preparation question: Foreign operations	–	–	35	135
40 Little (FA Pilot paper)	25	45	36	137
41 Small (FR, 5/03, amended)	25	45	38	139
42 Home group (FA 11/06)	10	18	39	142
43 ABC Group (5/11)	25	45	40	143

Group statements of cash flows

44 AH Group (FA 11/05)	25	45	41	146
45 EAG Group (FA 5/08)	25	45	42	149
46 MIC (Pilot paper)	25	45	44	152
47 LKL (FA 11/09, amended)	25	45	45	156

Part D: Analysis and interpretation of financial accounts

Ratio and trend analysis

48 LOP (11/10)	10	18	47	160
49 FGH Cash (3/11)	10	18	47	162
50 BCA (FA 11/09, amended)	25	45	48	163
51 BZJ (FA 5/06)	25	45	49	164
52 ABC (FA 5/06)	25	45	51	168
53 AXZ (FA 11/06)	25	45	52	170
54 DPC (FA 11/07)	25	45	53	172
55 FJK (FA 5/08)	25	45	55	175
56 BHG (FA 5/08)	25	45	56	178
57 Non-executive (FA 11/08)	25	45	57	180
58 XYZ (Pilot paper)	25	45	58	182
59 KER (5/10)	25	45	59	184
60 GD (11/10)	25	45	60	186
61 DFG (3/11)	25	45	62	189
62 CVB (5/11)	25	45	63	192

	Marks	Time allocation Mins	Page number Question	Page number Answer
Earnings per share				
63 JKL (FA Pilot paper)	10	18	64	194
64 CB (FA 5/05)	10	18	65	195
65 EPS ratio (FA 11/07)	10	18	66	196
66 AGZ (FA 11/08)	10	18	66	197
67 CSA (5/10)	10	18	66	198
Segment reporting				
68 *Preparation question: Operating segments*	–	–	67	200
69 STV (FA 11/05)	25	45	68	201
70 RG (FA 11/09, amended)	25	45	69	203
71 FGH (5/11)	10	18	70	206

Part E: Developments in external reporting

	Marks	Time allocation Mins	Page number Question	Page number Answer
Developments in financial reporting				
72 MNO (FA 5/06)	10	18	71	207
73 NGO (FA 5/09, amended)	25	45	71	208
Developments in non-financial reporting				
74 Environmental disclosure (Pilot paper)	10	18	73	211
75 FW (FA 5/05)	25	45	73	212
76 Intellectual capital (11/08)	10	18	74	214
77 Staff resource (11/10)	10	18	74	215
78 Service and knowledge (3/11)	10	18	75	217

Mock exam 1
Questions 79-85

Mock exam 2 (September 2011 resit examination)
Questions 86-92

Mock exam 3 (November 2011 examination)
Questions 93-99

Planning your question practice
Our guidance from page xviii shows you how to organise your question practice, either by attempting questions from each syllabus area or by **building your own exams** – tackling questions as a series of practice exams.

Topic index

Listed below are the key Paper F2 syllabus topics and the numbers of the questions in this Kit covering those topics.

If you need to concentrate your practice and revision on certain topics or if you want to attempt all available questions that refer to a particular subject you will find this index useful.

Syllabus topic	Question numbers
Actuarial deficits and surpluses	8-10
Asset valuation (alternative approaches to)	11-12
Consolidation	
• Acquisitions	15-21
• Associates	15, 20, 24, 26, 27, 28
• Income statement	15, 20, 25, 28
• Statement of comprehensive income	26
• Statement of changes in equity	15, 17
• Statement of financial position	21, 23, 24
• Changes in group structures	29, 33, 34, 36-38
• Foreign currency translation	39-43
• Group statement of cash flows	44–47
• Joint ventures	22-23
• Proportionate consolidation method	22-23
• More complex structures	30-32, 35
Earnings per share	63-67
Environmental issues	74–75
Financial instruments	2-7
Global Reporting Initiative	75
Human resource accounting	76-78
Hyperinflation	11
Intellectual capital	76-78
IAS 7	44–47
IAS 19	8-10, 13
IAS 21	1, 39-43
IAS 27	15-47
IAS 28	15, 20, 24, 26, 27, 28
IAS 31	22-23
IAS 32	4, 7
IAS 33	57–61
IAS 37	75
IAS 39	2-7
IFRS 2	13-14
IFRS 3	15-47
IFRS 8	68-71
Interpretation of financial statements	48-62
Operating and financial review	72
Pension schemes	8-10, 13

Syllabus topic	Question numbers
Ratio analysis	48-62
Retirement benefits	8-10, 13
Segment analysis	68-71
Substance over form	1
US GAAP/IFRS	73

Using your BPP Learning Media Practice and Revision Kit

Tackling revision and the exam

You can significantly improve your chances of passing by tackling revision and the exam in the right ways. Our advice is based on feedback from CIMA. We focus on Paper F2; we discuss revising the syllabus, what to do (and what not to do) in the exam, how to approach different types of question and ways of obtaining easy marks.

Selecting questions

We provide signposts to help you plan your revision.

- A full **question index**
- A **topic index**, listing all the questions that cover key topics, so that you can locate the questions that provide practice on these topics, and see the different ways in which they might be examined
- **BPP's question plan**, highlighting the most important questions
- **Build your own exams**, showing you how you can practise questions in a series of exams

Making the most of question practice

We realise that you need more than questions and model answers to get the most from your question practice.

- Our **Top tips** provide essential advice on tackling questions and presenting answers
- We show you how you can pick up **Easy marks** on questions, as picking up all readily available marks can make the difference between passing and failing
- We include **marking guides** to show you what the examiner rewards
- We summarise **Examiner's comments** to show you how students coped with the questions
- We refer to the **BPP 2011 Study Text** for detailed coverage of the topics covered in each question

Attempting mock exams

There are three mock exams that provide practice at coping with the pressures of the exam day. We strongly recommend that you attempt them under exam conditions, as they reflect the question styles and syllabus coverage of the exam. To help you get the most out of doing these exams, we provide guidance on how you should have approached the whole exam.

Our other products

BPP Learning Media also offers these products for practising and revising the F2 exam:

Passcards	Summarising what you should know in visual, easy to remember, form
Success CDs	Covering the vital elements of the F2 syllabus in less than 90 minutes and also containing exam hints to help you fine tune your strategy
i-Pass	Providing computer-based testing in a variety of formats, ideal for self-assessment
Interactive Passcards	Allowing you to learn actively with a clear visual format summarising what you must know

You can purchase these products by visiting www.bpp.com/learningmedia

Revising F2

The F2 exam

This will be a time-pressured exam that requires you to demonstrate knowledge as much as application. It is very important that you do not concentrate completely on the calculations at the expense of fully understanding the underlying issues involved.

Topics to revise

You need to be comfortable with **all areas of the syllabus** as all questions are compulsory. Question spotting will absolutely **not work** on this paper. It is better to go into the exam knowing a reasonable amount about most of the syllabus rather than concentrating on a few topics.

Group financial statements

- Preparation of consolidated financial statements (including consolidated statements of cash flows)
- Treatment of subsidiaries
- Treatment of associates
- Treatment of joint ventures
- Foreign currency translation

Issues in recognition and measurement

- Asset valuation
- Substance over form and revenue recognition
- Financial instruments
- Employee benefits
- Share based payments

Analysis and interpretation of financial accounts

- Ratios and their analysis
- Earnings per share
- Segment reporting

Developments in external reporting

- Financial reporting including environmental provisions
- Non-financial reporting including human resource accounting
- Major differences between IFRS and US GAAP

Question practice

Question practice under timed conditions is essential, so that you can get used to the pressures of answering exam questions in **limited time** and practise not only the key techniques but allocating your time between different requirements in each question. It's particularly important to do questions from both sections of the paper in full to see how the numerical and written elements balance in longer questions.

General exam support from BPP Learning Media

BPP Learning Media is committed to giving you the best possible support in your quest for exam success. With this in mind, we have produced **guidance** on how to revise and techniques you can apply to **improve your chances of passing** the exam. This guidance can be found on the BPP Learning Media web site at the following link:

www.bpp.com/cima/examtips/Revising-for-CIMA-exams.doc

A paper copy of this guidance is available by emailing learningmedia@bpp.com

As well as written guidance, an excellent presentation entitled '**Exam technique – advice from the experts at BPP Learning Media**' is available at the following link:

www.bpp.com/learningmedia/cima/cimaexamskills/player.html

Passing the F2 exam

Avoiding weaknesses

You will enhance your chances significantly if you ensure you avoid these mistakes:

- Little or no time spent practising questions
- Failure to read the question
- Lack of application of knowledge to question asked
- Failure to show clear workings
- Confusion of question details from different questions
- Time management – spending excessive time on strong areas or too long on areas you struggle with
- Poor English, structure and presentation
- Poor knowledge of basic concepts and calculations (basic consolidation workings, ratios)

Using the reading time

We recommend you spend the reading time looking at the compulsory Section B questions and planning your answers to these. Then look through the shorter Section A questions.

Choosing which questions to answer first

Choosing which questions to answer first is a matter of preference. You should practise different methods during your revision to decide which one suits you best.

Having read through the questions in Section B during the reading time you might feel quite confident about them. One option is to do these questions first. An alternative method is to do them in the paper order, that is, Section A and then Section B. The **most important** thing to remember is to spend **no longer** than 90 minutes on Section A, and 90 minutes on Section B!

Numerical questions

You are likely to see calculation questions covering:

- Consolidated financial statements (including consolidated statements of cash flows)
- Complex groups
- Ratio analysis
- Pensions, financial instruments and share-based payments
- Earnings per share

Even if you do make a mistake on the numbers, you will gain credit for the correct approach on these questions. A brief narrative explaining your approach to tricky calculations will help the marker.

You can expect to come across some very difficult things in the questions. You must learn to move on and do as much of the questions as possible.

Present your numbers neatly in a table format with key numbers underlined and clear workings.

Discussion questions

These often focus on interpretation of financial statements. As well as the limitations of your calculations, you should expect to discuss their results in the context of the organisation's wider situation and strategy. As well as discussing the ratios, be prepared also to bring relevant knowledge from other management level papers such as the risks affecting performance.

Remember that strategies you recommend must be suitable and feasible for the organisation, and acceptable to shareholders, managers and perhaps other stakeholders as well.

One important aspect of time allocation is not to spend excessive time on the calculations at the expense of the discussion parts. You need to be strict with yourself as you won't at this level see a question that purely consists of calculations.

Remember that the marking schemes for discussion questions will be fairly general, and you will gain credit for all relevant points. Good discussion focused on the question scenario, with evaluation of pros and cons supported by examples, will score well.

Gaining the easy marks

There will definitely be easy marks in some part of each question. However when you're using techniques such as ratio and trend analysis, you will generally be expected to comment on your calculations, so knowledge of the limitations of each technique will earn you marks.

There may be some discussion parts, such as the treatment of transactions according to IFRS, which are straightforward provided you revise those areas.

In the end the easiest marks may be gained (or avoided being lost) through following certain basic techniques:

- Setting out calculations and proformas clearly

- Clearly labelling the points you make in discussions so that the marker can identify them all rather than getting lost in the detail

- Providing answers in the form requested, particularly using report format if asked for and giving recommendations if required

The exam paper

Format of the paper

		Number of marks
Section A:	Five compulsory medium answer questions, each worth five marks. Short scenarios may be given, to which some or all questions relate	50
Section B:	One or two compulsory questions. Short scenarios may be given to which question relate.	50
		100

Time allowed: 3 hours, plus 20 minutes reading time

CIMA guidance

CIMA has stated that credit will be given for focusing on the right principles and making practical evaluations and recommendations in a variety of different business scenarios, including manufacturing, retailing and financial services.

A likely weakness of answers is excessive focus on details. Plausible alternative answers could be given to many questions, so model answers should not be regarded as all-inclusive.

Numerical content

The paper is likely to have about a 50% numerical content, mainly in questions relating to *Group financial statements* and *Analysis and interpretation of financial accounts.*

Questions may also include the interpretation of data.

Breadth of question coverage

Questions in *both* sections of the paper may cover more than one syllabus area.

Knowledge from other syllabuses

Candidates should also use their knowledge from other Management level papers. One aim of this paper is to prepare candidates for the Strategic level papers.

November 2011

Section A

1   Joint venture using proportionate consolidation; discussion of equity method.

2   Sale and repurchase of land; appropriate treatment of an equity's relationship with another entity.

3   Basic and diluted earnings per share calculation and explanation of why DEPS is needed.

4   Financial instruments; employee benefits.

5   Progress towards convergence.

Section B

6   Consolidated statement of comprehensive income with piecemeal acquisition and associate.

7   Financial analysis; limitations of ratio analysis.

This paper is Mock Exam 3 in this Kit

September 2011 resit exam

Section A

1　Calculation of key figures for the consolidated statement of financial position including a piecemeal acquisition.

2　Journal entries for an available for sale financial asset, discussion of accounting for a derivative, and journal entries for an equity-settled share-based payment.

3　Discussion of voluntary narrative disclosures.

4　Discussion of the substance of a consignment inventory arrangement and discussion of the drawbacks of using historical cost financial statements in times of high inflation.

5　Discussion of the comparability of four given ratios within a sector and international comparison.

Section B

6　Consolidated statement of cash flows including the acquisition of a subsidiary during the year.

7　Analysis of performance and position in the context of a loan application and discussion and calculation of earnings per share including a bonus issue.

This paper is Mock Exam 2 in this Kit

May 2011

Section A

1　Calculation of actuarial gains and losses on defined benefit pension scheme and accounting entries for a cash-settled share-based payment.

2　Consolidated statement of changes in equity including piecemeal acquisition.

3　Discussion of segment reporting.

4　Explanation and illustration of accounting treatment of a convertible bond and cumulative preference shares.

5　Discussion of voluntary narrative disclosures.

Section B

6　Consolidated statement of comprehensive income including a foreign subsidiary and an associate.

7　Analysis of performance and position for a potential investor in a company.

March 2011 resit exam

Section A

1　Consolidated income statement with a subsidiary and mid-year acquisition of an associate, including fair value and intragroup trading adjustments.

2　Discussion of human resource accounting.

3　Consolidated income statement with subsidiary and mid-year acquisition of an associate, including fair value and intragroup trading adjustments.

4　Explanation and illustration of accounting treatment of a derivative (forward contract).

5　Analysis of ratios provided for two potential takeover targets.

Section B

6　Consolidated statement of financial position with piecemeal acquisition during the accounting period.

7   Analysis of performance and position in the context of a loan application.

November 2010

Section A

1   Share-based payment – calculations, journal entries, and explanation of the recognition and measurement principles.

2   Discussion of human resource accounting.

3   Consolidated income statement with subsidiary and mid-year acquisition of an associate, including fair value and intragroup trading adjustments.

4   Explanation and illustration of accounting treatment of a derivative (forward contract).

5   Analysis of ratios provided for two potential takeover targets.

Section B

6   Consolidated statement of financial position with piecemeal acquisition during the accounting period.

7   Analysis of performance and position in the context of a loan application.

May 2010

Section A

1   Explanation of treatment of various investments in consolidated financial statements.
2   Discussion of treatment of a consignment inventory arrangement and accounting entries for share-based payment transaction.
3   Basic and diluted earnings per share calculations.
4   Calculation of goodwill, retained earnings and non-controlling interest figures for a consolidated statement of financial position.
5   Report on the progress of the convergence project.

Section B

6   Consolidated statement of comprehensive income with a mid-year acquisition of a subsidiary and a partial disposal of an investment in a subsidiary, with the remaining investment being an associate.
7   Analysis of financial performance and position of a company for an individual investor and a discussion of differences in accounting policies and estimates that can affect comparability between entities.

The examiner commented that the new exam format appeared to cause few problems and that the quality of written answers had generally improved compared with examinations set under the previous syllabus. The new technical areas, namely non-controlling interest on acquisition at fair value, share-based payments and the new disposal calculations were handled well.

The main concern highlighted was the inability of candidates to apply their consolidation knowledge to group income statements. It seems that candidates are rote learning consolidations as many were preparing workings that are only required if preparing a statement of financial position. This wastes valuable time.

The examiner also pointed out how the syllabus weighting and the format of the paper combine – approximately 35% of the exam will be weighted towards group accounts and the same for financial analysis. These areas are normally the focus of the 25 mark questions so it should not surprise candidates that both areas may also appear in Section A.

Two main recommendations were made relating to exam technique:

- Candidates are urged to show clear workings, including the figures used in ratio calculation

- The testing of higher skills requires that discussion and evaluation are core elements in the papers so candidates should prepare for this.

Specimen exam paper

Section A

1 Consolidated statement of comprehensive income with subsidiary and associate, including adjustment for actuarial gains and losses on pension scheme.
2 Discussion of arguments against voluntary disclosure of environmental information.
3 Convertible bonds and share-based payment.
4 Consolidated statement of financial position with a jointly controlled entity and adjustment for a sale and repurchase transaction.
5 Discussion of the defects of historical cost accounting and explanation of three current cost accounting adjustments.

Section B

6 Consolidated statement of cash flows including the acquisition of a subsidiary.
7 Analysis of financial information, comparing two potential takeover targets and discussion of the limitations of this type of analysis.

What the examiner means

The table below has been prepared by CIMA to help you interpret exam questions.

Learning objective	Verbs used	Definition	Examples in the Kit
1 Knowledge			
What you are expected to know	• List	• Make a list of	
	• State	• Express, fully or clearly, the details of/facts of	28
	• Define	• Give the exact meaning of	
2 Comprehension			
What you are expected to understand	• Describe	• Communicate the key features of	23
	• Distinguish	• Highlight the differences between	
	• Explain	• Make clear or intelligible/state the meaning or purpose of	31
	• Identify	• Recognise, establish or select after consideration	16
	• Illustrate	• Use an example to describe or explain something	
3 Application			
How you are expected to apply your knowledge	• Apply	• Put to practical use	
	• Calculate/compute	• Ascertain or reckon mathematically	4
	• Demonstrate	• Prove the certainty or exhibit by practical means	
	• Prepare	• Make or get ready for use	5
	• Reconcile	• Make or prove consistent/ compatible	
	• Solve	• Find an answer to	
	• Tabulate	• Arrange in a table	
4 Analysis			
How you are expected to analyse the detail of what you have learned	• Analyse	• Examine in detail the structure of	10
	• Categorise	• Place into a defined class or division	
	• Compare and contrast	• Show the similarities and/or differences between	7
	• Construct	• Build up or complete	
	• Discuss	• Examine in detail by argument	
	• Interpret	• Translate into intelligible or familiar terms	43
	• Prioritise	• Place in order of priority or sequence for action	
	• Produce	• Create or bring into existence	
5 Evaluation			
How you are expected to use your learning to evaluate, make decisions or recommendations	• Advise	• Counsel, inform or notify	15
	• Evaluate	• Appraise or assess the value of	22
	• Recommend	• Propose a course of action	

Planning your question practice

We have already stressed that question practice should be right at the centre of your revision. Whilst you will spend some time looking at your notes and the Paper F2 Passcards, you should spend the majority of your revision time practising questions.

We recommend two ways in which you can practise questions.

- Use **BPP Learning Media's question plan** to work systematically through the syllabus and attempt key and other questions on a section-by-section basis

- **Build your own exams** – attempt the questions as a series of practice exams

These ways are suggestions and simply following them is no guarantee of success. You or your college may prefer an alternative but equally valid approach.

BPP's question plan

The plan below requires you to devote a **minimum of 35 hours** to revision of Paper F2. Any time you can spend over and above this should only increase your chances of success.

 Review your notes and the chapter summaries in the Paper F2 **Passcards** for each section of the syllabus.

 Answer the key questions for that section. These questions have boxes round the question number in the table below and you should answer them in full. Even if you are short of time you must attempt these questions if you want to pass the exam. You should complete your answers without referring to our solutions.

 Attempt the other questions in that section. For some questions we have suggested that you prepare **answer plans or do the calculations** rather than full solutions. Planning an answer means that you should spend about 40% of the time allowance for the questions brainstorming the question and drawing up a list of points to be included in the answer.

 Attempt Mock exams 1, 2 and 3 under strict exam conditions.

Syllabus section	2011 Passcards chapters	Questions in this Kit	Comments	Done ☑
Substance over form and revenue recognition	1	1	Answer part (a) of Q1. This overlaps with group accounts and provides good practice in deciding the true nature of transactions.	☐
Financial instruments	2	4	Answer in full. A good past examination question on financial assets.	☐
		7	Answer in full. A good past examination question on financial Liabilities.	
Employee benefits and share-based payments	3,4	9	Answer in full. A good past examination question for this difficult topic.	☐
		14	A good recent examination question.	
Asset valuation and changing prices	5	11	Attempt part (a) only. This gives useful coverage of some key discussion topics.	☐
Consolidated financial statements	1, 2, 3	15	Answer in full. This will set the scene for more complicated questions.	☐
		19	A good test of some key calculations. Answer in full.	
		20	A good test of technique for the consolidated income statement. Answer in full.	
Associates and joint ventures	4	24	Answer in full. Useful question that provides revision of the treatment of an associate in the statement of financial position.	☐
		23	Answer in full. Excellent question on joint ventures.	
Changes in group structures; more complex group structures	10, 11	32	Answer in full. Longer than current exam questions but excellent coverage of calculations and techniques.	☐
		34 35	Try to find time to answer both of these short questions to make sure you understand how the issue of whether or not control is lost affects the treatment of a disposal.	
Foreign currency translation	12	39	Answer in full. A good preparation question.	☐
		43	Answer in full. Gives good practice in translating a company's statement of financial position and preparing consolidated accounts.	

Syllabus section	2011 Passcards chapters	Questions in this Kit	Comments	Done ☑
Group statements of cash flows	13	47	Answer in full. A good preparation question.	☐
		39	Answer in full. Lots of information to plough through. Looks complicated but is straightforward if you work through it logically.	
Ratio and trend analysis	14	62	Answer in full. Remember to write a report (use the correct format). Only quote those ratios that are relevant to the report. Remember to include all ratios used as an appendix to the report.	☐
		61	Do an answer plan only.	
Earnings per share	15	66	Answer in full. A thorough and very practical test of IAS 33.	☐
Segment reporting	16	69	Answer in full. A useful exercise in report writing, as well as testing your knowledge of IFRS 8.	☐
International issues	17	73	Answer part (c) only. A good discussion question on US GAAP/IFRS convergence.	☐
Environmental issues and human resource accounting	18	75	Do an answer plan only. A comprehensive question, covering everything you are likely to meet. Do an answer plan but learn our answer carefully.	☐
		77	Answer in full. Useful past exam question.	

Build your own exams

Having revised your notes and the BPP Passcards, you can attempt the questions in the Kit as a series of practice exams, making them up yourself or using the mock exams that we have listed below.

	Practice exams					
	1	2	3	4	5	6
Section A						
1	12	1	2	3	4	5
2	16	13	10	14	17	18
3	23	9	19	20	23	25
4	15	26	27	28	34	36
5	6	42	48	63	71	78
Section B						
6	59	35	61	70	51	75
7	32	60	38	62	73	55

Whichever practice exams you use, you must attempt **Mock exams 1, 2 and 3** at the end of your revision.

QUESTIONS

ISSUES IN RECOGNITION AND MEASUREMENT

Questions 1 to 14 cover issues in recognition and measurement, the subject of Part A of the BPP Study Text for Paper F2.

---

1   ETH (FA 11/09)   18 mins

Scenario (a)

ETH set up a company, SX, to operate its distribution activities. The managing director wishes to avoid having to consolidate SX and so has arranged for 100% of the ordinary share capital of SX to be held by the distribution director of SX. The shares held by the distribution director do not carry any voting rights. An agreement has been signed by both parties stating that the operating and financial decisions of SX will be determined by ETH and that all of the profits and losses of SX will flow to ETH. In addition, the agreement states that ETH will guarantee any finance that SX raises in order to continue its operating activities. ETH paid $200,000 to SX to help get the business started. ETH has recorded this under distribution costs as a management charge.

Scenario (b)

ETH has a subsidiary, ZAB, that operates across Centraland, where the local currency is "landers". ETH sources the raw materials for ZAB from one of its suppliers and the goods purchased are paid for in US dollars. ZAB recruits a local workforce and pays all wages and operating expenses in landers. The majority of sales income is received in landers. The management of ZAB operates with a high degree of autonomy and is responsible for raising any finance required to fund operations. ETH has sent a memo to ZAB requesting it to adopt US dollars as its functional currency for ease of consolidation.

Required

Discuss how appropriate the proposed accounting treatment is in respect of the above scenarios and identify any changes to the accounting treatment that are required. Your answer should make reference to any relevant international accounting standards

(Total = 10 marks)

(For Scenario A = 6 marks)
(For Scenario B = 4 marks)

---

2   AZG (FA 5/08)   18 mins

On 1 February 20X7, the directors of AZG decided to enter into a forward foreign exchange contract to buy 6 million florins at a rate of $1 = 3 florins, on 31 January 20Y0. AZG's year end is 31 March.

Relevant exchange rates were as follows:

1 February 20X7 $1 = 3 florins
31 March 20X7 $1 = 2. 9 florins
31 March 20X8 $1 = 2. 8 florins

Required

(a)   Identify the three characteristics of a derivative financial instrument as defined in IAS 39 *Financial Instruments: Recognition and Measurement*.   **(3 marks)**

(b)   Describe the requirements of IAS 39 in respect of the recognition and measurement of derivative financial instruments.   **(2 marks)**

(c)   Prepare relevant extracts from AZG's income statement and statement of financial position to reflect the forward foreign exchange contract at 31 March 20X8, with comparatives. (Note: ignore discounting when measuring the derivative).   **(5 marks)**

(Total = 10 marks)

3 RP (Pilot paper)   18 mins

Convertible bonds

RP issued $4 million 5% convertible bonds on 1 October 20X8 for $3.9 million. The bonds have a four year term and are redeemable at par. At the time the bonds were issued the prevailing market rate for similar debt without conversion rights was 7%. The effective interest rate associated with the bonds is 7% and the liability is measured, in accordance with IAS 39 Financial Instruments: recognition and measurement, at amortised cost. The interest due was paid and recorded within finance costs during the year.

Share options

RP granted share options to its 300 employees on 1 October 20X7. Each employee will receive 1,000 share options provided they continue to work for RP for the following three years from the grant date. The fair value of the options at the grant date was $1.10 each. In the year ended 30 September 20X8, 10 employees left and another 30 were expected to leave over the next two years. For the year ended 30 September 20X9, 20 employees left and another 15 are expected to leave in the year to 30 September 20Y0.

Required

(a)   Prepare the accounting entries to record the issue of the convertible bonds and to record the adjustment required in respect of the interest expense on the bonds for the year ended 30 September 20X9.

(5 marks)

(b)   Discuss the accounting treatment to be adopted for the share options and calculate the amount to be recognised in the income statement in respect of these options for the year ended 30 September 20X9. Prepare appropriate accounting entries. **(5 marks)**

(Total = 10 marks)

4 DG (FA 11/09)   18 mins

Financial Instrument (a)

DG acquired 500,000 shares in HJ, a listed entity, for $3.50 per share on 28 May 20X9. The costs associated with the purchase were $15,000 and were included in the cost of the investment. The directors plan to realise this investment before the end of 20X9. The investment was designated on acquisition as held for trading. There has been no further adjustment made to the investment since the date of purchase. The shares were trading at $3.65 each on 30 June 20X9.

Financial Instrument (b)

DG purchased a bond with a par value of $5 million on 1 July 20X8. The bond carries a 5% coupon, payable annually in arrears and is redeemable on 30 June 20Y3 at $5.8 million. DG fully intends to hold the bond until the redemption date. The bond was purchased at a 10% discount. The effective interest rate on the bond is 10.26%. The interest due for the year was received and credited to investment income in the income statement.

Required

Explain how financial instruments (a) and (b) should be classified, initially measured and subsequently measured. Prepare any journal entries required to correct the accounting treatment for the year to 30 June 20X9.

(Total = 10 marks)

5 BCL (11/10)   18 mins

BCL entered into a forward contract on 31 July 20X0 to purchase B$2 million at a contracted rate of A$1: B$0.64 on 31 October 20X0. The contract cost was nil. BCL prepares its financial statements to 31 August 20X0. At 31 August 20X0 an equivalent contract for the purchase of B$2 million could be acquired at a rate of A$1: B$0.70.

Required:

(a) **Explain** how this financial instrument should be classified and prepare the journal entry required for its measurement as at 31 August 20X0.   **(6 marks)**

(b) Assume now that the instrument described above was designated as a hedging instrument in a cash flow hedge, and that the hedge was 100% effective.

    (i) **Explain** how the gain or loss on the instrument for the year ended 31 August 20X0 should now be recorded and why different treatment is necessary.

    (ii) **Prepare** an extract of the statement of total comprehensive income for BCL for the year ended 31 August 20X0, assuming the profit for the year of BCL was A$1 million, before accounting for the hedging instrument.   **(4 marks)**

(Total = 10 marks)

6 MNB (3/11)   18 mins

(a) MNB acquired an investment in a debt instrument on 1 January 20X0 at its par value of $3 million. Transaction costs relating to the acquisition were $200,000. The investment earns a fixed annual return of 6%, which is received in arrears. The principal amount will be repaid to MNB in 4 years' time at a premium of $400,000. The investment has been correctly classified as held to maturity. The investment has an effective interest rate of approximately 7.05%.

Required:

    (i) **Explain** how this financial instrument will be initially recorded AND subsequently measured in the financial statements of MNB, in accordance with IAS 39 *Financial Instruments: Recognition and Measurement*.

    (ii) **Calculate** the amounts that would be included in MNB's financial statements for the year to 31 December 20X0 in respect of this financial instrument.   **(6 marks)**

(b) MNB acquired 100,000 shares in AB on 25 October 20X0 for $3 per share. The investment resulted in MNB holding 5% of the equity shares of AB. The related transaction costs were $12,000. AB's shares were trading at $3.40 on 31 December 20X0. The investment has been classified as held for trading.

Required:

Prepare the journal entries to record the initial AND subsequent measurement of this financial instrument in the financial statements of MNB for the year to 31 December 20X0.   **(4 marks)**

(Total = 10 marks)

7   QWE (5/11)   18 mins

(a)   QWE issued 10 million 5% convertible $1 bonds 20X5 on 1 January 20X0. The proceeds of $10 million were credited to non-current liabilities and debited to bank. The 5% interest paid has been charged to finance costs in the year to 31 December 20X0.

The market rate of interest for a similar bond with a five year term but no conversion terms is 7%.

Required:

Explain AND **demonstrate** how this convertible instrument would be initially measured in accordance with IAS 32 *Financial Instruments: Presentation* AND subsequently measured in accordance with IAS 39 *Financial Instruments: Recognition and Measurement* in the financial statements for the year ended 31 December 20X0.   **(7 marks)**

(b)   The directors of QWE want to avoid increasing the gearing of the entity. They plan to issue 5 million 6% cumulative redeemable $1 preference shares in 20X1.

Required:

Explain how the preference shares would be classified in accordance with IAS 32 *Financial Instruments: Presentation*, AND the impact that this issue will have on the gearing of QWE.   **(3 marks)**

(Total = 10 marks)

8   Preparation question: Defined benefit scheme

Brutus Co operates a defined benefit pension plan for its employees conditional on a minimum employment period of 6 years. The present value of the future benefit obligations and the fair value of its plan assets on 1 January 20X1 were $110 million and $150 million respectively.

In the financial statements for the year ended 31 December 20X0, there were unrecognised actuarial gains of $43 million. (Brutus Co's accounting policy is to use the 10% corridor approach to recognition of actuarial gains and losses).

The pension plan received contributions of $7m and paid pensions to former employees of $10m during the year.

Extracts from the most recent actuary's report show the following:

	31 December 20X1
Present value of pension plan obligation	$116m
Market value of plan assets	$140m
Present cost of pensions earned in the period	$13m
Yield on high quality corporate bonds for the period	10%
Long term expected return on scheme assets for the period	12%

On 31 December 20X1, the rules of the pension plan were changed to improve benefits for plan members, vesting immediately. The actuary has advised that this will cost $20 million in total.

The average remaining working life of plan members at 31 December 20X1 is 7 years. This tends to remain static as people leave and join.

Required

Produce the extracts for the financial statements for the year ended 31 December 20X1.

Assume contributions and benefits were paid on 31 December.

Helping hand

Use the proformas below as a guidance to the work required.

INCOME STATEMENT EXTRACT

<u>Defined benefit expense recognised in profit or loss</u>

$'m

Current service cost
Interest cost
Expected return on plan assets
Net actuarial (gains)/losses recognised
Past service cost
_____

STATEMENT OF FINANCIAL POSITION EXTRACT

<u>Net defined benefit liability recognised in the statement of financial position</u>

$'m

Present value of defined benefit obligation
Fair value of plan assets
_____

Unrecognised actuarial gains
_____

Workings

<u>Changes in the present value of the defined benefit obligation</u>

$'m

Opening defined benefit obligation

<u>Changes in the fair value of plan assets</u>

$'m

Opening fair value of plan assets

<u>Recognised/unrecognised actuarial gains and losses</u>

$'m

9   BGA (FA 11/07)   18 mins

The following information relates to the defined benefits pension scheme of BGA, a listed entity:

The present value of the scheme obligations at 1 November 20X6 was $18,360,000, while the fair value of the scheme assets at that date was $17,770,000. During the financial year ended 31 October 20X7, a total of $997,000 was paid into the scheme in contributions. Current service cost for the year was calculated at $1,655,000, and actual benefits paid were $1,860,300. The applicable interest cost for the year was 6.5% and the expected return on plan assets was 9.4%.

The present value of the scheme obligations at 31 October 20X7 was calculated as $18,655,500, and the fair value of scheme assets at that date was $18,417,180.

BGA adopts the '10% corridor' criterion in IAS 19 *Employee benefits* for determining the extent of recognition of actuarial gains and losses. The average remaining service life of the employees was 10 years. Net unrecognised actuarial losses on 1 November 20X6 were $802,000.

Required

(a)   Calculate the actuarial gain or loss on BGA's pension scheme assets and liabilities for the year ended 31 October 20X7.   **(8 marks)**

(b)   Calculate the extent to which, if at all, actuarial gains or losses should be recognised in BGA's profit or loss for the year ended 31 October 20X7, using the '10% corridor' criterion.   **(2 marks)**

                             (Total = 10 marks)

10   EAU (5/11)   18 mins

(a)   EAU operates a defined benefit pension plan for its employees. At 1 January 20X2 the fair value of the pension plan assets was $2,600,000 and the present value of the plan liabilities was $2,900,000.

The actuary estimates that the current and past service costs for the year ended 31 December 20X2 is $450,000 and $90,000 respectively. The past service cost is caused by an increase in pension benefits. The plan liabilities at 1 January and 31 December 20X2 correctly reflect the impact of this increase.

The interest cost on the plan liabilities is estimated at 8% and the expected return on plan assets at 5%.

The pension plan paid $240,000 to retired members in the year to 31 December 20X2. EAU paid $730,000 in contributions to the pension plan and this included $90,000 in respect of past service costs.

At 31 December 20X2 the fair value of the pension plan assets is $3,400,000 and the present value of the plan liabilities is $3,500,000.

In accordance with the amendment to IAS 19 *Employee Benefits*, EAU recognises actuarial gains and losses in other comprehensive income in the period in which they occur.

Required:

Calculate the actuarial gains or losses on pension plan assets and liabilities that will be included in other comprehensive income for the year ended 31 December 20X2. (Round all figures to the nearest $000).   **(5 marks)**

(b)   EAU granted 1,000 share appreciation rights (SARs), to its 300 employees on 1 January 20X1. To be eligible, employees must remain employed for 3 years from the date of issue and the rights must be exercised in January 20X4, with settlement due in cash.

- In the year to 31 December 20X1, 32 staff left and a further 35 were expected to leave over the following two years.

- In the year to 31 December 20X2, 28 staff left and a further 10 were expected to leave in the following year.

- No actual figures are available as yet for 20X3.

The fair value of each SAR was $8 at 31 December 20X1 and $12 at 31 December 20X2.

Required:

Prepare the accounting entry to record the expense associated with the SARs, for the year to 31 December 20X2, in accordance with IFRS 2 *Share-based Payments*. **(5 marks)**

(Total = 10 marks)

11 Leisure (FR, 5/01, amended) — 45 mins

(a) There are several measurement systems which can be used in accounting. The most important single characteristic which distinguishes them is whether they are based on historical cost or current value. A further related issue is that of general price changes which affect the significance of reported profits and the ownership interest. It is often stated that a measurement system based on current values is superior to one based on historical cost and that accounting practice should develop by greater utilisation of current values. Current value accounting can utilise replacement cost accounting and net realisable value techniques, which use entry and exit values respectively. If general inflation is a problem, it is possible to eliminate the effect by producing a 'real terms' measure of total gains and losses, where a current value system of accounting is adjusted for the effects of changes in General Purchasing Power (GPP).

Required

Describe the problems associated with replacement cost accounting and net realisable value accounting techniques. **(7 marks)**

(b) You are the management accountant of Leisure. On 1 January 20X0, the entity set up a subsidiary in Urep – a country whose currency is orbits. The investment by Leisure was 50 million orbits. The foreign subsidiary invested all the initial capital in a hotel complex and this complex is effectively the sole asset of the subsidiary. The hotel complex is not being depreciated by the subsidiary. Relevant exchange rates at 1 January 20X0 and 31 December 20X2 – the accounting date for Leisure and its subsidiary – were as follows.

Date	Number of orbits per $
1 January 20X0	25
31 December 20X2	220

The retail price index in Urep was 100 on 1 January 20X0 and 1,000 on 31 December 20X2.

Required

(i) Discuss the effects that hyper-inflation can have on the usefulness of financial statements, and explain how entities with subsidiaries that are located in hyper-inflationary economies should reflect this fact in their consolidated financial statements. You should restrict your discussion to financial statements that have been prepared under the historical cost convention. **(10 marks)**

(ii) Compute the carrying value of the hotel complex in the consolidated financial statements of Leisure at 31 December 20X2:

- Assuming the economy of Urep is not a hyper-inflationary economy
- Assuming the economy of Urep is a hyper-inflationary economy

Critically evaluate the results you have obtained. **(8 marks)**

(Total = 25 marks)

12   BG (Pilot paper)   18 mins

BG is an entity with several overseas operations. One of its subsidiaries, DG operates in a country which experiences relatively high rates of inflation in its currency, the Dez. Most entities operating in that country voluntarily present two versions of their financial statements: one at historic cost, and the other incorporating current cost adjustments. DG complies with this accepted practice.

Extracts from the income statement of DG, including adjustments for current costs for the year ended 30 June 20X9 are shown below:

	Dez'000
Historical cost profit from operations	926
Current cost adjustments:	
Cost of sales adjustment	(82)
Depreciation adjustment	(37)
Monetary working capital adjustment	(9)
Current cost profit from operations	798

Required

(a)   Discuss the defects of historical cost accounting in times of increasing prices.   **(4 marks)**

(b)   Explain how EACH of the three current cost accounting adjustments shown above contributes to the maintenance of capital.   **(6 marks)**

(Total = 10 marks)

13   JKL (3/11)   18 mins

(a)   JKL granted share options to its 300 employees on 1 January 20X1. Each employee will receive 1,000 share options provided they continue to work for JKL for 3 years from the grant date. The fair value of each option at the grant date was $1.22.

The actual and expected staff movement over the 3 years to 31 December 20X3 is provided below:

20X1 25 employees left and another 40 were expected to leave over the next two years.

20X2 A further 15 employees left and another 20 were expected to leave the following year.

Required:

(i)   **Calculate** the charge to JKL's income statement for the year ended 31 December 20X2 in respect of the share options and **prepare** the journal entry to record this.

(ii) **Explain** how the recognition and measurement of a share-based payment would differ if it was to be settled in cash rather than in equity, in accordance with IFRS 2 *Share-based Payments*.

(6 marks)

(b)   JKL operates a defined benefit pension plan. The fair value of the plan assets at 31 December 20X2 was $13.1 million. The present value of the plan liabilities at 31 December 20X2 was $13.9 million. JKL currently adopts the corridor approach for the treatment of actuarial gains and losses. Unrecognised actuarial losses as at 31 December 20X2 totalled $0.5 million.

Required:

(i)   **Calculate** the net pension asset or liability that would be included in JKL's statement of financial position as at 31 December 20X2.

(ii) **Explain** what other options the directors have for the treatment of actuarial gains or losses, in accordance with IAS 19 *Employee Benefits*.   **(4 marks)**

(Total = 10 marks)

14 LBP (11/10)   18 mins

LBP granted share options to its 600 employees on 1 October 20X5. Each employee will receive 500 share options provided they continue to work for LBP for four years from the grant date. The fair value of each option at the grant date was $1.48.

The actual and expected staff movement over the 4 years to 30 September 20X9 is given below:

20X6 20 employees left and another 50 were expected to leave over the next three years.

20X7 A further 25 employees left and another 40 were expected to leave over the next two years.

20X8 A further 15 employees left and another 20 were expected to leave the following year.

20X9 No actual figures are available to date.

The sales director of LBP has stated in the board minutes that he disagrees with the treatment of the share options. No cash has been paid out to employees, therefore he fails to understand why an expense is being charged against profits.

Required:

(a)   **Calculate** the charge to the income statement for the year ended 30 September 20X8 for LBP in respect of the share options and **prepare** the journal entry to record this.   **(6 marks)**

(b)   **Explain** the principles of recognition and measurement for share-based payments as set out in *IFRS 2 Share-based Payments* so as to address the concerns of the sales director.   **(4 marks)**

(Total = 10 marks)

15 Preparation question: Simple consolidation

P acquired 80% of S on 1 January 20X4 for $20,000,000 when its equity was $13,800,000 (share capital $1,500,000, retained earnings $12,300,000). The fair value of S at that date was $1,200,000 more than its book value, the difference being attributable to the value of the property, plant and equipment, being depreciated over a remaining useful life of 10 years from 1 January 20X4. P acquired 30% of A on 1 January 20X6 for $1,900,000 when the balance on its equity was $4,000,000 (share capital $1,000,000, retained earnings $3,000,000).

During the year ended 31 December 20X7, S sold goods to P which cost $1,000,000 for $1,500,000. One quarter of these goods remain unsold at the end of the year. A sold goods to P which cost $500,000 for $700,000. All of the goods remain unsold at the end of the year.

An impairment test conducted at the year end revealed impairment losses of $800,000 relating to the recognised goodwill of S. No impairment losses had previously been recognised. The Group recognises impairment losses in other expenses. No impairment losses to date have been necessary for the investment in A.

INCOME STATEMENTS FOR THE YEAR ENDED 31 DECEMBER 20X7

	P $'000	S $'000	A $'000
Revenue	200,000	150,000	44,000
Cost of sales	(120,000)	(90,000)	(31,000)
Gross profit	80,000	60,000	13,000
Other expenses	(30,000)	(30,000)	(4,000)
Profit before tax	50,000	30,000	9,000
Income tax expense	(20,000)	(10,500)	(3,000)
Profit for the year	30,000	19,500	6,000

STATEMENT OF CHANGES IN EQUITY FOR THE YEAR ENDED 31 DECEMBER 20X7

	Total equity		
	P $'000	S $'000	A $'000
Balance at 01.01.20X7	51,100	20,500	11,000
Profit for the year	30,000	19,500	6,000
Balance at 31.12.20X7	81,100	40,000	17,000

Equity at 31 December 20X7 comprises:

	P	S	A
Share capital	2,900	1,500	1,000
Retained earnings	78,200	38,500	16,000
	81,100	40,000	17,000

It is the group's policy to value non-controlling interest at acquisition at its proportionate share of the fair value of the subsidiary's identifiable net assets.

Required

Prepare the consolidated income statement and statement of changes in equity (total) for the year ended 31 December 20X7.

P GROUP
CONSOLIDATED INCOME STATEMENT FOR THE YEAR ENDED 31 DECEMBER 20X7

	$'000
Revenue	
Cost of sales	————
Gross profit	
Other expenses	
Share of profit of associate	————
Profit before tax	
Income tax expense	————
Profit for the year	════
Profit attributable to:	
Owners of the parent	
Non-controlling interest	————
	════

CONSOLIDATED STATEMENT OF CHANGES IN EQUITY FOR THE YEAR ENDED 31 DECEMBER 20X7

	Equity attributable to equity holders of the parent $'000	Non-controlling interest $'000	Total equity $'000
Balance at 1 January 20X7			
Profit for the year	————	————	————
Balance at 31 December 20X7	════	════	════

16 ABC and DEF (FA11/05 amended)   18 mins

ABC is currently expanding its portfolio of equity interests in other entities. On 1 January 20X5, it made a successful bid for a controlling interest in DEF, paying a combination of shares and cash in order to acquire 80% of DEF's 100,000 issued equity shares. The terms of the acquisition were as follows.

In exchange for each $1 ordinary share purchased, ABC issued one of its own $1 ordinary shares and paid $1.50 in cash. In addition to the consideration paid, ABC agreed to pay a further $1.40 per share on 1 January 20X7, on condition that the profits of DEF for the year ended 31 May 20X6 will exceed $6,000,000. Allowing for the likelihood of DEF's profits exceeding the target, and the time value of money, the fair value of the contingent consideration is estimated at $80,000. The market value of a $1 share in ABC at January 20X5 was $3.50, rising to $3.60 at ABC's 31 May 20X5 year end.

The fair value of the non-controlling interest on 1 January 20X5 was $115,000.

Total legal, administrative and share issue costs associated with the acquisition were $60,000. This figure included $20,000 paid to external legal and accounting advisors, an estimated $10,000 in respect of ABC's own administrative overhead and $30,000 in share issue costs.

The carrying value of DEF's net assets at 1 January 20X5 was $594,000. Carrying value was regarded as a close approximation to fair value, except in respect of the following.

(a)   The carrying value of DEF's property, plant and equipment at 1 January 20X5 was $460,000. Market value at that date was estimated at $530,000.

(b)   DEF had a contingent liability in respect of a major product warranty claim with a fair value of $100,000.

(c)   The cost of reorganising DEF's activities following acquisition was estimated at $75,000.

(d)   DEF's inventories included goods at an advanced stage of work-in-progress with a carrying value of $30,000. The sales value of these goods was estimated at $42,000 and further costs to completion at $6,000.

(e)   DEF measures non-controlling interests on acquisition at full fair value.

Required

Calculate goodwill on the acquisition of DEF, in accordance with the requirements of IFRS 3 (revised) *Business combinations*, explaining your treatment of the legal, administrative, share issue and reorganisation costs.

(10 marks)

17   AAY (FA 5/08)   18 mins

Summarised statements of changes in equity for the year ended 31 March 20X8 for AAY and its only subsidiary, BBZ, are shown below:

	AAY $'000	BBZ $'000
Balance at 1 April 20X7	662,300	143,700
Profit for the year	81,700	22,000
Dividends	(18,000)	(6,000)
Balance at 31 March 20X8	726,000	159,700

Notes

(1)   AAY acquired 80% of the issued share capital of BBZ on 1 April 20X5, when BBZ's total equity was $107.7 million. The first dividend BBZ has paid since acquisition is the amount of $6 million shown in the summarised statement above. The profit for the year of $81,700 in AAY's summarised statement of changes in equity above does not include its share of the dividend paid by BBZ.

(2)   The only consolidation adjustment required is in respect of intra-group trading. BBZ regularly supplies goods to AAY. The amount included in the inventory of AAY in respect of goods purchased from BBZ at the beginning and end of the accounting period was as follows:

1 April 20X7 $2 million
31 March 20X8 $3 million

BBZ earns a profit on intra-group sales of 25% on cost.

It is group policy to measure NCI at acquisition at the proportionate share of the fair value of the net assets.

Required

Prepare a summarised consolidated statement of changes in equity for the AAY Group for the year ended 31 March 20X8.

(10 marks)

18   DNT (FA 11/08)   18 mins

At its year end on 31 August 20X8, DNT held investments in two subsidiaries, CM and BL.

Details of the investments were as follows:

1   Several years ago DNT purchased 850,000 of CM's 1 million ordinary $1 shares when CM's retained earnings were $1,775,000 (there were no other reserves). At 31 August 20X8, CM's retained earnings were $2,475,000. The fair value of the non-controlling interest at acquisition was $520,000.

2   On 31 May 20X8, DNT purchased 175,000 of BL's 250,000 $1 ordinary shares. The fair value of the non-controlling interest at this date was $386,000. At 1 September 20X7, BL's retained earnings were $650,000 (there were no other reserves). During the year ended 31 August 20X8, BL made a loss after tax of $40,000. It can be assumed that BL's revenue and expenses accrue evenly throughout the year.

No adjustments to fair value of the subsidiaries' net assets were required at either of the acquisitions.

DNT measures non-controlling interests at fair value at the date of acquisition.

On 1 March 20X7 CM sold an item of machinery to DNT for $75,000. The carrying amount of the item at the date of sale was $60,000, and CM recorded a profit on disposal of $15,000. The remaining useful life of the item at the date of sale was 2.5 years. The group depreciation policy in respect of machinery is the straight line basis with a proportionate charge in the years of acquisition and of disposal.

DNT's retained earnings balance at 31 August 20X8 was $2,669,400.

Required

Calculate the amounts of consolidated retained earnings and non-controlling interest for inclusion in the DNT group's statement of financial position at 31 August 20X8.   **(10 marks)**

19   MX (5/10)   18 mins

MX acquired 80% of the 1 million issued $1 ordinary share capital of FZ on 1 May 20X9 for $1,750,000 when FZ's retained earnings were $920,000.

The carrying value was considered to be the same as fair value with the exception of the following:

•   The carrying value of FZ's property, plant and equipment at 1 May 20X9 was $680,000. The market value at that date was estimated at $745,000. The remaining useful life of the property, plant and

equipment was estimated at 5 years from the date of acquisition.

•   FZ had a contingent liability with a fair value of $100,000. There was no change to the value of this liability at the year-end.

MX estimates that the costs of reorganising the combined entity following acquisition will be $200,000.

MX depreciates all assets on a straight line basis over their estimated useful lives on a monthly basis.

FZ sold goods to MX with a sales value of $300,000 during the 8 months since the acquisition. All of these goods remain in MX's inventories at the year end. FZ makes 20% gross profit margin on all sales.

The retained earnings reported in the financial statements of MX and FZ as at 31 December 20X9 are $3.2 million and $1.1 million respectively. There has been no impairment to goodwill since the date of acquisition.

The group policy is to measure non-controlling interest at fair value at the date of acquisition. The fair value of non-controlling interest at 1 May 20X9 was $320,000.

Required

Calculate the amounts that will appear in the consolidated statement of financial position of the MX Group as at 31 December 20X9 for:

(i)   Goodwill;
(ii)   Consolidated retained earnings; and
(iii)   Non-controlling interest.

                                                                       (10 marks)

20   AB Group (11/10)   18 mins

The income statements for AB, CD and EF for the year ended 30 June 20X9 are shown below.

	AB	CD	EF
	$000	$000	$000
Revenue	2,000	1,500	800
Cost of sales	(1,200)	(1,000)	(500)
Gross profit	800	500	300
Distribution costs	(400)	(120)	(80)
Administrative expenses	(240)	(250)	(100)
Other income	40	-	-
Profit before tax	200	130	120
Income tax expense	(50)	(40)	(20)
Profit for the year	150	90	100

Additional information

1.   AB acquired 80% of the ordinary share capital of CD on 1 July 20X7 for $4,100,000. At the date of acquisition the fair value of the net assets of CD was $5,000,000. The group policy is to value non-controlling interest at fair value and at the date of acquisition the fair value of the non-controlling interest was $1,100,000. No impairment of goodwill arose in the year ended 30 June 20X8, however, an impairment review conducted on 30 June 20X9 showed goodwill had been impaired by 15%. Impairment is charged to administrative expenses.

2.   AB acquired 20% of the ordinary share capital of EF on 1 October 20X8. The interest acquired enables AB to exercise significant influence over the operating and financial policies of EF.

3.   During the year to 30 June 20X9, AB and CD paid ordinary dividends of $100,000 and $50,000 respectively. Income from investments is shown in "Other income".

4.   Included in the fair value uplift on the acquisition of CD were depreciable assets with a remaining useful life at the acquisition date of 12 years. The fair value of these assets was found to be $240,000 higher than book value. The group policy is to depreciate non-current assets on a straight line basis over their estimated economic useful life. Depreciation is charged to administrative expenses.

5.   EF sold goods to AB on 1 May 20X9 with a sales value of $80,000. Half of these goods remain in AB's inventories at the year end. EF makes 25% profit margin on all sales.

Required:

Prepare the consolidated income statement for the AB Group for the year ended 30 June 20X9.

(Total = 10 marks)

21   ERT (3/11)   45 mins

The statements of financial position for ERT and BNM as at 31 December 20X0 are provided below:

	ERT	*BNM*
ASSETS	*$000*	*$000*
Non-current assets		
Property, plant and equipment	12,000	4,000
Available for sale investment (note 1)	4,000	-
	16,000	4,000
Current assets		
Inventories	2,200	800
Receivables	3,400	900
Cash and cash equivalents	800	300
	6,400	2,000
Total assets	22,400	6,000

EQUITY AND LIABILITIES

Equity

Share capital ($1 equity shares)	10,000	1,000
Retained earnings	7,500	4,000
Other reserves	200	-
Total equity	17,700	5,000
Non-current liabilities		
Long term borrowings	2,700	-
Current liabilities	2,000	1,000
Total liabilities	4,700	1,000
Total equity and liabilities	22,400	6,000

Additional information:

1.   ERT acquired a 75% investment in BNM on 1 May 20X0 for $3,800,000. The investment has been classified as available for sale in the books of ERT. The gain on its subsequent measurement as at 31 December 20X0 has been recorded within other reserves in ERT's individual financial statements. At the date of acquisition BNM had retained earnings of $3,200,000.

2.   It is the group policy to value non-controlling interest at fair value at the date of acquisition. The fair value of the non-controlling interest at 1 May 20X0 was $1,600,000.

3.   As at 1 May 20X0 the fair value of the net assets acquired was the same as the book value with the following exceptions:

The fair value of property, plant and equipment was $800,000 higher than the book value. These assets were assessed to have an estimated useful life of 16 years from the date of acquisition. A full year's depreciation is charged in the year of acquisition and none in the year of sale.

The fair value of inventories was estimated to be $200,000 higher than the book value. All of these inventories were sold by 31 December 20X0.

On acquisition ERT identified an intangible asset that BNM developed internally but which met the recognition criteria of IAS 38 Intangible Assets. This intangible asset is expected to generate economic benefit from the date of acquisition until 31 December 20X1 and was valued at $150,000 at the date of acquisition.

A contingent liability, which had a fair value of $210,000 at the date of acquisition, had a fair value of $84,000 at 31 December 20X0.

4.   An impairment review was conducted at 31 December 20X0 and it was decided that the goodwill on the acquisition of BNM was impaired by 20%.

5.   ERT sold goods to BNM for $300,000. Half of these goods remained in inventories at 31 December 20X0. ERT makes 20% margin on all sales.

6.   No dividends were paid by either entity in the year ended 31 December 20X0.

Required:

(a)   **Explain** how the fair value adjustments identified above will impact *BOTH* the calculation of goodwill on the acquisition of BNM *AND* the consolidated financial statements of the ERT group for the year ended 31 December 20X0.   **(7 marks)**

(b)   **Prepare** the consolidated statement of financial position as at 31 December 20X0 for the ERT Group.
                                                                                           (18 marks)

(Total = 25 marks)

22 Preparation question: Joint venture

	Top Co $'000	Notch Co $'000
Non-current assets		
Property, plant and equipment	70,000	45,000
Investment in Notch	12,000	
	82,000	45,000
Current assets	93,000	52,000
	175,000	97,000
Equity		
Share capital	50,000	5,000
Retained earnings	74,000	65,000
	124,000	70,000
Current liabilities	51,000	27,000
	175,000	97,000

Top Co acquired a 25% interest in Notch Co six years ago when the balance on Notch Co's retained earnings was $35,000,000. Top Co has joint control of Notch together with three other parties.

Required

Prepare the consolidated statement of financial position of Top Co incorporating Notch under the proportionate consolidation method. No impairment losses have been necessary to date.

> **Helping hand**
>
> Use the proforma below as a guide to the figures you need to determine.

TOP GROUP CONSOLIDATED STATEMENT OF FINANCIAL POSITION

	$'000
Non-current assets	
Property, plant and equipment	
Goodwill	_____
Current assets	_____
	======
Equity	
Share capital	
Retained earnings	_____
Current liabilities	_____
	======

23 JKA (Pilot paper)   18 mins

JKA acquired 50% of the issued ordinary share capital of CBX, an entity set up under a contractual agreement as a joint venture between JKA and one of its customers. JKA adopts a policy of proportionate consolidation in accounting for joint ventures.

The statements of financial position for JKA and CBX as at 31 May 20X9 are provided below:

	JKA $000	CBX $000
ASSETS		
Non-current assets		
Property, plant and equipment	11,000	7,500
Investment in CBX	2,000	–
	13,000	7,500

	JKA $000	CBX $000
Current assets		
Inventories	3,100	1,200
Receivables	3,300	1,400
Cash and cash equivalents	600	400
	7,000	3,000
Total assets	20,000	10,500
EQUITY AND LIABILITIES		
Equity		
Share capital ($1 ordinary shares)	10,000	4,000
Revaluation reserve	1,500	500
Other reserves	500	–
Retained earnings	2,000	4,500
Total equity	14,000	9,000
Non-current liabilities	2,000	–
Current liabilities	4,000	1,500
Total liabilities	6,000	1,500
Total equity and liabilities	20,000	10,500

Additional information:

1. Intra-group trading

    During the year to 31 May 20X9 CBX sold goods to JKA with a sales value of $200,000. 25% of the goods remain in JKA's inventories at the year end. CBX makes 20% margin on all sales. The final invoice amount of $34,000 remains unpaid at the year end.

2. Sale of land

    On 31 May 20X9 JKA sold a piece of land to DEX Finance for $500,000 when the carrying value of the land was $520,000 (the original cost of the asset). Under the terms of the sale agreement JKA has the option to repurchase the land within the next three years for between $560,000 and $600,000 depending on the date of repurchase. The land must be repurchased for $600,000 at the end of the three year period if the option is not exercised before that time.

    JKA has derecognised the land and recorded the subsequent loss within profit for the year ended 31 May 20X9.

Required

(a) Explain how the sale of the land should be accounted for in accordance with the principles of IAS 18 *Revenue* and the *Framework for Preparation and Presentation of Financial Statements*   **(4 marks)**

(b) Prepare the consolidated statement of financial position for JKA as at 31 May 20X9   **(6 marks)**

(Total = 10 marks)

24 AJ (FA 5/05)   45 mins

AJ is a law stationery business. In 20X2, the majority of its board of directors was replaced. The new board decided to adopt a policy of expansion through acquisition. The statements of financial position at 31 March 20X5 of AJ and of two entities in which it holds substantial investments are shown below.

	AJ $'000	$'000	BK $'000	$'000	CL $'000	$'000
Non-current assets						
Property, plant and equipment	12,500		4,700		4,500	
Investments	18,000		–		1,300	
		30,500		4,700		5,800

Current assets					
Inventories	7,200		8,000		–
Trade receivables	6,300		4,300		3,100
Financial assets	–		–		2,000
Cash	800		–		900
		14,300		12,300	6,000
		44,800		17,000	11,800
Equity					
Called up share capital					
($1 shares)		10,000		5,000	2,500
Retained earnings		14,000		1,000	4,300
		24,000		6,000	6,800
Non-current liabilities					
Loan notes		10,000		3,000	–
Current liabilities					
Trade payables	8,900		6,700		4,000
Income tax	1,300		100		600
Short-term borrowings	600		1,200		400
		10,800		8,000	5,000
		44,800		17,000	11,800

NOTES TO THE STATEMENTS OF FINANCIAL POSITION

Notes

(1)   Investment by AJ in BK

On 1 April 20X2, AJ purchased $2 million loan notes in BK at par.

On 1 April 20X3, AJ purchased 4 million of the ordinary shares in BK for $7.5 million cash, when BK's reserves were $1.5 million.

At the date of acquisition of the shares, BK's property, plant and equipment included land recorded at a cost of $920,000. At the date of acquisition the fair value of the land was $1,115,000. No other adjustments in respect of fair value were required to BK's assets and liabilities upon acquisition. BK has not recorded the fair value in its own accounting records.

(2)   Investment by AJ in CL

On 1 October 20X4, AJ acquired 1 million shares in CL, a book distributor, when the reserves of CL were $3.9 million. The purchase consideration was $4.4 million. Since the acquisition, AJ has had the right to appoint one of the five directors of CL. The remaining shares in CL are owned principally by three other investors.

No fair value adjustments were required in respect of CL's assets or liabilities upon acquisition.

(3)   Goodwill on consolidation

Since acquiring its investment in BK, AJ has adopted the requirements of IFRS 3 Business combinations in respect of goodwill on consolidation. During March 20X5, it conducted an impairment review of goodwill. As a result, the goodwill element of the investment in CL is unaltered, but the value of goodwill on consolidation in respect of BK is now $1.7 million.

It is group policy to measure NCI at acquisition at the proportionate share of the fair value of the net assets.

(4)   Intra-group trading

BK supplies legal books to AJ. On 31 March 20X5, AJ's inventories included books purchased at a total cost of $1 million from BK. BK's mark-up on books is 25%.

Required

(a)   Explain, with reasons, how the investments in BK and CL will be treated in the consolidated financial statements of the AJ group.   **(5 marks)**

(b)   Prepare the consolidated statement of financial position for the AJ group at 31 March 20X5. Full workings should be shown.   **(20 marks)**

(Total = 25 marks)

25 ST (FA 5/06)   18 mins

The income statements of ST and two entities in which it holds investments are shown below for the year ended 31 January 20X6.

	ST	UV	WX
	$'000	$'000	$'000
Revenue	1,800	1,400	600
Cost of sales	(1,200)	(850)	(450)
Gross profit	600	550	150
Operating expenses	(450)	(375)	(74)
Finance cost	(16)	(12)	–
Interest income	6	–	–
Profit before tax	140	163	76
Income tax expense	(45)	(53)	(26)
Profit for the year	95	110	50

Notes

(1)   Investments by ST

Several years ago ST acquired 70% of the issued ordinary share capital of UV. On 1 February 20X5, ST acquired 50% of the issued share capital of WX, an entity set up under a contractual arrangement as a joint venture between ST and one of its suppliers. The directors of ST have decided to adopt a policy of proportionate consolidation wherever appropriate and permitted by International Financial Reporting Standards.

(2)   UV's borrowings

During the financial year ended 31 January 20X6, UV paid the full amount of interest due on its 6% debenture loan of $200,000. ST invested $100,000 in the debenture when it was issued three years ago.

(3)   Intra-group trading

During the year, WX sold goods to ST for $20,000. Half of the goods remained in ST's inventories at 31 January 2006. WX's gross profit margin on the sale was 20%.

It is the group's policy to value non-controlling interest at acquisition at its proportionate share of the fair value of the subsidiary's identifiable net assets.

Required

Prepare the consolidated income statement of the ST group for the year ended 31 January 20X6.   **(10 marks)**

26 AB (Pilot paper)   18 mins

The statements of comprehensive income for AB, CD and EF for the year ended 31 May 20X9 are shown below:

	AB	CD	EF
	$000	$000	$000
Revenue	6,000	3,000	1,000
Cost of sales	(4,800)	(2,400)	(800)
Gross profit	1,200	600	200
Distribution costs	(64)	(32)	(10)
Administrative expenses	(336)	(168)	(52)
Finance costs	(30)	(15)	(5)
Profit before tax	770	385	133
Income tax expense	(204)	(102)	(33)
PROFIT FOR THE YEAR	566	283	100
Other comprehensive income:			
Revaluation of property	200	100	30
Tax effect of revaluation	(42)	(21)	(6)
Other comprehensive income for the year, net of tax	158	79	24
TOTAL COMPREHENSIVE INCOME FOR THE YEAR	724	362	124

Additional information:

1.   AB operates a defined benefit pension plan for its employees. At the year end, there is an actuarial loss of $52,000 on the pension plan liabilities and an actuarial gain of $40,000 on pension plan assets. These amounts are not reflected in the above statements. In accordance with the amendment to IAS 19 *Employee Benefits*, AB recognises actuarial gains and losses from the defined benefit plan in other comprehensive income in the period that they occur.

2.   AB holds a 15% investment in XY which is designated as available for sale. The fair value of this investment at 31 May 20X9 was $106,000. The investment is currently recorded in the financial statements at $92,000.

3.   AB owns 80% of the ordinary share capital of CD and exercises control over its operating and financial policies. AB owns 30% of the ordinary share capital of EF and exerts significant influence over its operating and financial policies.

Required

Prepare the consolidated statement of comprehensive income for the AB Group, taking account of the information provided in the notes above. Ignore any further taxation effects of notes 1 and 2.   **(10 marks)**

27   DF (5/10)   18 mins

DF is preparing its consolidated financial statements for the year ended 31 December 20X9. DF has a number of investments in other entities. Details of some of these investments are provided below:

Investment in AB

DF acquired 90% of the issued ordinary share capital of AB on 1 July 20X9 for $6 million, when the book value of the net assets was $5.8 million. The fair value of these net assets was estimated at $6.8 million at the date of acquisition. The difference between the fair value and book value of the net assets related to depreciable property with a remaining useful life at the date of acquisition of 40 years.

Investment in GH

DF acquired 40% of the issued ordinary share capital of GH on 1 January 20X8 for $2 million, when the book value of the net assets was $5.5 million. The fair value of these net assets was estimated at $6 million at the date of acquisition.

Investment in JK

At the date of acquisition of AB, AB held 65% of the issued ordinary share capital of JK. The operations of JK do not fit within the strategic plans of DF and so the directors plan to sell this investment. The investment is currently being actively marketed with a view to selling it within the next 4 months.

Investment in LM

DF acquired 15% of the issued ordinary share capital of LM on 1 January 20X4 for $1 million. On 1 October 20X9, DF acquired a further 40% of issued ordinary share capital for $4.5 million. The fair value of the net assets at 1 October 20X9 was $12 million and on 1 January 20X4 was $8 million. The previously held interest had a fair value on 1 October 20X9 of $1.7 million.

The group policy is to value non-controlling interest at the date of acquisition at the proportionate share of the fair value of the net assets.

Required

(a)   Explain the basis on which each of the investments should be accounted for in the consolidated financial statements of the DF Group for the year ended 31 December 20X9 (**calculations are not required**).

                                                                (8 marks)

(b)   Briefly explain the impact of the investment in AB, in the consolidated income statement for the year ended 31December 20X9.   **(2 marks)**

                                                  (Total = 10 marks)

28   PQ (FA11/09 amended)

The income statements of PQ, ST and AC for the year ended 30 June 20X9 are provided below:

	PQ $'000	ST $'000	AC $'000
Revenue	900	560	505
Cost of sales	(630)	(345)	(310)
Gross profit	270	215	195
Distribution costs	(90)	(39)	(60)
Administrative expenses	(60)	(30)	(72)
Profit from operations	120	146	63
Investment income	32	–	15
Profit before tax	152	146	78
Income tax expense	(42)	(38)	(10)
Profit for the year	110	108	68

PQ's investment in ST

PQ acquired 80% of the ordinary share capital of ST on 1 November 20X8 for $700,000, when the fair value of the net assets was $650,000. These fair values were the same as the book values with the exception of property, plant and equipment, which required an uplift of $120,000 in respect of buildings. ST had already depreciated the buildings for 10 of their 50 year estimated useful economic life and had charged the depreciation through administrative expenses.

An impairment review has indicated that goodwill was impaired by 20% at the year end. Impairment losses are charged to administrative expenses.

Group policy is to measure non-controlling interests at acquisition at the proportionate share of fair value of net assets.

ST paid a final dividend of $40,000 before the year end.

PQ's investment in AC

PQ acquired 25% of the ordinary share capital of AC on 1 July 20X5. The fair value of the net assets was equal to the book value at the date of acquisition. No impairment of the investment in AC was evident.

AC sold goods to PQ during the year with a total sales value of $180,000. $40,000 of these goods remains in the inventory of PQ at the year end. AC makes 20% margin on all sales.

Profit of all three entities can be assumed to accrue evenly throughout the year.

Required

Prepare the consolidated income statement for the PQ group for the year ended 30 June 20X9. (Round to the nearest $'000.)

(Total = 10 marks)

> **MORE COMPLEX GROUP TOPICS**
>
> Questions 29 to 47 cover more complex group topics, the subject of Part C of the BPP Study Text for Paper F2.

29 Preparation question: Part disposal

> **BPP note**. In this question, proformas are given to you to help you get used to setting out your answer. You may wish to transfer them to a separate sheet or to use a separate sheet for your workings.

Angel Co bought 70% of the share capital of Shane Co for $120,000 on 1 January 20X6. At that date Shane Co's retained earnings stood at $10,000.

The statements of financial position at 31 December 20X8, summarised income statements to that date and movement on retained earnings are given below:

	Angel Co $'000	Shane Co $'000
STATEMENTS OF FINANCIAL POSITION		
Non-current assets		
Property, plant and equipment	200	80
Investment in Shane Co	120	–
	320	80
Current assets	890	140
	1,210	220
Equity		
Share capital – $1 ordinary shares	500	100
Retained reserves	400	90
	900	190
Current liabilities	310	30
	1,210	220
SUMMARISED INCOME STATEMENTS		
Profit before interest and tax	100	20
Income tax expense	(40)	(8)
Profit for the year	60	12
Other comprehensive income, net of tax	10	6
Total comprehensive income for the year	70	18
MOVEMENT IN RETAINED RESERVES		
Balance at 31 December 20X7	330	72
Total comprehensive income for the year	70	18
Balance at 31 December 20X8	400	90

Angel Co sells one half of its holding in Shane Co for $120,000 on 30 June 20X8. At that date, the fair value of the 35% holding in Shane was slightly more at $130,000 due to a share price rise. The remaining holding is to be dealt with as an associate. This does not represent a discontinued operation.

No entries have been made in the accounts for the above transaction.

Assume that profits accrue evenly throughout the year.

It is the group's policy to value the non-controlling interest at acquisition at fair value. The fair value of the non-controlling interest on 1 January 20X6 was $51,000.

Required

Prepare the consolidated statement of financial position, statement of comprehensive income and a reconciliation of movement in retained reserves for the year ended 31 December 20X8.

Ignore income taxes on the disposal. No impairment losses have been necessary to date.

Helping hands

1   Set out a proforma like the one below or use the one we have provided.

2   As 'no entries have been made in the accounts for the above transaction', you will need to calculate the gain on disposal.

3   Consolidate 100% Share Co's profit and income tax expense for the number of months Angel Co had control.

PART DISPOSAL PROFORMA

ANGEL GROUP
CONSOLIDATED STATEMENT OF FINANCIAL POSITION
AS AT 31 DECEMBER 20X8

	$'000
Non-current assets	
Property, plant and equipment	
Investment in Shane	_____
	_____
Current assets	_____
	_____
Equity attributable to owners of the parent	
Share capital	
Retained earnings	_____
	_____
Current liabilities	_____
	_____

CONSOLIDATED STATEMENT OF COMPREHENSIVE INCOME
FOR THE YEAR ENDED 31 DECEMBER 20X8

	$'000
Profit before interest and tax	
Profit on disposal of shares in subsidiary	
Share of profit of associate	_____
Profit before tax	
Income tax expense	_____
Profit for the year	_____
Other comprehensive income net of tax	
Share of other comprehensive income of associate	
Other comprehensive income for the year	
Total comprehensive income for the year	
Profit attributable to:	
Owners of the parent	
Non-controlling interest	_____
	_____
Total comprehensive income attributable to	
Owners of the parent	
Non-controlling interests	_____
	_____

CONSOLIDATED RECONCILIATION OF MOVEMENT IN RETAINED RESERVES

	$'000
Balance at 31 December 20X7	
Total comprehensive income for the year	
Balance at 31 December 20X8	_____
	_____

30 Preparation question: 'D' shaped group statement of financial position

BPP note. In this question, a proforma is given to you for Part (a) to help you get used to setting out your answer. You may wish to transfer it to a separate sheet or to use a separate sheet for workings.

Below are the statements of financial position of three companies as at 31 December 20X9.

	Bauble Co $'000	Jewel Co $'000	Gem Co $'000
Non-current assets			
Property, plant and equipment	720	60	70
Investments in group companies	185	100	–
	905	160	70
Current assets	175	95	90
	1,080	255	160
Equity			
Share capital – $1 ordinary shares	400	100	50
Retained earnings	560	90	65
	960	190	115
Current liabilities	120	65	45
	1,080	255	160

You are also given the following information:

(1) Bauble Co acquired 60% of the share capital of Jewel Co on 1 January 20X2 and 10% of Gem on 1 January 20X3. The cost of the combinations were $142,000 and $43,000 respectively. Jewel Co acquired 70% of the share capital of Gem Co on 1 January 20X3.

(2) The retained earnings balances of Jewel Co and Gem Co were:

	1 January 20X2 $'000	1 January 20X3 $'000
Jewel Co	45	60
Gem Co	30	40

(3) No impairment loss adjustments have been necessary to date.

(4) It is the group's policy to value the non-controlling interest at acquisition at its proportionate share of the fair value of the subsidiary's identifiable net assets.

Required

Prepare the consolidated statement of financial position for Bauble Co and its subsidiaries as at 31 December 20X9.

> **Helping hands**
>
> 1 Use the proforma below as a guide to the layout needed and figures required.
>
> 2 Using the information in note 1, draw the group structure (as a 'D').
>
> 3 Consolidate together 100% the three balances for property, plant and equipment as there is control.
>
> 4 Determine the date when the group gained control of Gem Co. Using the information in note 2 you can then establish the pre-acquisition retained earnings figure.

BAUBLE – CONSOLIDATED STATEMENT OF FINANCIAL POSITION AS AT 31 DECEMBER 20X9

$'000

Non-current assets
Property, plant and equipment
Goodwill

Current assets

Equity attributable to owners of the parent
Share capital – $1 ordinary shares
Retained earnings

Non-controlling interest

Current liabilities

31 Preparation question: 'D' shaped group income statement

Upper Co owns 75% of the ordinary shares of Middle Co and 20% of Lower.

Middle Co owns 60% of the ordinary shares of Lower Co.

The summarised income statements for the year ended 31 December 20X9 are as follows:

	Upper Co $'000	Middle Co $'000	Lower Co $'000
Profit before tax	1,500	750	150
Income tax expense	500	250	50
Profit for the year	1,000	500	100
Dividends declared during the period	300	100	40

Dividends have not been accounted for in the books of the recipient companies although they were declared before the year end.

Required

Prepare the summarised consolidated income statement extract for the year ended 31 December 20X9 for Upper Co.

Helping hand

Use the proforma below as a guide to the layout needed and figures required.

UPPER GROUP CONSOLIDATED INCOME STATEMENT FOR THE YEAR ENDED 31 DECEMBER 20X9

$'000

Profit before tax
Income tax expense
Profit for the year

Profit attributable to:
Owners of the parent
Non-controlling interest

32 Big Group   54 mins

The statements of financial position of Big, Small and Tiny at 30 September 20X9 (the accounting date for all three entities) are given below.

	Big $'000	Big $'000	Small $'000	Small $'000	Tiny $'000	Tiny $'000
Non-current assets						
Property, plant and equipment	56,000		66,000		56,000	
Investments (Notes 1-3)	104,000		29,000		–	
		160,000		95,000		56,000
Current assets						
Inventories (Note 5)	45,000		44,000		25,000	
Trade receivables (Note 6)	40,000		30,000		16,000	
Cash in hand	8,000		6,000		3,000	
		93,000		80,000		44,000
		253,000		175,000		100,000
Equity						
Share capital (Notes 2 and 3)		90,000		80,000		32,000
Retained earnings		69,000		59,000		19,000
		159,000		139,000		51,000
Long-term loans		50,000				25,000
Current liabilities						
Trade payables (Note 5)	25,000		20,000		11,000	
Tax payable	7,000		6,000		4,000	
Bank overdraft	12,000		10,000		9,000	
		44,000		36,000		24,000
		253,000		175,000		100,000

Notes to the financial statements

(1)   On 1 October 20X3, when the retained earnings of Small showed a balance of $22 million, Big purchased 64 million of Small's $1 equity shares for a consideration of $91.5 million, payable in cash. On 1 October 20X3, a large property owned by Small had a statement of financial position value of $7 million and a fair value to Big of $11 million. With the exception of this property, the fair values of all the identifiable net assets of Small were the same as their carrying values in the statement of financial position of Small. The property that had a fair value of $11 million on 1 October 20X3 was sold by Small on 30 June 20X7.

(2)   On 1 April 20X5, when the retained earnings of Tiny stood at $10m, Big purchased 8 million of Tiny's $1 equity shares for a cash consideration of $12.5 million. A fair-value exercise was carried out but all of the net identifiable assets of Tiny at 1 April 20X5 had a fair value that was the same as their carrying values in the statement of financial position of Tiny.

(3)   On 1 April 20X9, Small purchased 16 million of Tiny's $1 equity shares for a cash consideration of $29 million (equivalent to the fair value of $1.8125 per share acquired on that date). A fair-value exercise was carried out but all of the net identifiable assets of Tiny at 1 April 20X9 had a fair value that was the same as their carrying values in the statement of financial position of Tiny. During the year ended September 20X9, Tiny made a profit after taxation of $8 million and paid no dividends. This profit accrued evenly over the year.

(4)   Big and Small both measure investments in subsidiaries and associates at cost in their separate financial statements.

(5)   A key reason behind the purchase of shares in Tiny by Big and Small was that Tiny supplied a component that was used by both entities. Until 1 April 20X9, the component was supplied by Tiny at cost plus a mark-up of 30 per cent. From 1 April 20X9, the mark-up changed to 20 per cent. On 30 September 20X9, the inventories purchased from Tiny (all purchases since 1 April) were as follows.

- In Big's books, $9 million
- In Small's books, $7.8 million

(6)   The trade payables of Big and Small show amounts of $6 million and $5 million respectively as being payable to Tiny, and these balances have been agreed. There was no other inter-group trading.

(7)   The policy of Big Group is to measure non-controlling interests at their proportionate share of the fair value of the identifiable net assets acquired.

You are the management accountant responsible for the consolidation of the Big group. Your assistant is aware of the basic principles and procedures to be followed in preparing consolidated financial statements. She is clear on what is required to consolidate Small but is much less sure of what to do with Tiny. She is particularly puzzled by the fact that both Big and Small made investments in Tiny and that one of these investments took place in the financial year.

Required

Prepare the consolidated statement of financial position of the Big group at 30 September 20X9.   **(30 marks)**

33   AZ (FA 5/06)   45 mins

The statements of financial position of AZ and two entities in which it holds substantial investments at 31 March 20X6 are shown below:

STATEMENT OF FINANCIAL POSITION AS AT 31 MARCH 20X6

	AZ		BY		CX	
	$'000	$'000	$'000	$'000	$'000	$'000
Non-current assets						
Property, plant and equipment	10,750		5,830		3,300	
Investments	7,650		–		–	
		18,400		5,830		3,300
Current assets						
Inventories	2,030		1,210		1,180	
Trade receivables	2,380		1,300		1,320	
Cash	1,380		50		140	
		5,790		2,560		2,640
		24,190		8,390		5,940
Equity						
Called up share capital ($1 shares)		8,000		2,300		2,600
Preferred share capital		–		1,000		–
Reserves		10,750		3,370		2,140
		18,750		6,670		4,740
Current liabilities						
Trade payables	3,770		1,550		1,080	
Income tax	420		170		120	
Suspense account	1,250		–		–	
		5,440		1,720		1,200
		24,190		8,390		5,940

Notes

(1)   Investments by AZ in BY

Several years ago AZ purchased 80% of BY's ordinary share capital for $3,660,000 when the reserves of BY were $1,950,000. In accordance with the group's policy goodwill was recorded at cost, and there has been no subsequent impairment.

At the same time as the purchase of the ordinary share capital, AZ purchased 40% of BY's preferred share capital at par. The remainder of the preferred shares are held by several private investors.

(2) <u>Investment by AZ in CX</u>

Several years ago AZ purchased 60% of CX's ordinary share capital for $2,730,000 when the reserves of CX were $1,300,000. Goodwill was recorded at cost and there has been no subsequent impairment.

On 1 October 20X5, AZ disposed of 520,000 ordinary shares in CX, thus losing control of CX's operations. However, AZ retains a significant influence over the entity's operations and policies. The proceeds of disposal, $1,250,000, were debited to cash and credited to a suspense account. No other accounting entries have been made in respect of the disposal. The fair value of the remaining investment in CX at the date of disposal was $2,800,000. An investment gains tax of 30% of the profit on disposal will become payable by AZ within the twelve months following the year end of 31 March 20X6, and this liability should be accrued.

CX's reserves at 1 April 20X5 were $1,970,000. The entity's profits accrued evenly throughout the year.

(3) <u>Additional information</u>

No fair value adjustments were required in respect of assets or liabilities upon either of the acquisitions of ordinary shares. The called up share capital of both BY and CX has remained the same since the acquisitions were made. It is the group's policy to value non-controlling interest at acquisition at its proportionate share of the fair value of the subsidiary's identifiable net assets.

(4) <u>Intra-group trading</u>

During the year ended 31 March 20X6, BY started production of a special line of goods for supply to AZ. BY charges a mark-up of 20% on the cost of such goods sold to AZ. At 31 March 20X6, AZ's inventories included goods at a cost of $180,000 that had been supplied by BY.

Required

(a) Calculate the profit or loss on disposal after tax of the investment in CX that will be disclosed in

    (i) AZ's own financial statements

    (ii) The AZ group's consolidated financial statements   **(6 marks)**

(b) Calculate the consolidated reserves of the AZ group at 31 March 20X6.   **(5 marks)**

(c) Prepare the consolidated statement of financial position of the AZ group at 31 March 20X6.   **(14 marks)**

Full workings should be shown.   **(Total = 25 marks)**

---

34   RW (FA 5/05)   18 mins

RW held on 1 Jan 20X4 80% of the 1,000,000 ordinary shares of its subsidiary, SX. Summarised income statements of both entities for the year ended 31 December 20X4 are shown below.

	RW	SX
	$'000	$'000
Revenue	6,000	2,500
Operating costs	(4,500)	(1,700)
Profit before tax	1,500	800
Income tax expense	(300)	(250)
Profit for the year	1,200	550

RW purchased 800,000 of SX's $1 shares in 20X3 for $3.2 million, when SX's reserves were $2.4 million. Goodwill has been carried at cost since acquisition and there has been no subsequent impairment.

On 1 July 20X4, RW disposed of 400,000 shares in SX for $3 million. SX's reserves at 1 January 20X4 were $2.9 million, and its profits accrued evenly throughout the year. The fair value of the investment retained is $1m. RW is liable to income tax of $40,000 on the gain on disposal of the investment in SX.

The effects of the disposal are not reflected in the income statements shown above.

It is the group's policy to value the non-controlling interest at acquisition at its proportionate share of the fair value of the subsidiary's net assets.

Required

Prepare the summarised consolidated income statement for RW for the year ended 31 December 20X4.

(10 marks)

35 AD (FA 11/06)   45 mins

The statements of financial position of three entities, AD, BE and CF at 30 June 20X6, the year end of all three entities, are shown below.

	AD		BE		CF	
	$'000	$'000	$'000	$'000	$'000	$'000
ASSETS						
Non-current assets						
Property, plant and equipment	1,900		680		174	
Financial assets						
Investments in equity shares	880		104		–	
Other (Note 3)	980		–		–	
		3,760		784		174
Current assets						
Inventories	223		127		60	
Trade receivables	204		93		72	
Other financial asset (Note 4)	25		–		–	
Cash	72		28		12	
		524		248		144
		4,284		1,032		318
EQUITY AND LIABILITIES						
Equity						
Called up share capital ($1 shares)	1,000		300		100	
Reserves	2,300		557		122	
		3,300		857		222
Non-current liabilities		600		–		–
Current liabilities						
Trade payables	247		113		84	
Income tax	137		62		12	
		384		175		96
		4,284		1,032		318

Notes

(1)   Investment by AD in BE

AD acquired 80% of the ordinary shares of BE on 1 July 20X3 for $880,000 when BE's reserves were $350,000. It is group policy to measure non-controlling interests at acquisition at their proportionate share of the subsidiary's net assets. Goodwill on acquisition continues to be unimpaired.

(2)   Investment by BE in CF

BE acquired 40% of the ordinary shares of CF on 1 January 20X6 for $104,000. BE appoints one of CF's directors and, since the acquisition, has been able to exert significant influence over CF's activities. CF's reserves at the date of acquisition were $102,000.

(3)   Non-current financial asset

AD's other non-current financial asset is a debenture with a fixed interest rate of 5%. AD invested $1 million in the debenture at par on its issue date, 1 July 20X4. The debenture is redeemable at a premium on 30 June 20X8; the applicable effective interest rate over the life of the debenture is 8%. The full annual interest amount was received and recorded by AD in June 20X5 and June 20X6, and the appropriate finance charge was recognised in the financial year ended 30 June 20X5. However, no finance charge has yet been calculated or recognised in respect of the financial year ended 30 June 20X6.

(4) Current financial asset

The current financial asset of $25,000 in AD represents a holding of shares in a major listed company. AD maintains a portfolio of shares held for trading. At 30 June 20X6, the only holding in the portfolio was 4,000 shares in DG, a major listed company with 2.4 million ordinary shares in issue. The investment was recognised on its date of purchase, 13 May 20X6, at a cost of 625c per share. At 30 June 20X6, the fair value of the shares had risen to 670c per share.

(5) Intra-group trading

BE supplies goods to both AD and CF. On 30 June 20X6, CF held inventories at a cost of $10,000 that had been supplied to it by BE. BE's profit margin on the selling price of these goods is 30%.

On 30 June 20X6, AD's inventories included no items supplied by BE. However, BE's receivables on 30 June 20X6 included $5,000 in respect of an intra-group balance relating to the supply of goods to AD. No equivalent balance was included in AD's payables because it had made a payment of $5,000 on 27 June 20X6, which was not received and recorded by BE until after the year end.

Required

(a) Explain the accounting treatment in the statement of financial position and income statement for the financial assets described in Notes 3 and 4 above, as required by IAS 39 *Financial Instruments: recognition and Measurement*. **(5 marks)**

(b) Prepare the consolidated statement of financial position for the AD Group at 30 June 20X6. **(20 marks)**

(Total = 25 marks)

36   RBE (5/11)   18 mins

RBE owns 70% of the ordinary share capital of DCA. The total group equity as at 31 December 20X1 was $4,000,000, which included $650,000 attributable to non-controlling interest.

RBE purchased a further 20% of the ordinary share capital of DCA on 1 October 20X2 for $540,000.

During the year to 31 December 20X2, RBE issued 2 million $1 ordinary shares, fully paid, at $1.30 per share.

Dividends were paid by both group entities in April 20X2. The dividends paid by RBE and DCA were $200,000 and $100,000, respectively.

Total comprehensive income for the year ended 31 December 20X2 for RBE was $900,000 and for DCA was $600,000. Income is assumed to accrue evenly throughout the year.

Required:

(a) **Explain** the impact of the additional 20% purchase of DCA's ordinary share capital by RBE on the equity of the RBE Group. **(3 marks)**

(b) **Prepare** the consolidated statement of changes in equity for the year ended 31 December 20X2 for the RBE Group, showing the total equity attributable to the parent and to the non-controlling interest. **(7 marks)**

(Total = 10 marks)

37 SOT Group (5/10)   45 mins

The statements of comprehensive income for three entities for the year ended 30 September 20X9 are presented below:

	SOT $'000	PB $'000	UV $'000
Revenue	6,720	6,240	5,280
Cost of sales	(3,600)	(3,360)	(2,880)
Gross profit	3,120	2,880	2,400
Administrative expenses	(760)	(740)	(650)
Distribution costs	(800)	(700)	(550)
Investment income	80	–	–
Finance costs	(360)	(240)	(216)
Profit before tax	1,280	1,200	984
Income tax expense	(400)	(360)	(300)
Profit for the year	880	840	684
Other comprehensive income			
Actuarial gains on defined benefit pension plan	110	–	40
Tax effect of other comprehensive income	(30)	–	(15)
Other comprehensive income for the year, net of tax	80	–	25
Total comprehensive income for the year	960	840	709

Additional information

1. SOT acquired 160,000 of the 200,000 $1 issued ordinary share capital of PB on 1 May 20X9 for $2,800,000. The reserves of PB at 1 May 20X9 were $2,050,000. A year end impairment review indicated that goodwill on acquisition of PB was impaired by 10%. The group policy is to charge impairment losses to administrative expenses. The group policy is to value the non-controlling interest at the proportionate share of the fair value of the net assets at the date of acquisition.

    The fair value of the net assets acquired was the same as the book value with the exception of property, plant and equipment, which was higher by $960,000. The uplift in value related to a depreciable property with an estimated total useful life of 50 years. At the date of acquisition PB had owned and used this property for 10 years. The group policy is to charge depreciation on buildings to administrative expenses on a monthly basis from the date of acquisition to the date of disposal.

2. SOT disposed of 40,000 $1 ordinary shares of UV on 1 July 20X9 for $960,000. SOT had acquired 75,000 of the 100,000 $1 issued ordinary share capital of UV for $980,000 on 1 November 20X6, when the balance on reserves was $1,020,000. The fair value of the shareholding retained at 1 July 20X9 was $792,000. There was no evidence of goodwill having been impaired since the date of acquisition. The reserves of UV at 1 October 20X8 were $1,300,000.

3. PB paid a dividend of $100,000 on 1 September 20X9 and SOT has recorded its share in investment income.

4. SOT holds several available for sale investments, and accounts for these in accordance with IAS 39 *Financial Instruments: recognition and measurement*. Gains on subsequent measurement of $46,000 occurred in the year. The financial controller, however is unsure how this should be presented within the statement of comprehensive income and so has yet to include it.

5. SOT also disposed of an available for sale investment during the year to 30 September 20X9 for $630,000, when the carrying value of the investment was $580,000. The gain on disposal of $50,000 is included in administrative expenses. Previously recognised gains associated with this investment of $40,000 still remain in other reserves.

    Assume that all income and gains for the three entities accrue evenly throughout the year.

    Ignore any further tax impact of available for sale investments.

    Round all figures to the nearest $000.

    Required

    Prepare the consolidated statement of comprehensive income for the SOT group for the year ended 30 September 20X9.   **(Total = 25 marks)**

38 ROB Group (11/10)   45 mins

The statements of financial position for ROB and PER as at 30 September 20X3 are provided below:

	ROB $000	PER $000
ASSETS		
Non-current assets		
Property, plant and equipment	22,000	5,000
Available for sale investment (note 1)	4,000	-
	26,000	5,000
Current assets		
Inventories	6,200	800
Receivables	6,600	1,900
Cash and cash equivalents	1,200	300
	14,000	3,000
Total assets	40,000	8,000
EQUITY AND LIABILITIES		
Equity		
Share capital ($1 equity shares)	20,000	1,000
Retained earnings	7,500	5,000
Other components of equity	500	-
Total equity	28,000	6,000
Non-current liabilities		
5% Bonds 20X6 (note 2)	3,900	-
Current liabilities	8,100	2,000
Total liabilities	12,000	2,000
Total equity and liabilities	40,000	8,000

Additional information:

1. ROB acquired a 15% investment in PER on 1 May 20X1 for $600,000. The investment was classified as available for sale and the gains earned on it have been recorded within other reserves in ROB's individual financial statements. The fair value of the 15% investment at 1 April 20X3 was $800,000.

    On 1 April 20X3, ROB acquired an additional 60% of the equity share capital of PER at a cost of $2,900,000. In its own financial statements, ROB has kept its investment in PER as an available for sale asset recorded at its fair value of $4,000,000 as at 30 September 20X3.

2. ROB issued 4 million $1 5% redeemable bonds on 1 October 20X2 at par. The associated costs of issue were $100,000 and the net proceeds of $3.9 million have been recorded within non-current liabilities. The bonds are redeemable at $4.5 million on 30 September 20X6 and the effective interest rate associated with them is approximately 8.5%. The interest on the bonds is payable annually in arrears and the amount due has been paid in the year to 30 September 20X3 and charged to the income statement.

3. An impairment review was conducted at the year end and it was decided that the goodwill on the acquisition of PER was impaired by 10%.

4. It is the group policy to value non-controlling interest at fair value at the date of acquisition. The fair value of the non-controlling interest at 1 April 20X3 was $1.25 million.

5. The profit for the year of PER was $3 million, and profits are assumed to accrue evenly throughout the year.

6. PER sold goods to ROB for $400,000. Half of these goods remained in inventories at 30 September 20X3. PER makes 20% margin on all sales.

7. No dividends were paid by either entity in the year to 30 September 20X3.

Required:

(a) **Explain** how the investment in PER should be accounted for in the consolidated financial statements of ROB, following the acquisition of the additional 60% shareholding.   **(5 marks)**

(b) **Prepare** the consolidated statement of financial position as at 30 September 20X3 for the ROB Group.
                                                                                               (20 marks)

                                                                                        (Total = 25 marks)

39 Preparation question: Foreign operations

Standard Co acquired 80% of Odense SA for $520,000 on 1 January 20X4 when the reserves of Odense were 2,100,000 Danish Krone.

An impairment test conducted at the year end revealed impairment losses of 168,000 Danish Krone relating to Odense's recognised goodwill. No impairment losses had previously been recognised.

It is group policy to measure NCI at acquisition at the proportionate share of the fair value of the net assets.

Required

Prepare the consolidated statement of financial position, income statement and statement of changes in equity (attributable to owners of the parent *only*) for the Standard Group for the year ended 31 December 20X6.

> **Helping hand**
>
> Fill in the blanks in the proformas below.

STATEMENTS OF FINANCIAL POSITION AS AT 31 DECEMBER 20X6

	S	O	Rate	O	Consol
	$'000	Kr'000		$'000	$'000
Property, plant and equipment	1,285	4,400	8.1	543	
Investment in Odense	520	–		–	
Goodwill	–	–		–	_____
	1,805	4,400		543	
Current assets	410	2,000	8.1	247	_____
	2,215	6,400		790	
Share capital	500	1,000	9.4	106	
Retained reserves	1,115				
Pre-acquisition		2,100	9.4	224	
Post-acquisition	–	2,200	Bal	324	_____
	1,615	5,300		654	
Non-controlling interest					_____
Loans	200	300	8.1	37	
Current liabilities	400	800	8.1	99	_____
	600	1,100		136	
	2,215	6,400		790	

Exchange rates were as follows:

	Kr to $1
1 January 20X4	9.4
31 December 20X5	8.8
31 December 20X6	8.1
Average 20X6	8.4

STATEMENTS OF COMPREHENSIVE INCOME FOR YEAR ENDED 31 DECEMBER 20X6

	S	O	Rate	O	Consol
	$'000	Kr'000		$'000	$'000
Revenue	1,125	5,200	8.4	619	
Cost of sales	(410)	(2,300)	8.4	(274)	_____
Gross profit	715	2,900		345	
Other expenses	(180)	(910)	8.4	(108)	
Impairment loss	–	–		–	
Dividend received from Odense	40				
Profit before tax	575	1,990		237	_____
Income tax expense	(180)	(640)	8.4	(76)	
Profit for the year	395	1,350		161	

Other comprehensive income:
Exchange differences on translating foreign operations _____
Total comprehensive income _____

	Consol $'000
Profit attributable to:	
Owners of the parent	
Non-controlling interest	
	‗‗‗‗‗
Total comprehensive income attributable to:	
Owners of the parent	
Non-controlling interest	
	‗‗‗‗‗

STATEMENTS OF CHANGES IN EQUITY FOR THE YEAR

	S $'000	O Kr'000
Balance at 1 January 20X6	1,415	4,355
Profit for the year	395	1,350
Dividends paid	(195)	(405)
Balance at 31 December 20X6	1,615	5,300

CONSOLIDATED STATEMENT OF CHANGES IN EQUITY (ATTRIBUTABLE TO OWNERS OF THE PARENT) FOR THE YEAR ENDED 31 DECEMBER 20X6

	$'000
Balance at 1 January 20X6	
Total comprehensive income for the year	
Dividends paid	
Balance at 31 December 20X6	‗‗‗‗‗

40   Little (FA Pilot paper)   45 mins

Little was incorporated over twenty years ago, operating as an independent entity for fifteen years until 20X1 when it was taken over by Large. Large's directors decided that the local expertise of Little's management should be utilised as far as possible, and since the takeover they have allowed the subsidiary to operate independently, maintaining its existing supplier and customer bases. Large exercises 'arm's length' strategic control, but takes no part in day-to-day operational decisions.

The statements of financial position of Large and Little at 31 March 20X7 are given below. The statement of financial position of Little is prepared in francos (F), its reporting currency.

	Large $'000	Large $'000	Little F'000	Little F'000
Non-current assets				
Property, plant and equipment	63,000		80,000	
Investments	12,000		–	
		75,000		80,000
Current assets				
Inventories	25,000		30,000	
Trade receivables	20,000		28,000	
Cash	6,000		5,000	
		51,000		63,000
		126,000		143,000
Equity				
Share capital (50c/1 Franco shares)		30,000		40,000
Retained earnings		35,000		34,000
Revaluation reserve		–		6,000
		65,000		80,000

	Large $'000	Large $'000	Little F'000	Little F'000
Non-current liabilities				
Long-term borrowings	20,000		25,000	
Deferred tax	6,000		10,000	
		26,000		35,000
Current liabilities				
Trade payables	25,000		20,000	
Tax	7,000		8,000	
Bank overdraft	3,000		–	
		35,000		28,000
		126,000		143,000

NOTES TO THE STATEMENTS OF FINANCIAL POSITION

(1)   Investment by Large in Little

On 1 April 20X1 Large purchased 36,000,000 shares in Little for 72 million francos. The accumulated profits of Little at that date were 26 million francos. There was no impairment of goodwill.

(2)   Intra-group trading

Little sells goods to Large, charging a mark-up of one-third on production cost. At 31 March 20X7, Large held $1 million (at cost to Large) of goods purchased from Little in its inventories. The goods were purchased during March 20X7 and were recorded by Large using an exchange rate of $1 = 5 francos. (There were minimal fluctuations between the two currencies during March 20X7.) At 31 March 20X6, Large's inventories included no goods purchased from Little. On 29 March 20X7, Large sent Little a cheque for $1 million to clear the intra-group payable. Little received and recorded this cash on 3 April 20X7.

(3)   Accounting policies

The accounting policies of the two companies are the same, except that the directors of Little have decided to adopt a policy of revaluation of property, whereas Large includes all property in its statement of financial position at a depreciated historical cost. Until 1 April 20X6, Little operated from rented warehouse premises. On that date, the entity purchased a leasehold building for 25 million francos, taking out a long-term loan to finance the purchase. The building's estimated useful life at 1 April 20X6 was 25 years, with an estimated residual value of nil, and the directors decided to adopt a policy of straight-line depreciation. The building was professionally revalued at 30 million francos on 31 March 20X7, and the directors have included the revalued amount in the statement of financial position. No other property was owned by Little during the year.

Large measures non-controlling interests at acquisition at the proportionate share of the fair value of the subsidiary's net assets.

(4)   Exchange rates

Date	Exchange rate Francos to $1
1 April 20X1	6.0
31 March 20X6	5.5
31 March 20X7	5.0
Weighted average for the year to 31 March 20X7	5.2
Weighted average for the dates of acquisition of closing inventory	5.1

Required

(a)   Explain (with reference to relevant accounting standards to support your argument) how the financial statements (statement of financial position and income statement) of Little should be translated into $s for the consolidation of Large and Little.   **(5 marks)**

(b)   Translate the statement of financial position of Little at 31 March 20X7 into $s and prepare the consolidated statement of financial position of the Large group at 31 March 20X7.   **(20 marks)**

Note. Ignore any deferred tax implications of the property revaluation and the intra-group trading.

(Total = 25 marks)

41 Small (FR, 5/03, amended) 45 mins

Small was incorporated 18 years ago and prior to its acquisition by Big had built up its own customer base and local supplier network. This was not disturbed when Small became a subsidiary of Big as the directors of Big were anxious that the local expertise of the management of Small should be utilised as much as possible. Therefore all the day-to-day operational decisions regarding Small continued to be made by the existing management, with the directors of Big exercising 'arm's length' strategic control.

The statements of financial position of Big and Small at 31 March 20X9 are given below. The statement of financial position of Small is prepared in florins, the reporting currency for Small.

	Big		Small	
	$000	$000	Fl'000	Fl'000
Non-current assets				
Property, plant and equipment	60,000		80,000	
Investments	9,500		–	
		69,500		80,000
Current assets				
Inventories	30,000		40,000	
Trade receivables	25,000		32,000	
Cash	3,000		4,000	
		58,000		76,000
		127,500		156,000
Equity				
Share capital (50 cents/1/2 florin shares)		30,000		40,000
Retained earnings		34,500		44,000
Revaluation reserve		15,000		–
		79,500		84,000
Non-current liabilities				
Long-term borrowings	15,000		30,000	
Deferred tax	5,000		9,000	
		20,000		39,000
Current liabilities				
Trade payables	12,000		15,000	
Tax	16,000		18,000	
		28,000		33,000
		127,500		156,000

NOTES TO THE STATEMENTS OF FINANCIAL POSITION

(1) Investment by Big in Small

On 1 April 20X3, Big purchased 60 million shares in Small for 57 million florins. The retained earnings of Small showed a balance of 20 million florins at that date. The accounting policies of Small are the same as those of Big except that Big revalues its land, whereas Small carries its land at historical cost. Small's land had been purchased on 1 April 20X0. On 1 April 20X3, the fair value of the land of Small was 6 million florins higher than its carrying value in the individual financial statements of that enterprise. By 31 March 20X9, the difference between fair value and carrying value had risen to 11 million florins. Apart from this accounting policy difference, no other fair value adjustments were necessary when initially consolidating Small as a subsidiary.

Big measures non-controlling interests at acquisition at the proportionate share of the fair value of the subsidiary's net assets.

(2) Intra-group trading

On 6 March 20X9, Big sold goods to Small at an invoiced price of $6,000,000, making a profit of 25% on cost. Small recorded these goods in inventory and payables using an exchange rate of 5 florins to $1 (there were minimal fluctuations between the two currencies in the month of March 20X9). The goods remained in the inventory of Small at 31 March 20X9 but on 29 March 20X9 Small sent Big a cheque for 30 million florins to clear its payable. Big received and recorded this cash on 3 April 20X9.

(3)   Exchange rates

Date	Exchange rate Florins to $1
1 April 20X0	7.0
1 April 20X3	6.0
31 March 20X8	5.5
31 March 20X9	5.0
Weighted average for the year to 31 March 20X9	5.2
Weighted average for the dates of acquisition of closing inventory	5.1

Required

Translate the statement of financial position of Small at 31 March 20X9 into $s and prepare the consolidated statement of financial position of the Big group at 31 March 20X9.   **(25 marks)**

42 Home group (FA 11/06)   18 mins

The income statements for Home and its wholly owned subsidiary Foreign for the year ended 31 July 20X6 are shown below.

	Home $'000	Foreign Crowns '000
Revenue	3,000	650
Cost of sales	(2,400)	(550)
Gross profit	600	100
Distribution costs	(32)	(41)
Administrative expenses	(168)	(87)
Finance costs	(15)	(10)
Profit (loss) before tax	385	(38)
Income tax	(102)	10
Profit (loss) for the year	283	(28)

Notes

(1)   The presentation currency of the group is the $ and Foreign's functional currency is the Crown.

(2)   Home acquired 100% of the ordinary share capital of Foreign on 1 August 20X4 for 204,000 Crowns. Foreign's share capital at that date comprised 1,000 ordinary shares of 1 Crown each, and its reserves were 180,000 Crowns. In view of its subsidiary's losses, Home's directors conducted an impairment review of the goodwill at 31 July 20X6. They concluded that the goodwill had lost 20% of its value during the year (before taking exchange differences into account). The impairment should be reflected in the consolidated financial statements for the year ended 31 July 20X6.

(3)   On 1 June 20X6, Home purchased an item of plant for 32,000 Florins. At the year end, the payable amount had not yet been settled. No exchange gain or loss in respect of this item is reflected in Home's income statement above.

(4)   Exchange rates are as follows:

On 1 August 20X4:	1.7 Crowns = $1
On 31 July 20X6:	2.2 Crowns = $1
Average rate for year ended 31 July 20X6:	2.4 Crowns = $1
On 1 June 20X6:	1.5 Florins = $1
On 31 July 20X6:	1.6 Florins = $1

(5)   During the year, Foreign made sales of 50,000 Crowns to Home. None of the items remained in inventory at the year end.

Required

Prepare the consolidated income statement for the Home group for the year ended 31 July 20X6. (Work to the nearest $100)   **(10 marks)**

43 ABC Group (5/11)   45 mins

Extracts from the financial statements of A, its subsidiary, B and its associate, C for the year to 30 September 20X6 are presented below:

Summarised statement of comprehensive income	A	B	C
	A$000	B$000	A$000
Revenue	4,600	2,200	1,600
Cost of sales and operating expenses	(3,700)	(1,600)	(1,100)
Profit before tax	900	600	500
Income tax	(200)	(150)	(100)
Profit for the year	700	450	400
Other comprehensive income:			
Revaluation of property, plant and equipment	200	120	70
Total other comprehensive income	200	120	70
Total comprehensive income	900	570	470

Statement of financial position	A	B	C
	A$000	B$000	A$000
Assets			
Non-current assets			
Property, plant and equipment	7,000	4,000	2,000
Investment in B	5,200		
Investment in C	900		
	13,100	4,000	2,000
Current assets	3,000	2,000	1,000
Total assets	16,100	6,000	3,000
Equity and liabilities			
Share capital	2,000	1,000	1,000
Reserves	12,100	3,500	1,500
	14,100	4,500	2,500
Current liabilities	2,000	1,500	500
Total equity and liabilities	16,100	6,000	3,000

Additional information

1. The functional currency of both A and C is the A$ and the functional currency of B is the B$.

2. A acquired 80% of B on 1 October 20X3 for A$5,200,000 when the reserves of B were B$1,800,000. The investment is held at cost in the individual financial statements of A.

3. A acquired 40% of C on 1 October 20X1 for A$900,000 when the reserves of C were A$700,000. The investment is held at cost in the individual financial statements of A.

4. No impairment to either investment has occurred to date.

5. The group policy is to value the non-controlling interest at fair value at the date of acquisition. The fair value of the non-controlling interest of B at 1 October 20X3 was B$600,000.

6. Relevant exchange rates are as follows:

1 October 20X3	A$/B$0.5000
30 September 20X5	A$/B$0.7100
30 September 20X6	A$/B$0.6300
Average rate for year ended 30 September 20X6	A$/B$0.6500

Required:

Prepare the consolidated statement of comprehensive income for the A Group for the year ended 30 September 20X6 and the consolidated statement of financial position as at that date.

(Total = 25 marks)

44 AH Group (FA 11/05)   45 mins

Extracts from the consolidated financial statements of the AH group for the year ended 30 June 20X5 are given below.

AH GROUP CONSOLIDATED INCOME STATEMENT FOR THE YEAR ENDED 30 JUNE 20X5

	20X5 $'000
Revenue	85,000
Cost of sales	59,750
Gross profit	25,250
Operating expenses	5,650
Finance cost	1,400
Disposal of property (note 2)	1,250
Profit before tax	19,450
Income tax	6,250
Profit for the year	13,200
Profit attributable to:	
Owners of the parent	12,545
Non-controlling interest	655
	13,200

AH GROUP: EXTRACTS FROM STATEMENT OF CHANGES IN EQUITY FOR THE YEAR ENDED 30 JUNE 20X5

	Share capital $'000	Share premium $'000	Consolidated retained earnings $'000
Opening balance	18,000	10,000	18,340
Issue of share capital	2,000	2,000	
Profit for year			12,545
Dividends			(6,000)
Closing balance	20,000	12,000	24,885

AH GROUP STATEMENT OF FINANCIAL POSITION AT 30 JUNE 20X5

	20X5 $'000	$'000	20X4 $'000	$'000
ASSETS				
Non current assets				
Property, plant and equipment	50,600		44,050	
Intangible assets (note 3)	6,410		4,160	
		57,010		48,210
Current assets				
Inventories	33,500		28,750	
Trade receivables	27,130		26,300	
Cash	1,870		3,900	
		62,500		58,950
		119,510		107,160
EQUITY AND LIABILITIES				
Equity				
Share capital	20,000		18,000	
Share premium	12,000		10,000	
Consolidated retained earnings	24,885		18,340	
		56,885		46,340
Non-controlling interest		3,625		1,920
Non current liabilities				
Interest-bearing borrowings		18,200		19,200

	20X5		20X4	
	$'000	$'000	$'000	$'000
Current liabilities				
Trade payables	33,340		32,810	
Interest payable	1,360		1,440	
Tax	6,100		5,450	
		40,800		39,700
		119,510		107,160

Notes

(1) Several years ago, AH acquired 80% of the issued ordinary shares of its subsidiary, BI. On 1 January 20X5, AH acquired 75% of the issued ordinary shares of CJ in exchange for a fresh issue of 2 million of its own $1 ordinary shares (issued at a premium of $1 each) and $2 million in cash. The net assets of CJ at the date of acquisition were assessed as having the following fair values.

	$'000
Property, plant and equipment	4,200
Inventories	1,650
Receivables	1,300
Cash	50
Trade payables	(1,950)
Tax	(250)
	5,000

It is group policy to measure NC1 at acquisition at the proportionate share of the fair value of net assets.

(2) During the year, AH disposed of a non-current asset of property for proceeds of $2,250,000. The carrying value of the asset at the date of disposal was $1,000,000. There were no other disposals of non-current assets. Depreciation of $7,950,000 was charged against consolidated profits for the year.

(3) Intangible assets comprise goodwill on acquisition of BI and CJ (20X4: BI only). Goodwill has remained unimpaired since acquisition.

Required

Prepare the consolidated statement of cash flows of the AH Group for the financial year ended 30 June 20X5 in the form required by IAS 7 *Statement of cash flows*, and using the indirect method. Notes to the statement of cash flows are **not** required, but full workings should be shown.

(25 marks)

45 EAG Group (FA 5/08) — 45 mins

Extracts from the consolidated financial statements of the EAG Group for the year ended 30 April 20X8 are as follows:

EAG GROUP CONSOLIDATED INCOME STATEMENT FOR THE YEAR ENDED 30 APRIL 20X8

	$m
Revenue	30,750.00
Cost of sales	(26,447.50)
Gross profit	4,302.50
Distribution costs	(523.00)
Administrative expenses	(669.40)
Finance cost	(510.90)
Share of profit of associate	1.60
Profit on disposal of associate	3.40
Profit before tax	2,604.20
Income tax	(723.90)
Profit for the year	1,880.30
Profit attributable to:	
Owners of the parent	1,652.30
Non-controlling interests	228.00
	1,880.30

EAG GROUP STATEMENT OF FINANCIAL POSITION AT 30 APRIL 20X8

	20X8		20X7	
	$m	$m	$m	$m
ASSETS				
Non-current assets				
Property, plant and equipment	22,225.10		19,332.80	
Goodwill	1,662.70		1,865.30	
Intangible assets	306.50		372.40	
Investment in associate	–		13.80	
		24,194.30		21,584.30
Current assets				
Inventories	5,217.00		4,881.00	
Trade receivables	4,633.60		4,670.00	
Cash	62.50		88.30	
		9,913.10		9,639.30
		34,107.40		31,223.60
EQUITY AND LIABILITIES				
Equity				
Share capital	4,300.00		3,600.00	
Retained earnings	14,643.70		12,991.40	
		18,943.70		16,591.40
Non-controlling interest		2,010.50		1,870.50
Non-current liabilities				
Long-term borrowings		6,133.90		6,013.00
Current liabilities				
Trade payables	5,579.30		5,356.30	
Short-term borrowings	662.40		507.70	
Income tax	777.60		884.70	
		7,019.30		6,748.70
		34,107.40		31,223.60

Notes

(1)   Depreciation of $2,024. 7 million was charged in respect of property, plant and equipment in the year ended 30 April 20X8.

(2)   On 1 January 20X8 EAG disposed of the investment in associate for $18 million. The share of profit in the income statement relates to the period from 1 May 20X7 to 31 December 20X7. A dividend was received from the associate on 1 June 20X7. There were no other disposals, and no acquisitions, of investments in the accounting period.

(3)   Goodwill in one of the group's subsidiaries suffered an impairment during the year. The amount of the impairment was included in cost of sales.

(4)   The long-term borrowings are measured at amortised cost. The borrowing was taken out on 1 May 20X6, and proceeds of $6,000 million less issue costs of $100 million were received on that date. Interest of 5% of the principal is paid in arrears each year, and the borrowings will be redeemed on 30 April 20Y1 for $6. 55 million. All interest obligations have been met on the due dates. The effective interest rate applicable to the borrowings is 7%. The finance cost in the income statement includes interest in respect of both the long-term and the short-term borrowing. Short-term borrowing comprises overdrafts repayable on demand.

(5)   Amortisation of 25% of the opening balance of intangibles was charged to cost of sales. A manufacturing patent was acquired for a cash payment on 30 April 20X8.

(6)   An issue of share capital at par was made for cash during the year.

(7)   Dividends were paid to non-controlling interests during the year, but no dividend was paid to the equity holders of the parent entity.

Required

Prepare the consolidated statement of cash flows of the EAG Group for the financial year ended 30 April 20X8. The statement of cash flows should be presented in accordance with the requirements of IAS 7 *Statement of cash flows*, and using the indirect method. Notes to the financial statement are NOT required, but full workings should be shown.   **(25 marks)**

46   MIC (Pilot paper)   45 mins

The consolidated statement of financial position for MIC as at 31 March 20X9 and its comparative for 20X8 is shown below:

	20X9	20X8
	$000	$000
ASSETS		
Non-current assets		
Property, plant and equipment	16,800	15,600
Goodwill	2,900	2,400
Investment in associate	8,000	7,800
	27,700	25,800
Current assets		
Inventories	11,600	12,000
Receivables	9,400	8,200
Held for trading investment	2,200	1,800
Cash and cash equivalents	1,400	4,100
	24,600	26,100
Total assets	52,300	51,900
EQUITY AND LIABILITIES		
Equity attributable to owners of the parent		
Share capital ($1 ordinary shares)	12,000	10,000
Share premium	2,800	–
Other reserves	400	400
Retained earnings	7,300	6,300
	22,500	16,700
Non-controlling interest	6,500	6,100
Total equity	29,000	22,800
Non-current liabilities		
Long term loans	14,000	18,000
Current liabilities		
Payables	8,700	10,200
Income tax	600	900
	9,300	11,100
Total liabilities	23,300	29,100
Total equity and liabilities	52,300	51,900

The consolidated income statement for MIC for the year ended 31 March is shown below:

	$000
Revenue	12,000
Cost of sales	(8,400)
Gross profit	3,600
Distribution costs	(400)
Administrative expenses	(1,260)
Finance costs	(450)
Share of profit of associate	500
Profit before tax	1,990
Income tax expenses	(600)
PROFIT FOR THE YEAR	1,390
Attributable to:	
Owners of the parent	1,200
Non-controlling interest	190
	1,390

Additional information:

1.   There were no disposals of property, plant and equipment in the year. Depreciation charged in arriving at plant totalled $1,800,000.

2. MIC acquired 90% of the ordinary share capital of GH on 1 December 20X8 for a cash consideration of $460,000 plus the issue of 1 million $1 ordinary shares in MIC, which had a deemed value of $3.60 per share at the date of acquisition. The fair values of the net assets acquired were as follows:

	$000
Property, plant and equipment	800
Inventories	2,200
Receivables	700
Cash and cash equivalents	200
Payables	(500)
	3,400

MIC made no other purchases or sales of investments in the year. The group policy is to value the non-controlling interest at acquisition at the proportionate share of the fair value of the net assets.

3. Finance costs include interest on loans and any gains or losses on held for trading investments. All interest due was paid in the year.

Required

Prepare the consolidated statement of cash flows for MIC for the year ended 31 March 20X9. **(25 marks)**

47 LKL (FA 11/09, amended) 45 mins

The following extracts are from the consolidated financial statements of the LKL group. The consolidated financial statements for the year ended 31 March 20X9 are presented below.

Consolidated statement of financial position as at 31 March 20X9

	20X9 $m	20X8 $m
ASSETS		
Non-current assets		
Property, plant and equipment (Note 1)	847	840
Goodwill (Note 4)	108	75
Intangible assets (Note 2)	105	60
Investment in associate	240	200
Investments – available for sale (Note 3)	60	53
	1,360	1,228
Current assets		
Inventories	320	280
Trade receivables	360	310
Investments – held for trading (Note 3)	26	20
Cash and cash equivalents	52	36
	758	646
Total assets	2,118	1,874
EQUITY AND LIABILITIES		
Equity attributable to the owners of the parent		
Share capital ($1 ordinary shares)	450	300
Share premium	280	200
Other reserves	49	42
Retained earnings	447	380
	1,226	922
Non-controlling interest	164	120
Total equity	1,390	1,042
Non-current liabilities		
Long term borrowing	380	540
Deferred tax	78	70
Total non-current liabilities	458	610
Current liabilities		
Trade and other payables	230	190
Current tax payable	40	32
	270	222
Total equities and liabilities	2,118	1,874

Consolidated statement of comprehensive income for LKL group for the year ended 31 March 20X9

	20X9
Revenue	1,800
Cost of sales	(1,050)
Gross profit	750
Distribution costs	(256)
Administrative expenses (Note 2)	(305)
Finance costs	(140)
Share of profit of associate	50
Profit before tax (Note 1)	99
Income tax expense	(20)
Profit for the year	79
	20X9
Other comprehensive income	
Gains on available for sale financial assets	7
Total comprehensive income for the year	86
Profit attributable to:	
Owners of the parent	67
Non-controlling interests	12
	79
Total comprehensive income attributable to:	
Owners of the parent	74
Non controlling interests	12
	86

Additional information

Note 1. Depreciation of $130 million was charged in arriving at profit before tax. A number of the additions to plant and equipment were purchased abroad and a foreign exchange gain totalling $5 million arose on the settlement of the related payables. This has been included in administrative expenses.

Note 2. Intangible assets relate to development expenditure that has been capitalised in accordance with IAS 38 *Intangible Assets*. An amount of $30 million was amortised in the year and charged to administrative expenses.

Note 3. There were no purchases or disposals of the investments held as available for sale and those designated as held for trading. These investments have been accounted for in accordance with IAS 39 *Financial Instruments: recognition and measurement*. Gains on held for trading investments have been netted off against finance costs.

Note 4. LKL acquired 80% of the ordinary share capital of ZZ during the year. The consideration was made up of 100 million $1 shares with fair value of $1.50 plus $60 million cash. The net assets of ZZ at the date of acquisition were as follows:

	$m
Property, plant and equipment	70
Inventories	60
Receivables	70
Cash and cash equivalents	20
Trade and other payables	(30)
	190

LKL measures non-controlling interests at acquisition at their proportionate share of the fair value of the subsidiary's net assets.

An impairment review of purchased goodwill resulted in an impairment loss being charged to administrative expenses.

Required

Prepare the consolidated statement of cash flows for the LKL group for the year ended 31 March 20X9, in accordance with IAS 7 *Statement of cash flows* using the indirect method (notes are not required but full workings should be shown).   **(Total 25 marks)**

ANALYSIS AND INTERPRETATION OF FINANCIAL ACCOUNTS

Questions 48 to 71 cover reporting and analysing performance, the subject of Part D of the BPP Study Text for Paper F2.

48 LOP (11/10) 18 mins

LOP operates in the construction industry and prepares its financial statements in accordance with IFRS. It is listed on its local exchange. LOP is looking to expand its overseas operations by acquiring a new subsidiary. Two geographical areas have been targeted, Frontland and Sideland. Entity A operates in Frontland and entity B operates in Sideland. Both entities are listed on their local exchanges.

The financial highlights for entities A, B and LOP are provided below for the last trading period.

	A	B	LOP
Revenue	$160m	$300m	$500m
Gross profit margin	26%	17%	28%
Net profit	9%	11%	16%
Gearing	65%	30%	38%
Average rate of interest available in the respective markets	5%	9%	8%
P/E ratio	11.6	15.9	16.3

Required:

(a) **Analyse** the information provided by the key financial indicators above and **explain** the impact that each entity would have on the financial indicators of LOP. **(7 marks)**

(b) **Explain** the limitations of using this type of analysis to decide on a potential takeover target. **(3 marks)**

(Total = 10 marks)

49 FGH Cash (3/11) 18 mins

FGH has been trading for a number of years and is currently going through a period of expansion of its core business area.

The statement of cash flows for the year ended 31 December 20X0 for FGH is presented below.

Cash flows from operating activities	$000	$000
Profit before taxation	2,200	
Adjustments for:		
Depreciation	380	
Gain on sale of investments	(50)	
Loss on sale of property, plant and equipment	45	
Investment income	(180)	
Interest costs	420	
	2,815	
Increase in trade receivables	(400)	
Increase in inventories	(390)	
Increase in payables	550	
Cash generated from operations	2,575	
Interest paid	(400)	
Income taxes paid	(760)	
Net cash from operating activities		1,415

	$000	$000
Cash flows from investing activities		
Acquisition of subsidiary (net of cash acquired)	(800)	
Acquisition of property, plant and equipment	(340)	
Proceeds from sale of equipment	70	
Proceeds from sale of investments	150	
Interest received	100	
Dividends received	80	
Net cash used in investing activities		(740)
Cash flows from financing activities		
Proceeds from share issue	300	
Proceeds from long term borrowings	300	
Dividend paid to equity holders of the parent	(1,000)	
Net cash used in financing activities		(400)
Net increase in cash and cash equivalents		275
Cash and cash equivalents at the beginning of the period		110
Cash and cash equivalents at the end of the period		385

Required:

Analyse the above statement of cash flows for FGH, highlighting the key features of each category of cash flows.

(Total = 10 marks)

50   BCA (11/09, amended)   45 mins

BCA is a multinational entity and part of its business is the operation of power stations. Minimising pollution is of primary concern to the entity and therefore it has contracts with CAD, a relatively new and innovative entity, to undertake regular monitoring of the output of potentially hazardous gases from the stations.

CAD utilises sophisticated equipment that is highly sensitive to many gases. The equipment and related software were developed by CAD using innovative techniques created by the Chief Scientific Officer (CSO) who has extensive expertise in gas sensing and laser physics. A number of CAD's products have been patented. As the CSO is considered to be a vital part of the entity's ongoing success, CAD required her to sign a nine month contract. This contract prevents her from developing similar products for anyone else for a further 12 months. The CSO was also given a bonus this year, as the development of new technology helped to secure a lucrative four year contract with a new customer. It is likely to bring additional revenues from existing contracts over the next couple of years. The CSO has an equity stake in the business as does the Chief Executive.

Despite having another three key contracts, similar to the one with BCA, CAD is struggling financially and is desperately in need of investment. CAD is having difficulty raising finance as it has very few tangible assets on which security can be offered.

The directors of CAD have approached the board of BCA to ask for investment and have indicated that they would be willing to give up their controlling interest in CAD if the entity's future and their own, could be secured.

Summary financial information is provided below:

INCOME STATEMENT FOR THE YEAR ENDED
30 SEPTEMBER 20X9 FOR CAD

	20X9	20X8
	$'000	$'000
Revenue	4,330	3,562
Cost of sales	(3,702)	(2,810)
Gross profit	628	752
Other operating expenses	(465)	(580)
Finance costs	(13)	(2)
Profit before tax	150	170
Income tax expense	(42)	(45)
Profit for the year	108	125

STATEMENT OF FINANCIAL POSITION AS AT
30 SEPTEMBER 20X9 FOR CAD

	20X9 $'000	20X8 $'000
ASSETS		
Non-current assets		
Property, plant and equipment	52	78
Intangible assets	89	38
	141	116
Current assets		
Inventories	125	72
Trade receivables	1,091	587
Cash and cash equivalents	58	318
	1,274	977
Total assets	1,415	1,093
EQUITY AND LIABILITIES		
Equity attributable to equity owners of the parent		
Share capital ($1 ordinary shares)	4	4
Retained earnings	539	431
Total equity	543	435
Non-current liabilities		
Provisions	62	173
Current liabilities		
Trade and other payables	687	485
Short term borrowings	123	–
Total current liabilities	810	485
Total liabilities	872	658
Total equity and liabilities	1,415	1,093

Required

(a) Prepare a preliminary report for the board of BCA, highlighting the key considerations of CAD as a potential target for acquisition. Your report should include discussion of the key challenges that CAD faces and whether these would change if BCA were to acquire CAD. (5 marks are available for relevant ratios that can aid your discussion.) **(15 marks)**

(b) (i) Explain why there is increasing pressure to extend the scope of corporate reporting and why this may result in an increase in narrative reporting. **(4 marks)**

(ii) Discuss why a report, similar to the UK's Operating and Financial Review, might be helpful to potential investors in CAD. **(6 marks)**

(Total = 25 marks)

51 BZJ (FA 5/06)   45 mins

You advise a private investor who holds a portfolio of investments in smaller listed companies. Recently, she has received the annual report of the BZJ Group for the financial year ended 31 December 20X5. In accordance with her usual practice, the investor has read the chairman's statement, but has not looked in detail at the figures. Relevant extracts from the chairman's statement are as follows.

'Following the replacement of many of the directors, which took place in early March 20X5, your new board has worked to expand the group's manufacturing facilities and to replace non-current assets that have reached the end of their useful lives. A new line of storage solutions was designed during the second quarter and was put into production at the beginning of September. Sales efforts have been concentrated on increasing our market share in respect of storage products, and in leading the expansion into Middle Eastern markets.

The growth in the business has been financed by a combination of loan capital and the issue of additional shares. The issue of 300,000 new $1 shares was fully taken up on 1 November 20X5, reflecting, we believe, market confidence in the group's new management. Dividends have been reduced in 20X5 in order to increase profit retention to fund the further growth planned for 20X6. The directors believe that the implementation of their medium– to long-term strategies will result in increased returns to investors within the next two to three years.'

The group's principal activity is the manufacture and sale of domestic and office furniture. Approximately 40% of the product range is bought in from manufacturers in other countries.

Extracts from the annual report of the BZJ Group are as follows:

BZJ GROUP
CONSOLIDATED INCOME STATEMENT FOR THE YEAR ENDED 31 DECEMBER 20X5

	20X5 $'000	20X4 $'000
Revenue	120,366	121,351
Cost of sales	(103,024)	(102,286)
Gross profit	17,342	19,065
Operating expenses	(11,965)	(12,448)
Interest payable	(1,469)	(906)
Profit before tax	3,908	5,711
Income tax expense	(1,125)	(1,594)
Profit for the year	2,783	4,117
Profit attributable to:		
Owners of the parent	2,460	3,676
Non-controlling interest	323	441
	2,783	4,117

BZJ GROUP
SUMMARISED CONSOLIDATED STATEMENT OF CHANGES IN EQUITY
FOR THE YEAR ENDED 31 DECEMBER 20X5 (ATTRIBUTABLE TO OWNERS OF THE PARENT)

	Retained earnings $'000	Share capital $'000	Share premium $'000	Reval. reserve $'000	Total 20X5 $'000	Total 20X4 $'000
Opening balance	18,823	2,800	3,000		24,623	21,311
Surplus on revaluation of properties				2,000	2,000	
Profit for the period	2,460				2,460	3,676
Issue of share capital		300	1,200		1,500	–
Dividends paid 31/12	(155)				(155)	(364)
Closing balance	21,128	3,100	4,200	2,000	30,428	24,623

BZJ GROUP
CONSOLIDATED STATEMENT OF FINANCIAL POSITION AS AT 31 DECEMBER

	20X5 $'000	$'000	20X4 $'000	$'000
Non-current assets				
Property, plant and equipment	40,643		21,322	
Goodwill	1,928		1,928	
Trademarks and patents	1,004		1,070	
		43,575		24,320
Current assets				
Inventories	37,108		27,260	
Trade receivables	14,922		17,521	
Cash	–		170	
		52,030		44,951
		95,605		69,271
Equity				
Share capital ($1 shares)	3,100		2,800	
Share premium	4,200		3,000	
Retained earnings	21,128		18,823	
Revaluation reserve	2,000		–	
		30,428		24,623
Non-controlling interest		2,270		1,947
Non-current liabilities				
Interest bearing borrowings		26,700		16,700

	20X5		20X4	
	$'000	$'000	$'000	$'000
Current liabilities				
Trade and other payables	31,420		24,407	
Income tax	1,125		1,594	
Short-term borrowings	3,662		–	
		36,207		26,001
		95,605		69,271

Required

(a) Calculate the earnings per share figure for the BZJ Group for the years ended 31 December 20X5 and 20X4, assuming that there was no change in the number of ordinary shares in issue during 20X4.

(3 marks)

(b) Produce a report for the investor that:

    (i) Analyses and interprets the financial statements of the BZJ Group, commenting upon the group's performance and position **(17 marks)**

    (ii) Discusses the extent to which the chairman's comments about the potential for improved future performance are supported by the financial statement information for the year ended 31 December 20X5 **(5 marks)**

(Total = 25 marks)

52 ABC (FA 5/06) — 45 mins

You are the assistant to the Chief Financial Officer (CFO) of ABC, a light engineering business based in Bolandia. ABC, a listed entity, has expanded over the last few years with the successful introduction of innovative new products. In order to further expand its product range and to increase market share, it has taken over several small, unlisted, entities within its own country.

ABC's directors have recently decided to expand its markets by taking over entities based in neighbouring countries. As the first step in the appraisal of available investment opportunities the CFO has asked you to prepare a brief report on the position and performance of three possible takeover targets: entity W based in Winlandia, entity Y based in Yolandia and entity Z based in Zeelandia. These three countries share a common currency with Bolandia, and all three target entities identify their principal activity as being the provision of light engineering products and services. The report is to comprise a one page summary of key data and a brief written report providing an initial assessment of the targets. The format of the summary is to be based upon the one generally used by ABC for its first-stage assessment of takeover targets, but with the addition of

(a) Price/earnings ratio information (because all three target entities are listed in their own countries)
(b) Some relevant country-specific information

You have produced the one-page summary of key data, given below, together with comparative information for ABC itself, based on its financial statements for the year ended 31 March 20X6.

	ABC	W	Y	Z
Country of operation	Bolandia	Winlandia	Yolandia	Zeelandia
Date of most recent annual report	31 March 20X6	31 January 20X6	30 June 20X5	30 June 20X5
Financial statements prepared in compliance with:	IFRS	IFRS	Yolandian GAAP	IFRS
Revenue	$263.4m	$28.2m	$24.7m	$26.3m
Gross profit margin	19.7%	16.8%	17.3%	21.4%
Operating profit margin	9.2%	6.3%	4.7%	8.3%
Return on total capital employed	11.3%	7.1%	6.6%	12.3%
Equity	$197.8m	$13.6m	$14.7m	$16.7m
Long-term borrowings	$10.4m	$6.2m	$1.3m	$0.6m
Average interest rate applicable to long-term borrowings by listed entities	7.5%	6%	8%	10%
Income tax rate	30%	28%	31%	38%
Inventories turnover	47 days	68 days	52 days	60 days

Receivables turnover	44 days	42 days	46 days	47 days
Payables turnover	46 days	50 days	59 days	73 days
Current ratio	1.4 : 1	0.7 : 1	1.1 : 1	0.9 : 1
P/E ratio	18.6	12.6	18.3	15.2

ABC has a cash surplus and would seek to purchase outright between 90% and 100% of the share capital of one of the three entities. The directors of ABC do not intend to increase the gearing of the group above its existing level. Upon acquisition they would, as far as possible, retain the acquired entity's management and its existing product range. However, they would also seek to extend market share by introducing ABC's own products.

Required

Prepare a report to accompany the summary of key data. The report should:

(a) Analyse the key data, comparing and contrasting the potential takeover targets with each other and with ABC itself. **(13 marks)**

(b) Discuss the extent to which the entities can be validly compared with each other, identifying the limitations of inter-firm and international comparisons. **(12 marks)**

(Total = 25 marks)

53   AXZ (FA 11/06)   45 mins

AXZ is a rapidly expanding entity that manufactures and distributes hair care and other beauty products. Its directors are currently considering expansion into foreign countries by means of acquisitions of similar entities. Two acquisition possibilities are to be considered at the next board meeting: DCB, an entity operating in Lowland, and GFE which operates in Highland. The target acquisitions are of similar size, and operate within similar economic parameters and the same currency, although their tax regimes differ substantially. Neither entity is listed. Neither Lowland nor Highland requires unlisted entities to comply with IFRS, and consequently both entities comply with local GAAP. Local GAAP in both countries is, in most respects, similar to IFRS but there are some differences that must be taken into account when making comparisons between financial statements produced in the two countries. AXZ is listed, and complies with IFRS.

The directors of both DCB and GFE have co-operated fully in providing detailed information about their businesses. Provided that a reasonable price is offered for the shares, takeover is unlikely to be resisted by either entity. AXZ can afford to fund one acquisition but not both.

The most recent income statements of the three entities are provided below, together with some relevant statement of financial position totals.

INCOME STATEMENTS FOR THE YEAR ENDED 30 SEPTEMBER 20X6

	AXZ	DCB	GFE
	$'000	$'000	$'000
Revenue	8,300	1,900	2,200
Cost of sales	(5,600)	(1,300)	(1,400)
Gross profit	2,700	600	800
Distribution costs	(252)	(60)	(65)
Administrative expenses	(882)	(180)	(250)
Finance costs	(105)	(25)	(65)
Profit before tax	1,461	335	420
Income tax expense	(366)	(134)	(105)
Profit for the year	1,095	201	315

EXTRACTS FROM STATEMENT OF FINANCIAL POSITION AT 30 SEPTEMBER 20X6

	AXZ	DCB	GFE
	$'000	$'000	$'000
Total equity	4,820	1,350	1,931
Non-current liabilities (borrowings)	1,500	500	650
Non-current assets	9,950	1,680	2,400

Notes

(1)   It is customary for entities complying with local GAAP in Lowland to adopt the rates of depreciation used by the tax authorities. Tax depreciation is calculated on the straight-line basis in all cases, at a rate of 12.5% each year on all non-current assets. DCB's non-current assets have been held, on average, for three years, and none are fully depreciated. The age profile of non-current assets held by AXZ and GFE is very similar to that of DCB, but both entities charge an average of 10% straight line depreciation each year.

All depreciation in all three entities has been charged to cost of sales.

(2)   Accounting for financial instruments is similar under Lowland GAAP and IFRS. However, Highland's GAAP takes a less prescriptive approach. GFE has $100,000 of 5% non-participating shares included in equity. Under IFRS, these shares would be classified as non-current liabilities. The 5% fixed charge on these shares has been reflected in the statement of changes in equity; under IFRS it would be shown as part of finance costs. This charge would not, however, be allowable against income tax in Highland.

(3)   The directors of AXZ plan to finance the acquisition through a combination of equity and debt that will be similar, proportionately, to the existing capital structure. When assessing possible takeover targets the following key accounting ratios are of especial interest:

Gross profit margin
Profit before tax as a percentage of sales
Return on equity
Return on total capital employed
Non-current asset turnover
Gearing (long-term debt as a percentage of equity)

Their policy is to consider targets for takeover only if the above ratios for the combined group would not be adversely affected to any material extent.

Required

(a)   Calculate and tabulate for each entity the key ratios listed in Note 3, both before and after taking the information in Notes 1 and 2 above into account.   **(15 marks)**

(b)   Write a concise report for the directors of AXZ, which analyses the financial statement information and interprets the ratios calculated in your answer to part (a). You should also include in your analysis any additional ratios that are likely to be useful to the directors of AXZ in making their decision.   **(10 marks)**

(Total = 25 marks)

54   DPC (FA 11/07)   45 mins

The directors of DPC, a listed entity, have been approached by three out of the five shareholders of PPS, an unlisted competitor. The PPS shareholders are nearing retirement age, and would like to realise their investment in the business. The two remaining shareholders do not object, but would like to retain between them at least a significant influence over the business.

The directors of DPC are currently concerned about the threat of a takeover bid for DPC itself. Although they would like to acquire an interest in PPS as it would help them to increase DPC's market share, they do not want to take any action that would adversely affect their financial statements and certain key accounting ratios (EPS, gearing [calculated as debt/equity], and non-current asset turnover).

There are two possibilities for consideration:

(1)   DPC could purchase 40% of the ordinary shares of PPS, giving it significant influence, but not control. The cost of this would be $3.5 million, to be settled in cash. DPC would pay $1 million out of its cash resources and would increase its existing long-term borrowings for the balance.

(2)   DPC could purchase 60% of the ordinary shares of PPS, giving it control. The cost of this would be $6 million, to be settled in cash. DPC would pay $3 million out of its cash resources, and would increase its existing long-term borrowings for the balance.

The purchase would take place on the first day of the new financial year, 1 January 20X8. Projected summary income statements for the 20X8 financial year, and projected summary statement of financial position at 31 December 20X8 are shown below. The DPC figures are consolidated to include its existing 100% held subsidiaries (it currently holds no interests in associates). The projected financial statements for PPS are for that entity alone.

SUMMARY PROJECTED INCOME STATEMENTS FOR THE YEAR ENDED 31 DECEMBER 20X8

	DPC consolidated Projected: 20X8 $'000	PPS entity Projected: 20X8 $'000
Revenue	60,300	10,200
All expenses including income tax	(55,300)	(9,500)
Profit for the period attributable to owners of parent	5,000	700

SUMMARY PROJECTED STATEMENTS OF FINANCIAL POSITION AT 31 DECEMBER 20X8

	DPC consolidated Projected: 20X8 $'000	PPS entity Projected: 20X8 $'000	Notes
Non-current assets	50,400	9,800	2
Current assets	82,000	16,000	
	132,400	25,800	
Equity	31,400	4,000	3 & 4
Long-term liabilities	10,000	9,300	
Current liabilities	91,000	12,500	
	132,400	25,800	

Notes

(1) DPC's consolidated projected financial statements at 31 December 20X8 do not take into account the proposed acquisition of PPS.

(2) DPC's non-current asset figure includes goodwill on acquisition of various subsidiaries.

(3) PPS's equity comprises 100,000 ordinary shares of $1 each, $3,200,000 of retained earnings brought forward on 1 January 20X8 and $700,000 profit for the period.

(4) DPC will have 10 million ordinary shares of $1 each on 1 January 20X8. No issues of shares will be made during 20X8.

Required

(a) Prepare draft projected financial statements for the DPC group for the year ending 31 December 20X8 under each of the following assumptions:

(i) DPC acquires 40% of the ordinary shares of PPS on 1 January 20X8;
(ii) DPC acquires 60% of the ordinary shares of PPS on 1 January 20X8.

It can be assumed that no impairment of either investment would have taken place by 31 December 20X8 and that DPC would measure non-controlling interests at their proportionate share of the subsidiary's net assets at acquisition. **(14 marks)**

(b) Calculate EPS, gearing and non-current asset turnover ratios based on the draft projected 31 December 20X8 financial statements for:

(i) DPC and its existing subsidiaries
(ii) DPC including the acquisition of an associate interest in PPS
(iii) DPC including the acquisition of a subsidiary interest in PPS **(6 marks)**

(c) Discuss the differences in the accounting ratios under the different scenarios, identifying reasons for the most significant differences. **(5 marks)**

(Total = 25 marks)

55 FJK (FA 5/08)   45 mins

Several years ago, on leaving university, Fay, Jay and Kay set up a business, FJK, designing and manufacturing furniture for sale to retailers. When FJK was established, Fay and Jay each took 45% of the share capital, with Kay holding the remaining 10%. This arrangement has remained unchanged. Fay and Jay have always worked full-time in the business and remain its sole directors. Kay's role was initially part-time, but after the first two years she transferred to full-time work in her own consultancy business. Her contribution to FJK in recent years has been limited to occasionally providing advice. The relationship between the three shareholders has remained good, but all three are so busy that Kay rarely meets the others. FJK has been successful, and in February of each year, with the exception of 20X8, has paid a substantial dividend to its three shareholders.

Kay's consultancy business has also been successful and she now employs 20 staff. You are Kay's financial adviser.

During 20X6, the two directors decided to expand FJK's international sales, by establishing sales forces in two neighbouring countries. By early 20X7, orders were starting to come in from the new countries. The expansion strategy has been very successful. Last week, Kay attended a meeting with Fay and Jay, to discuss the future of FJK. Fay and Jay explained that the business now requires more capital in order to fund further expansion, and the purpose of the meeting with Kay was to request her to inject capital of $250,000 into the business.

Kay was provided with a draft income statement for the year ended 31 March 20X8 and a statement of financial position at that date (given below). The draft statements are unaudited, but the figures are not expected to change, except for the income tax expense figure for 20X8. FJK's accountant has not yet completed a tax calculation and so the 20X7 figure of $164,000 has been used as an estimate. No statement of changes in equity has been provided, but the only movements on it would be in respect of a revaluation of property, plant and equipment that took place during the year, and the movement on retained earnings for profit for the period.

Kay, who has a reasonably good understanding of financial statements, is impressed by the revenue and profit growth. However, she has asked you, as her financial adviser, to look at the figures, in order to identify possible risks and problem areas.

FJK DRAFT INCOME STATEMENT FOR THE YEAR ENDED 31 MARCH 20X8

	20X8	20X7
	$'000	$'000
Revenue	5,973	3,886
Cost of sales	(4,318)	(2,868)
Gross profit	1,655	1,018
Distribution costs	(270)	(106)
Administrative expenses	(320)	(201)
Finance costs	(97)	(40)
Profit before tax	968	671
Income tax expense	(164)	(164)
Profit for the year	804	507

FJK DRAFT STATEMENT OF FINANCIAL POSITION AT 31 MARCH 20X8

	20X8		20X7	
	$'000	$'000	$'000	$'000
ASSETS				
Non-current assets				
Property, plant and equipment		3,413		1,586
Current assets				
Inventories	677		510	
Trade and other receivables	725		553	
Cash	–		12	
		1,402		1,075
		4,815		2,661

	20X8		20X7	
	$'000	$'000	$'000	$'000
EQUITY AND LIABILITIES				
Equity				
Called up share capital ($1 shares)	1		1	
Retained earnings	2,166		1,362	
Revaluation reserve	167		–	
		2,334		1,363
Non-current liabilities				
Long-term borrowings		763		453
Current liabilities				
Loans and borrowings	327		103	
Trade and other payables	1,227		578	
Income tax	164		164	
		1,718		845
		4,815		2,661

Required

Prepare a report for Kay that

(a)   analyses and interprets the draft financial statements and discusses FJK's performance and position.

(19 marks)

(b)   discusses possible risks and problem areas revealed by the financial statements, and the actions that the directors could take to address these risks and problems. **(6 marks)**

(Up to 8 marks are available for the calculation of relevant accounting ratios.)

(Total = 25 marks)

56   BHG (FA 5/08)   45 mins

BHG is a successful listed entity that designs and markets specialist business software. BHG's directors have decided to adopt a policy of expansion into overseas territories through the acquisition of similar software businesses possessing established shares of their domestic markets. BHG's aim is to obtain control, or at the minimum, significant influence (represented by at least 40% of issued share capital) of investee entities. Target investee entities are likely to be listed entities in their own countries, but the acquisition of unlisted entities is not ruled out.

You are a senior accountant in BHG, and you have been asked by the Chief Financial Officer (CFO) to establish a set of key accounting ratios for use in:

(1)   the initial appraisal of potential acquisitions;
(2)   on-going appraisal following acquisitions.

The ratios will be used as part of a suite of quantitative and non-quantitative measurements to compare businesses with each other. The CFO has suggested that it would be appropriate to identify no more than 5-7 key financial ratios.

One of your assistants has suggested a list of 5 key accounting ratios as suitable for both initial and on-going appraisal and comparison. She has provided reasons to support the case for their inclusion as key ratios.

(1)   Earnings per share: 'one of the most important investor ratios, widely used by all classes of investor to assess business performance'.

(2)   Dividend yield: 'this ratio provides a very useful measurement that allows comparison with yields from other equity and non-equity investments'.

(3)   Gearing: 'this is of critical importance in determining the level of risk of an equity investment'.

(4)   Gross profit margin: 'allows investors to assess business performance, and is of particular use over several accounting periods within the same organisation. It is also very useful for comparing performances between businesses'.

(5)   Asset turnover ratios: 'allow the investor to compare the intensity of asset usage between businesses, and over time'.

Required

(a)   Discuss the extent to which each of the 5 suggested accounting ratios is likely to be useful to BHG for both initial and on-going appraisal and comparison, and the extent to which your assistant's assessments of the value of the ratios are justified.   **(15 marks)**

(b)   Explain the problems and limitations of accounting ratio analysis in making inter-firm and international comparisons.   **(10 marks)**

(Total = 25 marks)

57 Non-executive (FA 11/08)   45 mins

Ned is a recently appointed non-executive director of ABC Corp, a listed entity. ABC's corporate governance arrangements permit non-executives to seek independent advice on accounting and legal matters affecting the entity, where they have any grounds for concern. Ned has asked you, an independent accountant, for advice because he is worried about certain aspects of the draft financial statements for ABC's year ended 30 September 20X8.

The ownership of most of ABC's ordinary share capital is widely dispersed, but the three largest institutional shareholders each own around 10% of the entity's ordinary shares. In meetings with management, these shareholders have made it clear that they expect improvements in the entity's performance and position. ABC appointed a new Chief Financial Officer (CFO) at the start of the 20X7/X8 financial year, and the board has set ambitious financial targets for the next five years.

The 20X7/X8 targets were expressed in the form of three key accounting ratios, as follows:

- Return on capital employed (profit before interest as a percentage of debt + equity): 7%
- Net profit margin (profit before tax as a percentage of revenue): 5%
- Gearing (long-term and short-term debt as a percentage of the total of debt + equity): below 48%

The draft financial statements include the following figures:

	$
Revenue	31,850,000
Profit before interest	2,972,000
Interest	1,241,000
Equity	22,450,800
Debt	18,253,500

The key ratios, based on the draft financial statements, are as follows:

Return on capital employed	7.3%
Net profit margin	5.4%
Gearing	44.8%

Ned's copies of the minutes of board meetings provide the following relevant information:

1   On 1 October 20X7 ABC sold an item of plant for $1,000,000 to XB, an entity that provides financial services to businesses. The carrying value of the plant at the date of sale was $1,000,000. XB has the option to require ABC to repurchase the plant on 1 October 20X8 for $1,100,000. If the option is not exercised at that date, ABC will be required under the terms of the agreement between the entities to repurchase the plant on 1 October 20X9 for $1,210,000. ABC has continued to insure the plant and to store it on its business premises. The sale to XB was recognised as revenue in the draft financial statements and the asset was derecognised.

2   A few days before the 30 September 20X8 year end, ABC entered into a debt factoring agreement with LM, a factoring business. The terms of the agreement are that ABC is permitted to draw down cash up to a maximum of 75% of the receivables that are covered under the factoring arrangement. However, LM is able to require repayment of any part of the receivables that are uncollectible. In addition, ABC is obliged to pay interest at an annual rate of 10% on any amounts it draws down in advance of cash being received from customers by LM. As soon as the agreement was finalised, ABC drew down the maximum cash available in respect of the $2,000,000 receivables it had transferred to LM as part of the agreement. This amount was accounted for by debiting cash and crediting receivables.

3   In October 20X7, ABC issued 2,000,000 $1 preference shares at par. The full year's dividend of 8% was paid before the 30 September 20X8 year end, and was recognised in the statement of changes in equity. The preference shares are redeemable in 20Y5, and the entity is obliged to pay the dividend on a fixed date each year. The full $2,000,000 proceeds of the issue were credited to equity capital.

Required

(a)   Discuss the accounting treatment of the three transactions, identifying any errors that you think have been made in applying accounting principles with references, where appropriate, to IFRS. Prepare the adjustments that are required to correct those errors and identify any areas where you would require further information.

(15 marks)

(b)   Calculate the effect of your adjustments on ABC's key accounting ratios for the year ended 30 September 20X8.

(7 marks)

(c)   Explain, briefly, the results and the implications of your analysis to the non-executive director. **(3 marks)**

(Total = 25 marks)

---

58   XYZ (Pilot paper)   45 mins

XYZ has a strategy of growth by acquisition. Two entities, A and B, have been identified and will be considered at the next board meeting. The target entities are of a similar size and operate within similar economic parameters. Neither entity is listed. The entities are subject to different tax regimes. Takeover is unlikely to be resisted by either entity, provided a reasonable price is offered for the shares.

XYZ can afford to fund only one acquisition and the board are asking for a review of the financial statements of both entities together with a recommendation on which of the entities looks a more promising prospect. In previous acquisitions, the board focussed mainly on key benchmarks of profitability, efficiency and risk and to that end it is expecting any report to include analysis of the following key financial ratios:

- Gross profit percentage
- Profit before tax as a percentage of revenue
- Return on capital employed
- Non-current asset turnover
- Gearing (debt/equity)

The most recent income statements for both A and B are presented below, together with extracts from their statements of financial position.

	A	B
	$000	$000
Revenue	3,800	4,400
Cost of sales	(2,700)	(2,820)
Gross profit	1,100	1,580
Distribution costs	(375)	(420)
Administrative expenses	(168)	(644)
Finance costs	(25)	(32)
Profit before tax	532	484
Income tax expense	(148)	(170)
PROFIT FOR THE YEAR	384	314

Extracts from statement of financial position	$000	$000
Total equity	950	1,500
Non-current liabilities (borrowings)	500	650
Non-current assets	1,700	1,500

Additional information:

1. A's administrative expenses include a gain of $350,000 on the disposal of non-current assets, following a major restructuring of the entity. The refocusing of the business activities also resulted in some capital investment which was undertaken near the end of its financial period.

2. A has a Held for Trading investment on the statement of financial position. Entity A made a gain on this investment of $20,000 in the period and this has been deducted from finance costs.

Required

(a) Prepare a report for presentation to the board of XYZ, which analyses the financial information provided and recommends the most suitable takeover target. (8 marks are available for the calculation of ratios).

(18 marks)

(b) Explain the limitations of analysis when comparing two entities, using A and B as examples.   **(7 marks)**

(Total = 25 marks)

59   KER (5/10)   45 mins

A friend is seeking advice on one of his investments, KER. KER manufactures stationery supplies. The entity appointed a new Chairman in 20X8 and since then has been implementing an expansion strategy aimed at pursuing new markets with its existing product base.

The Chairman's report included in the 20X9 annual report announces the success of the expansion plan, citing increased revenues and profits as evidence of the entity's success, and noting that the entity has invested in non-current assets to ensure revenue continues to increase. Your friend is intending to retain his investment in KER based on the positive chairman's report but has asked you to consider the financial information to assess whether the figures support the chairman's claims.

The statement of financial position as at 31 December 20X9 and its comparative is shown below:

	20X9 $m	20X8 $m
ASSETS		
Non-current assets		
Property, plant and equipment	480	404
Investment in associate	177	–
Available for sale investments	150	140
	807	544
Current assets		
Inventories	145	65
Receivables	247	134
Cash and cash equivalents	–	22
	392	221
Total assets	1,199	765
EQUITY AND LIABILITIES		
Equity		
Share capital	100	100
Revaluation reserve	74	32
Other reserves	32	22
Retained earnings	457	333
Total equity	663	487
Non-current liabilities		
Loans	400	210
Current liabilities		
Payables	99	68
Overdraft	37	–
	136	68
Total liabilities	536	278
Total equity and liabilities	1,199	765

The statement of comprehensive income for the year ended 31 December 20X9 and its comparative is shown below:

	20X9 $m	20X8 $m
Revenue	1,430	1,022
Cost of sales	(1,058)	(705)
Gross profit	372	317
Administrative expenses	(74)	(62)
Distribution costs	(158)	(100)
Finance costs	(60)	(30)
Share of profit of associate	80	–
Profit before tax	160	125
Income tax expense	(40)	(33)
Profit for the year	120	92
Other comprehensive income:		
Revaluation gain on property, plant and equipment	45	15
Gains on available for sale investments	16	6
Tax effects of other comprehensive income	(14)	(5)
Other comprehensive income for the year, net of tax	47	16
Total comprehensive income for the year	167	108

Required

(a)   Analyse the financial performance and financial position of KER for the year to 31 December 20X9 and comment on the Chairman's claims on expansion (8 marks are available for the calculation of relevant ratios).   **(20 marks)**

(b)   Differences in accounting policies and estimates can affect the comparison of financial statements of two or more entities. Discuss three examples of where such differences could affect comparability between entities.   **(5 marks)**

(Total = 25 marks)

60   GD (11/10)   45 mins

GD is an entity that operates in the packaging industry across a number of different markets and activities. GD has applied to the financial institution where you are employed, for a long term loan of $150 million. Your immediate supervisor was working on the report and recommendation in response to GD's request, but has fallen ill and you have been asked to complete the analysis and prepare the supporting documentation for the next management meeting to discuss applications for lending.

Extracts from the consolidated financial statements of GD are provided below:

Statement of financial position as at 30 June	20X8 $m	20X7 $m
Non-current assets		
Property, plant and equipment	548	465
Goodwill	29	24
	577	489
Current assets		
Inventories	146	120
Receivables	115	125
Held for trading investments	31	18
Cash and cash equivalents	-	41
	292	304
Total assets	869	793
EQUITY AND LIABILITIES		
Equity attributable to owners of the parent		
Share capital ($1 shares)	120	120
Revaluation reserve	18	-
Retained earnings	293	183
	431	303
Non-controlling interest	65	61
Total equity	496	364

	20X8 $m	20X7 $m
Non-current liabilities		
Long term loans	<u>90</u>	<u>180</u>
Current liabilities		
Payables	185	160
Bank overdraft	50	-
Income tax payable	<u>48</u>	<u>89</u>
	283	249
Total liabilities	<u>373</u>	<u>429</u>
Total equity and liabilities	<u>869</u>	<u>793</u>

Statement of comprehensive income for the year ended 30 June	20X8 $m	20X7 $m
Revenue	1,200	1,400
Cost of sales	<u>(840)</u>	<u>(930)</u>
Gross profit	360	470
Distribution costs	(40)	(45)
Administrative expenses	(130)	(120)
Finance costs	<u>(11)</u>	<u>(15)</u>
Profit before tax	179	290
Income tax expense	<u>(50)</u>	<u>(85)</u>
PROFIT FOR THE YEAR	<u>129</u>	205
Other comprehensive income		
Revaluation of property	<u>18</u>	<u>-</u>
Total comprehensive income (net of tax)	<u>147</u>	<u>205</u>
Profit for the year attributable to:		
Owners of the parent	121	195
Non-controlling interest	<u>8</u>	<u>10</u>
	<u>129</u>	<u>205</u>
Total comprehensive income attributable to:		
Owners of the parent	139	195
Non-controlling interest	<u>8</u>	<u>10</u>
	<u>147</u>	<u>205</u>

Additional information

1.   In August 20X7, a new competitor entered one of GD's markets and pursued an aggressive strategy of increasing market share by undercutting GD's prices and prioritising volume sales. The directors had not anticipated this as GD had been the market leader in this area for the past few years.

2.   The minutes from the most recent meeting of the Board of Directors state that the directors believe they can implement a new strategy to regain GD's market position in this segment, providing long term funding can be secured. GD acquired a subsidiary during the year as part of the new strategy and revenue is forecast to increase by the second quarter of 20X9.

3.   A meeting is scheduled with GD's main suppliers to discuss a reduction in costs for bulk orders.

4.   The existing long-term loan is due to be repaid on 1 August 20X9.

5.   Gains of $9 million generated by the held for trading investments have been offset against administrative expenses.

Required:

(a)   **Analyse** the financial performance and financial position of GD and recommend whether or not GD's application for borrowing should be considered further
Note: 8 marks are available for the calculation of relevant ratios.   **(21 marks)**

(b)   **Explain** what further information might be useful in assessing the future prospects of GD and its ability to service a new long term loan.   **(4 marks)**

(Total = 25 marks)

61 DFG (3/11)   45 mins

A friend has approached you looking for some advice. He has been offered the position of Sales Director within an entity, DFG, which supplies the building trade. He commented that he had reviewed the information on DFG's website and there were lots of positive messages about the entity's future, including how it had secured a new supplier relationship in 20X1 resulting in a significant improvement in margins.

He has been offered a lucrative remuneration package to implement a new aggressive sales strategy, but has been with his current employer for six years and wants to ensure his future would be secure. He has provided you with the finalised financial statements for DFG for the year ended 31 December 20X1, with comparatives.

The financial statements for DFG are provided below:

Statement of Financial Position at 31 December	20X1	20X0
ASSETS	$m	$m
Non-current assets		
Property, plant and equipment	254	198
Investment in associate	24	-
	278	198
Current assets		
Inventories	106	89
Receivables	72	48
Cash and cash equivalents	-	6
	178	143
Total assets	456	341
EQUITY AND LIABILITIES		
Equity		
Share capital ($1 equity shares)	45	45
Retained earnings	146	139
Revaluation reserve	40	-
Total equity	231	184
Non-current liabilities		
Long term borrowings	91	91
	91	91
Current liabilities		
Trade and other payables	95	66
Short term borrowings	39	-
	134	66
Total liabilities	225	157
Total equity and liabilities	456	341

Statement of comprehensive income for the year ended 31 December	20X1	20X0
	$m	$m
Revenue	252	248
Cost of sales	(203)	(223)
Gross profit	49	25
Distribution costs	(18)	(13)
Administrative expenses	(16)	(11)
Share of profit of associate	7	-
Finance costs	(12)	(8)
Profit before tax	10	(7)
Income tax expense	(3)	2
Profit for the year	7	(5)
Other comprehensive income:		
Revaluation gain on PPE	40	-
Total other comprehensive income	40	-
Total comprehensive income	47	(5)

Additional information:

1. **Long term borrowings**

   The long term borrowings are repayable in 20X3.

2. **Contingent liability**

   The notes to the financial statements include details of a contingent liability of $30 million. A major customer, a house builder, is suing DFG, claiming that it supplied faulty goods. The customer had to rectify some of its building work when investigations discovered that a building material, which had recently been supplied by DFG, was found to contain a hazardous substance. The initial assessment from the lawyer is that DFG is likely to lose the case although the amount of potential damages could not be measured with sufficient reliability at the year-end date.

3. **Revaluation**

   DFG decided on a change of accounting policy in the year and now includes its land and buildings at their revalued amount. The valuation was performed by an employee of DFG who is a qualified valuer.

Required

(a) **Analyse** the financial performance of DFG for the year to 31 December 20X1 and its financial position at that date AND briefly **discuss** DFG's suitability as a secure employer for your friend (8 marks are available for the calculation of relevant ratios). **(20 marks)**

(b) **Explain** the potential limitations of using traditional ratio analysis as a means of decision making, using DFG's situation to illustrate your answer. **(5 marks)**

(Total = 25 marks)

---

62 CVB (5/11)   45 mins

A friend has recently inherited some money and has approached you seeking investment advice. She has an interest in fashion and has decided to invest in the fashion retail sector. She has performed some initial research which concentrated on the social and economic policies of a number of entities. She has selected a listed entity, CVB, for potential investment as she was particularly impressed with the fact that they had recently introduced a new line of fair-trade clothing.

She has asked that you help with a review of the financial information before she makes her final decision to invest. CVB's current share price is $1.25 per share, which is 40% lower than at the same time last year.

The financial statements for CVB are provided below:

CONSOLIDATED STATEMENT OF FINANCIAL POSITION AS AT 30 SEPTEMBER	20X1	20X0
ASSETS	$m	$m
Non-current assets		
Property, plant and equipment	262	235
Investment in associate	14	16
	276	251
Current assets		
Inventories	140	87
Trade and other receivables	75	63
Cash and cash equivalents	–	9
	215	159
Held for sale assets	4	–
Total assets	495	410
EQUITY AND LIABILITIES		
Equity attributable to owners of the parent		
Share capital ($1 shares)	30	30
Share premium	48	48
Retained reserves	179	164
	257	242

	20X1	20X0
	$m	$m
Non-controlling interest	16	14
Total equity	273	256
Non-current liabilities		
Long-term borrowings	55	58
Deferred tax provision	5	1
	60	59
Current liabilities		
Trade and other payables	144	95
Short-term borrowings	18	–
	162	95
Total liabilities	222	154
Total equity and liabilities	495	410

CONSOLIDATED STATEMENT OF COMPREHENSIVE INCOME FOR THE YEAR ENDED 30 SEPTEMBER	2010	2009
	$m	$m
Revenue	453	412
Cost of sales	(305)	(268)
Gross profit	148	144
Sales and marketing costs	(66)	(60)
Administrative expenses	(62)	(64)
Finance costs	(8)	(5)
Share of (loss)/profit of associate	(2)	3
Profit before tax	10	18
Income tax expense	(2)	(5)
Profit for the year	8	13
Other comprehensive income		
Revaluation gains from property (net of tax)	14	–
Total comprehensive income	22	13
Profit for the year attributable to:		
Equity holders of the parent	7	11
Non-controlling interest	1	2
	8	13
Total comprehensive income attributable to:		
Equity holders of the parent	21	11
Non-controlling interest	1	2
	22	13

Required:

(a) **Analyse** and **prepare** a report on the financial performance and financial position of CVB. *(8 marks are available for the calculation of **relevant** ratios.)* **(20 marks)**

(b) **Explain** what further financial information may assist your friend in deciding whether or not to invest in CVB. **(5 marks)**

(Total = 25 marks)

63   JKL (FA Pilot paper)   18 mins

JKL is a listed entity preparing financial statements to 31 August. At 1 September 20X3, JKL had 6,000,000 50c shares in issue. On 1 February 20X4, the entity made a rights issue of 1 for 4 at 125c per share; the issue was successful and all rights were taken up. The market share price of one share immediately prior to the issue was 145c per share. Earnings after tax for the year ended 31 August 20X4 were $2,763,000.

Several years ago, JKL issued a convertible loan of $2,000,000. The loan carries an interest rate of 7% and its terms of conversion (which are at the option of the stockholder) are as follows:

For each $100 of loan stock:

Conversion at 31 August 20X8:   105 shares
Conversion at 31 August 20X9:   103 shares

JKL is subject to an income tax rate of 32%.

Required

(a)   Calculate basic earnings per share and diluted earnings per share for the year ended 31 August 20X4.

(7 marks)

(b)   The IASB *Framework for the Preparation and Presentation of Financial Statements* states that the objective of financial statements is to provide information that is:

'useful to a wide range of users in making economic decisions'.

Explain to a holder of ordinary shares in JKL both the usefulness and limitations of the diluted earnings per share figure.

(3 marks)

(Total = 10 marks)

64   CB (FA 5/05)   18 mins

On 1 February 20X4, CB, a listed entity, had 3,000,000 ordinary shares in issue. On 1 March 20X4, CB made a rights issue of 1 for 4 at $6.50 per share. The issue was completely taken up by the shareholders.

Extracts from CB's financial statements for the year ended 31 January 20X5 are presented below.

CB EXTRACTS FROM STATEMENT OF COMPREHENSIVE INCOME FOR THE YEAR ENDED 31 JANUARY 20X5

	$'000
Operating profit	1,380
Finance cost	400)
Profit before tax	980
Income tax expense	(255)
Profit for the year	725
Other comprehensive income:	
Gains on property revaluation	900
Total comprehensive income for the year	1,625

CB EXTRACTS FROM SUMMARISED STATEMENT OF CHANGES IN EQUITY
FOR THE YEAR ENDED 31 JANUARY 20X5

	$'000
Balance at 1 February 20X4	7,860
Issue of share capital	4,875
Total comprehensive income for the year	1,625
Equity dividends	(300)
Balance at 31 January 20X5	14,060

Just before the rights issues, CB's share price was $7.50, rising to $8.25 immediately afterwards. The share price at close of business on 31 January 20X5 was $6.25.

At the beginning of February 20X5, the average price earnings (P/E) ratio in CB's business sector was 28.4, and the P/E of its principal competitor was 42.5.

Required

(a)   Calculate the earnings per share for CB for the year ended 31 January 20X5, and its P/E ratio at that date.

(6 marks)

(b)   Discuss the significance of P/E ratios to investors and CB's P/E ratio relative to those of its competitor and business sector.

(4 marks)

(Total = 10 marks)

65   EPS ratio (FA 11/07)   18 mins

Earnings per share (EPS) is generally regarded as a key accounting ratio for use by investors and others. Like all accounting ratios, however, it has its limitations. You have been asked to make a brief presentation to CIMA students on the topic.

Required

(a)   Explain why EPS is regarded as so important that the IASB has issued an accounting standard on its calculation.   **(2 marks)**

(b)   Explain the general limitations of the EPS accounting ratio and its specific limitations for investors who are comparing the performance of different entities.   **(8 marks)**

                                                              (Total = 10 marks)

66   AGZ (FA 11/08)   18 mins

AGZ is a listed entity. You are a member of the team drafting its financial statements for the year ended 31 August 20X8. Extracts from the draft income statement, including comparative figures, are shown below:

	20X8 $million	20X7 $million
Profit before tax	276.4	262.7
Income tax expense	85.0	80.0
Profit for the year	191.4	182.7

At the beginning of the financial year, on 1 September 20X7, AGZ had 750 million ordinary shares of 50¢ in issue. At that date the market price of one ordinary share was 87.6¢.

On 1 December 20X7, AGZ made a bonus issue of one new ordinary 50¢ share for every three held.

In 20X6, AGZ issued $75 million convertible bonds. Each unit of $100 of bonds in issue will be convertible at the holder's option into 200 ordinary 50¢ shares on 31 August 20Y2. The interest expense relating to the liability element of the bonds for the year ended 31 August 20X8 was $6.3 million (20X7 – $6.2 million). The tax effect related to the interest expense was $2.0 million (20X7 – $1.8 million).

There were no other changes affecting or potentially affecting the number of ordinary shares in issue in either the 20X8 or 20X7 financial years.

Required

(a)   Calculate earnings per share and diluted earnings per share for the year ended 31 August 20X8, including the comparative figures.   **(8 marks)**

(b)   Explain the reason for the treatment of the bonus shares as required by IAS 33 *Earnings per Share*.
                                                                   (2 marks)

                                                              (Total = 10 marks)

67   CSA (5/10)   18 mins

On 1 January 20X9 CSA, a listed entity, had 3,000,000 $1 ordinary shares in issue. On 1 May 20X9, CSA made a bonus issue of 1 for 3.

On 1 September 20X9, CSA issued 2,000,000 $1 ordinary shares for $3.20 each. The profit before tax of CSA for the year ended 31 December 20X9 was $1,040,000. Income tax expense for the year was $270,000.

The basic earnings per share for the year ended 31 December 20X8 was 15.4 cents.

On 1 November 20X9 CSA issued convertible loan stock. Assuming the conversion was fully subscribed there would be an increase of 2,400,000 ordinary shares in issue. The liability element of the loan stock is $4,000,000 and the effective interest rate is 7%.

CSA is subject to income tax at a rate of 30%.

Required

(a) Calculate the basic earnings per share to be reported in the financial statements of CSA for the year ended 31 December 20X9, including comparative, in accordance with the requirements of IAS 33 *Earnings Per Share*. **(4 marks)**

(b) Calculate the diluted earnings per share for the year ended 31 December 20X9, in accordance with the requirements of IAS 33 *Earnings Per Share*. **(3 marks)**

(c) Briefly explain why the bonus issue and issue at full market value are treated differently in arriving at basic earnings per share. **(3 marks)**

(Total = 10 marks)

68 Preparation question: Operating segments

The Multitrade Group has three divisions, A, B and C. Details of their revenue, results and assets are given below.

	$'000
Division A	
Sales to B	304,928
Other sales (home)	57,223
Middle East export sales	406,082
Pacific fringe export sales	77,838
	846,071
Division B	
Sales to C	31,034
Export sales to Europe	195,915
	226,949
Division C	
Export sales to North America	127,003

	Head office $'000	Division A $'000	Division B $'000	Division C $'000
Operational profit/(loss) before tax		162,367	18,754	(8,303)
Re-allocated costs from				
Head office		48,362	24,181	24,181
Interest costs		3,459	6,042	527
Non-current assets	49,071	200,921	41,612	113,076
Current assets	47,800	121,832	39,044	92,338

Required

(a) Prepare a segmental report in accordance with IFRS 8 *Operating segments* for publication in Multitrade's group accounts in so far as the information permits.

(b) Comment on what the user of the accounts does and does not learn from this segmental report.

Helping hands

1 The calculations are very straightforward in this question, but be careful with your layout.

2 Make sure you show all the categories necessary for disclosure under IFRS 8.

3 As with all financial information, you have to be able to put it to good use for it to have a value, which is the point in part (b). Your answer should be in point form.

69 STV (FA 11/05)   45 mins

One of your colleagues has recently inherited investments in several listed entities and she frequently asks for your advice on accounting issues. She has recently received the consolidated financial statements of STV, an entity that provides haulage and freight services in several countries. She has noticed that note 3 to the financial statements is headed 'Segment information'.

Note 3 explains that STV's primary segment reporting format is business segments of which there are three: in addition to road and air freight, the entity provides secure transportation services for smaller items of high value. STV's *Operating and Financial Review* provides further background information: the secure transport services segment was established only three years ago. This new operation required a sizeable investment in infrastructure which was principally funded through borrowing. However, the segment has experienced rapid revenue growth in that time, and has become a significant competitor in the industry sector.

Extracts from STV's segment report for the year ended 31 August 20X5 are as follows.

	Road haulage		Air freight		Secure transport		Group	
	20X5	20X4	20X5	20X4	20X5	20X4	20X5	20X4
	$m	$m	$m	$m	$m	$m	$m	$m
Revenue	653	642	208	199	98	63	959	904
Segment result	169	168	68	62	6	(16)	243	214
Unallocated corporate expenses							(35)	(37)
Operating profit							208	177
Interest expense							(22)	(21)
Share of profits of associates	16	12					16	12
Profit before tax							202	168
Income tax							(65)	(49)
Profit							137	119
Other information								
Segment assets	805	796	306	287	437	422	1,548	1,505
Investment in equity method associates	85	84					85	84
Unallocated corporate assets							573	522
Consolidated total assets							2,206	2,111
Segment liabilities	345	349	176	178	197	184	718	711
Unallocated corporate liabilities							37	12
Consolidated total liabilities							755	723

Your colleague finds several aspects of this note confusing:

'I thought I'd understood what you told me about consolidated financial statements; the idea of aggregating several pieces of information to provide an overall view of the activities of the group makes sense. But the segment report seems to be trying to disaggregate the information all over again. What is the point of doing this? Does this information actually tell me anything useful about STV? I know from talking to you previously that financial information does not always tell us everything we need to know. So, what are the limitations in this statement?'

Required

(a)   Explain the reasons for including disaggregated information about business segments in the notes to the consolidated financial statements.   **(5 marks)**

(b)   Analyse and interpret STV's segment disclosures for the benefit of your colleague, explaining findings in a brief report.   **(12 marks)**

(c)   Explain the general limitations of segment reporting, illustrating your answer where applicable with references to STV's segment report.   **(8 marks)**

(Total = 25 marks)

70 RG (FA 11/09, amended)   45 mins

RG, a listed entity, invested significantly in one of its many operating segments in 20X8, by acquiring property, plant and equipment and developing a new distribution network in an attempt to increase market share. The network has been put in place (distribution costs have been incurred within the set budget) and a new sales team has been hired and has just recently completed its product training. The first orders from the new customers were received in June 20X9 and were higher than expected.

Extracts from the financial statements for RG for the year ended 30 June 20X9 are presented below.

Statement of comprehensive income for the RG group

	20X9 $m	20X8 $m
Revenue	576	573
Cost of sales	(422)	(428)
Gross profit	154	145
Distribution costs	(56)	(40)
Administrative expenses (including profit on disposal of investment)	(37)	(22)
Finance costs	(6)	(8)
Share of profit of associate	5	–
Profit before tax	60	75
Income tax expense	(15)	(14)
Profit for the year	45	61
Other comprehensive income		
Gains on available for sale financial assets	6	-
Gains reclassified to profit or loss on disposal of available for sale financial assets	(4)	-
Other comprehensive income for the year, net of tax	2	0
Total comprehensive income for the year	47	61
Profit attributable to:		
Owners of the parent	37	52
Non-controlling interests	8	9
	45	61
Total comprehensive income attributable to:		
Owners of the parent	39	52
Non controlling interests	8	9
	47	61

Statement of changes in equity

	Share capital	Share premium	Other components of equity	Retained earnings	Non-controlling interest	Total
1 July 20X8	80	4	8	372	11	475
Total comprehensive income for the year			2	37	8	47
Dividends				(50)	(5)	(55)
Issue of share capital	30	18	—	—	—	48
30 June 20X9	110	22	10	359	14	515

Statement of financial position as at 30 June 20X9

	20X9 $m	20X8 $m
ASSETS		
Non-current assets		
Property, plant and equipment	371	346
Investment in associate	85	–
Available for sale investments	65	140
	521	486
Current assets		
Inventories	133	82
Receivables	109	76
Cash and cash equivalents	12	137
	254	295
Total assets	775	781

EQUITY AND LIABILITIES
Attributable to owners of the parent:

Called up share capital ($1 shares)	110	80
Share premium	22	4
Other components of equity	10	8
Retained earnings	359	372
	501	464
Non-controlling interest	14	11
Total equity	515	475
Non-current liabilities		
Long-term loan	154	205
Current liabilities		
Trade payables	91	87
Income tax payable	15	14
	106	101
Total equity and liabilities	775	781

A close friend of yours has inherited a portfolio of investments which includes a holding in RG. He is contemplating whether to retain or sell his shareholding. As he does not have a financial background he is looking for your advice. In his email to you he appeared to be focusing his initial conclusions on the decreased profitability of the business but wanted your opinion on the profitability and financial health of RG. He also wants your thoughts on its future prospects. He mentioned that he had had a quick look at the segmental information provided in the financial statements but was confused by the volume of numerical information and was questioning whether a review of the segmental information was relevant for his purposes. To help with your review he has sent through extracts from the financial statements, shown above, but has not provided any segmental information.

Required

(a) Prepare a report that analyses the financial performance and position of RG to assist your friend in his decision making. (8 marks are available for the calculation of **relevant** ratios). **(21 marks)**

(b) Briefly discuss how useful segmental analysis could be in the analysis of RG's financial statements.

(4 marks)

(Total 25 marks)

71 FGH (5/11)   18 mins

The directors of FGH have agreed as part of their strategic plan to list the entity's equity shares on the local stock exchange.

At a recent board meeting, the directors discussed, in overview, the additional compliance that would be required upon listing. This included compliance with the requirements of IFRS 8 *Operating Segments* (IFRS 8). The managing director commented that adherence to the requirements of IFRS 8 would be time-consuming and costly due to the additional financial information that the entity would have to prepare.

Required:

(a) **Discuss** whether the managing director's comment is accurate in respect of the operating segment analysis that is required in accordance with IFRS 8. **(4 marks)**

(b) (i) **Explain** why the information that is presented for operating segments is likely to be highly relevant to investors

(ii) **Discuss** the potential limitations of operating segment analysis as a tool for comparing different entities. **(6 marks)**

(Total = 10 marks)

DEVELOPMENTS IN EXTERNAL REPORTING

Questions 72 to 78 cover developments in external reporting, the subject of Part E of the BPP Study Text for Paper F2.

72 MNO (FA 5/06)   18 mins

You are the assistant to the Finance Director of MNO, a medium-sized listed entity that complies with International Financial Reporting Standards. One of MNO's directors has proposed the publication of an Operating and Financial Review (OFR) as part of the annual financial statements. Most of the directors know very little about the OFR, and the Finance Director has asked you to produce a short briefing paper on the topic for their benefit.

Required

Write the briefing paper, which should discuss the following issues.

(a)   Any relevant regulatory requirements for an OFR
(b)   The purpose and, in outline, the typical content of an OFR
(c)   The advantages and drawbacks of publishing an OFR from the entity's point of view   **(10 marks)**

73 NGO (FA 5/09 amended)   45 mins

NGO has retailing and warehousing operations in several countries and prepares its consolidated financial statements in accordance with IFRS. The directors' expansion strategy over the last few years has been highly successful and has included both organic growth and growth through acquisition. The directors have four key financial ratios that they believe their acquisition targets must meet or exceed, if their strategy is to stay on course.

The current acquisition target is TRP, an entity which operates in Highpark, a fictitious country. The country has a buoyant market and NGO is keen to exploit the opportunities that TRP has available to it. The country does not have its own accounting standard setter and TRP has been preparing its financial statements in accordance with US GAAP.

The financial controller of NGO has prepared a preliminary report on TRP, including the calculation of the four key ratios used in the selection process. The ratios presented below are for TRP based on its published financial statements for the year ended 31 December 20X8. They are shown alongside those calculated for NGO. The directors wish to pursue entities that will not significantly affect the key ratios of NGO in an adverse way. The ratios show that two of the four will have an adverse effect, and on that basis the financial controller made a recommendation that the interest in TRP should not be taken further.

Key ratios:	TRP	NGO
Gearing (debt/equity)	54·5%	52·6%
Return on assets (operating profit/total assets)	9·1%	7·9%
Basic earnings per share	20·6c	102·6c
Current ratio	2·2 : 1	1·2 : 1

The Financial Director has since pointed out that the financial statements are prepared under different accounting rules and they should be compared as if both had adopted IFRS. He added that, although the convergence project had been successful in reducing the significant differences between IFRS and US GAAP, there were three relevant areas where the policies continued to differ and where there may be a significant effect on the financial statements of TRP:

1   NGO has a policy of revaluing property, plant and equipment in the financial statements to reflect current market values. Included within property, plant and equipment of TRP is land held at cost of $4 million. This land had an estimated market value of $5·4 million as at 31 December 20X8.

2   NGO accounts for all inventories using FIFO in accordance with IAS 2 Inventories. TRP's inventories have been valued using LIFO. The value of these inventories, had FIFO been adopted, is $3·6 million.

3   TRP issued $6 million 4% convertible bonds in December 20X8 and in accordance with US GAAP it is classified as a non-current liability. Under IFRS, the instrument would be classified in accordance with IAS 32 Financial instruments: presentation. The bonds have a seven-year term and were issued at par. At the time the bonds were issued, the prevailing market interest rate for similar debt without conversion rights was 6%. As the issue was made close to the year end, no interest is to be accrued in respect of these bonds.

The Financial Director has asked that the financial statements of TRP be brought into line with the policies adopted by NGO and the ratios subsequently recalculated.

The statement of financial position of TRP as at 31 December 20X8 is as follows:

STATEMENT OF FINANCIAL POSITION

	$'000	$'000
Assets		
Non-current assets		
Property, plant and equipment	8,600	
Investment in associate	4,200	
		12,800
Current assets		
Inventories	3,300	
Trade receivables	3,100	
Cash and cash equivalents	1,200	
		7,600
Total assets		20,400

	$'000	$'000
Equity and liabilities		
Equity		
Share capital ($1 ordinary shares)	8,000	
Other reserves	500	
Retained earnings	2,500	
		11,000
Non-current liabilities		
4% Convertible bonds 20Y5		6,000
Current liabilities		
Trade and other payables		3,400
Total equity and liabilities		20,400

Extracts from the income statement of TRP for the year ended 31 December 20X8:

	$'000
Operating profit	1,848
Share of profit of associate	402
Finance income	60
Profit before tax	2,310
Taxation charge	(660)
Profit for the year	1,650

Required

(a)   (i)   Explain how the convertible bonds are accounted for under IAS 32 *Financial Instruments: Presentation.*

(ii)   Prepare a revised statement of financial position for TRP, taking account of all the necessary adjustments required to comply with the requirements of IFRS.   **(9 marks)**

(b)   Recalculate the ratios and provide a brief analysis on how suitable TRP is as an acquisition target for NGO. (Do NOT calculate diluted earnings per share.)   **(9 marks)**

(C)   Your Finance Director has commented on the convergence project and the progress that has been made. Explain the process that is being adopted to pursue convergence and identify FOUR examples of where progress has been achieved.   **(7 marks)**

(Total = 25 marks)

74 Environmental disclosure (Pilot paper) — 18 mins

Shareholders are becoming increasingly interested in the environmental policies, impacts and practices of business entities, however financial statements have not traditionally provided this information. As a result, there has been significant growth in entities providing narrative environmental information on a voluntary basis.

Required

Identify and explain the principal arguments against voluntary disclosures by business entities of their environmental policies, impacts and practices. **(10 marks)**

75 FW (FA 5/05) — 45 mins

FW is a listed entity involved in the business of oil exploration, drilling and refining in three neighbouring countries. Aye, Bee and Cee. The business has been consistently profitable, creating high returns for its international shareholders. In recent years, however, there has been an increase in environmental lobbying in FW's three countries of operation. Two years ago, an environmental group based in Cee started lobbying the government to take action against FW for alleged destruction of valuable wildlife habitats in Cee's protected wetlands and the displacement of the local population. At the time, the directors of FW took legal advice on the basis of which they assessed the risk of liability at less than 50%. A contingent liability of $500 million was noted in the financial statements to cover possible legal costs, compensation to displaced persons and reinstatement of the habitats, as well as fines.

FW is currently preparing its financial statements for the year ended 28 February 20X5. Recent advice from the entity's legal advisors has assessed that the risk of a successful action against FW has increased, and must now be regarded as more likely than not to occur. The board of directors has met to discuss the issue. The directors accept that a provision of $500 million is required, but would like to be informed of the effects of the adjustment on certain key ratios that the entity headlines in its annual report. All of the directors are concerned about the potentially adverse effect on the share price, as FW is actively engaged in a takeover bid that would involve a substantial share exchange. In addition, they feel that the public's image of the entity is likely to be damaged. The chief executive makes the following suggestion:

> 'Many oil business now publish an environmental and social report, and I think it may be time for us to do so. It would give us the opportunity to set the record straight about what we do to reduce pollution, and could help to deflect some of the public attention from us over this law suit. In any case, it would be a good public relations opportunity; we can use it to tell people about our equal opportunities programme. I was reading about something called the Global Reporting Initiative [GRI]. I don't know much about it, but it might give us some help in structuring a report that will get the right message across. We could probably pull something together to go out with this year's annual report.'

The draft financial statements for the year ended 28 February 20X5 include the following information relevant for the calculation of key ratios. All figures are before taking into account the $500 million provision. The provision will be charged to operating expenses.

	$m
Net assets (before long-term loans) at 1 March 20X4	9,016
Net assets (before long-term loans) at 28 February 20X5	10,066
Long-term loans at 28 February 20X5	4,410
Share capital + reserves at 1 March 20X4	4,954
Share capital + reserves at 28 February 20X5	5,656
Revenue	20,392
Operating profit	2,080
Profit before tax	1,670
Profit for the period	1,002

The number of ordinary shares in issue throughout the years ended 29 February 20X4 and 28 February 20X5 were 6,000 million shares of 25c each.

FW's key financial ratios for 20X4 financial year (calculated using financial statements for the year ended 29 February 20X4) were:

Return on equity (using average equity):	24.7%
Return on net assets (using average net assets):	17.7%
Gearing (debt as a percentage of equity):	82%
Operating profit margin:	10.1%
Earnings per share:	12.2c per share

Required

In your position as assistant to FW's Chief Financial Officer produce a briefing paper that

(a)   Analyses and interprets the effects of making the environmental provision on FW's key financial ratios. You should take into account the possible effects on the public perception of FW.   **(12 marks)**

(b)   Identifies the advantages and disadvantages to FW of adopting the Chief Executive's proposal to publish an environmental and social report.   **(7 marks)**

(c)   Describes the three principal sustainability dimensions covered by the GRI's framework of performance indicators.   **(6 marks)**

(Total = 25 marks)

76   Intellectual capital (11/08)   18 mins

CIMA's Official Terminology defines intellectual capital as 'knowledge which can be used to create value'.

Currently, IFRS permit the recognition of only a limited range of internally generated intellectual assets including, for example, copyrights.

Required

(a)   Explain the advantages that could be gained by entities and their stakeholders if the scope of IFRS were expanded to permit the recognition in the statement of financial position of intellectual assets, such as know-how, the value of the workforce, and employee skills.   **(5 marks)**

(b)   Explain the principal reasons why IFRS do not currently permit the recognition in the statement of financial position of intellectual assets such as know-how, the value of the workforce, and employee skills.   **(5 marks)**

(Total for Question Five = 10 marks)

77   Staff resource (11/10)   18 mins

A relative of yours has retired recently from the business world and has decided to invest some of his money in the stock market. You have received an email from him asking for advice:

"I have set aside some funds and wish to make some investments in the stock market. There are a number of entities that have caught my attention and I have been comparing their performance and financial position using their latest financial statements. The management commentary and chairman's statement for one entity in particular, mentions staff being a key resource and a substantial asset."

Required

Discuss why the narrative elements of financial statements are likely to include comments about staff resource being a key asset and the issues of recognition that prevent such assets from being included in the statement of financial position.   **(10 marks)**

78 Service and knowledge (3/11)   18 mins

A friend who likes to invest in the stock market made the following statement to you recently, "I don't invest in entities that operate in service or knowledge-based industries because their financial statements don't really reflect the true value of the entity. This makes it very difficult for me to make informed decisions about whether to invest or not."

Required:

(a) **Discuss** why an investor may arrive at the conclusion that the financial statements of entities operating in service and knowledge based industries are not useful for making investment decisions.   **(5 marks)**

(b) **Explain** the recognition criteria that prevent human capital being recognised as an asset in the financial statements.   **(5 marks)**

(Total = 10 marks)

ANSWERS

78

1 ETH

> **Text reference.** Substance over form is covered in Chapter 1 of the study text, group financial statements and the definition of control is covered in Chapter 6 and foreign currency translation is covered in Chapter 12.
>
> **Top tips.** This question shows how different topics from different parts of the syllabus can be combined in one question. You need to have a **basic** knowledge of all of the syllabus areas, **read** the requirements carefully and then **apply** your knowledge to the specific question.
>
> **Easy marks.** There were some marks available here for demonstrating your basic knowledge of the relevant accounting standards.
>
> **Examiner's comments.** The majority of candidates identified that consolidation was unavoidable and correctly applied substance over form. Candidates did not have to identify that it was a special purpose entity to get full marks. In part (b) some candidates misunderstood the requirement and wasted time describing the method of translating the financial statements.

(a)   SX undertakes activities that ETH would have to do itself if SX did not exist. Ownership of the majority of equity shares normally implies that the holder has control, as per IAS 27 *Consolidated and separate financial statements* and IFRS 3 *Business combinations*, unless there is evidence to the contrary. The director of SX does not have any voting rights and this indicates that ETH as may have control. Furthermore, the agreement that exists between the two entities states that the operating and financial policies of SX are determined by ETH and therefore ETH controls SX. In addition, ETH uses that control to ensure that economic benefit flows from SX to ETH and guarantees any finance that SX has to raise, exposing ETH to any risk arising from default.

SX represents a special purpose entity and the substance of the relationship is that ETH controls SX and it should therefore consolidate it. The $200,000 is not a management charge but the cost of the investment in the subsidiary.

(b)   Functional currency should be determined by the rules within IAS 21 *The effects of changes in foreign exchange rates*. It cannot be selected. The functional currency should be the currency of the primary economic environment in which the entity operates. In determining its functional currency, ZAB should consider the guidelines set down by IAS 21 :

   (i)   The currency that principally influences selling prices for goods and services;

   (ii)   The currency that influences labour, material and other costs;

   (iii)   Which country's competitive forces and regulations principally determine the selling prices of the goods and services;

   (iv)   In which currency funds for financing are generated; and

   (v)   If the foreign enterprise operates autonomously or as an extension of the parent.

In the case of ZAB, the materials are purchased in dollars but it is landers that influence other expenses, sales and labour costs. ZAB also operates with autonomy and arranges its own finance. Therefore the functional currency of ZAB is landers not dollars.

2 AZG

> **Text reference.** Financial instruments are covered in Chapter 2 of the study text.
>
> **Top tips.** Many questions in section A of the paper contain both written and numerical requirements, Don't underestimate the importance of the written parts. They are often the easiest parts so make sure you spend time on them before tacking the numerical part.
>
> **Easy marks.** The easiest marks here are in parts (a) and (b) where you could get credit for knowledge of definitions and other basic points.

> **Examiner's comments.** Candidates who had studied the basics of accounting for derivatives could gain marks here very quickly. Other candidates who clearly knew little about derivatives wasted time on guesswork and writing about other aspects of financial instruments,

(a) According to IAS 39, a financial instrument or other contract is a derivative if it has the following three characteristics.

    (i) Its value changes in response to the change in a specified interest or exchange rate, or in response to the change in a price, rating, index or other variable.

    (ii) It requires no initial net investment or a very small net investment compared to the net investment that other types of contract would require in order to have the same response to changes in the value of the underlying instrument.

    (iii) It is settled at a future date.

    The futures contract meets all three characteristics and it is therefore a derivative.

(b) IAS 39 requires that derivative financial instruments should be recognised as either assets or liabilities. They should be measured at fair value both upon initial recognition and subsequently on the statement of financial position, and changes in their fair value should be recognised in profit or loss unless they qualify for hedge accounting treatment as effective hedging instruments, or when the underlying instrument is an unquoted equity instrument.

(c) <u>AZG: extract from statement of comprehensive income for the year ended 31 March 20X7</u>

	20X7	*20X6*
Gain on derivative	$73,891	$68,966

<u>AZG: extract from statement of financial position at 31 March 20X7</u>

	20X7	*20X6*
Derivative asset	$142,857	$68,966

Workings

The dollar fair value of the forward foreign exchange contract at the relevant dates will be:

27 February 20X6	Fair value: FI 6,000,000/3	=	$2,000,000
31 March 20X6	Fair value: FI 6,000,000/2.9	=	$2,068,966
31 March 20X7	Fair value: FI 6,000,000/2.8	=	$2,142,857

			$
Gain recognised in year ended 31 March 20X6: $2,068,966 − $2,000,000	=		68,966
Gain recognised in year ended 31 March 20X7: $2,142,857 − $2,068,966	=		73,891
Derivative asset at fair value at 31 March 20X7: $68,966 + $73,891	=		142,857

3 RP

> **Text reference.** Financial instruments are covered in Chapter 2 and share-based payment is covered in Chapter 4.
>
> **Top tips.** Make sure that you know the basics of all of the accounting standards in the syllabus, and that you can show the **double entry** needed to apply them, as this is a favourite requirement of the examiner.
>
> **Easy marks.** There are not many easy marks here, but you will start to earn marks as soon as you show some knowledge of the basic principles of each of these transactions, such as splitting the convertible bond into its debt and equity elements (even if the calculations go wrong) and for recognising an expense and a credit to equity for the share-based payment.

(a) <u>Convertible bonds</u>

Present value factor at 7% for 4 years = 0.763

Cumulative present value factor at 7% for 4 years = 3.387

	$
Present value of the principal ($4m × 0.763)	3,052,000
Present value of the interest ($4m × 5%× 3.387)	677,400
Total liability component	3,729,400
Equity component (balancing figure)	170,600
Proceeds of the bond issue	3,900,000

Therefore the accounting entries on issue are:

DEBIT	Bank	3,900,000	
CREDIT	Liability		3,729,400
	Equity		170,600

	$
Opening carrying value at 1.10.2008	3,729,400
Finance cost (7.0% × 3,729,400)	261,058
Interest paid (5% × 4,000,000)	(200,000)
Closing carrying value at 30.09.2009	3,790,458

The interest paid of $200,000 should have already gone through the books, therefore the adjustment required is:

DEBIT	Finance costs	61,058	
CREDIT	Liability		61,058

(b)   Share options

This is an equity-settled share-based payment transaction. Under IFRS 2, the entity estimates the number of options expected to vest and bases the amount that it recognises as an expense and in equity each year on that estimate, spread over the vesting period, that is the three years from the date of the grant on 1 October 2007. The value used for each option is the fair value as at the grant date. The estimate of the total number of options that will vest is updated at each year end.

2008	$
Equity c/d and P/L expense	
((300 – 10 – 30) × 1,000 × $1.10 × 1/3)	95,333

2009	$
Equity b/d	95,333
∴ Profit or loss expense	91,667
Equity c/d ((300 – 10 – 20 – 15) × 1,000 × $1.10 × 2/3)	187,000

Therefore the accounting entries for the year ended 30 September 2009 are:

DEBIT	Staff costs	$91,667	
CREDIT	Equity (other reserves)		$91,667

4   DG

Text reference. Financial instruments are covered in chapter 2 of the text.

Top tips On questions about financial instruments it is worth thinking through the basics:

– identify whether the item is an asset or a liability

– decide which classification it falls into

– apply the correct measurement rules, for initial measurement and subsequent measurement

This should help to get you on the right track.

Easy marks. Basic knowledge of this area should have gained you the main marks for the "explain" part of the requirement.

> **Examiner's comments**. Candidates who scored well addressed all parts of the requirement. The most common errors were failing to treat the held for trading investment as fair value through profit or loss, and calculating the effective interest on the bond on its par value instead of the net proceeds.

Purchase of Held for Trading Investment

The held for trading investment should be classified as an asset held at fair value through profit or loss. It is initially measured at fair value, in this case the cost of $1.75 million (500,000 shares x $3.50). The transaction costs should not be included in the cost of the investment and should be written off to the income statement as a period cost. The investment is subsequently measured (at 30 June 20X9) at fair value of $1.825 million (500,000 shares x $3.65). The following adjustments are therefore required:

DEBIT	Administrative expenses	$15,000
CREDIT	HFT Investment	$15,000

Being the correction in respect of transaction costs

DEBIT	HFT Investment	$75,000
CREDIT	Gain on investment (P/L)	$75,000

Being the gain on the investment being credited to the income statement

Purchase of a bond

The bond purchased by DG should be classified as a held to maturity investment as DG intends to hold it to redemption. It is initially recorded at the net cost of $4.5 million and then subsequently measured at amortised cost using the effective interest rate. Only the interest received of $250,000 (5% x face value of $5 million) has been recorded in the income statement. The following adjustment is therefore required:

DEBIT	HTM Asset	$211,700
CREDIT	Investment income	$211,700

Being the additional investment income to be recognised in profit or loss

Working

	$'000
1 July 20X8 Purchased ($5m x 90%)	4,500
Interest to 30 June 20X9 at effective rate ($4.5m x 10.26%)	461.7
Coupon interest received ($5m x 5%)	(250)
30 June 20X9 Balance c/d	4,711.7

The investment will be held at $4.71 million and a further $211,700 ($461,700 - $250,000) will be credited to the income statement.

5   BCL

> **Text reference**. Financial instruments are dealt with in Chapter 2 of the text.
>
> **Top tips**. Take time to read the detail in this question very carefully. It would be very easy to misunderstand the exchange rates and get the calculations back to front. Derivatives and hedging have not been examined frequently but this question emphasises the importance of studying the syllabus widely.
>
> **Easy marks**. This is a challenging question but there are some easy marks available for applying some basic points about financial instruments. Think through the basic points, such as "is it an asset or liability" and the classifications set out in IAS 39.

(a)   Explanation

This forward contract is a **derivative**. It is a **financial liability** because it is **unfavourable** at the year end.

Under the forward contract, BCL has to pay A$3.125 million (B$2m ÷ 0.64).

At the year end, an equivalent contract would only have cost A$2.857 million (B$2m ÷ 0.7).

Therefore, the contract is standing at a loss of A$0.268 million at the year end. This is why it is a financial liability.

Normally derivatives are treated as being **held for trading** so this contract will be treated as a **financial liability at fair value through profit or loss**.

Journal entry:

| DEBIT | Profit or loss | $0.268m |
| CREDIT | Financial liability | $0.268m |

Being the recognition of the liability and loss on forward contract

(b)   (i)   Recording the gain or loss

If the forward contract is to be treated as a hedging instrument, it should still be measured at its fair value of A$0.268 million but the loss should be recognised in **other comprehensive income** instead of profit or loss.

Why different treatment is necessary

The reason for hedging is to try to **offset the gain/loss on the hedged item** with the **corresponding loss/gain on the hedging instrument**.

With a **cash flow hedge**, the hedged item is often a future or forecast transaction which has not yet been recorded in the financial statements. If the normal accounting treatment was applied the loss on this hedging instrument would be recognised in profit or loss in one period and the gain on the hedged item would be recognised in profit or loss in a later period, so the offsetting effect would not be reflected.

When the gain on the hedged item occurs and is recognised in profit or loss, the loss on the forward contract should be **reclassified** from other comprehensive income to profit or loss. This matches the gain and loss and better reflects the offsetting that was the purpose of the transaction.

(ii)   EXTRACT FROM STATEMENT OF COMPREHENSIVE INCOME FOR THE YEAR ENDED 31 AUGUST 20X0

	A$m
Profit for the year	1
Other comprehensive income	
Loss on forward contract	(0.268)
Total comprehensive income	0.732

Marking scheme

		Marks
(a)		
	Explanation	2
	Calculations	2
	Journal	2
		6
(b)	Explanation	2
	Extract from statement of comprehensive income	2
		4
		10

6 MNB

Text reference. This topic is covered in Chapter 2 of the text.

Top tips. Make sure you analyse each requirement to identify all of the tasks you are being asked to carry out. In part (a) you had to explain a treatment and calculate figures. In part (b) you were asked to prepare journal entries at two different points.

The amortised cost calculations that feature in part (a) come up regularly in financial instruments questions. You need to learn a methodical working to deal with the steps in the calculation.

Easy marks.

The easiest marks were for the explanation in part (a).

Examiner's comments. Candidates still struggle to apply the accounting principles for financial instruments although the questions tend to have a regular format. In part (a) some candidates treated the held to maturity asset as a liability, or wrongly concluded that it was a compound instrument but still earned marks for the principle of amortised cost. In part (b) one mistake was to include the transaction costs in the initial measurement. The most worrying errors were the numbers of journal entries that made no sense, with debits to equity/share capital and credits to investment.

(a) (i) MNB has acquired a financial asset and the question states that it has been correctly classified as **held to maturity**.

The requirements in respect of this category of financial asset under IAS 39 *Financial instruments: recognition and measurement* are as follows:

Initial measurement

The asset should be recorded at its fair value, plus of transaction costs.

The initial value of MNB's investment is $2,800,000 ($3,000,000 - $200,000).

Subsequent measurement

The asset should be measured using the **amortised cost** method. Interest should be accrued using the **effective interest rate** (allocating the true interest earned over the term of the investment, including the actual interest received each year and the premium received on maturity at a constant rate). The effective interest is added to the carrying value of the asset in each accounting period and any cash flows received from the investment will be deducted from its carrying value.

(ii) The financial statements for the year ended 31 December 20X0 will include:

- a financial asset of $2,817,400 (in the statement of financial position)

- interest income of $197,400 (in profit or loss, in the statement of comprehensive income)

Working

	$
1 January 20X0	3,200,000
31 December 20X0 effective interest ($3,200,000 × 7.05%)	225,600
31 December 20X0 coupon interest received ($3,000,000 × 6%)	(180,000)
Balance c/fwd 31 December 20X0	3,245,600

(b) The investment is classified as **held for trading,** so it will be measured at fair value through profit or loss. The journal entries will be:

Initial measurement:

DEBIT	Financial asset	$300,000	
DEBIT	Profit or loss	$12,000	
CREDIT	Cash		$312,000

Subsequent measurement at 31 December 20X0:

DEBIT	Financial asset	$40,000	
CREDIT	Profit or loss		$40,000

Working

	$
25 October 20X0 (200,000 × $3) *(see Note)*	600,000
Gain (balancing figure)	80,000
Balance c/fwd 31 December 20X0	680,000

Notes:

(1) Transaction costs are **excluded** from the initial fair value of a financial asset that is classified as **held for trading**. These costs are charged to profit or loss immediately.

7 QWE

Text reference. Financial instruments are covered in Chapter 2 of the study text.

Top tips. In part (a) don't get so bogged down in the numbers that you run out of time and don't write any **explanation**. You must always tackle all of the parts of each requirement.

Easy marks. In both parts of this question there were easy marks available for demonstrating knowledge of the basic principles of accounting for financial instruments. In part (a) the easier marks were to be found in the written part of the requirement.

Examiner's comments. Candidates have finally taken heed of previous comments on how this area will be examined, concentrating on initial recognition and measurement and subsequent measurement. Part (a) was answered exceptionally well. Part (b) was generally answered well but some candidates wrongly concluded that since the instruments were described as 'shares' they would not affect gearing.

(a) Convertible bonds

A convertible instrument is considered part liability and part equity. IAS 32 requires that each part is measured separately on initial recognition. The liability element is measured by estimating the present value of the future cash flows from the instrument (interest and potential redemption) using a discount rate equivalent to the market rate of interest for a similar instrument with no conversion terms. The equity element is then the balance, calculated as follows:

	$
PV of the principal amount $10m at 7% redeemable in 5 yrs ($10m x 0.713)	7,130,000
PV of the interest annuity at 7% for 5 yrs (5% x $10m) x 4.100	2,050,000
Total value of liability element	9,180,000
Equity element (balancing figure)	820,000
Total proceeds raised	10,000,000

The equity will not be remeasured, however the liability element will be subsequently remeasured at amortised cost recognising the finance cost using the effective interest rate of 7% and deducting the coupon interest paid. The financial statements will include:

Statement of comprehensive income for the year ended 31 December 20X0 (within profit or loss)

	$
Finance cost (7% x 9,180,000)	642,600

Statement of financial position as at 31 December 20X0

	$
Equity	820,000
Liability (W)	18,472,320

Working

	$
Liability recognised 1.1.20X0	9,180,000
Interest to 31.12.20X0 (7% × 9,180,000)	642,600
Interest paid (5% × 10,000,000)	(500,000)
At 31.12.20X0	9,322,600

(b)   Cumulative redeemable preference shares

IAS 32 requires that financial instruments are classified according to their **substance**, rather than their legal form.

The main distinguishing feature of a **liability** is that it contains an **obligation** to transfer economic benefit.

In this case the preference shares are **redeemable** so the company can be compelled to pay back the capital to the shareholders.

Therefore, these preference shares should be classified as **liabilities** and this will **increase the gearing** of QWE.

8   Preparation question: Defined benefit scheme

INCOME STATEMENT NOTE

Defined benefit expense recognised in profit or loss

	$'m
Current service cost	13
Interest cost (10% × 110)	11
Expected return on plan assets (12% × 150)	(18)
Recognised actuarial gains (Working)	(4)
Past service cost	20
	22

STATEMENT OF FINANCIAL POSITION NOTES

Net defined benefit liability recognised in the SOFP

	$'m
Present value of pension obligation	116
Fair value of plan assets	(140)
	(24)
Unrecognised actuarial gains/(losses) (Working)	42
	18

Changes in the present value of the defined benefit obligation

	$'m
Opening defined benefit obligation	110
Interest cost (10% × 110)	11
Current service cost	13
Benefits paid	(10)
Past service cost	20
Actuarial gain (balancing figure)	(28)
Closing defined benefit obligation	116

Changes in the fair value of plan assets

	$'m
Opening fair value of plan assets	150
Expected return on plan assets (12% × 150)	18
Contributions	7
Benefits paid	(10)
Actuarial loss (balancing figure)	(25)
Closing fair value of plan assets	140

Working

Recognised/unrecognised actuarial gains and losses

	$'m	$'m
Corridor limits, greater of:		
10% of pension obligation b/d (10% × 110)	11	
10% of plan assets b/d (10% × 150)	15	
⇒ Corridor limit	15	
Unrecognised gains b/d		43
Gain recognised in I/S [(43 – 15)/7]		(4)
Gain on obligation in the year		28
Loss on assets in the year		(25)
Unrecognised gains c/d		42

9 BGA

Text reference. These topics are covered in Chapter 3.

Top tips. Accounting for defined benefit pension schemes under IAS 19 *Employee benefits* is one of the most complex areas of financial reporting.

Make sure you follow a careful step by step approach. First set out the gain or loss on the **obligation**, calculating the actuarial gain or loss on the obligation as a balancing figure. Then set out the gain or loss on **plan assets**, again calculating the actuarial gain or loss on the plan assets as a balancing figure.

Consider the corridor limit to determine the amount to be recognised in the income statements.

Easy marks. You will gain a substantial proportion of the marks for setting out correctly the constituent elements of the gain or loss on the obligation and the constituent elements of the gain or loss on the plan assets. Show your workings and identify the balancing figure to ensure you gain the remaining two marks.

Gains or loss on obligation

	$
Present value of obligation at start of year	18,360,000
Interest cost (6.5% × $18,360,000)	1,193,400
Current service cost	1,655,000
Benefits paid	(1,860,300)
Actuarial gain on obligation (balancing figure)	(692,600)
Present value of obligation at the end of the year	18,655,500

Gains or loss on plan assets

	$
Fair value of plan assets at start of year	17,770,000
Expected return on plan assets (9.4% × $17,770,000)	1,670,380
Contributions	997,000
Benefits paid	(1,860,300)
Actuarial loss on assets (balancing figure)	(159,900)
Fair value of plan assets at the end of the year	18,417,180

(a) The **actuarial loss** for the year ended 31 October 20X7 on BGA's assets is $159,900 and actuarial gains of $692,600 on the **defined benefit obligation**.

(b) At the start of the year, ie on 1 November 20X6, the net cumulative unrecognised actuarial gains were $802,000.

This means that the amount of **actuarial gains** and **losses** to be recognised in the income statement for year ended 31 October 20X7 will be calculated through the steps set out below. First we need to consider the corridor limits.

Do the **net cumulative unrecognised actuarial gains and losses** exceed 10% of the greater of:

(i) The present value of the obligation before deducting plan assets
10% × 18,360,000 = $1,836,000

(ii)   The fair value of the plan assets
       10% × 17,770,000 = $1,777,000

As the **net cumulative unrecognised actuarial gains** at the start of the year of $802,000 were less than 10 per cent of the greater of:

(i)   The **present value** of the **obligation** before deducting **plan assets**
(ii)   The **fair value** of any **plan assets**

No actuarial gains and losses will be recognised in the income statement during the year ending 31 October 20X7.

Marking scheme

			Marks
(a)	Gain/loss on obligation:		4
	Gain/loss on assets		4
(b)	10% of PV of obligation	0.5	
	10% of PV of asset	0.5	
	Net cumulative unrecognised actuarial gains less than greater of 10% of above	1.0	2
			10

10 EAU

Text reference. Accounting for defined benefit pension schemes is covered in Chapter 3 of the study text.

Top tips. You should learn the standard workings for both of these topics. If you do that, both defined benefit pensions and share-based payment calculations become very mechanical.

Easy marks. In part (a) the calculations should have been fairly easy as the basic calculation of the actuarial gains and losses forms part of all defined benefit pension questions, irrespective of the company's policy for recognising these gains and losses.

Examiner's comments. Many candidates scored full marks on this question. The main error is part (a) was preparing the income statement calculations, which were not required here. The most common errors in part (b) were failing to update the fair value used at the end of the year, as this was a cash-settled share-based payment, and forgetting to use the correct fractions for each year.

(a)

Gains or loss on plan assets

	$
Fair value of plan assets at 1.1.20X2	2,600
Expected return on plan assets (5% × $2,600)	130
Contributions	730
Benefits paid	(240)
Actuarial gain on assets (balancing figure)	180
Fair value of plan assets at 31.12.20X2	3,400

Gains or loss on obligation

	$'000
Present value of obligation at 1.1.20X2	2,900
Current service cost	450
Past service cost	90
Interest cost (8% × $2,900)	232
Benefits paid	(240)
Actuarial loss on obligation (balancing figure)	68
Present value of obligation at 31.12.20X2	3,500

The net actuarial gain that will be recognised in other comprehensive income is $112,000 ($180,000 - $68,000).

(b)   <u>Share appreciation rights</u>

	$
20X1	
Liability c/d and P/L expense ((300 – 32 – 35) × 1,000 × $8 × 1/3)	621,333

	$
20X2	
Liability b/d	621,333
∴ Profit or loss expense	1,218,667
Liability c/d ((300 – 32 – 28 – 10) × 1,000 × $12 × 2/3)	1,840,000

The accounting entries for the year ended 30 September 20X2 are:

DEBIT	Staff costs	$1,218,667	
CREDIT	Liability		$1,218,667

11   Leisure

Text reference. Changes in price levels are covered in Chapter 5.

Top tips. This question illustrates quite well the principal difficulties associated with the production of financial statements adjusted for price level changes (the complexity of the calculations and the problem of explaining the results to the management of an entity). It is unlikely that you would get a full 25 mark question on inflation in the exam.

Easy marks. Part (a) contains easy marks for just listing out material from your Study Text. Likewise Part (b) (i).

(a)   <u>Disadvantages of replacement cost accounting</u>

   (i)   The indices used to value assets can be unreliable or inappropriate.

   (ii)   The asset values used may relate to new types of assets (not those currently in use) and hence the statement of financial position values may not reflect the technology actually in use.

   (iii) RCA does not take into account changes in general price levels nor gains or losses arising from holding monetary liabilities or assets.

   (iv) The term 'replacement cost' is imprecise, it could mean the cost of an equivalent asset for example.

<u>Disadvantages of net realisable value accounting</u>

   (i)   It is only relevant if the asset is expected to be sold in an active market. Net realisable values may not be readily available for specialist items with no alternative uses.

   (ii)   Net realisable values have little relevance if the asset is expected to continue to be used by an entity.

   (iii) There is a real problem in valuing intangible assets such as goodwill and also liabilities.

   (iv) If a firm is not a going concern additional liabilities may emerge which can be very difficult to value such as closure costs. Should liabilities be included at contractual amounts or the amounts required to settle the liabilities?

   (v)   The use of the NRV method implies that a business may not be a going concern, this can give an unfortunate appearance for an entity's financial statements.

   (vi) NRV does not account for general price level changes.

(b)   (i)   <u>The effects of hyperinflation on the financial statements</u>

Hyperinflation can reduce the usefulness of financial statements in the following ways:

   (1)   The amounts at which assets are stated in the statement of financial position are unlikely to reflect their current values.

   (2)   The level of profit for the year may be misleading. Income appears to increase rapidly, while expenses such as depreciation may be based on out of date costs and are artificially low.

(3)   It is therefore difficult to make any meaningful assessment of an entity's performance as assets are understated and profits are overstated.

These are well known disadvantages of basing financial statements on historic cost and they affect most entities. However, where there is hyperinflation these problems are exacerbated. In addition, where an entity's financial statements are translated into dollars, hyperinflation often gives rise to significant exchange differences which may absorb reserves.

How hyperinflation should be dealt with in the financial statements

IAS 29 does not provide a definition of hyperinflation. However, it does include guidance as to characteristics of an economic environment of a country in which hyperinflation may be present. These include, but are not limited to, the following.

(1)   The general population prefers to keep its wealth in non-monetary assets or in a relatively stable foreign currency

(2)   Interest rates, wages and prices are linked to a price index

(3)   The cumulative inflation rate over three years is approaching, or exceeds, 100%

IAS 29 states that the financial statements of an entity that reports in the currency of a hyperinflationary economy should be restated in terms of the measuring unit current at the reporting date. This involves remeasuring assets and liabilities by applying a general price index. The gain or loss on the net monetary position is included in net income and separately disclosed. The fact that the financial statements have been restated should also be disclosed, together with details of the index used.

IAS 21 *The effects of changes in foreign exchange rates* states that where there is hyperinflation, the financial statements of a foreign operation should be restated in accordance with the requirements of IAS 29 before they are translated into the currency of the reporting entity. In this way users are made aware of the effect of hyperinflation on the results and net assets of the entity.

(ii)   Carrying value of hotel complex at 31 December 20X2

Assuming the economy of Urep is not a hyperinflationary economy

The closing rate is used. This produces a value of:

50 million ÷ 220 = $227,273

Use of the closing rate without adjustments produces an amount based on the original cost. Because the exchange rate has increased from 25 to 220 over the life of the complex, there is a cumulative exchange loss of $1,772,727 (50 million ÷ 25 – 227,273). The hotel complex appears to be worth much less at 31 December 20X0 than when it was first acquired.

Assuming the economy of Urep is a hyperinflationary economy

Before the cost of the hotel complex is translated into dollars it is restated using the retail price index. This produces a value of:

50 million × 1000/100 ÷ 220 = $2,272,727

This method adjusts the value of the complex to reflect the effect of ten-fold inflation over the two year period. In this way the 'disappearing assets' problem is overcome. In fact the asset now appears to be worth more than when it was first acquired.

12 BG

(a)   Defects of historical cost accounting

In times of increasing prices, historical cost accounting has the following defects:

(i)   Cost of sales reflect historical costs but sales revenue reflects current values. Therefore **cost of sales are understated** and so profits are overstated.

(ii) Property, plant and equipment values at historical cost will be less than current value. This will affect depreciation since this will be calculated on the lower historical cost figure. Since **depreciation is too low**, expenses are understated and so profits are overstated.

(iii) Monetary assets and liabilities will be settled at historical rather than current cost values. Therefore **gains and losses will be made by holding these items**, which are not reflected in historical cost accounting.

(iv) Historical cost profits may be under or over stated in terms of current values. This will affect **performance ratios** and give a misleading picture of profitability.

(b)   Maintenance of capital

(i) The **cost of sales adjustment** increases cost of sales to the current value. This is used to reduce profits and helps to protect capital by ensuring that funds are available to continue to operate at the current levels.

(ii) The **depreciation adjustment** increases depreciation to that on the current value of property, plant and equipment. This gives a more realistic estimate of the costs used in earning current revenue. Once again profit is reduced to protect capital.

(iii) The **monetary working capital adjustment**, reflects the gains or losses involved in holding working capital. In this case DG must have been holding net monetary assets so has made a loss, and so profits are again reduced to protect capital.

If DG uses the adjusted profits for dividend decisions, **distributions will be reduced**, helping to maintain the capital that is needed to continue trading in a time of rising prices.

13 JKL

Text reference. Share-based payments are covered in Chapter 4. Employee benefits are covered in Chapter 3.

Top tips. Questions on accounting for share-based payments all tend to be quite similar so you need to learn and practise your workings and method. It is also important to read the question carefully to make sure you understand the significance of the dates. In this example you are asked to calculate the expense that would be recognised in the **second** year after the grant of the options.

Easy marks. The easiest marks were probably for the explanations in part (ii) of both of the requirements where marks were available for demonstrating some basic knowledge of the rules for the relevant transactions. You must not ignore or underplay the written parts of questions as these often contain the easiest marks.

The numerical requirement of part (b) was also very straightforward as no calculations were involved. As long as you understood the information given in the question, all you had to do was combine the numbers provided.

Examiner's comments. The IFRS 2 calculation and journal in part (a) were well-answered. A number of candidates tried to answer part (ii) with an explanation of the principle of IFRS 2, which was not required. This was a worrying indication that candidates had studied the previous exam paper and rote-learned the answer.

(a)   (i)   Income statement charge for the year ended 31 December 20X2

Charge $1,225,000 (working)

Journal entry:

DEBIT	Expense	$1,225,000
CREDIT	Equity	$1,225,000

Being the expense recognised in respect of employee share options for the year.

Workings

	$
Equity at 31.12.20X1 $(300 - 25 - 40) \times 1,000 \times \$1.22 \times \frac{1}{3}$ (Note 1)	95,567
Expense (balancing figure)	99,633
Equity at 31.12.20X2 $(300 - 25 - 15 - 20) \times 1,000 \times \$1.22 \times \frac{2}{3}$ (Note 2)	195,200

Notes:

(1) The cumulative amount recognised in equity up to the previous year end was calculated as the estimated number of employees expected to be entitled to options, the original 300 less the actual leavers in 20X1 and the estimate (as at 31.12.20X1) of future leavers. Each employee has 1,000 options, measured at the grant date fair value of $1.22, and up to 31.12.20X1, 1 year out of a total vesting period of 3 years have elapsed.

(2) The cumulative amount that would be recognised at 31.12.20X2 is calculated in a similar way, but using a new estimated number of employees (deducting the actual leavers in 20X1 and 20X2 and the new estimate of future leavers of 20). By 31.12.20X2, 2 of the 3 years of the vesting period have elapsed.

(ii) <u>Recognition and measurement of cash-settled share-based payments</u>

Recognition

As a cash settled share-based payment will result in a future outflow of cash, the entity has taken on an obligation at the grant date, so a **liability** must be recognised, instead of an amount in equity.

Measurement

The amounts recognised are measured at fair values, but unlike the equity-settled transaction, where the fair value is fixed as at the grant date, the fair value is **remeasured** at each reporting date, in order to reflect the best estimate of the amount of cash that will ultimately be paid out.

(b) (i) <u>Net pension liability</u>

	$m
PV of defined benefit plan liabilities	13.9
Less FV of defined benefit plan assets	(13.1)
	0.8
Unrecognised actuarial losses	(0.5)
Net pension liability	0.3

(ii) <u>Treatment of actuarial gains and losses</u>

The corridor method only establishes the minimum amount that is permitted to be recognised in profit or loss, so an entity could recognise the gains and losses **immediately in profit or loss** or through any other systematic method that gave **faster recognition** than the corridor.

The other permitted treatment is to recognise actuarial gains and losses **immediately in other comprehensive income**.

14 LBP

Text reference. Share-based payments are covered in Chapter 4.

Top tips. It's important to manage your time here so that you can answer **both** requirements. There might even be a case for writing an answer to part (b) first. That way you can't run out of time before you attempt it, and even one or two basic points will score marks here and mean that you can get away with some errors in the calculations in part (a) and still pass the question.

In part (a) you must **read** all of the detail very carefully, especially about the numbers of employees leaving and expected to leave during the vesting period. You should set out **clear workings** so that it is easy for the marker to follow what you have done and give you credit for each element that you have handled correctly.

Easy marks. Numerical questions on share-based payment always tend to be fairly similar and lend themselves to a methodical approach. If you have learned some standard workings to calculate the expense, it should be fairly easy to achieve most of the marks in part (a).

(a)   Income statement charge for the year ended 30 September 20X8

Charge $98,050 (working)

Journal entry:

DEBIT	Expense	$98,050
CREDIT	Equity	$98,050

Being the expense recognised in respect of employee share options for the year.

Workings

	$
Equity at 30.9.20X7 (600 – 20 – 25 – 40) × 500 × $1.48 × $\frac{2}{4}$ (Note 1)	190,550
Expense (balancing figure)	98,050
Equity at 30.9.20X8 (600 – 20 – 25 – 15 – 20) × 500 × $1.48 × $\frac{3}{4}$ (Note 2)	288,600

Notes:

(1)   The cumulative amount recognised in equity up to the previous year end was calculated as the estimated number of employees expected to be entitled to options, the original 600 less the actual leavers in 20X6 and 20X7 and the estimate (as at 30.9.20X7) of future leavers. Each employee has 500 options, measured at the grant date fair value of $1.48, and up to 30.9.20X7, 2 years out of a total vesting period of 4 years have elapsed.

(2)   The cumulative amount that would be recognised at 30.9.20X8 is calculated in a similar way, but using a new estimated number of employees (deducting the actual leavers in 20X8 and the new estimate of future leavers of 20). By 30.9.20X8, 3 of the 4 years of the vesting period have elapsed.

(b)   Principles of recognition and measurement for share-based payments

Recognition

Employee share options are a type of **equity-settled share-based payment** as defined in IFRS 2. The standard requires an **expense** to be recognised, with a corresponding increase in **equity**.

Although the company is not paying cash under this scheme, it is granting something of **value** to the employees, namely financial instruments carrying the **right to buy shares** in the company on potentially advantageous terms in the future.

The share options are part of the total amount of **remuneration** for the employees in the same way as wages, salaries, bonuses and other benefits, so they must be treated in the same way as the other types of remuneration.

Where there are **conditions** attached to the options, such as the requirement in this case to work for LBP for four years, the expense must be **spread over the vesting period** to match the expense with the revenues generated by the employees over the same period.

The increase in equity reflects the existence of instruments that may become shares in the future.

Measurement

The basic principle in IFRS 2 is that equity-settled share-based payments should be measured at the fair value of the goods or services acquired (this is known as the **direct** method of measurement). However, the standard says that this will not be possible for options issued in return for employees' services, as these do not have a reliable fair value. So the transaction must be measured at the **fair value of the options at the grant date** (the **indirect** method).

The options issued to employees are not traded so there will be no market-based fair value, but an **option pricing model** should be used to arrive at the fair value.

Marks

(a)

	Marks
Equity b/d	2
Equity c/d	2
Expense and journal entry	2
	6

(b) One mark for each relevant point

	Marks
Equity-settled share-based payment	1
Part of remuneration	1
Expense and equity	1
Fair value of option at the grant date	1
Spread over vesting period	1
Option pricing model	1
To a maximum of	4
	10

15 Preparation question: Simple consolidation

P GROUP
CONSOLIDATED INCOME STATEMENT FOR THE YEAR ENDED 31 DECEMBER 20X7

	$'000
Revenue (200,000 + 150,000 – 1,500)	348,500
Cost of sales (120,000 + 90,000 – 1,500 + (W2) 125 + (W3) 120)	(208,745)
Gross profit	139,755
Other expenses (30,000 + 30,000 + 800)	(60,800)
Share of profit of associate [(6,000 × 30%) – (W2) 60]	1,740
Profit before tax	80,695
Income tax expense (20,000 + 10,500)	(30,500)
Profit for the year	50,195
Profit attributable to:	
Owners of the parent	46,344
Non-controlling interest [(19,500 – (W2) 125 – (W3) 120) × 20%]	3,851
	50,195

CONSOLIDATED STATEMENT OF CHANGES IN EQUITY FOR THE YEAR ENDED 31 DECEMBER 20X7

	Equity attributable to owners of the parent	Non-controlling interest	Total equity
	$'000	$'000	$'000
Balance at 01.01.20X7 (2,900 + (W4) 55,372) / (W5)	58,272	4,268	62,540
Profit for the year	46,344	3,851	50,195
Balance at 31.12.20X7 (2,900 + (W6) 101,716) / (W7)	104,616	8,119	112,735

Workings

(1) Group structure and goodwill

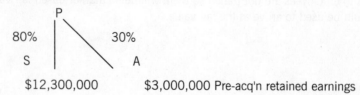

	$'000	$'000
Consideration transferred		20,000
Non-controlling interests (20% × 15,000)		3,000
Net assets acquired represented by:		
Share capital	1,500	
Pre-acquisition retained earnings	12,300	
Fair value adjustment (W3)	1,200	
		(15,000)
		8,000
Impairment		(800)
Goodwill		7,200

(2) PUP adjustments

	$'000
S ⇒ P (1,500 – 1,000) × ¼	125
A ⇒ P (700 – 500) × 30%	60

(3) Fair value adjustment

	Difference at acquisition	Movement*	Difference at SOFP date
	$'000	$'000	$'000
Property, plant and equipment	1,200	(480)	720
	1,200	(480)	720

* Additional depreciation $= \frac{1,200}{10} = 120$ per annum × 4 years = 480

(4) Retained earnings at 01.01.20X7

	P	S	A
	$'000	$'000	$'000
Per Q at 31.12.20X7	78,200	38,500	16,000
Profit for 20X7	(30,000)	(19,500)	(6,000)
Less: Fair value adjustment (3 × (W3) 120)		(360)	
Less: Pre-acquisition retained earnings		(12,300)	(3,000)
	48,200	6,340	7,000
Share of post acquisition retained earnings			
S (6,340 × 80%)	5,072		
A (7,000 × 30%)	2,100		
	55,372		

(5) Non-controlling interest at 01.01.20X7

	$'000
At acquisition (W1)	3,000
Share of post acquisition retained earnings (20% × 6,340 (W4))	1,268
	4,268

(6) Retained earnings at 31.12.20X7

	P	S	A
	$'000	$'000	$'000
Per Q	78,200	38,500	16,000
Less: PUP (W2)	(60)	(125)	
Less: Fair value adjustment (W3)		(480)	
Less: Pre-acquisition retained earnings		(12,300)	(3,000)
	78,140	25,595	13,000
Share of post acquisition retained earnings			
S (25,595 × 80%)	20,476		
A (13,000 × 30%)	3,900		
Goodwill impairment losses to date (S)	(800)		
	101,716		

(7) <u>Non-controlling interest at 31.12.20X7</u>

	$'000
At acquisition (W1)	3,000
Share of post-acquisition retained earnings (20% × 25,595 (W6))	5,119
	8,119

16 ABC and DEF

<u>Fair value of consideration</u>

	$
Ordinary shares issued 80,000 × $3.50	280,000
Cash 80,000 × $1.50	120,000
Contingent consideration (at fair value)	80,000
	480,000

<u>Fair value of net assets</u>

	$
Carrying value	594,000
Add revaluation (530,000 – 460,000)	70,000
Less contingent liability	(100,000)
Add work in progress (36,000 – 30,000)	6,000
	570,000

<u>Goodwill</u>

	$
Fair value of consideration	480,000
Non-controlling interest (at full fair value)	115,000
Fair value of net assets acquired	(570,000)
Goodwill	25,000

Under IFRS 3 (revised) all the costs of the transaction should be written off to profit or loss, so the **legal fees** and the **administrative fees** are excluded from the consideration total and will be treated as expenses.

Costs of issuing financial instruments must be accounted for in accordance with IASs 32 and 39. The **share issue costs** should be deducted from the proceeds of the equity issue.

There is **no present obligation** to incur the **reorganisation costs** as at the date of acquisition. Therefore they do not meet the definition of a liability and therefore they should not be recognised as part of the fair value adjustment.

17 AAY

Text references. This topic is covered in Chapter 8 of your Study Text.

Top tips. Points to watch are:

Often the best way to answer a requirement relating to the statement of changes in equity is to use the same reserves workings that you would use to prepare a statement of financial position then add on the share capital. In this question, the equity figure is not split into share capital and reserves, so you must simply work with this total, but using the same layouts that you would normally use for a reserves working.

Notice the unrealised profit adjustment here, the adjustment to opening inventories adjusts opening equity, the adjustment to closing inventories adjusts closing equity, and the effect on the profit for the year is the net effect of the two adjustments.

You should also spot that there is no need to set out a working for closing equity. Once you have worked out the opening figures and dealt with the profit and dividends for the year the totals on the statement will represent the closing balance.

> **Easy marks**. As long as you know the proforma for the statement of changes in equity and the basic workings for equity and non-controlling interest, you should have been able to get most of the key figures in place.

AAY Group Consolidated statement of changes in equity for the year ended 31 March 20X8

	Equity attributable to owners of the parent $'000	Non-controlling interest $'000	Total $'000
Balance at 1 April 20X7	690,780 (W4)	28,660 (W5)	719,440
Profit for the year (W2)	99,140	4,360	103,500
Dividend paid (6,000 × 20%)	(18,000)	(1,200)	(19,200)
Balance at 31 March 20X8	771,920	31,820	803,740

Workings

(1)   Group structure

AAY

1/4/X5   80%

BBZ   Pre-acquisition equity = $107.7m

(2)   Adjustment for intra-group trading

	$'000
Unrealised profit in opening inventory 25/125 × $2m	400
Unrealised profit in closing inventory 25/125 × $3m	600
Increase in provision required	200

(3)   Profit for the year

	$'000
Consolidated profit (81,700 + (22,000 − 200 (W2)))	103,500
Profit attributable to:	
Owners of the parent (bal)	99,140
Non-controlling interest (22,000 − 200 (W2)) × 20%	4,360
	103,500

(4)   Group equity b/d

	AAY $'000	BBZ $'000
Per question	662,300	143,700
Unrealised profit (W2)		(400)
Pre-acquisition equity		(107,700)
		35,600
BBZ − Group share (35,600 × 80%)	28,480	
	690,780	

(5)   Non-controlling interest b/d

	$'000
NCI at acquisition (107,700 (W1) x 20%)	21,540
NCI share of post acquisition profits (35,600 x 20%)	7,120
	28,660

18 DNT

Text references. This topic is covered in Chapter 7 of your Study Text.

Top tips. Points to watch are:

BL makes a loss in the year. Make sure you take this into account when calculating retained earnings and working out how much of this is pre-acquisition.

The best way to approach the intergroup sale of the machinery is to take the unrealised profit given in the question, add back the element of that profit that is realised through depreciation then make the adjustment.

Easy marks. Easy marks. Even if you don't get the intragroup sale right, there are easy marks just for setting out the workings properly. It is essential that you learn our standard workings.

CONSOLIDATED STATEMENT OF FINANCIAL POSITION EXTRACTS

Retained earnings

	DNT $	CM $	BL $
Retained earnings: per question (W3)	2,669,400	2,475,000	610,000
Unrealised profit (W2)		(6,000)	
Pre acquisition: per question (W3)		(1,775,000)	(620,000)
		694,000	(10,000)
Group share: CM 85%	589,900		
BL 70%	(7,000)		
	3,253,300		

Non-controlling interest

	CM $	BL $
NCI at acquisition	520,500	386,000
NCI share of post acq'n reserves (see retained earnings calculation)		
(15% × 694,000)/ (30% × (10,000))	104,100	(3,000)
	624,600	383,000

Workings

1   Group structure

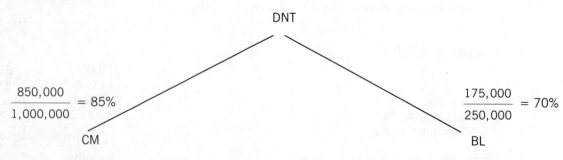

DNT

$$\frac{850,000}{1,000,000} = 85\%$$

CM

$$\frac{175,000}{250,000} = 70\%$$

BL

2   Unrealised profit on intragroup sale of machinery

	$
Profit on disposal per question	15,000
Realised through depreciation by 31 August 20X8	
$15,000 \times \dfrac{1.5\ \text{years}}{2.5\ \text{years}}$	(9,000)
Unrealised profit	6,000

Adjust in books of seller: CM

3   Retained earnings of BL

	$'000
Retained earnings at 1 September 20X7	650
Loss for year	(40)
Retained earnings at 31 August 20X8	610

At acquisition: $(650,000 – (9/12 × 40,000) = $620,000

19 MX

> **Text reference.** The consolidated statement of financial position and fair values are covered in Chapter 7.
>
> **Top tips.** Although the requirements here do not ask for a complete statement of financial position, think about how you would have used these three calculations as workings in a full SOFP question, and stick to the technique that you are familiar with.
>
> **Easy marks.** The easiest marks are for the basic steps in each of the workings, even if some of the fair value adjustments are omitted.

(i)   Goodwill (W2) $185,000
(ii)   Retained earnings (W3) $3,289,066
(iii) Non-controlling interest (W4) $342,267

(1)   Group structure

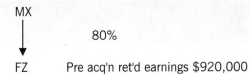

MX

                    80%

FZ   Pre acq'n ret'd earnings $920,000

(2)   Goodwill

	$	$
Consideration transferred		1,750,000
NCI at fair value		320,000
Less: Net assets acquired:		
Share capital	1,000,000	
Pre-acquisition retained earnings	920,000	
Fair value adjustment (W5)	(35,000)	
		(1,885,000)
Goodwill		185,000

(3)   Consolidated retained earnings

	MX	FZ
	$	$
Per SOFP	3,200,000	1,100,000
Pre-acq'n retained earnings		(920,000)
Additional depreciation on PPE (W5)		(8,667)
Unrealised profit (W6)		(60,000)
		111,333
Group share (80%)	89,066	
	3,289,066	

(4)   Non-controlling interest

		$
At acquisition		320,000
NCI share of post-acq retained earnings	(20% x 111,333 (W3))	22,267
		342,267

(5) <u>Fair values</u>

	Acq'n date	Movement	Year end
	$	$	$
PPE (745 −680) (65,000 × 1/5 × 8/12)	65,000	(8,667)	56,333
Contingent liability	(100,000)	–	(100,000)
	(35,000)	(8,667)	(43,667)

(6) <u>Provision for unrealised profit</u>

Intragroup sales by FZ $300,000

Margin (300,000 × 20%) = $60,000 (adjust in FZ's retained earnings)

Marking scheme

		Marks
Goodwill		4
Consolidated retained earnings		3
Non controlling interest		3
		10

---

20 AB Group

Text reference. These topics are dealt with in Chapters 8 and 9 of the text.

Top tips. Take time to identify the group structure and the dates of investment. You needed to remember to time apportion the results of the associate. A timeline is often helpful here.

Easy marks. There were marks available here for dealing with the basics of consolidating a parent and an 80% subsidiary that was held for a full year. Further marks were available for demonstrating that you knew how to handle equity accounting for an associate in the income statement.

AB GROUP
CONSOLIDATED INCOME STATEMENT FOR THE YEAR ENDED 30 JUNE 20X9

	$'000
Revenue (2,000 + 1,500)	3,500
Cost of sales (1,200 + 1,000)	(2,200)
Gross profit	1,300
Distribution costs (400 + 120)	(520)
Administrative expenses (240 + 250 + 30 (W2) + 20 (W4))	(540)
Other income (40 – 40(W3))	0
Share of profit of associate (W6)	13
Profit before tax	253
Income tax expense (50 + 40)	(90)
Profit for the year	163
Profit attributable to:	
Owners of the parent (balance)	155
Non-controlling interest (W7)	8
	163

Workings

1   <u>Group structure and timeline</u>

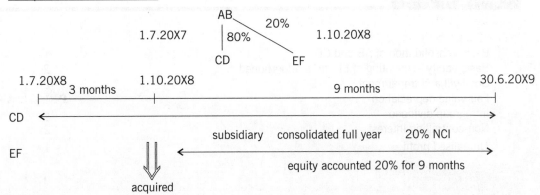

2   <u>Goodwill (to find impairment loss)</u>

	$'000
Consideration transferred	4,100
Non-controlling interest (at fair value)(20%)	1,100
Fair value of net assets acquired	(5,000)
	200
Impairment (15%)	(30)
	170

3   <u>Intragroup dividend income</u>

	$'000
Received from CD (80% × 50)	40

Cancelled out of "other income".

4   <u>Depreciation on fair value adjustment</u>

$240,000 / 12 = $20,000

Added to administrative expenses and adjust NCI

5   <u>Unrealised profit</u>

EF (associate) sells to AB (parent)

$80,000 × 25% × ½ = $10,000

Group share: $10,000 × 20% = $2,000

Deducted from "share of associate's profit".

6   <u>Share of profit of associate</u>

	$'000
Share of CD's profit after tax (20% × 100× 9/12)	15
Unrealised profit (W5)	(2)
	13

7   <u>Non-controlling interest</u>

	$'000
CD's profit for the year per question	90
Less: depreciation on fair value adjustment (W4)	(20)
Less: impairment loss (w2)	(30)
	40
NCI share (20%)	8

Marking scheme

	Marks
Basic consolidation of AB and CD	1
Basic equity accounting of EF, time-apportioned	2
Goodwill and impairment	2
Fair value depreciation	1
Intragroup dividend	1
Non-controlling interest	2
Unrealised profit	1
	10

21 ERT

Text reference. This topic is covered in Chapter 7 in the study text.

Top tips. Part (a) might have felt unfamiliar so it might have been easier to leave it until after you had done part (b). Once you had dealt with the fair value adjustments in the numerical part, it would have been easier to write about them as long as you had managed your time carefully and left enough time to deal with part (a). In part (b) the key to success was to use a methodical technique. Identify the group structure, then set up a pro-forma for the consolidated statement of financial position. Then you can work your way down the statements of financial position in the question putting the easy figures onto the face of the answer in brackets. The figures that need to be adjusted can be used to open up the main consolidation workings.

Then work through the other information making adjustments on the face of the answer or in the workings, as appropriate. If any individual adjustment seems difficult, it's better to leave it out and complete the bulk of the question than to get bogged down in one point. No one adjustment ever carries more than one or two marks.

Easy marks.

In part (a) easy marks are available for explaining the basics of the effect of the fair value adjustments, such as the effect of the fair value adjustments at the acquisition date on the goodwill calculation. In part (b) the easiest marks can be gained by dealing with the basics steps of the consolidation.

Examiner's comments.

Weaker candidates showed a lack of knowledge of basic principles by proportionally consolidating the subsidiary but the more common problems related to the failure to follow through adjustments to retained earnings and non-controlling interests. Candidates coped well with the fair value adjustments, both the explanations and the adjustments, except for including the intangible asset and contingent liability in the consolidated statement of financial position.

(a) Adjustment	Effect on goodwill calculation	Effect on the consolidated financial statements
Property, plant and equipment	The uplift of $800,000 increases the fair value of net assets acquired and so reduces goodwill by this amount.	Additional depreciation must be charged on the fair value uplift and this will be charged against post acquisition profits of the group, and the property, plant and equipment in the consolidated statement of financial position will be increased by the original uplift less the accumulated amount of additional depreciation charged to date.
Inventories	The uplift of $200,000 increases the fair value of net assets acquired and so reduces goodwill by this amount.	As the inventories had been sold by the reporting date, no adjustment will be required to the inventories balance in the consolidated statement of financial position. In the consolidated income statement an adjustment will be needed to increase cost of sales by this amount, as the 'opening' inventory, when the subsidiary was acquired is increased, and there is no corresponding increase in 'closing' inventories.
Intangible asset	The intangible asset must be recognised on consolidation so its value will increase the fair value of net assets acquired and reduce goodwill by this amount.	The asset must be amortised over its useful life of 20 months. Eight months' amortisation will be charged in the consolidated income statement and the value, net of amortisation, must be recognised in the consolidated statement of financial position.
Contingent liability	The contingent liability must be recognised on acquisition at its fair value. This liability will reduce the total fair value of net assets acquired and so will increase the goodwill on consolidation.	The fair value measured at the reporting date must be recognised in the consolidated statement of financial position. The reduction in the fair value from the acquisition date to the reporting date will be credited in the consolidated income statement.

(b)   CONSOLIDATED STATEMENT OF FINANCIAL POSITION AT 31 DECEMBER 20X0

	$'000
Non-current assets	
Property, plant and equipment (12,000 + 4,000 + 750 (W6))	16,750
Goodwill (W2)	208
Intangible asset (W6)	90
	17,048
Current assets	
Inventories (2,200 + 800 – 30 (W7))	2,970
Receivables (3,400 + 900)	4,300
Cash and cash equivalents (800 + 300)	1,100
	25,418
Equity attributable to owners of the parent	
Share capital ($1 equity shares)	10,000
Retained earnings (W4)	7,893
	17,893
Non-controlling interest (W5)	1,741
	19,634
Non-current liabilities	
Long term borrowings	2,700
Current liabilities (2,000 + 1,000 + 84 (W6))	3,084
	25,418

Workings

(1)   Group structure

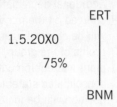

```
                        ERT
          1.5.20X0        |
             75%          |
                          |
                        BNM
```

Pre-acquisition retained earnings $3,200,000.

(2)   Goodwill

	$'000	$'000
Consideration transferred (4,000 – 200)		3,800
NCI at acquisition (fair value)		1,600
Net assets acquired:		
Share capital	1,000	
Ret'd reserves at acquisition	3,200	
Fair value adjustment (W6)	940	
		(5,140)
		260
Impairment losses to date (20%)		(52)
At reporting date		208

(3)   Consolidated retained reserves

	ERT	BNM
	$'000	$'000
Per question	7,500	4,000
Fair value movement (W6)		(184)
PUP (W7)	(30)	
Retained reserves at acquisition		(3,200)
		616
Group share		
BK (616 × 75%)	462	
Impairment losses to date (52(W2) × 75%) *(Note 1)*	(39)	
	7,893	

Note 1: As the non-controlling interest is measured at full fair value, part of the goodwill arising on consolidation is attributable to the non-controlling interest and only the parent's share of the impairment loss is charged to the group retained earnings. The non-controlling interest's share of the impairment loss is charged to the non-controlling interest (W5).

Note 2: The 'other reserves' balance shown in ERT's separate statement of financial position is eliminated on consolidation because the carrying value of the investment has to be restated to its fair value as at the acquisition date for consolidation purposes (see W2). As a result, the only reserve that appears in the group statement of financial position is retained earnings.

(5)   Non-controlling interest

	$'000
At acquisition (W2)	1,600
Share of post acq'n retained profits (25% × 616 (W4))	154
Share of impairment losses (52(W2) × 25%)	(13)
	1,741

(6)   Fair value adjustments

	At acquisition 1.5.20X0	Movement	At SOFP date 31.12.20X0
	$'000	$'000	$'000
Property, plant and equipment	800	(50)*	750
Inventories	200	(200)	0
Intangible asset	150	(60)**	90
Contingent liability	(210)	126	(84)
	940	(184)	756

* Additional depreciation on fair value adjustment (800 ÷ 16)

**Amortisation of intangible (150 × 8/20)

(7)   <u>Intragroup trading</u>

Unrealised profit (ERT → BNM) 300,000 × 20% × ½ = 30,000

Dr Retained reserves (ERT) 30,000

Cr Group inventories   30,000

22   Preparation question: Joint venture

TOP GROUP CONSOLIDATED STATEMENT OF FINANCIAL POSITION

	$'000
Non-current assets	
Property, plant and equipment (70,000 + (45,000 × 25%))	81,250
Goodwill (W2)	2,000
	83,250
Current assets (93,000 + (52,000 × 25%))	106,000
	189,250
Equity	
Share capital	50,000
Retained earnings (W3)	81,500
	131,500
Current liabilities (51,000 + (27,000 × 25%))	57,750
	189,250

Workings

(1)   <u>Group structure</u>

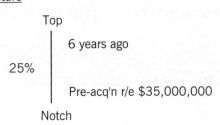

Top

6 years ago

25%

Pre-acq'n r/e $35,000,000

Notch

(2)   <u>Goodwill</u>

	$'000	$'000
Cost of combination		12,000
Net assets acquired		
Share capital	5,000	
Retained earnings	35,000	
	40,000	
25%		10,000
		2,000

(3)   <u>Retained earnings</u>

	Top Co	Notch Co
	$'000	$'000
Per Q	74,000	65,000
Pre-acquisition retained earnings		(35,000)
	74,000	30,000
Notch – share of post acquisition ret'd earnings (30,000 × 25%)	7,500	
	81,500	

23 JKA

> **Text reference**. The consolidated statement of financial position is covered in Chapter 7 and substance over form is covered in Chapter 1.
>
> **Top tips.** Time management is key here, as it would be easy to get bogged down in part (a). Aim to get a basic explanation down plus an attempt at the journal entry but make sure you leave time to attempt the consolidation in part (b).
>
> **Easy marks.** The easiest marks are in part (b) as long as you know how to apply **proportional consolidation**.

(a) **Sale of land**

The *Framework* principles include a requirement that financial statements should reflect the substance of transactions. There are features of this sale of land that suggest that its true substance is not a sale. The land is being sold to a finance company, at less than its carrying value in JKA's statement of financial position. There is also an agreement giving JKA an option to repurchase the land within three years, and requiring the entity to repurchase the land by the end of that period. This means that if the land increases in value, JKA can repurchase it at the agreed price and benefit from the increase in value, and that if the value of the land decreases, JKA will still be obliged to repurchase it and will suffer a loss.

The risks and rewards of owning the land remain with JKA so in substance the transaction is a refinancing exercise, so the land should remain on the statement of financial position, the proceeds of the sale should be treated as a loan, and the "loss" on the disposal should not be recognised.

Therefore JKA's accounting entries need to be reversed:

DEBIT	Property, plant and equipment	$520,000	
CREDIT	Liabilities		$500,000
CREDIT	Retained earnings		$20,000

(b) JKA GROUP
CONSOLIDATED STATEMENT OF FINANCIAL POSITION AS AT 31 MAY 2009

	$'000	$'000
Assets		
Non-current assets		
Property, plant and equipment (11,000 + (7,500 × 50%) + 520 (Part (a))		15,270
Current assets		
Inventories (3,100 + (50% × 1,200) – 5 (W3))	3,695	
Receivables (3,300 + (50% × 1,400) – 17 (W3))	3,983	
Cash and cash equivalents (600 + (50% × 400))	800	
		8,478
Total assets		23,748

	$'000	$'000
Equity and liabilities		
Equity		
Share capital	10,000	
Revaluation reserve (1,500 + (50% × 500))	1,750	
Other reserves	500	
Retained earnings (2,000 + (50% × 4,500) – 5(W1) + 20 (Part (a))		
	4,265	
		16,515
Non-current liabilities (2,000 + 500 (Part (a))		2,500
Current liabilities (4,000 + (50% × 1,500) – 17 (W3))		4,733
Total equity and liabilities		23,748

Workings

1   Group structure

JKA

| | 50% |

CBX   Pre acq'n ret'd earnings $0 (set up by JKA)

Note: Goodwill on acquisition is zero as CBX was set up by JKA.

Goodwill

	$'000
Cost of investment	2,000
Share of net assets acquired (50% × 4,000)	2,000
Goodwill	NIL

2   Consolidated retained earnings

	JKA	CBX
	$'000	$'000
Per question	2,000	4,500
Reversal of loss on sale of land (part (a))	20	
PUP (W3)	(5)	
Pre-acquisition retained earnings		(0)
	2,015	4,500
CBX – share of post acquisition earnings (4,500 × 50%)	2,250	
	4,265	

3   Unrealised profit in inventory

	$'000
Sales value (200,000 × 25%)	50,000
Unrealised profit (50,000 × 20%)	10,000
Intra-group share of unrealised profit (10,000 × 50%)	5,000

$34,000 still in intra-group balances, therefore need to reduce both receivables and payables by $17,000 ($34,000 × 50%).

24   AJ

Text reference. These topics are covered in Chapters 6, 7, and 9.

Top tips. The examiner has made it quite clear that consolidation questions are likely to appear frequently in Section B therefore it is a topic that candidates must be confident with. This is a fairly straightforward question with one subsidiary and an associate. Take care with the provision for unrealised profit as the profit has been made by the subsidiary. It is important to reflect this adjustment in the subsidiary's column in the retained earnings working so that only the group share is charged to consolidated reserves and the non-controlling share is allocated to the non-controlling interest.

Easy marks. 5 marks for this question are available for 'understanding the principles of consolidation'. This is as basic as setting out the proforma and adding items together. If you were to get bogged down in calculating the investment in associate, however, this would earn you 3 marks maximum. Understanding the group structure will earn you 5 marks. There are no hidden traps, so these 5 marks will be easy to gain.

Examiner's comments. Most candidates produced very good answers, but there are some who have not mastered group accounting and who are thus jeopardising their chances of success.

(a)   AJ owns 80% of the share capital of BK and as such this would imply that BK was a **subsidiary** of AJ. The deciding factor on subsidiary status is whether the parent has control of the subsidiary and there is nothing to imply here that AJ does not control BK. Therefore BK will be **consolidated using the acquisition method**.

The investment in CL of 40% of the share capital would normally indicate that CL is an **associate** of AJ. This will be the case if AJ has **significant influence, rather than control**, of CL. The fact that AJ has the right to appoint one of the five directors and that the remaining 60% of the shares are owned principally by three other investors implies that AJ does have significant influence. Therefore CL will be treated as an **associate** and **accounted for using the equity method**.

(b)   AJ GROUP
CONSOLIDATED STATEMENT OF FINANCIAL POSITION AT 31 MARCH 20X5

	$'000
Non-current assets	
Property, plant and equipment (12,500 + 4,700 + 195 (W6))	17,395
Goodwill (W2)	1,700
Investment in associate (W3)	4,560
Other financial assets (18,000 – 7,500 – 4,400 – 2,000 intragroup loan)	4,100
	27,755
Current assets	
Inventories (7,200 + 8,000 – 200 (W7))	15,000
Trade receivables (6,300 + 4,300)	10,600
Cash	800
	54,155
Equity attributable to owners of the parent	
Share capital	10,000
Reserves (W4)	13,156
	23,156
Non-controlling interest (W5)	1,199
	24,355
Non-current liabilities	
Loan notes (10,000 + 3,000 – 2,000 intragroup)	11,000
Current liabilities	
Trade payables (8,900 + 6,700)	15,600
Income tax (1,300 + 100)	1,400
Short term borrowings (600 + 1,200)	1,800
	54,155

Workings

(1)   Group structure

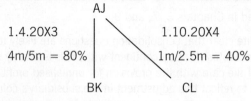

AJ

1.4.20X3   1.10.20X4

4m/5m = 80%   1m/2.5m = 40%

BK   CL

(2)   Goodwill (BK)

	$'000	$'000
Consideration transferred		7,500
NCI at acquisition (20% × 6,695)		1,339
Net assets acquired:		
Share capital	5,000	
Ret'd reserves at acquisition	1,500	
Fair value adjustment (W6)	195	
		(6,695)
		2,144
Impairment losses to date		(444)
At reporting date		1,700

(3) Investment in associate (CL)

	$'000
Cost of associate	4,400
Share of post-acquisition retained reserves ((4,300 – 3,900) × 40%)	160
	4,560

(4) Consolidated retained reserves

	AJ $'000	BK $'000	CL $'000
Per question	14,000	1,000	4,300
PUP (W7)		(200)	
Fair value movement (W6)		–	
Retained reserves at acquisition		(1,500)	(3,900)
		(700)	400
Group share			
BK ((700) × 80%)	(560)		
CL (400 × 40%)	160		
Impairment losses to date	(444)		
	13,156		

(5) Non-controlling interest (BK)

	$'000
At acquisition (W2)	1,339
Share of post acq'n retained losses (20% × (700)(W4))	(140)
	1,199

(6) Fair value adjustments (BK)

	At acquisition 1.4.20X3 $'000	Movement $'000	At SOFP date 31.5.20X5 $'000
Land (1,115 – 920)	195	–	195

(7) Intragroup trading

Unrealised profit (BK → AJ) 1,000,000 × 25/125	200,000
Dr Retained reserves (BK)	200,000
Cr Group inventories	200,000

25 ST

Text reference. Joint ventures are covered in Chapter 9.

Top tips. This is a fairly straightforward consolidation with the addition of the treatment of WX as a joint venture using proportionate consolidation. This basically means including just 50% of each income statement figure for WX. However this is complicated by the intra group sale from WX to ST. As ST is only consolidating 50% of WX's figures then adjustments for the intra group sale and unrealised profit are only 50% of the total figures.

Easy marks. Easy marks are available for setting out the proforma and adding across. Also, remember to split out the profit into parent and non-controlling interests.

ST GROUP
CONSOLIDATED INCOME STATEMENT FOR THE YEAR ENDED 31 JANUARY 20X6

	$'000
Revenue (W1)	3,490
Cost of sales (W2)	(2,266)
Gross profit	1,224
Operating expenses (450 + 375 + 74 × 50%)	(862)
Finance cost (16 + (12 − 6))	(22)
Profit before tax	340
Income tax expense (45 + 53 + 26 × 50%)	(111)
Profit for the year	229

Profit attributable to:	
Owners of the parent (bal fig)	196
Non-controlling interest (110 × 30% (UV))	33
	229

Workings

(1)   Revenue

		$'000
ST		1,800
UV		1,400
WX (600 × 50%)	300	
Less intra-group trading 20 × 50%	(10)	
		290
		3,490

(2)   Cost of sales

	$'000
ST	1,200
UV	850
Less intra-group trading (20 × 50%)	(10)
WX (450/2)	225
Add unrealised profit (20 × 20% × ½) × 50%	1
	2,266

26   AB

> **Text reference.** The consolidated statement of comprehensive income is covered in Chapter 8, financial instruments are covered in Chapter 2 and accounting for retirement benefits is covered in Chapter 3.
>
> **Top tips.** The examiner likes to combine a range of syllabus areas in each question. Make sure you don't spend too long on any one issue.
>
> **Easy marks.** The easiest marks here are for demonstrating that you can deal with the basics of consolidating a subsidiary and equity accounting an associate in the statement of comprehensive income.

AB GROUP
CONSOLIDATED STATEMENT OF COMPREHENSIVE INCOME FOR THE YEAR ENDED 31 MAY 2009

	$'000	$'000
Revenue (6,000 + 3,000)		9,000
Cost of sales (4,800 + 2,400)		(7,200)
Gross profit		1,800
Distribution costs (64 + 32)		(96)
Administrative expenses (336 + 168)		(504)
Finance costs (30 +15)		(45)
Share of profit of associate (30% × 100)		30
Profit before tax		1,185
Income tax expense (204 + 102)		(306)
Profit for the year		879

Other comprehensive income:

Revaluation of property (200 + 100)	300
Tax effect of revaluation of property (42 + 21)	(63)
Actuarial loss on pension plan liabilities	(52)
Actuarial gain on pension plan assets	40
Gain on available for the sale investment (106 – 92)	14
Share of other comprehensive income of associate (24 × 30%)	7
	246
Total comprehensive income for the year	1,125

Profit for the year attributable to:

Owners of parent	822
Non-controlling interest (20% × 283)	57
	879

Total comprehensive income for the year attributable to:

Owners of parent	1,053
Non-controlling interest (20% × 362)	72
	1,125

Workings

1   Group structure

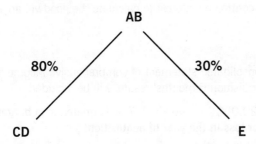

AB controls CD and so CD is a subsidiary. AB has significant influence over EF and so EF is an associate.

27   DF

> **Text reference**. These topics are covered in Chapters 6, 8, 9 and 10.
>
> **Top tips.** The examiner has clearly stated that at least half of this exam is likely to involve narrative answers. You must be prepared to **explain** the issues relating to all areas of the syllabus, including consolidations.
>
> It was important to **read the requirements carefully.** Part (a) stated that **no calculations** were required. If you did not spot this, you could have wasted time and perhaps missed some of the basic points that would have scored marks.
>
> **Easy marks.** In part (a) easy marks were available for the ability to identify a subsidiary and an associate from simple information and for outlining that these would be fully consolidated and equity accounted respectively.
>
> **Examiner's comments.** This question was well answered. Difficult points that many candidates missed were the treatment of the subsidiary that was held for sale, and the gain on a bargain purchase in part (b).

(a)   <u>Investment in AB</u>

DF has acquired 90% of the issued ordinary share capital of AB. Therefore it has **control** of AB, which should be **fully consolidated as a subsidiary** under the provisions of IAS 27 *Investments in subsidiaries*.

<u>Investment in GH</u>

DF has acquired 40% of the issued ordinary share capital of GH. Therefore it can exercise **significant influence** over GH, which should be treated **as an associate** under the provisions of IAS 28 *Investments in associates*. GH will be included in the group's financial statements using **equity accounting**. The investment should have been measured at cost on initial recognition and then in each subsequent period the group share of GH's post acquisition retained reserves should be added on.

Investment in JK

Although AB holds 65% of the issued ordinary share capital of JK, the investment is **held exclusively with a view to sale** within the next four months. Therefore the holding will be included in the group's financial statements **as a discontinued operation** under the provisions of IFRS 5 *Non-current assets held for sale and discontinued operations*.

As DF intends to sell the investment in the next four months and is actively marketing it, the assumption must be that it meets the IFRS 5 criteria to be treated as **held for sale.** The assets and liabilities of JK will be treated as a disposal group and measured at the **lower of carrying value and fair value less costs to sell.** JK will not be consolidated line by line, but rather as two single amounts, assets held for sale and liabilities held for sale. In the consolidated statement of comprehensive income the minimum required is to show as a single line entitled "discontinued operations" the profit or loss for the year of JK and any gain or loss on remeasuring the investment to fair value less costs to sell.

Investment in LM

After the second acquisition on 1 October, DF holds a total of 55% of the issued ordinary share capital of LM and so has **control of LM from that date.** The holding will be treated as an **investment** up to 30 September and **as a subsidiary** from 1 October under the provisions of IFRS 3 *Business combinations*.

In a step acquisition where control is acquired, IFRS 3 requires that the original investment is treated as being realised at its fair value. This fair value is added to the consideration paid for the controlling interest in the subsidiary and the (proportionate) non-controlling interest to calculate the goodwill arising on the acquisition.

(b)   Impact on the income statement

AB was acquired on 1 July 20X9 so in the consolidated statement of comprehensive income its results will be time apportioned and only the post acquisition 6 months' results will be included.

DF acquired AB with negative goodwill of $120,000 (see working). This is treated as a **bargain purchase** and the $120,000 will be **credited to profit or loss in the year of acquisition.**

In addition, the fair value uplift of $1m relates to property. This will result in **additional depreciation of $25,000 each year** ($1m/40). The depreciation should be time apportioned so in 20X9 only $12,500 (6/12 × $25,000) will be charged.

Working

	$'000	$'000
Consideration transferred		6,000
Non-controlling interests (10% × 6,800)		680
		6,680
Less: fair value of net assets		
Book value	5,800	
Fair value adjustment	1,000	
		6,800
Goodwill		(120)

Marking scheme

		Marks
(a) Explanation of accounting for investments		
AB - subsidiary	2	
GH - associate	2	
JK – subsidiary held for sale	3	
LM – subsidiary (step acquisition)	3	
Maximum available		8
(b) Impact of AB on the income statement		2
		10

28 PQ

Text reference. The consolidated income statement is covered in Chapter 8 and the treatment of associates is covered in Chapter 9 of the text.

Top tips. Take time to analyse the group structure and it helps to draw up a timeline when there has been an acquisition part way through the year.

Easy marks. The easiest marks are for the basic consolidation of PQ and ST, including ST's results for only 8 months.

Examiner's comments. Most candidates correctly time-apportioned the results of the subsidiary but few carried this through to the calculation of the NCI. The most common mistake was including the $120,000 as a fair value **adjustment** in the goodwill working, despite the question giving the **fair value of the net assets acquired**. Many candidates did not treat the unrealised profit on transactions with the associate correctly.

CONSOLIDATED INCOME STATEMENT FOR THE PQ GROUP FOR THE YEAR ENDED 30 JUNE 20X9

	$'000
Revenue $900,000 + (8/12 x $560,000)	1,273
Cost of sales $630,000 + (8/12 x $345,000)	(860)
Gross profit	413
Distribution costs $90,000 + (8/12 x $39,000)	(116)
Administrative expenses $60,000 + (8/12 x $30,000) + $36,000 (W2) + $2,000 (W3)	(118)
Profit from operations	179
Share of profit of associate (W4)	15
Profit before tax	194
Income tax expense $42,000 + (8/12 x $38,000)	(67)
Profit for the year	127
Profit attributable to:	
Owners of the parent (balancing figure)	113
Non-controlling interest (W5)	14
	127

Workings

1   Group structure and timeline

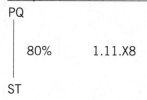

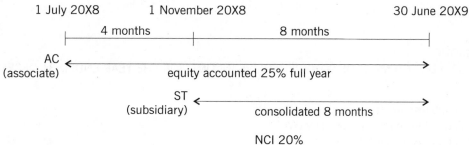

2   Impairment of goodwill

	$'000
Consideration transferred	700
NCI at acquisition (650 × 20%)	130
Net assets at acquisition	(650)
Goodwill on acquisition	180
Impairment 20%	36

3   Additional depreciation on fair value adjustment

Fair value adjustment of $120,000/ (50-10 years) = $3,000

$3,000 × 8 months = $2,000

4   Share of profit of associate

	$'000
Profit after tax of AC	68
Group share 25%	17
less: PUP (20% × 40k) × 25%	(2)
	15

5   Non-controlling interest

	$'000
Profit after tax	108
Fair value adjustment	(3)
	105
Profit for 8 months (105K x 8/12)	70
NCI share 20%	14

6   Intra-group dividend

PQ has recognised its share of the dividend paid by ST (80% × $40k) $32k. This is eliminated on consolidation.

29   Preparation question: Part disposal

ANGEL GROUP
CONSOLIDATED STATEMENT OF FINANCIAL POSITION AS AT 31 DECEMBER 20X8

	$'000
Non-current assets	
Property, plant and equipment	200.00
Investment in Shane (W3)	133.15
	333.15
Current assets (890 + 120)	1,010.00
	1,343.15
Equity attributable to owners of the parent	
Share capital	500.00
Retained earnings (W4)	533.15
	1,033.15
Current liabilities	310.00
	1,343.15

ANGEL GROUP
CONSOLIDATED STATEMENT OF COMPREHENSIVE INCOME FOR THE YEAR ENDED 31 DECEMBER 20X8

	$'000
Profit before interest and tax [100 + (20 × 6/12)]	110.00
Profit on disposal of shares in subsidiary (W6)	80.30
Share of profit of associate (12 × 35% × 6/12)	2.10
Profit before tax	192.40
Income tax expense [40 + (8 × 6/12)]	(44.00)
Profit for the year	148.40
Other comprehensive income net of tax [10 + (6 × 6/12)]	13.00
Share of other comprehensive income of associate (6 × 35% × 6/12)	1.05
Other comprehensive income for the year	14.05
Total comprehensive income for the year	162.45

	$'000
Profit attributable to:	
Owners of the parent	146.60
Non-controlling interests (12 × 6/12 × 30%)	1.80
	148.40
Total comprehensive income attributable to:	
Owners of the parents	159.75
Non controlling interests (18 × 6/12 × 30%)	2.70
	162.45

ANGEL GROUP
CONSOLIDATED RECONCILIATION OF MOVEMENT IN RETAINED RESERVES

	$'000
Balance at 31 December 20X7 (W5)	373.40
Total comprehensive income for the year	159.75
Balance at 31 December 20X8 (W4)	533.15

Workings

(1)   Group structure and timeline

Shane
|
70% reduced to 35% on 30.6.X8
|
Angel
|

1.1.X8	30.6.X8	31.12.X8

SOC ←————————————→←————————————→

Subsidiary – 6/12   Associate – 6/12

Group gain
on disposal

Equity account
in SOFP

(2)   Goodwill – Shane

	$'000	$'000
Consideration transferred		120
Non-controlling interests (FV)		51
Less:		
Share capital	100	
Retained earnings	10	
		(110)
		61

(3)   Investment in associate

	$'000
Fair value at date control lost	130.00
Share of post 'acquisition' retained reserves (W4)	3.15
	133.15

(4)   Group retained earnings

	Angel	Shane 70%	Shane 35% retained
Per qu/date of disposal (90 – (18 × 6/12))	400.00	81	90
Group profit on disposal (W6)	80.30		
Less retained earnings at acquisition/date of disposal		(10)	(81)
		71	9
Shane: 70% x 71	49.70		
Shane: 35% × 9	3.15		
	533.15		

(5) Retained earnings b/f

	Angel $'000	Shane $'000
Per Q	330.0	72
Less: Pre-acquisition retained reserves		(10)
	330.0	62
Shane – Share of post acquisition ret'd reserves (62 × 70%)	43.4	
	373.4	

(6) Group profit on disposal of Shane

	$'000	$'000
Fair value of consideration received		120.0
Fair value of 35% investment retained		130.0
Less share of carrying value when control lost		
Net assets (190 – (18 × 6/12)) × 70%	126.7	
Goodwill belonging to owners of the parent: 61 × 70% (W2)	43.0	
		(169.7)
		80.3

30 Preparation question: 'D' shaped group statement of financial position

BAUBLE GROUP
CONSOLIDATED STATEMENT OF FINANCIAL POSITION AS AT 31 DECEMBER 20X9

	$'000
Non-current assets	
Property, plant and equipment (720 + 60 + 70)	850
Goodwill (W2)	111
	961
Current assets (175 + 95 + 90)	360
	1,321
Equity attributable to owners of the parent	
Share capital – $1 ordinary shares	400
Retained earnings (W3)	600
	1,000
Non-controlling interest (W4)	91
	1,091
Current liabilities (120 + 65 + 45)	230
	1,321

Workings

(1) Group Structure

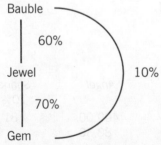

Bauble interest in Gem	– direct	% 10
	– indirect (60% × 70%)	42
		52
Non-controlling interest in Gem		48

(2)   <u>Goodwill</u>

	Jewel		Gem	
	$'000	$'000	$'000	$'000
Consideration transferred – Bauble		142		43.0
Consideration transferred – Jewel			60% × 100	60.0
NCI	40% × 145	58	48% × 90	43.2
Net assets at acq'n as represented by:				
Share capital	100		50	
Ret'd earnings	45		40	
		(145)		(90.0)
Goodwill		55		56.2

Total goodwill = $111,200

(3)   <u>Consolidated retained earnings</u>

	B	J	G
	$'000	$'000	$'000
Per Q	560	90	65
Less: pre-acquisition ret'd earnings		(45)	(40
		45	25
J – share of post acquisition ret'd earnings (45 × 60%)	27		
G – share of post acquisition ret'd earnings (25 × 52%)	13		
	600		

(4)   <u>Non-controlling interests</u>

	Jewel	Gem
	$'000	$'000
NCI at acquisition (W2)	58	43.2
NCI in investment in Gem (100 × 40%)	(40)	
NCI share of post acquisition retained earnings:		
Jewel ((W3) 45 × 40%)	18	
Gem ((W3) 25 × 48%)		12.0
	36	55.2

91.2

31   Preparation question: 'D' shaped group income statement

UPPER GROUP CONSOLIDATED INCOME STATEMENT FOR THE YEAR ENDED 31 DECEMBER 20X9

	$'000
Profit before tax (1,500 + 750 + 150)	2,400
Income tax expense (500 + 250 + 50)	800
Profit for the year	1,600
Profit attributable to:	
Owners of the parent	1,440
Non-controlling interest (W)	160
	1,600

Working

Group structure

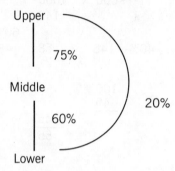

Non-controlling interest in Lower		
Direct		20%
Indirect (25% × 60%)		15%
		35%
Therefore, non-controlling interest		35%
Non-controlling interest in profit for the year		$'000
Middle (500 × 25%)		125
Lower (100 × 35%)		35
		160

32   Big Group

> **Text reference.** More complex group structures are covered in Chapter 11.
>
> **Top tips.** Do not panic at the amount of information thrown at you. Work through the information logically. Set up a proforma statement of financial position and slot the figures in as you can. Do not forget to detail your workings for items such as goodwill and reserves. Bear in mind that this question is longer than you would get in an exam.

At the beginning of the year, Big had a 25% holding in Tiny. This gives Big a significant influence over Tiny but not control. Tiny is an associate of Big. Tiny's results for the first six months of the year will be treated as an associate under the rules of IAS 28 (the equity method). A further purchase of shares was made by Small on 1 April 20X9. This is therefore a 'piecemeal' acquisition where control is achieved in stages. The group structure is now as follows:

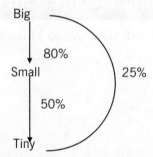

Big now owns 65% of Tiny (25% directly + (80% × 50%) via Small). So for the second six months of the year, Big **controls** Tiny and it is treated as a **subsidiary**.

BIG GROUP
CONSOLIDATED STATEMENT OF FINANCIAL POSITION AS AT 30 SEPTEMBER 20X9

	$'000
Non-current assets	
Property, plant and equipment (56,000 + 66,000 + 56,000)	178,000
Goodwill (W2)	13,850
	191,850
Current assets	
Inventories (45,000 + 44,000 + 25,000 – (W6) 2,800)	111,200
Trade receivables (40,000 + 30,000 + 16,000 – 6,000 – 5,000 intragroup)	75,000
Cash in hand (8,000 + 6,000 + 3,000)	17,000
	395,050
Equity attributable to owners of the parent	
Share capital	90,000
Retained earnings (W3)	98,180
	188,180
Non-controlling Interest (W4)	38,870
	227,050
Non-current liabilities	
Long-term loans (50,000 + 25,000)	75,000
Current liabilities	
Trade payables (25,000 + 20,000 + 11,000 – 6,000 – 5,000 intragroup)	45,000
Tax payable (7,000 + 6,000 + 4,000)	17,000
Bank overdraft (12,000 + 10,000 + 9,000)	31,000
	395,050

Workings

(1) Group structure

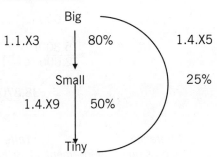

	%
Big's effective interest in Tiny [(80% x50%) indirect +25% direct]	65
Therefore, non-controlling interest	35
	100

When Tiny becomes a subsidiary, the existing investment is remeasured to fair value, and a gain or loss recognised in profit or loss. This fair value, along with the group share of the consideration paid by Small, plus the non-controlling interest is compared with Tiny's net assets at acquisition to calculate goodwill.

(2) Goodwill

	Small		Tiny	
	$'000	$'000	$'000	$'000
Consideration transferred		91,500	(80% × $29m)	23,200
Non-controlling interest (20% × 106,000)		21,200	(35% × $47m)	16,450
Fair value of previously held equity interest			(8m × $1.8125)	14,500
Fair value of NA acquired:				
Share capital	80,000		32,000	
Retained earnings	22,000		15,000	
Fair value adjustment (W5)	4,000		–	
		(106,000)		(47,000)
		6,700		7,150

Note

	$'000
Retained earnings at 30.9.X9	19,000
Less: profits after tax for period since acquisition (8,000,000 × 6/12)	(4,000)
Retained earnings at 1.4.X9	15,000

Consolidated goodwill 6,700 + 7,150 = 13,850

(3) Retained earnings

	Big	Small	Tiny 25%	Tiny 65%
	$'000	$'000	$'000	$'000
Retained earnings per question/date control obtained	69,000	59,000	15,000	19,000
Less: Unrealised profit (W6)				(2,800)
Fair value movement (W5)		(4,000)	–	–
Gain on derecognition of equity investment (W7)	750			
Pre-acquisition retained earnings		(22,000)	(10,000)	(15,000)
		33,000	5,000	1,200
Small: (33,000× 80%)	26,400			
Tiny: (5,000 × 25%)	1,250			
(1,200 × 65%)	780			
	98,180			

(4) Non controlling interest

	Small $'000	Tiny $'000
Non-controlling interests at acquisition	21,200	16,450
Share of post-acquisition retained earnings		
Small (20% × 33,000(W3))	6,600	
Tiny (35% × 1,200(W3))		420
Less: NCI in investment in Tiny (20% × $29m)	(5,800)	
	22,000	16,870
		38,870

(5) Fair value adjustment – Small

	Difference at acquisition $'000	Movement $'000	Difference at SOFP date $'000
Property (11,000 – 7,000)	4,000	(4,000)	0
	4,000	(4,000)	0

(6) Provision for unrealised profit

	$'000
Big $\left(\dfrac{9,000}{120}\times20\right)$	1,500
Small $\left(\dfrac{7,800}{120}\times20\right)$	1,300
	2,800

(7) Gain on derecognition of equity investment

	$'000	$'000
At fair value (8m × $1.8125)		14,500
Carrying value (equity method)		
Cost	12,500	
Share of post-acquisition retained earnings		
25% (15,000 (W2) – 10,000)	1,250	
		13,750
Gain on remeasurement to fair value		750

33 AZ

> **Text reference**. Disposals are covered in Chapter 10.
>
> **Top tips.** This is a fairly straightforward disposal and consolidated statement of financial position question which leads you through the processes step by step. Take care in Part (a) that you use the correct percentages for the disposal and that you bring in the fair value of the investment retained.
>
> **Easy marks.** Most of the 25 marks are for preparing the consolidated statement of financial position. Even if you got the calculations wrong in Part (a) and (b), you will get the marks for carrying your figures over correctly into Part (c).

(a) Shareholding in CX originally = 60% × 2,600,000 shares = 1,560,000 shares

Sale of 520,000 shares leaves remaining shareholding of 1,040,000 shares = 40%

(i) <u>Profit on disposal in AZ's own financial statements</u>

	$'000
Fair value of consideration received	1,250
Less carrying value of investment disposed of (2,730 × 20/60)	(910)
	340
Less tax (340 × 30%)	(102)
Profit after tax	238

(ii) <u>Profit on disposal in AZ's consolidated financial statements</u>

	$'000
Fair value of consideration received	1,250
Fair value of 40% investment retained	2,800
Less share of carrying value when lost	
Net assets: 60% × $4,655,000 (W2)	(2,793)
Goodwill belonging to owners of the parent (W3)	(390)
Profit on disposal before tax	867
Less tax (Part (a) (i))	(102)
Consolidated profit on disposal	765

Workings

(1) <u>Group structure</u>

Originally

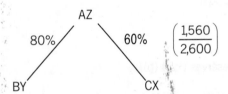

After the disposal of shares in CX on 1 October 20X5, AZ owns 1,040,000 shares. The remaining holding of 40%, and the fact that AZ has retained 'significant influence' mean that CX will be treated as an associate as from 1 October 20X5.

(2) <u>Net assets disposed of</u>

	$'000
Share capital	2,600
Reserves at 1 April 20X5	1,970
Profit to 1 October 20X5 (2,140 − 1,970 × 6/12)	85
Net assets at date of disposal	4,655

(3)   <u>Goodwill in CX</u>

	$'000	$'000
Consideration transferred		2,730
Non-controlling interest: 40% × 3,900		1,560
Less net assets acquired		
Share capital	2,600	
Reserves	1,300	
		(3,900)
		390

(b)   <u>Consolidated reserves at 31 March 20X6</u>

	AZ $'000	BY $'000	CX 60% $'000	CX retained 40% $'000
Per question/date of disposal (2,140 – 85 (Part (a) W2))	10,750	3,370	2,055	2,140
Group profit on disposal (Part (a)(i))	765			
Provision for unrealised profit (180,000 × 20/120)		(30)		
	11,515			
Less at acquisition/date of disposal		(1,950)	(1,300)	(2,055)
		1,390	755	85
Share of BY: 80% × 1,390	1,112			
Share of CX: 60% × 755	453			
40% × 85	34			
	13,114			

(c)   AZ GROUP
CONSOLIDATED STATEMENT OF FINANCIAL POSITION AS AT 31 MARCH 20X6

	$'000	$'000
Non-current assets		
Property, plant and equipment (10,750 + 5,830)		16,580
Goodwill (W1)		260
Investment in associate (W2)		2,834
Other investments (W3)		860
		20,534
Current assets		
Inventory (2,030 + 1,210 – (180 × 20/120))	3,210	
Trade receivables (2,380 + 1,300)	3,680	
Cash (1,380 + 50)	1,430	
		8,320
Equity		28,854
Share capital		8,000
Consolidated reserves (Part (b))		13,114
		21,114
Non-controlling interest (W4)		1,728
Current liabilities		
Trade payables (3,770 + 1,550)	5,320	
Income tax (420 + 170 + 102 (Part a))	692	
		6,012
		28,854

Workings

(1) <u>Goodwill in BY</u>

	$'000	$'000
Considerations transferred		3,660
Non-controlling interest: 20% × 4,250		850
Net-assets acquired		
Share capital	2,300	
Reserves	1,950	
		4,250
Goodwill		260

Note. The group share of preferred shares is separately cancelled out, leaving only the non-controlling share.

(2) <u>Investment in associate</u>

	$'000
Fair value at date control lost	2,800
Share of post 'acquisition' retained reserves: $885,000 (Part (b)) × 40%	34
	2,834

(3) <u>Other investments</u>

	$'000
Investments per SOFP	7,650
Less investment in BY	(3,660)
Less investment in BY preference shares	(400)
Less investment in CX	(2,730)
Other investments	860

(4) <u>Non-controlling interest</u>

	$'000	$'000
In preferences shares of BY: 60% × $1,000,000		600
In equity of BY:		
At acquisition (W1)	850	
BY's post acq'n. retained reserves		
20% × $1,390,000 (part (b))	278	
		1,128
		1,728

34 RW

> **Text reference.** Changes in the group structures are covered in Chapter 10.
>
> **Top tips.** This question involves a partial disposal where the remaining investment is dealt with as an associate and the preparation of a consolidated income statement. A good approach might be as follows.
>
> **Step 1** Draw a time line to identify the changes over the year.
>
> **Step 2** Set up the income statement proforma and insert the basic figures for the group and non-controlling interest.
>
> **Step 3** Calculate the goodwill on consolidation.
>
> **Step 4** Calculate the gain on disposal and transfer this to the proforma income statement. Ensure you include the unimpaired goodwill relating to the disposal in the disposal profit and loss calculation.
>
> **Step 5** Calculate the share of the associate's profit.
>
> **Step 6** Complete the income statement.
>
> **Easy marks.** The obvious easy marks in this question are for setting out the proforma and adding things together. Otherwise the marks are fairly evenly distributed between goodwill, tax, share of net assets at disposal, preparation of income statement (including profit on disposal) and non-controlling interest.

> **Examiner's comment.** The most common error in this question was to consolidate only a proportion of SX's revenue and costs. Adjustments must then be made for the profit on sale and for the non-controlling interest. Even if candidates could not correctly deal with the disposal aspects of the question they could pick up marks for calculations such as goodwill and non-controlling interest.

RW GROUP: CONSOLIDATED INCOME STATEMENT FOR THE YEAR ENDING 31 DECEMBER 20X4

	$'000
Revenue: 6,000 + (6/12 × 2,500)	7,250
Operating costs: 4,500 + (6/12 × 1,700)	(5,350)
	1,900
Profit on disposal of investment (W3)	180
Share of profit of associate: 40% × 6/12 × 550	110
Profit before tax	2,190
Income tax: 300 + (6/12 × 250) + 40	(465)
	1,725
Attributable to:	
Owners of the parent	1,670
Non-controlling interest 550 × 20% × 6/12	55
	1,725

Workings

(1) <u>Group structure</u>

RW

| 80% reduced to 40% on 1/7/20X4

SX

Time line

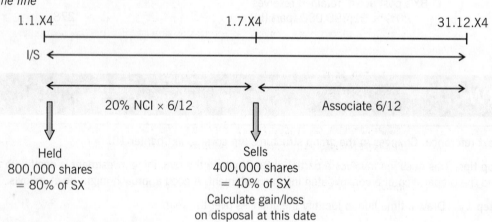

(2) <u>Goodwill</u>

	$'000	$'000
Consideration transferred		3,200
Non-controlling interest: 20% × 3,400		680
Net assets acquired		
Share capital	1,000	
Pre-acquisition reserves	2,400	
		(3,400)
Goodwill		480

(3) <u>Consolidated profit on disposal</u>

	$'000
Fair value of consideration received	3,000
Fair value of 40% investment retained	1,000
Less share of carrying value when control lost	
[1,000 + (2,900 + (550 × 6/12)] × 80%	(3,340)
Goodwill belonging to owners of the parent (W2)	(480)
	180

35 AD

Text reference. Financial instruments are covered in Chapter 2. Changes in group structure are covered in Chapter 10.

Top tips. Do not spend too long working out the figures in part (a). You will gain marks for explaining the treatment. In part (b), it helps if you learn our layout for reserves and non-controlling interest workings.

Easy marks. Setting out the proforma and having workings in place will earn you marks, even if you slip up on the unrealised profit and other details. There will be marks available for the basic consolidation of parent and direct subsidiary. As for the indirectly held associate, there will be basic marks for not treating it as a subsidiary and for showing an understanding of equity accounting.

Examiner's comments. Candidates generally found it more difficult to deal with the non-current financial asset than the current financial asset.

(a) <u>Non-current financial asset – Note 3</u>

The non-current financial asset is an investment in a **debenture**. The accounting treatment of this investment will depend upon how it is **classified**. If AD intends to hold the debenture until maturity it will be classified as a **'held-to-maturity'** investment and accounted for at **amortised cost**. This means that each year the effective interest is credited to the income statement and added to the value of the investment. The actual interest income of $50,000 is deducted from the investment value.

In the year ending June 20X5 the asset would have been valued at $1,030,000 (see working) and it would appear that in the current year the interest received of $50,000 has been credited to the investment to give a statement of financial position value of $980,000. At 30 June 20X6 this asset value will have increased by $82,000 to $1,062,000 and the income statement credited with this same amount.

<u>Current financial asset – Note 4</u>

The **current asset investment** in shares in DG would be classified as a financial asset at **fair value through profit or loss** as it is part of a portfolio held for trading and as such would be **revalued to fair value** at the reporting date. Therefore it would appear in the statement of financial position at $26,800 (4,000 × $6.70) with the **gain** of $1,800 since acquisition taken to the **income statement**.

<u>Working: Investment in debenture</u>

	$'000
1.7.20X4 cost	1,000
Effective interest to 30.6.20X5	80
(1,000 × 8%)	
Coupon interest received 30.6.20X5	(50)
(1,000 × 5%)	
∴ b/f 1.7.20X5	1,030
Coupon interest received 30.6.20X6	(50)
Figure as per question	980
Effective interest to 30.6.20X6	
(1,030 × 8%) (see note)	82
	1,062

Note. The effective interest is calculated on the carrying value of $1,030,000 which stood throughout the year until the coupon interest was received on 30 June 20X6.

(b) AD GROUP CONSOLIDATED STATEMENT OF FINANCIAL POSITION AS AT 30 JUNE 20X6

	$'000	$'000
ASSETS		
Non-current assets		
Property, plant and equipment (1,900 + 680)		2,580.0
Financial assets		
Investment in associate (W3)		110.8
Debenture (part a)		1,062.0
Goodwill (W2)		360.0
		4,112.8
Current assets		
Inventories (223 + 127)	350.0	
Trade receivables (204 + 93 – 5*)	292.0	
Other financial asset (part a)	26.8	
Cash (72 + 28 + 5*)	105.0	
		773.8
		4,886.6

*Cash in transit

	$'000	$'000
EQUITY AND LIABILITIES		
Equity		
Called up share capital		1,000.0
Reserves (W4)		2,554.8
		3,554.8
Non-controlling interest (W5)		172.8
		3,727.6
Non-current liabilities		600.0
Current liabilities		
Trade payables (247 + 113)	360.0	
Income tax (137 + 62)	199.0	
		559.0
		4,886.6

Workings

(1) <u>Group structure</u>

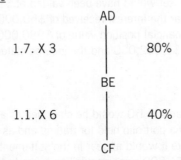

CF is a sub-associate. It will be equity accounted using the 40% held by BE (and thus controlled by AD) and added to the net assets of BE when the non-controlling interest is calculated (see W4).

(2) <u>Goodwill</u>

	$'000	$'000
Consideration transferred		880
Non-controlling interest 20% × 650		130
Net assets acquired		
Share capital	300	
Pre-acquisition reserves	350	
		(650)
Goodwill		360

(3)   Investment in associate

	$'000
Cost	104.0
Group share post acquisition profits	
40% × (122 – 102)	8.0
Less: unrealised profit on inventory	
(10,000 × 30%) × 40%	–
	110.8

(4)   Consolidated reserves

	AD $'000	BE $'000	CF $'000
Per question	2,300.0	557.0	122.0
Increase in fair value of asset	1.8		
Effective interest on debenture	82.0		
Less: unrealised profit on inventory (W3)		(1.2)	
Pre acquisition		(350.0)	(102.0)
		205.8	20.0
Share of BE			
80% × 205.8	164.6		
Share of CF (32% × 20.0)	6.4		
	2,554.8		

(5)   Non-controlling interest in BE

	$'000
NCI at acquisition (W2)	130.0
NCI share of post acquisition reserves of BE (W4) (20% × 205.8)	41.2
Add: NCI share of post acquisition reserves of associate (8% × 20 (W4))	1.6
	172.8

Note: The non-controlling interests in BE own 20% of BE's 40% of CF, so their effective interest is 8%.

Marking scheme

			Marks
(a)	Note 3: debenture	1	
	amortised cost	1	
	value	1	
			3
	Note 4: fair value	1	
	gain to income statement	1	
			2
(b)	Goodwill	3	
	Investment in associate	2	
	Reserves	3	
	Non-controlling interest	2	
			10
All other items (10 items): 1 mark each			10
			25

36 RBE

Text reference. Changes in group structure are covered in Chapter 10 of the study text.

Top tips. As in any group accounting question, it is important to identify the group structure. It also helps to set out the proforma for the SOCIE so that you can slot in the easy figures first.

Easy marks. The opening balances are stated in the question, and the calculations for the share issue and dividends paid are straightforward.

Examiner's comments. Part (a) was done well. Many candidates identified that this was a piecemeal acquisition but many of them could not apply this in part (b). Only a minority calculated the adjustment to parent's equity. Many also failed to show only the dividends paid to the owners of the parent in the parent column of the SOCIE.

(a)

RBE already controls DCA with its 70% investment, so DCA is already a subsidiary and would be fully consolidated. In substance, this is not an acquisition. Instead, it is treated in the group accounts as a transaction between the group shareholders i.e. the parent has purchased a 20% shareholding from NCI. No goodwill is calculated on the additional investment.

The value of the NCI needs to be worked out at the date of the additional investment (1 October 20X2), and the proportion purchased by the parent needs to be removed from NCI. The difference between the consideration transferred and the amount of the reduction in the NCI is included as an adjustment to parent equity.

(b)

RBE Group Consolidated statement of changes in equity for the year ended 31 December 20X2

	Equity attributable to owners of the parent $'000	Non-controlling interest $'000	Total $'000
Balance at 1 January 20X2	3,350	650	4,000
Total comprehensive income for the year (W2)	1,350	150	1,500
Share issue (2m x $1.30)	2,600	-	2,600
Dividends paid (100 × 30%)	(200)	(30)	(230)
Adjustment to equity	(37)	(503)	(540)
(on additional purchase of 20% of DCA's shares) (W3 and 4)			
Balance at 31 December 20X2	7,063	267	7,330

Workings

(1) Group structure

RBE

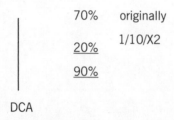

70%	originally
20%	1/10/X2
90%	

DCA

(2 Total comprehensive income

NCI share:

	$'000
To 1 October 20X2 (30% × 600 × 9/12)	135
To 31 December 20X2 (10% × 600 × 9/12)	15
NCI share of TCI	150

Parent share:

	$'000
Parent share of TCI of DCA (600 − 150)	450
TCI of RBE	900
NCI share of TCI	1,350

(3)   <u>Decrease in NCI</u>

	$000
NCI b/f 1 January 20X2	650
Share of TCI to 1 October 20X2 (W2)	135
Less: share of dividend paid (April 20X2) (30% × 100)	(30)
NCI at 1 October 20X2	755
Decrease in NCI on transfer of shares to parent (755× 20/30)	503

(4)   <u>Adjustment to equity</u>

	$000
Consideration transferred	(540)
Decrease in NCI on acquisition (W3)	503
Adjustment to parent's equity	(37)

In RBE's individual statement of financial position, the purchase of the 20% in DCA would have been recorded as follows:

	$000	$000
Dr Investment	540	
Cr Cash		540

Then in the group accounts, the adjustment to equity would be recorded as follows:

	$000	$000
Dr (reduce) NCI	503	
Dr (reduce) Parent's retained earnings	37	
Cr (cancel) Investment *		540

37   SOT Group

> **Text reference**. Changes in group structure are covered in Chapter 10. Financial instruments are covered in Chapter 2.
>
> **Top tips**. Take time to identify the group structure and the dates of the changes. A timeline is a useful way to sort this out.
>
> **Easy marks**. Once you have identified the changes, set up a proforma and get the basic time-apportioning and adding together set up in brackets on the face of the answer.
>
> **Examiner's comments**. The main concern was the inability of candidates to apply their consolidation knowledge when preparing a group income statement. Many were preparing workings that would only be required if preparing a statement of financial position – this wasted valuable exam time.

SOT GROUP
CONSOLIDATED STATEMENT OF COMPREHENSIVE INCOME FOR THE YEAR ENDED 30 SEPTEMBER 20X9

	$'000	$'000
Revenue (6,720 + (6,240 x 5/12) + (5,280 x 9/12))		13,280
Cost of sales (3,600 + (3,360 x 5/12) + (2,880 x 9/12))		(7,160)
Gross profit		6,120
Administrative expenses (760 + (740 x 5/12) + (650 x 9/12) + 23 (W1) + 10 (W5) − 40 recycled AFS gains)		(1,549)
Distribution costs (800 + (700 x 5/12) + (550 x 9/12))		(1,505)
Gain on disposal of investment in UV (W6)		163
Finance costs (360 + (240 x 5/12) + (216 x 9/12))		(622)
Share of profit of associate (684 x 3/12 x 35%)		60

Profit before tax		2,667
Income tax expense (400 + (360 x 5/12) + (300 x 9/12))		(775)
Profit for the year		1,892

Other comprehensive income:		
Actuarial gains on defined benefit pension plan (110 + (40 x 9/12))	140	
Tax effect of other comprehensive income (30 + (15 x 9/12))	(41)	
Recognised gains on AFS investments	46	
Recycling of previously recognised gains on AFS investment	(40)	
Share of other comprehensive income of associates, net of tax (25 x 3/12 x 35%)	2	
Other comprehensive income for the year, net of tax		107
Total comprehensive income for the year		1,999

Profit for the year attributable to:	
Owners of the parent	1,696
Non-controlling interest (W2)	196
	1,892

Total comprehensive income for the year attributable to:	
Owners of the parent	1,798
Non-controlling interest (W2)	201
	1,999

Workings

(1) Group structure

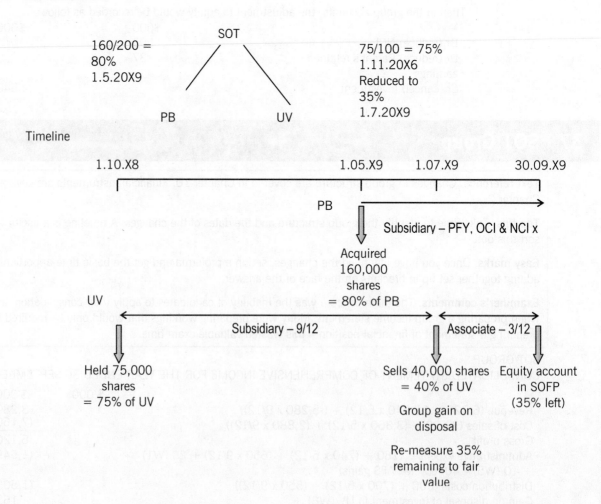

(2) <u>Non-controlling interests</u>

	PFY $'000	TCI $'000
PB		
Per Q (840 x 5/12)	350	
Additional depreciation on fair value adjustment (W4)	(10)	
	340	
NCI share (NCI in TCI is the same as PB has no OCI)	x 20%	
	= 68	= 68
UV		
Per Q (684 x 9/12)/(709 x 9/12)	513	532
	x 25%	x 25%
	= 128	= 133
Total NCI	196	201

(3) <u>Goodwill on consolidation of PB</u>

	$'000	$'000
Consideration transferred		2,800
NCI at proportionate share of fair value (20% × 3,210)		642
Less: Net assets acquired:		
Share capital	200	
Reserves	2,050	
Fair value uplift on PPE	960	
		3,210
Goodwill		232
Impairment (10%)		23

(4) <u>Goodwill on acquisition of UV</u>

	$'000	$'000
Consideration transferred		980
NCI at proportionate share of fair value (25% ×1,120)		280
Less: Net assets acquired:		
Share capital	100	
Reserves	1,020	
		1,120
Goodwill		140

(5) <u>Fair value adjustments (PB)</u>

	At acq'n 1.5.X9 $'000	Movement $'000	At year end 30.9.X9 $'000
PPE	960	(960/40 × 5/12) (10)	950

(6) <u>Group profit on part disposal of UV</u>

	$'000	$'000	$'000
Fair value of consideration received			960
Fair value of 35% investment retained			792
Less: Share of consolidated carrying value when control lost			
Net assets			
Share capital	100		
Retained earnings b/f	1,300		
TCI to 1.7.X9 (709 × $\frac{9}{12}$)	532		
	1,932		
Group share (75%)		1,449	
Goodwill (W3)		140	
			(1,589)
			163

Marking scheme

		Marks
Basic preparation of statement of comprehensive income		
Consolidation of SOT plus time apportioned results of subsidiaries	3	
Goodwill impairment	2	
Fair value adjustment	1	
Elimination of intragroup dividend	1	
Other comprehensive income	2	
Treatment of available for sale investments	2	
		11
Disposal of subsidiary	4	
Equity accounting for remaining investment	4	
		8
Non-controlling interest and allocation of profit between parent and NCI		6
		25

38 ROB Group

> **Text reference.** Changes in group structure are covered in Chapter 10. Financial instruments are covered in Chapter 2.
>
> **Top tips.** Don't neglect part (a). Once you have sorted out the group structure, make sure that you try to explain the basic points about the treatment of PER before you get into the detail of the numbers in part (b). In part (b) the most important thing is to stick to a methodical approach and set out clear workings. It is also important not to get bogged down and waste too much time on any one detail. For instance, if you were not sure what to do about the bond, the best approach would be miss it out and get on with the rest of the consolidation.
>
> **Easy marks.** There will be marks available for the basic consolidation of a parent and a subsidiary. Make sure you get the basic figures onto the statement of financial position quickly. The unrealised profit adjustment is similar to those in many other questions, so you should have been able to deal with it. There will also be marks available for every step you show in the main workings for goodwill, retained earnings and non-controlling interest.

(a) <u>Treatment of PER in the consolidated financial statements of ROB</u>

The acquisition of the additional 60% shareholding on 1 April 20X3 brings ROB's total investment in PER to 75%, and PER must be **consolidated**.

This is a **mid-year acquisition** so the results of PER would have to be **pro-rated** and only the post acquisition 6 months' results included in the statement of comprehensive income and in group retained earnings.

In the consolidated **statement of financial position**, 100% of PER's assets and liabilities must be consolidated with a 25% non-controlling interest.

This **piecemeal acquisition** involves a change in status for PER from a **financial asset** (where ROB had no significant influence) to a **subsidiary**. The change in investment from 15% to 75% crosses the 50% **control boundary**, so:

- The substance of the transaction is that the 15% financial asset has been « sold », so it must be restated to its fair value at the date of the change in status and the gain or loss recognised in profit or loss.

- ROB had treated the original investment as an **available for sale financial asset**, so the gain had already been recognised in 'other comprehensive income' (and other components of equity). This must be **reclassified** to profit or loss (and retained earnings).

- In substance ROB has acquired a 75% subsidiary on 1 April 20X3. Goodwill should be calculated as if the full 75% were acquired on that date.

(b) ROB GROUP CONSOLIDATED STATEMENT OF FINANCIAL POSITION AS AT 30 SEPTEMBER 20X3

	$'000	$'000
ASSETS		
Non-current assets		
Property, plant and equipment (22,000 + 5,000)		27,000.0
Goodwill (W2)		405.0
		27,405.0
Current assets		
Inventories (6,200 + 800 – 40(W7))	6960.0	
Trade receivables (6,600 + 1900)	8500.0	
Cash (1200 + 300)	1,500.0	
		16,960.0
		44,365.0
EQUITY AND LIABILITIES		
Equity		
Share capital ($1 ordinary shares)		20,000.0
Retained earnings (W3)		8,629.75
		28,629.75
Non-controlling interest (W4)		1603.75
		30,233.5
Non-current liabilities		
5% bonds 20X6 (W6)		4,031.5
Current liabilities (8,100 + 2,000)		10,100.0
		44,365.0

Workings

(1) <u>Group structure</u>

ROB

	15%	1.5.20X1	Financial asset
	60%	1.4.20X3	Subsidiary
	75%		

PER

<u>Pre acquisition retained earnings:</u>

	$'000
At 30.9 20X3	5,000
Less: 6 months' profit (1.4.20X3 – 30.9.20X3) ($3m × 6/12)	(1,500)
At 1.4.20X3	3,500

(2) <u>Goodwill (at full fair value)</u>

	$'000	$'000
Consideration transferred		2,900
Fair value of previously held investment		800
Non-controlling interest (25%) (at fair value)		1,250
Less: fair value of net assets		
Share capital	1,000	
Pre-acquisition reserves (W1)	3,500	
		(4,500)
Goodwill		450
Impairment (10%)		(45)
		405

(3) Consolidated retained earnings

	ROB $'000	PER $'000
Per question	7,500.0	5,000.0
Gain realised on derecognition of financial asset (W5)	200.0	
Finance cost on bond (W6)	(131.5)	
Less: unrealised profit on inventory (W7)		(40.0)
Pre acquisition (W1)		(3,500.0)
		1,460.0
Share of PER (75% × 1,460)	1,095	
Share of impairment loss (75% × 45 (W2))	(33.75)	
	8,629.75	

(4) Non-controlling interest

	$'000
NCI at acquisition (W2)	1,250.0
NCI share of post acquisition reserves (25% × 1,460 (W3))	365.0
NCI share of impairment loss (25% × 45 (W2))	(11.25)
	1,603.75

(5) Other components of equity

	$'000
ROB per question	500
Realised on derecognition of financial asset (800 – 600)	(200)
Fair value gain from 1.4.X3 to 30.9.X3: eliminate on consolidation	
(4,000 – 2,900 – 800)	(300)
	0

Note: The gain recognised on the original (15%) investment in PER is realised and reclassified to profit or loss (and so to retained earnings) when ROB takes control of PER. The further gain on the investment (both the original 15% and the new 60%) from 1.4.20X3 to 30.9.20X9 is eliminated on consolidation as the consideration transferred must be measured at its fair value on the acquisition date.

(6) Bonds

	$'000
1.10.20X8 Net proceeds	3,900.0
Effective interest to 30.9.20X9	331.5
(3,900 × 8.5%)	
Coupon interest paid 30.9.20X9	(200)
(4,000 × 5%)	
30.9.20X9 Balance c/d	4,031.5

The adjustment required to recognise the full effective finance cost (331,500 – 200,000) is:

DEBIT	Finance costs (Retained earnings)	$131,500
CREDIT	Non-current liability	$131,500

(7) Provision for unrealised profit

PER (subsidiary) sold to ROB (parent).

Unrealised profit = $400,000 × 20% × ½ = $40,000

The adjustment required is:

DEBIT	PER's retained earnings	$40,000
CREDIT	Inventories	$40,000

Marks

(a)	One mark for each relevant point	
	Mid-year acquisition	2
	Piecemeal acquisition	2
	Treatment of previously held investment	1
		5
(b)	Goodwill and impairment	5
	Retained earnings	4
	Non-controlling interest	3
	Bond	2
	Unrealised profit	2
	Other figures on SOFP	4
		20
		25

39 Preparation question: Foreign operations

STANDARD GROUP
CONSOLIDATED STATEMENT OF FINANCIAL POSITION AS AT 31 DECEMBER 20X6

	S $'000	O Kr'000	Rate	O $'000	Consol $'000
Property, plant and equipment	1,285	4,400	8.1	543	1,828
Investment in Odense	520	–		–	–
Goodwill (W2)	–	–		–	277
	1,805	4,400		543	2,105
Current assets	410	2,000	8.1	247	657
	2,215	6,400		790	2,762
Equity	500	1,000	9.4	106	500
Retained reserves (W3)	1,115				1,395
Pre-acq'n	–	2,100	9.4	224	–
Post-acq'n	–	2,200	Bal fig	324	–
	1,615	5,300		654	1,895
Non-controlling interest (W6)					131
					2,026
Loans	200	300	8.1	37	237
Current liabilities	400	800	8.1	99	499
	600	1,100		136	736
	2,215	6,400		790	2,762

CONSOLIDATED STATEMENT OF COMPREHENSIVE INCOME FOR THE YEAR ENDED 31 DECEMBER 20X6

	S $'000	O Kr'000	Rate	O $'000	Consol $'000
Revenue	1,125	5,200	8.4	619	1,744
Cost of sales	(410)	(2,300)	8.4	(274)	(684)
Gross profit	715	2,900		345	1,060
Other expenses	(180)	(910)	8.4	(108)	(288)
Impairment loss (W2)					(21)
Dividend received from Odense	40				–
Profit before tax	575	1,990		237	751
Income tax expense	(180)	(640)	8.4	(76)	(256)
Profit for the year	395	1,350		161	495

Other comprehensive income:
Exchange difference on translating foreign operations (W4)	72
Total comprehensive income	567

Profit attributable to:
Owners of the parent (balance)	463
Non-controlling interest (161 × 20%)	32
	495

Total comprehensive income attributable to:
Owners of the parent (balance)	525
Non-controlling interest (161 + 48 (W4)) × 20%)	42
	567

CONSOLIDATED STATEMENT OF CHANGES IN EQUITY (ATTRIBUTABLE TO OWNERS OF THE PARENT) FOR THE YEAR ENDED 31 DECEMBER 20X6

	$'000
Balance at 1/1/X6 (500 + (W5) 1,065)	1,565
Total comprehensive income for the year	525
Dividends paid (Standard)	(195)
Balance at 31/12/X6 (per SOFP)	1,895

Workings

(1) Group structure

Standard

1.1.X4	80%

Pre-acquisition ret'd reserves 2,100,000 Krone

Odense

(2) Goodwill

	Kr'000	Kr'000	Rate	$'000
Consideration transferred ($520,000 × 9.4)		4,888	9.4	520
NCI (20% × Kr 3,100,000)		620	9.4	66
Share capital	1,000			
Retained earnings	2,100			
		(3,100)	9.4	(330)
		2,408	9.4	256
Exchange differences 20X4-20X5		–	β	18
At 31.12.X5		2,408	8.8	274
Impairment losses 20X6		(168)	8.1	(21)
Exchange differences 20X6		–	β	24
At 31.12.X6		2,240	8.1	277

(3) Consolidated retained reserves carried forward

	Standard $'000	Odense $'000
Per question (O: 224 + 324)	1,115	548
Pre-acquisition		(224)
		324
Group share (324 × 80%)	259	
	1,374	
Less: Goodwill impairment losses (W2)	(21)	
Add: Goodwill exchange differences ((W2) 18 + 24))	42	
	1,395	

(4)   <u>Exchange differences in period</u>

	$'000	$'000
On translation of net assets (gross)		
Closing NA @ CR	654	
Opening NA @ OR (4,355 @ 8.8)	(495)	
Less retained profit as translated (W5)	(111)	
Exchange gain		48
On goodwill (W2)		24
		72

(5)   <u>Retained profit of Odense</u>

	$'000
Profit for the period (as translated)	161
Dividend for year (40/80 × 100)	(50)
	111

Per the consolidated income statement, Standard has received $40,000 dividend from Odense. This is 80% of the total dividend paid.

(6)   <u>Non-controlling interest</u>

	$'000
At acquisition (W2)	66
Share of post acquisition retained earnings	
– per translated SOFP (20% × 324 (W3))	65
	131

(7)   <u>Consolidated retained reserves b/f proof</u>

	Standard	Odense
	$'000	$'000
Per question (per question)/[224 + 324 – 161 + 50 – (W4) 48)]	915	389
Pre-acquisition		(224)
		165
Group share (165 × 80%)	132	
	1,047	
Less: Goodwill impairment losses (W2)	(0)	
Add: Goodwill exchange differences (W2)	18	
	1,065	

40   Little

> **Text reference**. Foreign currency consolidations are covered in Chapter 12.
>
> **Top tips.** Since this question was set, the standard has changed such that Part (a) is not as important. Nevertheless, you will need to know the mechanics of translation at the closing rate.
>
> We strongly advise you to set out your goodwill working in the format given in (W5) below. This is easy to understand and brings out the FX gain as a balancing figure.
>
> **Easy marks.** Students are often frightened of FX questions. However, there are easy marks to be gained just for straightforward translation and adding together, before you do the fiddly bits like the FX gain.

(a)   From the information in the question it is clear that Little operates on a largely independent basis from Large with its own supplier and customer bases and no day to day part being played by Large in operational decisions. Therefore the cash flows of Little will not have a day to day impact on those of Large. As such IAS 21 *The effects of changes in foreign exchange rates* requires that the financial statements of Little for consolidation purposes should be translated using the **presentation currency** or **closing rate** or **net investment method**. Under this method the statement of financial position assets and liabilities are translated at the **spot rate** of exchange on the **reporting date** and the income statement is translated at a **weighted average rate** of exchange for the year. Any exchange differences are not reported in profit or loss, as they have no impact on the cash flows of the group, but instead are reported as other comprehensive income.

(b) <u>Translation of Little statement of financial position into $</u>

	F000	Rate	$'000
Non-current assets			
Property, plant and equipment			
(80,000 – 6,000 revaluation adjustment)	74,000	5	14,800
Current assets			
Inventories	30,000	5	6,000
Trade receivables	28,000	5	5,600
Cash	5,000	5	1,000
	137,000		27,400
Equity			
Share capital	40,000	6	6,667
Revaluation surplus (6,000 – 6,000)			
Pre acquisition retained reserves	26,000	6	4,333
Post acquisition retained reserves			
(34,000 – 26,000)	8,000	Bal	3,800
	74,000		14,800
Non-current liabilities			
Long-term borrowings	25,000	5	5,000
Deferred tax	10,000	5	2,000
Current liabilities			
Trade payables	20,000	5	4,000
Tax	8,000	5	1,600
	137,000		27,400

CONSOLIDATED STATEMENT OF FINANCIAL POSITION AS AT 31 MARCH 20X7

	$'000	$'000
Non-current assets		
Goodwill (W2)		2,520
Property, plant and equipment (63,000 + 14,800)		77,800
Current assets		
Inventories (25,000 + 6,000 – (1,000 × 25%))	30,750	
Trade receivables (20,000 + 5,600 – 1,000)	24,600	
Cash (6,000 + 1,000 + 1,000 cash in transit)	8,000	
		63,350
		143,670
Equity		
Called up share capital		30,000
Retained earnings (W3)		38,615
Non-controlling interest (W4)		1,455
		70,070
Non-current liabilities		
Long-term borrowings (20,000 + 5,000)	25,000	
Deferred tax (6,000 + 2,000)	8,000	
		33,000
Current liabilities		
Trade payables (25,000 + 4,000)	29,000	
Tax (7,000 + 1,600)	8,600	
Bank overdraft	3,000	
		40,600
		143,670

Workings

(1)   Group structure

Investment in Little = 36,000/40,000 = 90%

Large

I.4.XI $\dfrac{36,000}{40,000}$ 90%

Little

Pre-acquisition retained earnings 26m francos

(2)   Goodwill

	F000	F000	Rate	$'000
Consideration transferred (12,000 × 6)		72,000	6	12,000
Non-controlling interest				
(66,000 × 10%)		6,600	6	1,100
Share capital	40,000			
Pre acquisition ret'd earnings	26,000			
		(66,000)		(11,000)
At 1.4.20X1		12,600	6	2,100
Foreign exchange gain		–	Bal	420
At 31.3.20X7		12,600	5	2,520

(3)   Retained earnings

	$'000
Large	35,000
Little – post acquisition (3,800 (from Little's $ SOFP) × 90%)	3,420
Unrealised profit (90% × 250)	(225)
Foreign exchange gain on goodwill (W2)	420
	38,615

(4)   Non controlling interest

	$'000
At acquisition (W2)	1,100
Share of post acquisition retained earnings	
((translated SOFP 3,800 – PUP 250) × 10%)	335
	1,455

Note: PUP on inventory. As mark-up is 25%, this is 25% profit on cost. So the unrealised profit on the inventory of 1,000 is 25%, ie 250.

41   Small

Text reference. Foreign currency translation is covered in Chapter 12.

Top tips. This is a fairly straightforward question on producing a consolidated statement of financial position, including a foreign currency translation.

You are required to carry out the translating and prepare the consolidated statement of financial position. **Do not forget to adjust for the accounting policy difference** before doing the translation. Remember to eliminate intra-group balances and unrealised profits before consolidating. The final step is to calculate the capital and retained earnings.

Adjustment to net assets for change in accounting policy

	Adjusted figure at acquisition	Adjusted figure at reporting date
	Fl'000	Fl'000
Share capital ($^{1}/_{2}$ Fl shares)	40,000	40,000
Revaluation reserve	6,000	11,000
Retained earnings	20,000	44,000
	66,000	95,000

> **Top tips.** You are not told the share capital at acquisition and you are not told that there have been any movements in the share capital since acquisition. Therefore assume that the share capital of Small at acquisition was Fl 40m. This equates to 80m shares. As Big purchased 60m shares, this is a 75% shareholding (60/80).

Translation of Small's statement of financial position

	Fl'000	Rate	$'000
Property, plant and equipment (80 + 11)	91,000	5	18,200
Inventories	40,000	5	8,000
Trade receivables	32,000	5	6,400
Cash	4,000	5	800
	167,000		33,400
Share capital	40,000	6	6,667
Revaluation reserve: pre-acquisition	6,000	6	1,000
post-acquisition (11 – 6)	5,000	5	1,000
Retained earnings: pre-acquisition	20,000	6	3,333
post acquisition (44 – 20)	24,000	(balance)	7,000
	95,000		19,000
Long term borrowings	30,000	5	6,000
Deferred tax	9,000	5	1,800
Trade payables	15,000	5	3,000
Current tax	18,000	5	3,600
	167,000		33,400

Consolidated statement of financial position

BIG GROUP
CONSOLIDATED STATEMENT OF FINANCIAL POSITION
AS AT 31 MARCH 20X9

	$'000	$'000
Non-current assets		
Property, plant and equipment (60 + 18.2)		78,200
Intangible assets (W2)		1,500
		79,700
Current assets		
Inventory (30 + 8 – 1.2 (W3))	36,800	
Trade receivables (25 + 6.4 – 6 (W4))	25,400	
Cash (3 + 0.8 + 6 (W4))	9,800	
		72,000
		151,700

	$'000	$'000
Equity attributable to owners of the parent		
Share capital (Big only)		30,000
Retained earnings (W5)		38,800
Revaluation reserve (15 + 75% × 1)		15,750
		84,550
Non-controlling interest (W6)		4,750
		89,300
Non-current liabilities		
Long term borrowings (15 + 6)	21,000	
Deferred tax (5 + 1.8)	6,800	
		27,800
Current liabilities		
Trade payables (12 + 3)	15,000	
Tax (16 + 3.6)	19,600	
		34,600
		151,700

Workings

(1) Group structure

Big

| 75%

Small

(2) Unrealised profit

Sales from Big to Small: $6m × $\dfrac{25}{125}$ = $1,200,000

(3) Goodwill on consolidation

	FI'000	FI'000	Rate	$'000
Consideration transferred		57,000	6	9,500
Non-controlling interest				
(66,000 × 25%)		16,500	6	2,750
Less: Share capital	40,000			
Revaluation reserve	6,000			
Pre-acq'n retained earnings	20,000			
		(66,000)	6	(11,000)
At 1.4.20X8		7,500	6	1,250
Foreign exchange gain		–	Bal	250
At 31.3.20X9		7,500		1,500

(4) Trade receivables and cash

	Receivables	Cash
	$'000	$'000
Big	25,000	3,000
Small	6,400	800
Cash in transit	(6,000)	6,000
	25,400	9,800

(5) Retained earnings

	Big	Small
	$'000	$'000
Per question/part (b)(ii)	34,500	7,000
Unrealised profit (W3)	(1,200)	
	33,300	
Share of Small's post-acquisition reserves		
75% × $7,000,000	5,250	
Exchange gain on retranslation of goodwill (W2)	250	
	38,800	

(6) <u>Non-controlling interest</u>

	$'000
NCI at acquisition (W3)	2,750
NCI share of post acq'n retained earnings (25% × 7,000 (W5))	1,750
NCI share of post acq'n revaluation reserve (25% × 1,000 (per translated SOFP))	250
	4,750

Marking scheme

		Marks
Net adjustments to net assets for change in accounting policy:		
At acquisition, 1 mark each		3
At reporting date, 1 mark each		3
Small's SOFP – correct translation of each item, 1 mark each		13
Consolidated SOFP – goodwill	1	
– retained earnings	1	
– non controlling interest	1	
– all other items, 0.5 mark each	5	
	8	
Maximum available		6
		25

42   Home group

> **Text reference**. This topic is covered in Chapter 12.
>
> **Top tips.** Make sure you use the average rate to translate the income statement. Do not spend too long on the impairment of goodwill.
>
> **Easy marks.** These are available for setting out the proforma, translating and adding together.
>
> **Examiner's comments.** Although the question was generally well answered, some candidates thought that no adjustment was required for intra-group sales on the grounds that the inventory purchased had been sold to third parties outside the group.

HOME GROUP – CONSOLIDATED INCOME STATEMENT FOR YEAR ENDED 31 JULY 20X6

	$'000
Revenue (3,000 + 270.8 (W1) – (50/2.4))	3,250.0
Cost of sales (2,400 + 229.2 (W1) – (50/2.4))	(2,608.4)
Gross profit	641.6
Distribution costs (32 + 17.1) (W1)	(49.1)
Administrative expenses (168 + 36.3) (W1)	(204.3)
Impairment of goodwill (W2)	(1.9)
Exchange difference (W3)	1.3
Finance costs (15 + 4.2) (W1)	(19.2)
Profit before tax	368.4
Income tax (102 – 4.2) (W1)	(97.8)
Profit for year	270.6

Workings

(1) <u>Translation of Foreign</u>

	Foreign Crowns 000	*Exchange rate*	*Foreign $'000*
Revenue	650	2.4	270.8
Cost of sales	550	2.4	229.2
Distribution costs	41	2.4	17.1
Administrative exp	87	2.4	36.3
Finance costs	10	2.4	4.2
Income tax (credit)	10	2.4	4.2

(2) <u>Goodwill</u>

	Crowns	*Crowns*	*Rate*	*$*
Consideration transferred		204,000	1.7	120,000
Less fair value of net assets				
acquired				
Share capital	1,000			
Reserves	180,000			
		(181,000)	1.7	(106,471)
		23,000	1.7	13,529
Impairment loss: 20%		(4,600)	2.4	(1,917)
Exchange difference			balance	(3,248)
At 31 July 20X6		18,400	2.2	8,364

(3) <u>Exchange difference on plant</u>

	$
Purchase price 32,000 florins /1.5	21,333
Year end re-translation 32,000 florins/1.6	20,000
Exchange gain	1,333

43 ABC Group

Text reference. Consolidation of foreign subsidiaries is covered in Chapter 12 of the study text.

Top tips. As with all consolidations, a methodical approach, setting up proformas for the answer and making sure you get the easy marks first will help you score well on this type of question. It's important to avoid getting bogged down in the complexities of calculating the exchange difference, so you should aim to complete as much of the rest of the question as you can before tackling this.

Easy marks. As long as you have learned the rules about which exchange rates to use, there will always be some easy marks available for the translation of the foreign subsidiary's financial statements. Also, once you have translated the figures, more easy marks are available for the basic steps in the consolidation.

Examiner's comments. Many candidates completely ignored the translation of the subsidiary or made no attempt to calculate the gain or loss on translation. This had a significant impact on the marks. Workings were poorly constructed and rarely completed, giving the impression that candidates were at a loss as to how to deal with the translation of the subsidiary. There was confusion over whether to divide or multiply on translation but candidates were not penalised for this as it was the principles of IAS 21 and the selection of the correct rates that was being tested.

A GROUP– CONSOLIDATED STATEMENT OF COMPREHENSIVE INCOME FOR THE YEAR ENDED 30 SEPTEMBER 20X6

	$'000
Revenue (4,600 + 3,385 (W2))	7,985
Cost of sales and operating expenses (3,700 + 2,462 (W2))	(6,162)
Share of associate's profit (400 × 40%)	160
Profit before tax	1,983
Income tax (200 + 231(W2))	(431)
Profit for the year	1,552

	$'000
Other comprehensive income:	
Revaluation of property, plant and equipment (200 + 185(W2))	385
Share of associate's other comprehensive income (70 × 40%)	28
Exchange difference on translating foreign operations (W7)	803
Other comprehensive income for the year	1,216
Total comprehensive income	2,768

Profit for the year attributable to:	
Owners of the parent (1,552 – 138)	1,414
Non-controlling interest (692(W2) × 20%)	138
	1,552

Total comprehensive income for the year attributable to:	
Owners of the parent (2,768 – 336)	2,432
Non-controlling interest (W8)	336
	2,768

CONSOLIDATED STATEMENT OF FINANCIAL POSITION AS AT 30 SEPTEMBER 20X6

	$'000
Non-current assets	
Property, plant and equipment (7,000 + 6,349 (W2))	13,349
Goodwill (W3)	635
Investment in associate (W6)	1,220
	15,204
Current assets (3,000 + 3,175 (W2))	6,175
	21,379
Equity attributable to owners of the parent	
Share capital	2,000
Reserves (W4)	13,522
	15,522
Non-controlling interest (W5)	1,476
Total equity	16,998
Current liabilities (2,000 + 2,381 (W2))	4,381
Total equity and liabilities	21,379

Workings

(1) Group structure

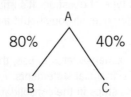

80%	40%
B	C

Note: B is a subsidiary but has a different functional currency to A, so must be translated into A$ and then consolidated.

C is an associate, and uses the same functional currency as A so no translation is required. It will be equity accounted.

(2) Translation of B's SOCI

	B$'000	Exchange rate Ave.rate	A$'000
Revenue	2,200	0.6500	3,385
Cost of sales and operating expenses	(1,600)	0.6500	(2,462)
Income tax	(150)	0.6500	(231)
Profit for the year			692
Revaluation	120	0.6500	185
Total comprehensive income	570		877

Translation of B's statement of financial position

	B$'000	Exchange rate	A$'000
Property, plant and equipment	4,000	CR 0.6300	6,349
Current assets	2,000	CR 0.6300	3,175
	6,000		9,524
Share capital	1,000	HR 0.5000	2,000
Reserves: pre-acquisition	1,800	HR 0.5000	3,600
post-acquisition (3,500 – 1,800)	1,700	(bal. figure)	1,543
	4,500		7,143
Current liabilities	1,500	CR 0.6300	2,381
	6,000		9,524

(3)   Goodwill

	B$'000	B$'000	Rate	A$'000
Consideration transferred		2,600	HR 0.5000	5,200
Non-controlling interest (FV)		600	HR 0.5000	1,200
Less fair value of net assets acquired				
Share capital	1,000			
Reserves	1,800			
		(2,800)	HR 0.5000	(5,600)
Goodwill at 1 October 20X3		400	HR 0.5000	800
Forex loss (balancing figure)				(237)
Goodwill at 1 October 20X5		400	OR 0.7100	563
Forex gain (balancing figure)				72
Goodwill at 1 October 20X6		400	CR 0.6300	635

(4)   Retained earnings

	A$'000
A per question	12,100
Share of B's post-acquisition reserves (80% × 1,543 (W2))	1,234
Share of C's post-acquisition reserves (40% × (1,500 - 700))	320
Group share of net exchange loss on retranslation of goodwill (80% × (237 - 72)(W3))	(132)
	13,522

(5)   Non-controlling interest (SOFP)

	A$'000
NCI at acquisition (W3)	1,200
NCI share of post acq'n reserves (20% × 1,543 (W2))	309
NCI share of net exchange loss on retranslation of goodwill (20% × (237 - 72)(W3))	(33)
	1,476

(6)   Investment in associate

	A$'000
Cost	900
Group share of post acquisition retained reserves 40% × (1,500 – 700)	320
	1,220

(7)   Exchange differences in period

	A$'000	A$'000
On translation of net assets (gross)		
Closing NA @ CR (W2)	7,143	
Opening NA @ OR ((4,500 – 570) @ 0.7100)	(5,535)	
Less TCI as translated (W2)	(877)	
Exchange gain		731
On goodwill (W3)		72
Total forex gains		803

(8)   Non-controlling interest in B's TCI

	A$'000
TCI as translated (W2)	877
Exchange gains (W7)	803
	1,680
NCI (20% × 1,680)	336

44 AH Group

Text reference. Consolidated statements of cash flows are covered in Chapter 13.

Top tips. This was a consolidated statement of cash flows. It is unusual to have both group accounts questions on non-mainstream consolidation topics. Students often dislike group statements of cash flows, but this one did not present any hidden traps. The trickiest parts were the acquisition of a subsidiary during the year, the payment of dividends to the non-controlling shareholders and the disposal of a property.

Easy marks. With all group statements of cash flows there are easy marks to be had for just doing the statement of cash flows aspects, leaving aside the fact that it is a group. Knowing the proforma, knowing whether to add or subtract increase/decrease in receivables etc, all topics you have studied for Paper F1.

Examiner's comment. Most candidates did well on this question. Common errors includes failure to take the acquisition into account in calculating movements in working capital items. Some included cash items in the statement of cash flows; for example, many candidates included the profit on the sale of the property rather than the proceeds of sale in cash flows from investing activities.

AH GROUP CONSOLIDATED STATEMENT OF CASH FLOWS FOR THE YEAR ENDED 30 JUNE 20X5

	$'000	$'000
Cash flows from operating activities		
Profit before taxation	19,450	
Adjustment for		
Depreciation	7,950	
Profit on disposal of property	(1,250)	
Interest expense	1,400	
	27,550	
Decrease in trade receivables (27,130 − 26,300 − 1,300) (W3)	470	
Increase in inventories (33,500 − 28,750 − 1,650) (W3)	(3,100)	
Decrease in trade payables (33,340 − 32,810 − 1,950) (W3)	(1,420)	
Cash generated from operations	23,500	
Interest paid (W6)	(1,480)	
Income taxes paid (W7)	(5,850)	
Net cash from operating activities		16,170
Cash flows from investing activities		
Acquisition of subsidiary, net of cash acquired (2,000 − 50)	(1,950)	
Purchase of property, plant and equipment (W1)	(11,300)	
Proceeds from sale of property	2,250	
Net cash used in investing activities		(11,000)
Cash flows from financing activities		
Repayment of interest-bearing borrowings	(1,000)	
Dividends paid (6,000 + (W5) 200)	(6,200)	
Net cash used in financing activities		(7,200)
Net decrease in cash and cash equivalents		(2,030)
Cash and cash equivalents at beginning of period		3,900
Cash and cash equivalents at end of period		1,870

Note. Dividends paid could also be shown under financing activities and dividends paid to non-controlling interest could also be shown under either operating activities or under financing activities.

Workings (two styles of workings are shown – you should use a consistent method, either T-accounts or the schedules throughout)

(1) Acquisition of property, plant and equipment

PROPERTY, PLANT AND EQUIPMENT

	$'000		$'000
Opening balance	44,050	Depreciation	7,950
On acquisition of subsidiary	4,200	Disposal	1,000
Acquisitions (bal fig)	11,300	Closing balance	50,600
	59,550		59,550

	$'000
B/d	44,050
Disposal	(1,000)
Depreciation	(7,950)
Acquisition of subsidiary	4,200
	39,300
Additions (balancing figure)	11,300
C/d	50,600

(2) Goodwill

GOODWILL

	$'000		$'000
Balance b/f	4,160		
On acquisition of subsidiary	2,250*	Balance c/f	6,410
	6,410		6,410

* Goodwill arising on acquisition

	$'000
Cost of combination	
Shares (2m @ $2) ($1 shares at a premium of $1)	4,000
Cash	2,000
	6,000
Less net assets acquired (5,000 × 75%)	(3,750)
	2,250

	$'000
B/d	4,160
Acquisition of subsidiary	2,250
C/d	6,410

(3) Inventories, trade receivables and trade payables

	Inventories	*Receivables*	*Payables*
	$'000	*$'000*	*$'000*
B/d	28,750	26,300	32,810
Acquisition of subsidiary	1,650	1,300	1,950
	30,400	27,600	34,760
Increase/(decrease) (balancing figure)	3,100	(470)	(1,420)
C/d	33,500	27,130	33,340

(4) Issue of ordinary share capital

SHARE CAPITAL

	$'000		$'000
Closing balance (20,000 + 12,000)	32,000	Opening balance (18,000 + 10,000)	28,000
		Issued on acquisition of subsidiary (2m × $2)	4,000
		Issued for cash (balancing figure)	0
	32,000		32,000

		$'000
B/d (18,000 + 10,000)		28,000
Acquisition of subsidiary (2m × $2)		4,000
		32,000
Issue for cash (balancing figure)		0
C/d (20,000 + 12,000)		32,000

(5) <u>Dividends paid to non-controlling interest</u>

NON-CONTROLLING INTEREST

	$'000		$'000
Cash paid (bal fig)	200	Opening balance	1,920
		On acquisition (5,000 × 25%)	1,250
Closing balance	3,625	Income statement	655
	3,825		3,825

	$'000
B/d	1,920
Profit attributable to NCI	655
On acquisition of subsidiary 25% × 5,000	1,250
	3,825
Dividends paid to non-controlling interests (balancing figure)	(200)
C/d	3,625

(6) <u>Interest paid</u>

INTEREST PAYABLE

	$'000		$'000
B/d			
Cash paid (bal fig)	1,480	Opening balance	1,440
Closing balance	1,360	Income statement	1,400
C/d	2,840		2,840

	$'000
B/d	1,440
Income statement	1,400
	2,840
Interest paid (balancing figure)	(1,480)
C/d	1,360

(7) <u>Income taxes paid</u>

INCOME TAXES PAYABLE

	$'000		$'000
Cash paid (bal fig)	5,850	Opening balance	5,450
		On acquisition of subsidiary	250
Closing balance	6,100	Income statement	6,250
	11,950		11,950

	$'000
B/d	5,450
Income statement	6,250
On acquisition of subsidiary	250
	11,950
Tax paid (balancing figure)	(5,850)
C/d	6,100

Marking scheme

	Marks
Correct adjustments for movements in working capital, 2 marks each	6
Interest paid	2
Income taxes paid	2
Acquisition of subsidiary	2
Purchase of PPE	4
All other items, 1 mark each (max 9)	9
	25

45 EAG Group

Text reference. Consolidated statements of cash flows are covered in Chapter 13.

Top tips. This was an unusual question, including the disposal of an associate, plus a detailed calculation of interest on debt measured at amortised cost. The most important thing here was to stick to the methodical techniques you have learned for group statements of cash flows, and to avoid getting bogged down in the tricky details. Before you try to deal with the disposal of the associate, think about how associates are treated in the statement of financial position and income statement.

Easy marks. With all group statements of cash flows there are easy marks available for just doing the statement of cash flows aspects, and working methodically through the information.

Examiner's comment. Candidates who attempted this question answered it well. A common error was failing to calculate the opening and closing cash and cash equivalent figures correctly

EAG GROUP CONSOLIDATED STATEMENT OF CASH FLOWS FOR THE YEAR ENDED 30 APRIL 20X8

	$m	$m	Ref to workings
Cash flows from operating activities			
Profit before taxation		2,604.2	
Adjustments for:			
Depreciation	2,024.7		
Impairment of goodwill	202.6		2
Amortisation of intangibles	93.1		3
Interest expense	510.9		
Profit on disposal of associate	(3.4)		
Share of profit of associate	(1.6)		
		2,826.3	
		5,430.5	
Increase in inventories (5,217.0 – 4,881.0)		(336.0)	
Decrease in receivables (4,670.0 – 4,633.6)		36.4	
Increase in payables (5,579.3 – 5,356.3)		223.0	
Cash generated from operations		5,353.9	
Interest paid		(390.0)	7
Income taxes		(831.0)	8
Net cash from operating activities		4,132.9	
Cash flows from investing activities			
Purchase of property, plant & equipment	(4,917.0)		1
Purchase of intangibles	(27.2)		3
Proceeds from sale of associate	18.0		
Dividend received from associate	0.8		4
Net cash used in investing activities		(4,925.4)	
		(792.5)	

Cash flows from financing activities
Proceeds from issue of share capital
(4,300.0 – 3,600.0)   700.0   5
Dividends paid to non-controlling interest   (88.0)   6
Net cash used in financing activities   612.0
Net decrease in cash and cash equivalents   (180.5)
Cash at the beginning of the period (88.3 – 507.7)   (419.4)
Cash at the end of the period (62.5 – 662.4)   (599.9)

Workings (two styles of workings are shown – you should use a consistent method, either T-accounts or the schedules throughout)

(1)   Additions to PPE

PROPERTY, PLANT AND EQUIPMENT (NBV)

	$m		$m
NBV b/fwd	19,332.8	Depreciation charge	2,024.7
Additions (balancing fig.)	4,917.0	NBV c/fwd	22,225.1
	24,249.8		24,249.8

	$m
B/d	19,332.8
Depreciation	(2,024.7)
	17,308.1
Additions (balancing figure)	4,917.0
C/d	22,225.1

(2)   Goodwill impairment losses

GOODWILL

	$m		$m
b/d	1,865.3	Impairment loss (balancing figure)	202.6
		c/d	1,662.7
	1,865.3		1,865.3

	$m
B/d	1,865.3
Impairment loss Impairment loss/(balancing figure)	(202.6)
C/d	1,662.7

(3)   Purchase of intangibles

INTANGIBLES

	$m		$m
Balance b f/wd	372.4	Amortisation ($372.4m × 25%)	93.1
Purchase of patent(balancing fig)	27.2	Bal c/fwd	306.5
	399.6		399.6

	$m
B/d	372.4
Amortisation ($372.4m × 25%)	(93.1)
	279.3
Purchase of patent(balancing fig)	27.2
C/d	306.5

(4)   Dividend from associate

INVESTMENT IN ASSOCIATE

	$m		$m
Balance b/fwd	13.8	Disposal proceeds	18.0
Share of profit to 31.12.X7	1.6	Dividend received	
Profit on disposal	3.4	1.6.X7 (balancing figure)	0.8
	18.8		18.8

	$m
B/d	13.8
Share of profit to 31.12.X7	1.6
Profit on disposal	3.4
Disposal proceeds	(18.0)
	0.8
Dividend received 1.6.X7 (balancing figure)	(0.8)
C/d	0

(5)   Issue of ordinary share capital

SHARE CAPITAL

	$m		$m
Closing balance	4,300	Opening balance	3,600
		Issued for cash (balancing figure)	700
	4,300		4,300

	$m
B/d	3,600
Issue for cash (balancing figure)	700
C/d	4,300

(6)   Dividend paid to non-controlling interest

NON-CONTROLLING INTEREST

	$m		$m
Dividend paid (balancing figure)	88.0	Bal B/d	1,870.5
Balance c/fwd	2,010.5	Profit attributable to NCI	228.0
	2,098.5		2,098.5

	$m
B/d	1,870.5
Profit attributable to NCI	228.0
	2,098.5
Dividends paid to non-controlling interests (balancing figure)	(88.0)
C/d	2,010.5

(7)   Interest paid

	$m
Long-term borrowing 1.5.X6 (6,000 – 100)	5,900.0
Effective interest @ 7%	413.0
Cash paid (5% × 6,000)	(300.0)
30.4.X7	6,013.0
Effective interest @ 7%	420.9
Cash paid	(300.0)
	6,133.9
Total finance cost in income statement	510.9
Less interest on long-term borrowings	(420.9)
Balance = Interest on short-term borrowings	90.0

Total cash outflow in respect of interest: $90.0m + $300.0m = $390.0m

(8)   Income taxes paid

INCOME TAXES

	$m		$m
Paid (balancing figure)	831.0	Balance b/fwd	884.7
Balance c/fwd	777.6	Income statement: provision	723.9
	1,608.6		1,608.6

	$m
B/d	884.7
Income statement	723.9
	1,608.6
Paid (balancing figure)	(831.0)
C/d	777.6

46 MIC Group

> **Text reference**. This topic is dealt with in Chapter 13 of the text.
>
> **Top tips**. You need to have a methodical technique for statement of cash flows questions. Keep working through the steps that you have learned. Your aim should be to deal with as much of the information as you can but if there is a complication that you don't understand, it's often better to leave it out than to waste time puzzling it out at the expense of completing more of your answer.
>
> **Easy marks**. The easiest marks come from knowing the proforma and dealing with the calculations that appear in every question of this style, such as payments to purchase property, plant and equipment and the basic adjustments to the profit for the year.

MIC GROUP
CONSOLIDATED STATEMENT OF CASH FLOWS FOR THE YEAR ENDED 31 MARCH 20X9

	$'000	$'000
Cash flows from operating activities		
Profit before tax	1,990	
Adjustments for:		
Depreciation	1,800	
Goodwill impairment (W2)	500	
Share of profit of associate	(500)	
Interest expense (W10)	850	
Gain on trading investment (2,200 – 1,800 (W5))	(400)	
Operating profit before working capital changes	4,240	
Decrease in inventories (11,600 – 12,000 – 2,200) (W4)	2,600	
Increase in receivables (9,400 – 8,200 – 700) (W4)	(500)	
Decrease in payables (8,700 – 10,200 – 500) (W4)	(2,000)	
Cash generated from operations	4,340	
Income taxes paid (W9)	(900)	
Interest paid (W10)	(850)	
Net cash inflows from operating activities		2,590
Cash flows from investing activities		
Purchase of property, plant and equipment (W1)	(2,200)	
Purchase of subsidiary (460 – 200)	(260)	
Dividends from associate (W3)	300	
Net cash outflow from investing activities		(2,160)
Cash flows from financing activities		
Issue of ordinary share capital (12,000 + 2,800 – 10,000 – 3,600(W6))		
	1,200	
Repayment of loan (18,000 – 14,000)	(4,000)	
Dividends paid to owners of the parent (W7)	(200)	
Dividends paid to non-controlling interests (W8)	(130)	
Net cash outflow from financing activities		(3,130)
Net decrease in cash and cash equivalents		(2,700)
Cash and cash equivalents at 1 April 20X8		4,100
Cash and cash equivalents at 31 March 20X9		1,400

Workings (two styles of workings are shown – you should use a consistent method, either T-accounts or the schedules throughout)

1   Purchase of PPE

PPE (NBV)

	$'000		$'000
Opening balance (NBV)	15,600	Depreciation	1,800
Acquisition of subsidiary	800	Closing balance	16,800
Additions (balancing figure)	2,200		
	18,600		18,600

	$'000
B/d	15,600
Depreciation	(1,800)
Acquisition of subsidiary	800
	14,600
Additions (balancing figure)	2,200
C/d	16,800

2   Goodwill impairment

GOODWILL

	$'000		$'000
Opening balance	2,400	Impairment (balancing figure)	500
Arising on acquisition (see below)	1,000	Closing balance	2,900
	3,400		3,400

Acquisition

	$'000
Consideration transferred	
Cash	460
Issue of shares (1m × $3.60)	3,600
NCI (10% × 3,400)	340
	4,400
Fair value of assets acquired	(3,400)
Goodwill on acquisition	1,000

	$'000
B/d	2,400
Acquisition of subsidiary	1,000
	3,400
Impairment loss (balancing figure)	(500)
C/d	2,900

3   Dividends from associate

ASSOCIATE

	$'000		$'000
Opening balance	7,800	Dividend received(balancing figure)	300
Share of profit of associate	500	Closing balance	8,000
	8,300		8,300

	$'000
B/d	7,800
Share of profit	500
	8,300
Dividend received (balancing figure)	(300)
C/d	8,000

4   Inventories, trade receivables and trade payables

	Inventories $'000	Receivables $'000	Payables $'000
B/d	12,000	8,200	10,200
Acquisition of subsidiary	2,200	700	500
	14,200	8,900	10,700
Increase/(decrease) (balancing figure)	(2,600)	500	(2,000)
C/d	11,600	9,400	8,700

5   Held for trading investment

INVESTMENT

	$'000		$'000
Opening balance	1,800		
Gain (offset in finance costs (W10))	400	Closing balance	2,200
	2,200		2,200

	$'000
B/d	1,800
Gain (offset in finance costs)	400
C/d	2,200

6   Issue of ordinary share capital

SHARE CAPITAL

	$'000		$'000
Closing balance (12,000 + 2,800)	14,800	Opening balance	10,000
		Issue on acquisition of subsidiary (1m × $3.60)	3,600
		Issued for cash (balancing figure)	1,200
	14,800		14,800

	$'000
B/d	10,000
Acquisition of subsidiary (1m x $3.60)	3,600
	13,600
Issue for cash (balancing figure)	1,200
C/d (12,000 + 2,800)	14,800

7   Dividends paid to owners of the parent

RETAINED EARNINGS

	$'000		$'000
Dividends paid (balancing figure)	200	Opening balance	6,300
		Profit attributable to owners	
Closing balance	7,300	of parent	1,200
	7,500		7,500

	$'000
B/d	6,300
Profit attributable to owners of parent	1,200
	7,500
Dividends paid (balancing figure)	(200)
C/d	7,300

8   Dividends paid to non-controlling interests

NON-CONTROLLING INTERESTS

	$'000		$'000
Dividends paid (balancing figure)	130	Opening balance	6,100
Closing balance	6,500	Profit attributable to NCI	190
		On acquisition (W2)	340
	6,630		6,630

	$'000
B/d	6,100
On acquisition of subsidiary (W2)	340
Profit attributable to NCI	190
	6,630
Dividends paid to non-controlling interest (balancing figure)	(130)
C/d	6,500

9   Income taxes paid

TAX

	$'000		$'000
Cash paid	900	Opening balance	900
Closing balance	600	Charge to IS	600
	1,500		1,500

	$'000
B/d	900
Income statement	600
	1,500
Tax paid (balancing figure)	(900)
C/d	600

10   Interest paid

FINANCE COSTS

	$'000		$'000
Interest paid (balancing figure)	850	Opening balance	0
Closing balance	0	Gain on investment (W5)	400
		Income statement	450
	850		850

	$'000
B/d	0
Gain on investment (W5)	400
Income statement	450
	850
Interest paid (balancing figure)	(850)
C/d	0

Note: The finance cost shown in the income statement is net of the gain on the held for trading investment. On the statement of cash flows these have been dealt with separately.

47   LKL

CONSOLIDATED STATEMENT OF CASH FLOWS FOR THE YEAR ENDED 31 MARCH 20X9

	$m	$m
Cash flows from operating activities		
Profit before tax	99	
Adjustments for:		
Depreciation	130	
Foreign exchange gain (W1)	(5)	
Amortisation of intangibles (W4)	30	
Goodwill impairment (W2)	25	
Share of profit of associate	(50)	
Interest expense (W12)	146	
Gain on trading investment (26 – 20 (W7))	(6)	
Operating profit before working capital changes	369	
Decrease in inventories (320 – 280 – 60)	20	
Decrease in receivables (360 – 310 – 70)	20	
Increase in payables (230 – 190 – 30)	10	
Cash generated from operations	419	
Income taxes paid (W11)	(4)	
Interest paid (W12)	(146)	
Net cash inflows from operating activities		269
Cash flows from investing activities		
Purchase of property, plant and equipment (W1)	(62)	
Purchase of intangible assets (W4)	(75)	
Purchase of subsidiary (60 – 20)	(40)	
Dividends from associate (W5)	10	
Net cash outflow from investing activities		(167)

	$m	$m
Cash flows from financing activities		
Issue of ordinary share capital (W8)	80	
Repayment of loan (540 – 380)	(160)	
Dividends paid to non-controlling interests (W10)	(6)	
Net cash outflow from financing activities		(86)
Net decrease in cash and cash equivalents		16
Cash and cash equivalents at 1 April 20X8		36
Cash and cash equivalents at 31 March 20X9		52

Workings (two styles of workings are shown – you should use a consistent method, either T-accounts or the schedules throughout)

1   Purchase of PPE

PPE (NBV)

	$m		$m
Opening balance (NBV)	840	Depreciation	130
Acquisition of subsidiary	70	Closing balance	847
Additions (balancing figure)	67		
	977		977

Note: The amount paid for additions will be net of the foreign exchange gain on settling the related payable (67 – 5) = 62

Property, plant and equipment

	$m
B/d	840
Depreciation	(130)
Acquisition of subsidiary	70
	780
Additions (balancing figure)	67
C/d	847

2   Goodwill impairment

GOODWILL

	$m		$m
Opening balance	75	Impairment (balancing figure)	25
Arising on acquisition (see below)	58	Closing balance	108
	133		133

Acquisition

	$m
Consideration transferred	
Cash	60
Issue of shares (100m × $1.50)	150
NCI (20% × 190)	38
	248
Fair value of assets acquired	(190)
Goodwill on acquisition	58

	$m
B/d	75
Acquisition of subsidiary	58
Impairment loss (balancing figure)	(25)
C/d	108

3   Inventories, trade receivables and trade payables

	Inventories	Receivables	Payables
	$m	$m	$m
B/d	280	310	190
Acquisition of subsidiary	60	70	30
	340	380	220
Increase/(decrease) (balancing figure)	(20)	(20)	10
C/d	320	360	230

4   Purchase of intangible asset

INTANGIBLE ASSETS

	$m		$m
Opening balance	60	Amortisation	
			30
Additions (balancing figure)	75	Closing balance	105
	135		135

	$m
B/d	60
Amortised in year	(30)
	30
Purchased in year (balancing figure)	75
C/d	105

5   Dividends from associate

ASSOCIATE

	$m		$m
Opening balance	200	Dividend received(balancing figure)	10
Share of profit of associate	50	Closing balance	240
	250		250

	$m
B/d	200
SOCI	50
	250
Dividends received from associate (balancing figure)	(10)
C/d	240

6   Available for sale investment

INVESTMENT

	$m		$m
Opening balance	53		
Gain (OCI)	7	Closing balance	60
	60		60

Note: The gain of $7m has been credited to Other Reserves in the statement of financial position.

	$m
B/d	53
Gain recognised in OCI	7
C/d	60

7   Held for trading investment

INVESTMENT

	$m		$m
Opening balance	20		
Gain (offset in finance costs (W12))	6	Closing balance	26
	26		26

	$m
B/d	20
Gain (in other comprehensive income)	6
C/d	26

8   Issue of ordinary share capital

SHARE CAPITAL (+ SHARE PREMIUM)

	$m		$m
Closing balance (450 + 280)	730	Opening balance (300 + 200)	500
		Issue on acquisition of subsidiary (100m × $1.50)	150
		Issued for cash (balancing figure)	80
	730		730

		$m
B/d (300 + 200)		500
Acquisition of subsidiary (100m x $1.50)		150
		650
Issue for cash (balancing figure)		80
C/d (450 + 280)		730

9   Dividends paid to owners of the parent

RETAINED EARNINGS

	$m		$m
Dividends paid	–	Opening balance	380
		Profit attributable to owners	
Closing balance	447	of parent	67
	447		447

	$m
B/d	380
SOCI	67
C/d	447

10   Dividends paid to non-controlling interests

NON-CONTROLLING INTERESTS

	$m		$m
Dividends paid (balancing figure)	6	Opening balance	120
		Total comprehensive income	
Closing balance	164	attributable to NCI	12
		On acquisition (W2)	38
	170		170

	$m
B/d	120
TCI attributable to NCI	12
On acquisition of subsidiary (W2)	38
Dividends received from associate (balancing figure)	(6)
C/d	164

11   Income taxes paid

TAX

	$m		$m
Cash paid	4	Opening balance – deferred tax	70
		– current tax	32
Closing balance – deferred tax	78	Charge to SOCI	20
– current tax	40		
	122		122

	$m
B/d (70 + 32)	102
SOCI	20
	122
Tax paid (balancing figure)	(4)
C/d (78 + 40)	118

12   Interest paid

FINANCE COSTS

	$m		$m
Interest paid (balancing figure)	146	Opening balance	0
Closing balance	0	Gain on investment (W7)	6
		SOCI	140
	146		146

Note: The finance cost shown in the statement of comprehensive income is net of the gain on the held for trading investment. On the statement of cash flows these have been dealt with separately.

	$m
B/d	0
SOCI	140
Gain on investment	6
	146
Interest paid (balancing figure)	(146)
C/d	0

48 LOP

> **Text reference**. Ratio analysis is dealt with in Chapter 14 of the text.
>
> **Top tips**. Make sure you read **both** parts of the requirement carefully before you start. There are two reasons for this:
>
> – It might be more efficient to do part (b) first
> – it stops any risk of you duplicating points in (a)and (b)
>
> **Easy marks**. Part (b) has the easiest marks as this is such a common requirement. In part (a) there are marks available for stating fairly obvious points

(a)   Analysis

Size

The revenue figures indicate the respective size of the companies. Both of the potential targets are smaller than LOP. Entity B is 80% larger than Entity A.

Margins

Both of the potential target entities appear to be less efficient than LOP in respect of generating profits.

Entity A has a much stronger gross profit margin than Entity B. There may be less competitive pressure on pricing in its markets, or it may face lower costs for materials and labour.

Comparing their net profit margins, Entity B appears stronger. This could be due to the effect of interest charges on the profits of Entity A, which has higher gearing, but could also be due to the fixed elements of operating expenses having less impact on the profits of the larger company. The larger company is in a better position to benefit from economies of scale.

Gearing

Entity A has significantly higher gearing than either Entity B or LOP. This is probably because of the low rate of interest rate of interest available in Frontland (5%). High gearing is quite usual in the construction industry as debt finance is needed to fund heavy investment in assets. These assets then provide security for the entity's borrowings, making it easier to raise finance.

The higher gearing makes Entity A a riskier investment than Entity B. Interest commitments must be paid irrespective of trading conditions and profitability, unlike equity dividends which are discretionary. Also, if the borrowings are at variable rates, there is a risk that increases in the interest rates can damage profits in future.

P/E ratio

The higher P/E ratio of Entity B suggests that investors have more confidence in Entity B than Entity A. However, both entities have lower P/E ratios than LOP so if LOP which to maintain or improve their P/E ratio, they might wish to seek an alternative target.

Impact on indicators of LOP

Revenue

Entity B would have the more significant effect on LOP's revenue, increasing it by 60%.

Gross margin

Both entities would decrease the overall gross margin of LOP. Entity A would have only a marginal effect, but a combination with Entity B would result in a gross margin of 24%. (The total gross margins of LOP and B (($28\% \times 500$) + ($17\% \times 300$)) over the combined revenue of $800m.)

Net margin

Both entities would have an adverse effect on LOP's net profit margin. Here Entity A would have the more significant effect, reducing the net margin to 14%. (The total net margins of LOP and A (($16\% \times 500$) + ($9\% \times 160$)) over the combined revenue of $660m.)

Gearing

Entity A would increase LOP's gearing and risk exposure. Entity B would decrease LOP's gearing and risk exposure.

However, investing in Entity A would decrease the average rates of interest suffered by the group as a whole.

P/E ratio

It would appear that both entities would be likely to decrease the P/E ratio of LOP.

Conclusion

Both entities would have an adverse effect on the financial indicators of LOP, so it may be wiser not to invest in either of them.

If LOP wishes to expand in size, and is most interested in profitability in terms of the 'bottom line' net profit and is risk averse, then Entity B is the more attractive proposition.

(b) Limitations

Entity A and Entity B operate in two different geographical areas, Frontland and Sideland. A number of factors could undermine the above comparisons:

(i)   They may use **different accounting policies**. It is not clear whether either or both use IFRS and different policies for aspects such as the recognition of revenue and profits on construction contracts could have a major effect on the reported results.

(ii) They could be experiencing **very different market and political circumstances**.

(iii) **Exchange rate fluctuations** could have a significant effect on the two entities' overall impact in the group financial statements of LOP.

The two entities have very different capital structures, which makes comparison difficult.

The indicators only cover profitability and gearing. There are no measures of efficiency or liquidity and both of these are very important for an entity's survival.

The indicators only measure one year of performance. These could be very unrepresentative of the ongoing level of performance. This type of analysis is more reliable using several years figures so that longer term trends can be identified.

The indicators are based on historical information. For the purposes of a takeover, forward-looking information is more important. The main value of a construction company might be the profits still to be earned from contracts in progress, or the value of new contracts that have been signed but where work has not yet commenced.

Marking scheme

		Marks
(a)		
	Size	1
	Margins	3
	Gearing	2
	Impact on indicators of LOP	2
	Maximum	7
(b)	1 mark for each relevant point	
	Maximum	3
		10

---

49 FGH Cash

Text reference. Statements of cash flows are covered in chapter 13 of the text and ratio and trend analysis is covered in chapter 14.

Top tips. Analyse the requirement carefully and use it to structure a relevant answer. The obvious approach here is to split your answer into sections corresponding to the categories of cash flows.

Easy marks. There should be plenty of easy marks for stating fairly obvious points. The introduction to the question mentions that the entity is going through a period of expansion. The statement of cash flows should be easy to interpret, you need to spot the major receipts and payments of cash and try to explain those in the context of the expansion scenario.

Examiner's comments. Many candidates achieved full marks in this question, showing application of skills and understanding the scenario to suggest reasons for the cash flows. The most common errors related to misunderstanding the requirement and describing how the statement was prepared or why certain adjustments were added or deducted in the calculation of cash flows.

Cash from operating activities

The operating activities section of FGH's statement of cash flows shows that the business is not only profitable, but is generating healthy inflows of cash from its main operations.

A significant proportion of the cash generated from operations is utilised in paying tax and paying interest on borrowings. The amount needed to pay interest in future may increase as the company appears to be increasing its borrowings to fund its expansion.

The adjustments to profit show that receivables, inventories and payables are all increasing. This trend may reflect the expansion of the business but working capital management must be reviewed carefully to ensure that cash is collected promptly from receivables so that the company is able to meet its obligations to pay its suppliers and maintain good trading relationships.

Cash from investing activities

The two main investing outflows in the year were the net cash payment of $800,000 to acquire a new subsidiary and the payment of $340,000 to acquire new property, plant and equipment. These are a clear reflection of the strategy of expansion and may lead to increased profits and cash flows from operations in future years. This section also reflects cash received from the sale of equipment of $70,000 and the operating cash flows section shows that this equipment was sold at a loss. This suggests that the company may have acquired the new equipment to replace assets that were old and inefficient.

The most significant inflow in this section is an amount of $150,000 from the sale of investments. It is likely that this was done to help finance the acquisition and expansion. This type of cash flow is unlikely to recur in future and also means that the other inflows in this section, the interest and dividends received, are likely to cease or be reduced in future.

Cash from financing activities

The company has raised new finance totalling $600,000, which has probably been applied to the acquisition and expansion. The new finance comprises equal amounts of equity and borrowings so should not have had a detrimental effect on the company's gearing. The increased borrowings will mean that future interest expenses will increase which could threaten profitability in future if the expansion does not create immediate increases in operating profits.

This section also includes the largest single cash flow, a dividend payment of $1,000,000. This appears to be a very high payout (70% of the cash generated from operating activities) and raises the question as to why the company has taken on additional borrowings rather than retaining more profits to invest in the expansion. On the other hand, it may indicate that management are very confident that the expanded business will generate returns that will easily cover the additional interest costs and allow this level of dividend payment to continue in future.

50 BCA

(a) Preliminary report to Board

Subject: Potential acquisition of CAD

Profitability

The gross margin achieved by CAD has dropped significantly from 21% last year to 14.5% (see appendix 1 for ratios). This is likely to be due to the cost of the new technology and the bonus paid to the Chief Scientific Officer (CSO). Sales are up 22% and indications are that future periods will see further revenue increases due to the development of the new technology. The main challenge for CAD will be staying in business long enough to take advantage of these further revenues. We would have to consider if these future contracts might be compromised if we were to acquire CAD, as they may be with our competitors. The net profit is down slightly from 3.5% to 2.5% due mainly to the finance costs incurred in 20X9. The net profit fall is less than that of gross profit and indicates that other costs and expenses have been well controlled.

Efficiency

The receivables days are crippling the flow of cash in the business. The recovery of amounts due has risen from 60 days to 92 days. CAD's main challenge is dealing with large customers with a significant outstanding balance and may not have the credit control resources to manage these accounts or are not in a position to successfully negotiate because of size and relative dependency. If, however, BCA was to takeover CAD and implemented stricter credit control procedures then this could be eradicated. Cutting this back to 60 days would release more than $300,000 and would remove the need to rely on expensive short term funding. The interest paid in 20X9 is at approximately 10%. That is likely to be because CAD cannot offer the bank substantial amounts of tangible non-current assets on which security can be taken. This is likely to be less of an issue for BCA as we are an established multinational and would be able to secure funding at more competitive rates if required.

In addition, it is likely that CAD is unable to successfully negotiate with its customers for early payment as the contracts are all with large established companies, however again that may not be an issue if contracts were negotiated by BCA.

Payables looks high, however the payables days has stayed relatively static in the 60s and suppliers have continued to supply as inventories have increased so the delay in settlement seems not to be a problem. BCA may choose to reduce the payables level to avoid any negative impact on its credit rating.

Potential target entity

CAD appears to be a sound investment provided the future services of the CSO can be secured. CAD shareholders are willing to surrender control if the company's future and their own is secure. The business is profitable and future prospects look positive. The contracts that CAD has are with established companies and there appears to be an order book to provide future services for the next couple of years at least. The issues of funding and debt collection are likely to be able to be solved by BCA. The key personnel member appears to have been well tied into the business and so the current management team clearly know what is vital to the survival of their business.

Receivables days	$1,091K/$4,330K × 365 days = 92 days	$587K/$3,562K × 365 days = 60 days
Payables days	$687K/$3,702K × 365 days = 68 days	$485K/$2,810K × 365 days = 63 days
Finance costs – approximate rate	$13K/$123K = 10.6%	
Gross profit margin	$628K/$4,330K × 100 = 14.5%	$752K/$3,562K × 100 = 21%
Net profit margin	$108K/$4,330K × 100 = 2.5%	$125/$3,562K × 100 = 3.5%

(b) (i) It has been recognised that financial statements report historical events and transactions and are generally backward looking. They are therefore often of limited use to users that are focussed on the entity's future prospects and potential results. It is generally agreed that the relevance of financial information would be improved if some information about the entity's future objectives and challenges and the strategies in place to overcome those challenges was included. Information on the dynamics and risks of the entity would also be useful – eg reliance on key personnel or development of technology. However this information cannot be audited and therefore lacks reliability which is a key qualitative characteristic of financial statements.

This has led to the growth in narrative reporting in corporate reports. The entity should give a balanced report on the activities and performance of the period and expected performance for the immediate future and in turn shareholders must recognise that this information does not have the added comfort of an audit opinion.

(ii) An OFR type report would be helpful to potential investors in CAD as the financial statements do not provide the information that is key to this type of high-tech industry. The low levels of tangible non-current asset make it pointless to calculate traditional ratios like return on capital employed and so comparisons with other potential investments are restricted. It also makes it hard for these entities to raise external finance as there are few assets available as security. This is an example of where the value of the business lies in the intellectual property within the entity through the patents and the know-how and technical expertise of the staff.

However the key elements in the future viability of the entity lie in the patents and key personnel and the contracts – much of which is absent from the historical financial statements. A management commentary on these areas would be invaluable to investors and other lenders as it would help them understand the underlying business.

The relationships with the CSO would also be discussed under the risks and relationships section as losing the technical developer would have a significant effect on the long term prospects of the entity. The high receivables would also be explained and would enable the entity to explain the details of arrangements as some readers would assume, in the absence of any information to the contrary, that it is as a result of poor credit control.

A narrative report would give the management the opportunity to explain the dynamics of the business and the investment in future technological improvements that are not evident from the numerical information presented in the financial statements.

51 BZJ

Text reference. EPS is covered in Chapter 15. Financial analysis is covered in Chapter 14.

Top tips. Part a) is a very straightforward EPS calculation . In Part (b) there is a lot of information, so start by calculating some of the most basic ratios covering profitability, liquidity and gearing. These will soon give you an idea of where you will be going with your narrative. Remember to comment on the EPS figures that you will have calculated for Part (a). Do allow yourself time to produce a decent report as the marks will be available for the analysis rather than the calculation of the ratios. Make sure in Part (c) that you relate the Chairman's statement to the evidence you find in the financial statements.

Easy marks. Keep writing, as you can always find something to say. Even if your conclusions are different from the examiner's or you make a mistake in your calculations, you will gain easy marks.

(a)   Earnings per share

Year ended 31 December 20X4

$$EPS = \frac{\$3,676,000}{2,800,000}$$

$$= 131.3c$$

Year ended 31 December 20X5

$$EPS = \frac{\$2,460,000}{2,850,000}$$

$$= 86.3c$$

Working: number of shares 20X5

Date	Narrative	Shares	Time	Weighted Average
1.1.X5	b/f	2,800,000	$\times\ ^{10}/_{12}$	2,333,333
1.11.X5	Issue at full market price	300,000		
		3,100,000	$\times\ ^{2}/_{12}$	516,667
				2,850,000

(b)   REPORT

To: Investor
From: Advisor
Date: March 20X6
Subject: **BZJ Group financial statements year ended 31 December 20X5**

As requested I have considered the financial statements of the BZJ Group for the year ended 31 December 20X5 and have calculated various financial ratios for 20X5 and 20X4 which are included in an appendix to this report.

Profitability

There do appear to be some **concerns about the financial performance and profitability** of the group during 20X5. There has been no evidence of growth in performance and indeed a 0.8% **decrease in revenue** from last year despite the large investment in the group during 20X5. There has also been a significant decrease in return on total capital employed from 15.3% to 8.5% and in return on equity from 21.5% to 12.0%.

Reasons for fall in return

These decreases in overall return have been caused both by **decreases in operating profitability and reduced performance**. Both the gross profit margin and operating profit margin have shown significant decreases over the position in 20X4. It is possible that these reduced margins have been caused partly by increased depreciation charges due to the investment of approximately $18 million in additional property, plant and equipment. More worryingly, however, the fall in margins may be due to the new storage products or the Middle East market where margins may be lower. If this is the case, then it is possible that these lower profit margins will continue in the future.

Asset turnover

Both **asset turnover** and **non-current asset turnover** have shown **significant decreases** indicating that the additional investment in non-current assets and working capital have not resulted in increased turnover. However it should be borne in mind that the additional finance was only raised two months before the year end, and if the non-current asset additions were also made at the same time then they have had only a short period in which to be used effectively.

Liquidity

In overall terms the liquidity of the business certainly appears to be **less healthy** at 31 December 20X5 than it was a year earlier. The cash balances found a year ago have been replaced by substantial short term borrowings, and both the current ratio and acid test ratio have decreased significantly. Although there would appear to be no immediate liquidity crisis, there is a definite trend towards a lower level of liquidity in the group.

Inventory turnover

Inventory turnover at the end of 20X4 was already quite long at 97 days but this has **increased significantly** at the end of 20X5 to 131 days. This could be due to a build up of inventory prior to anticipated growth in turnover in 20X6 or alternatively may indicate that the new products are not selling as fast as was anticipated.

Receivables and payables

On the brighter side there has been an improvement in the trade receivables period meaning that money is being received more quickly from credit customers. However, the payables period of 111 days is very long (an increase from 87 days at the end of 20X4) although this could be partly due to the large amount of purchases from foreign countries.

Gearing

During the year, $10 million of loan finance has been raised together with over $3.5 million of short term borrowings. These increases have led to an already high debt/equity ratio of 62.9% at the end of 20X4 rising to 81.7% at the end of 20X5. The funds have clearly been used to fund part of the investment in additional property, plant and equipment and as noted above it may be that these assets are not yet being used to their full potential.

It must be noted, however, that the 300,000 shares issued in November 20X5 were fully subscribed for at a premium of $4 per share which would indicate that the market is not concerned about this **high level of gearing**.

Interest cost

The additional loan finance has obviously **affected** the **interest cost** in the income statement and interest cover has reduced from 7.3 times last year to 3.7 times at the end of 20X5. While this still gives the group a fairly reasonable margin of safety, if the interest charged in the income statement is compared to the short term and long term borrowings at the year end the average rate is only 5%. This indicates that the additional finance has not been in place for long and that therefore there is likely to be an increase in the interest charges in 20X6.

Investors

From an investor's point of view there has clearly been a **marked decrease in their returns**. Earnings per share has decreased from 131.3c to 86.3c and dividend per share has decreased from 13c to 5c. In line with the Chairman's comments, funds are clearly being retained within the business for expansion as dividend cover has increased from 10.1 times last year to 15.87 times this year.

Chairman's comments

The Chairman's statement indicates that the new management are investing in new products, new markets and new property, plant and equipment in order to expand and grow the business. It is clear that there is indeed a large investment in new non-current assets and in working capital but as yet this **investment has not fed through to improved performance** with all profitability measures in decline. However, the new product was not put into production until September 20X5 and the additional finance for the non-current asset investment was not raised until November 20X5, therefore it is likely that the 20X5 financial statements do not yet show the full extent of the results of this expansion programme. The reduced dividend indicates that funds are being retained within the business to fund the growth plans as the Chairman explains, and it is to be hoped that these plans will, as stated by the Chairman, lead to 'increased returns to investors within the next two to three years', although there is little evidence of this in the financial statements for 20X5.

Conclusion

There is concern about the profit margins in the group, the management of working capital and the uses to which the additional investment are being put. However, there would appear to be no immediate concerns about the position of the business and hope that management's **expansionary plans** may come to fruition in 20X6 and beyond.

Appendix – Financial Ratios

		20X5	*20X4*
(i)	<u>Profitability</u>		
	Gross profit margin		
	17,342/120,366 × 100	14.4%	
	19,065/121,351 × 100		15.7%
	Operating profit margin		
	5,377/120,366 × 100	4.5%	
	6,617/121,315 × 100		5.5%
	Return on total capital employed		
	5,377/30,428 + 2,270 + 26,700 + 3,662	8.5%	
	6,617/24,623 + 1,947 + 16,700		15.3%
	Asset turnover		
	120,366/30,428 + 2,270 + 26,700 + 3,662	1.91	
	121,315/24,623 + 1,947 + 16,700		2.80
	Non-current asset turnover		
	120,366/43,575	2.76	
	121,351/24,320		4.99
	Return on equity		
	2,908/30,428 + 2,270	12.0%	
	5,711/24,623 + 1,947		21.5%
(ii)	<u>Liquidity</u>		
	Current ratio		
	52,030/36,207	1.44	
	44,951/26,001		1.73
	Acid test ratio		
	14,922/36,207	0.41	
	17,691/26,001		0.68
	Inventory turnover		
	37,108/103,024 × 365	131 days	
	27,260/102,286 × 365		97 days
	Receivables turnover		
	14,922/120,366 × 365	45 days	
	17,521/121,351 × 365		53 days
	Payables turnover		
	31,420/103,024 × 365	111 days	
	24,407/102,286 × 365		87 days
(iii)	<u>Gearing</u>		
	Debt/equity ratio		
	26,700/30,428 + 2,270 × 100	81.7%	
	16,700/24,623 + 1,947 × 100		62.9%
	Interest cover		
	5,377/1,469	3.7	
	6,617/906		7.3
(iv)	<u>Investor ratios</u>		
	Dividend per share		
	155/3,100	5c	
	364/2,800		13c
	Dividend cover		
	2,460/155	15.87	
	3,676/364		10.1

52 ABC

> **Text reference**. Financial analysis is covered in Chapter 14.
>
> **Top tip.** In Part (a) use the list of key data given as a structure for your comparison and make sure that you do use each of the key pieces of data given in your answer. In Part (b) do not limit yourself to a list of the standard limitations of ratio analysis but apply it to an international stage and apply it to the particular scenario given.
>
> **Easy marks.** These may be obtained by making full use of the information given to you in the question. Do not be afraid to state the obvious, for example that the revenue and net assets are similar for all three companies.

REPORT

To: Directors of ABC
From: Assistant to CFO
Date: May 20X6
Subject: Possible takeover targets – W, Y and Z

As requested this report provides a comparison of the key data for the three potential takeover targets, W, Y and Z and our own similar data and also discussion of the validity of inter-firm and international comparisons.

(a)   Comparison of company performance

All three of the potential takeover targets have a **similar level of revenue and net assets**. In terms of both revenue and asset value they are all approximately **one tenth of the size of ABC**.

Profitability

Z appears to be clearly the **most profitable** with significantly higher gross profit margin, operating profit margin and return on total capital employed than the other two companies. Indeed its gross profit margin and return on total capital employed are both higher than those of ABC. However, these ratios are based upon pre-tax figures, and it should be noted that the income tax rate in Zeelandia is significantly higher than in Bolandia or the other two countries.

Assets and liabilities

All three companies have a significantly **lower current ratio than ABC,** with those of W and Z looking quite low indeed for a light engineering business. All three companies **hold their inventories for significantly longer than ABC** with the inventory turnover of W the highest at 68 days which may indicate slow-moving or obsolete inventory. **Receivables turnover** in all three companies is **similar** and also very similar to that of ABC probably reflecting the similar nature of the businesses and their customers. However, there is a much wider fluctuation in payables turnover periods with that of Z seeming high at 73 days. This may be a conscious policy, given Z's fairly low current ratio, or may be due to poor payables management.

Gearing

ABC's gearing level is very low with debt amounting to about 5% of equity and it is group policy that group gearing should not be increased. The level of gearing in Z is **even lower** than that of ABC which is possibly understandable given the higher level of interest rates in Zeelandia. However, **W** has a **much higher** level of gearing with debt being approximately 50% of equity, possibly due to the lower rate of interest in Winlandia. This gearing would increase the group gearing to approximately 8% if W were acquired, but of course upon acquisition ABC could decide to reduce the borrowings of W if these were not acceptable.

P/E ratios

As would be expected of four companies in the same type of business the four **P/E ratios are within a fairly narrow band**. The P/E ratio of W is lowest at 12.6, possibly indicating that the shares are relatively undervalued, or that the investment is viewed as more risky due to its gearing or that the most recent earnings figures (January 20X6) have not yet been reflected in the share price.

Conclusion

There do not appear to be any major problems with any of the three companies. However, on the basis of this basic, preliminary analysis company Z would appear to be the superior company in terms of performance and of our requirements for a takeover company. Before any conclusions are drawn, a great deal of further information and analysis would be required.

(b) Inter-firm and international comparisons

There are always limitations to the validity of inter-firm comparisons and these can be exacerbated when the comparison is being made between companies in different countries.

Accounting standards

The figures that appear in the financial statements, and therefore the financial ratios that are calculated from these figures, will be affected by the accounting standards followed by each company. In this case ABC, W and Z all use IFRS but the financial statements of Y have been prepared according to Yolandian GAAP. There may be significant differences between Yolandian GAAP and IFRS.

Accounting policies

Even if the financial statements are prepared using IFRS there could still be significant differences between the accounting policies of the companies. For example, if some companies value their property, plant and equipment at depreciated cost whereas others use the valuation model, then this will significantly affect the financial statements and the financial ratios calculated from those statements such as return on total capital employed.

Size of companies

The size of a company can affect the figures and ratios. In this case all three potential target companies are approximately the same size but they are all about 10% of the size of ABC. This may affect comparison of figures between the companies and ABC as ABC may well benefit from economies of scale.

Type of business

Although all four companies are said to be in the same business, provision of light engineering products and services, it is likely in practice that there could be considerable differences between the detailed patterns of business which affect comparison of the figures. For example some companies may provide products through hire or leasing which would change the profile of their financial statements.

Single period comparison

As with all comparisons of financial indicators a single period set of figures gives no indication of the trend of figures and on its own may be misleading.

Accounting date

The comparison has been based upon financial statements for all three companies for periods ending before those of ABC. In particular, those of Y and Z are based on financial statements nine months before those of ABC. Obviously a lot can change in a company in that sort of time period, and it could be argued that the financial figures for Y and Z are too out of date to be particularly meaningful.

International economies

Each of the four companies is based in a different country, although they at least share a common currency. Each of these countries exhibits considerable differences in interest rates and tax rates and each is likely to differ in terms of economic state. The economic cycle and regulatory regime of the country can have a significant effect on the figures in the financial statements reducing the value of comparison. Similarly the size and nature of the stock market in each country could affect the P/E ratios that have been quoted. In a small, illiquid stock market, share prices and therefore P/E ratios will tend to be lower than those in a larger more liquid market.

53 AXZ

Text reference. Financial analysis is covered in Chapter 14. International issues are covered in Chapter 17.

Top tips. There are a lot of ratios to crunch through. Be methodical. Set out your adjustments to the financial statements clearly first, then if you make a mistake, the marker can still give you credit in your ratio calculations and report.

Easy marks. There are quite a few marks for mechanical number crunching.

Examiner's comments. Many candidates had difficultly calculating return on equity and capital employed.

(a) <u>Accounting ratios before adjustments</u>

	AXZ	DCB	GFE
Gross profit margin			
$\frac{2,700}{8,300} \times 100; \frac{600}{1,900} \times 100; \frac{800}{2,200} \times 100$	32.5%	31.6%	36.4%
Profit before tax as a % of sales			
$\frac{1,461}{8,300} \times 100; \frac{335}{1,900} \times 100; \frac{420}{2,200} \times 100$	17.6%	17.6%	19.1%
Return on equity			
$\frac{1,095}{4,820} \times 100; \frac{201}{1,350} \times 100; \frac{315}{1,931} \times 100$	22.7%	14.9%	16.3%
Return on capital employed			
$\frac{1,461+105}{4,820+1,500} \times 100; \frac{335+25}{1,350+500} \times 100;$	24.8%	19.5%	
$\frac{420+65}{1,931+650} \times 100$			18.8%
Non-current asset turnover			
$\frac{8,300}{9,950}; \frac{1,900}{1,680}; \frac{2,200}{2,400}$	0.83 times	1.13 times	0.92 times
Gearing			
$\frac{1,500}{4,820} \times 100; \frac{500}{1,350} \times 100; \frac{650}{1,931} \times 100$	31.3%	37.0%	33.7%

<u>Accounting ratios after adjustments</u>

	AXZ	DCB	GFE
Gross profit margin			
$\frac{2,700}{8,300} \times 100; \frac{667}{1,900} \times 100; \frac{800}{2,200} \times 100$	32.5%	35.1%	36.4%
Profit before tax as a % of sales			
$\frac{1,461}{8,300} \times 100; \frac{402}{1,900} \times 100; \frac{415}{2,200} \times 100$	17.6%	21.2%	18.9%
Return on equity			
$\frac{1,095}{4,820} \times 100; \frac{268}{1,552} \times 100; \frac{310}{1,831} \times 100$	22.7%	17.3%	16.9%
Return on capital employed			
$\frac{1,461+105}{4,820+1,500} \times 100; \frac{402+25}{1,552+500} \times 100;$	24.8%	20.81%	
$\frac{415+70}{1,831+750} \times 100$			18.8%

	AXZ	DCB	GFE

Non-current asset turnover

$$\frac{8,300}{9,950}; \frac{1,900}{1,882}; \frac{2,200}{2,400}$$

	0.83 times	1.00 times	0.92 times

Gearing

$$\frac{1,500}{4,820} \times 100; \frac{500}{1,552} \times 100; \frac{750}{1,831} \times 100$$

	31.1%	32.2%	40.1%

Workings

(1) Reworked figures after accounting adjustments

	DCB	GFE
	$'000	$'000
Revenue	1,900	2,200
Cost of sales (W2)	(1,233)	(1,400)
Gross profit	667	800
Distribution costs	(60)	(65)
Administrative expenses	(180)	(250)
Finance costs (W3)	(25)	(70)
Profit before tax	402	415
Income tax expense	(134)	(105)
Profit for the year	268	310

	DCB	GFE
	$'000	$'000
Total equity (1,350 + 202)	1,552	
(1,931 – 100)		1,831
Non-current liabilities	500	
(650 + 100)		750
Non-current assets (W2)	1,882	2,400

(2) Depreciation adjustment – DCB

Non-current assets

$1,680 = \text{Cost} - ((12.5\% \times \text{cost}) \times 3)$

Let cost= x
$1,680 = x - 37.5\%x$
$1,680 = 62.5\%x$
$x= 2,688$

Net book value of non-current assets adjusted:

$2,688 - ((2,688 \times 10\%) \times 3 = 1,882$

Therefore, adjustment to equity $= 1882 - 1,680 = 202$

Depreciation charge for year was $2,688 \times 12.5\% = 336$

Adjusted depreciation charge $2,688 \times 10\% = 269$

Cost of sales $= 1,300 - 336 + 269 = 1,233$

(3) Finance cost adjustment – GFE

GFE finance costs $= 65 + (\$100,000 \times 5\%) = 70$

No effect on equity as this was charged in the statement of changes in equity. However, equity will be reduced by $100,000 as the shares are moved to borrowings.

Non-current liabilities increase to $750,000

(b)   REPORT

To:	Directors of AXZ
From:	Management Accountant
Date:	November 20X6
Subject:	Potential acquisition targets

I have assessed the financial statement information provided for DCB and GFE as requested and have calculated our key accounting ratios (see Part (a)) for these companies both based upon their original figures provided and based upon figures that are adjusted to bring their financial statements into line with IFRS.

<u>Before adjusting for IFRS and local GAAP</u>

On balance the **preferred investment would probably have been GFE** as its gross and operating profit margins were higher than ours whereas DCB's were either lower or the same as ours. However the drawback with GFE is that its **return on equity** and **return on capital employed** are both considerably **lower** than our own and would reduce our figures significantly.

<u>After adjusting for IFRS and local GAAP</u>

After adjusting the figures to bring them in line with IFRS the picture is somewhat **different**. These show a dramatic **improvement in the profitability** figures for **DCB** which now has a higher gross profit margin than ourselves (although still lower than that of GFE) and a higher operating profit margin than both ourselves and GFE. Perhaps more importantly the return on equity and return on capital employed for DCB are now only slightly lower than our own therefore would have only a marginal effect on our own ratios when combined.

Based upon the adjusted figures **GFE does not seem to be an appropriate target** as the return ratios for GFE are all considerably lower than our own despite its higher profit ratios. The reason for GFE's poor level or return can be seen if the total asset turnover is considered rather than the non-current asset turnover:

	AXZ	DCB	GFE
Total asset turnover	1.31 times	0.99 times	0.85 times

As we can see both companies are **less efficient** than ourselves in the use of their total funding but GFE is considerably so.

On top of that the **gearing level of GFE is considerably higher than our own** and a combination with GFE would increase our own gearing level to 33.5%. Whereas a combination with DCB would only increase our combined gearing level to 31.4%.

<u>Conclusion</u>

On the basis of the figures provided and the adjustments made to bring the accounting treatments in line with IFRS on balance an **investment in DCB would be preferred**. This would increase our gross and operating profit margins and only marginally reduce our return on equity and return on total capital employed. There would also only be a very slight increase in our overall gearing level.

54 DPC

Text references. The topics in this answer are covered in Chapters 1–4 and 14.

Top tips. You are required to prepare draft projected financial statements for DPC assuming first that PPS becomes an associate of DPC or alternatively under the second option or subsidiary.

Given the summary financial statements part (a) should be straightforward provided you note and properly account for the fact that the acquisition is to be settled from existing cash resources and an increase in borrowings.

The ratios in part (b) are also straightforward although their calculation relies on the correct preparation of part (a). For part (c) make sure you identify the *reasons* for the differences between the ratios under the different scenarios.

Easy marks. It should be fairly easy to gain full marks for part (a). Make sure you show your workings clearly for both parts (a) and (b). You will gain most of the marks for part (b) if your approach is correct even if some of the numbers from part (a) are not quite right.

A reasonably detailed discussion and identification of the reasons for the differences in ratios should help you gain most of the marks for part (c).

(a) (i) <u>DPC acquires 40% of the ordinary shares of PPS on 1 January 20X8</u>

STATEMENT OF FINANCIAL POSITION

	$'000	$'000
Non-current assets		50,400
Investment in associate		
Cost	3,500	
Share of post-acquisition profits (40% × 700,000)	280	
		3,780
Current assets ($82m-$1m payment out of cash resources)		81,000
		135,180
Equity (31,400,000 + 280,000)		31,680
Long-term liabilities (10,000,000 + 2,500,000)		12,500
Current liabilities		91,000
		135,180

INCOME STATEMENT

	$'000
Revenue	60,300
Share of profits of PPS	280
	60,580
All expenses including income tax	(55,300)
	5,280

(ii) <u>DPC acquires 60% of the ordinary shares of PPS on 1 January 20X8</u>

STATEMENT OF FINANCIAL POSITION

	$'000
Goodwill (W1)	4,020
Non-current assets (50,400 + 9,800)	60,200
Current assets (82,000 + 16,000 − 3,000)	95,000
	159,220
Issued equity capital	10,000
Retained earnings (W3)	21,820
	31,820
Non-controlling interest (W2)	1,600
	33,420
Long-term liabilities (10,000 + 93,000 + 3,000)	22,300
Current liabilities	103,500
	159,220

Workings

(1) <u>Goodwill calculation</u>

	$'000	$'000
Consideration transferred		6,000,000
Non-controlling interest (40% × 3,300,000)		1,320,000
Net assets at the date of acquisition		
Issued share capital	100,000	
Retained earnings	3,200,000	
		3,300,000
Goodwill		4,020,000

(2) <u>Non-controlling interest</u>

	$'000
At acquisition (W1)	1,320,000
Share of post acquisition retained earnings (40% × 700,000)	280,000
	1,600,000

(3) <u>Consolidated retained earnings</u>

	$'000
Retained earnings of DPC	21,400,000
60% of post-acquisition retained earnings of PPS	420,000
	21,820,000

INCOME STATEMENT

	$'000
Revenue (60,300,000 + 10,200,000)	70,500
All expenses including income tax (55,300,000 + 9,500,000)	(64,800)
Profit for the year	5,700

	$ 000
Profit attributable to:	
Owners of the parent	5,420
Non-controlling interest (40% × 700,000)	280
	5,700

(b) The EPS is calculated as follows:

$$EPS = \frac{Earnings}{Number\ of\ shares}$$

The EPS for the three cases is shown in the table below. The number of shares remains the same in all three cases. Consolidated earnings when DPC acquires 60% of PPS are defined as net of non-controlling interest.

	DPC and its existing subsidiaries	DPC including the acquisition of an associate interest in PPS	DPC including the acquisition of a subsidiary interest in PPS
Earnings	$5,000,000	$5,280,000	$5,420,000
Number of shares	10,0000,000	10,0000,000	10,0000,000
EPS	$0.5	$5,280	$0.54

The gearing ratio is defined as:

$$\frac{Total\ long\text{-}term\ debt}{Equity}$$

	DPC and its existing subsidiaries	DPC including the acquisition of an associate interest in PPS	DPC including the acquisition of a subsidiary interest in PPS
Total long-term debt	$10,000,000	$12,500,000	$22,300,000
Equity	$31,400,000	$31,680,000	$31,820,000
Ratio	31.85%	39.46%	70.08%

The non-current asset turnover ratio is defined as:

$$\frac{Revenues}{Non\text{-}current\ assets}$$

	DPC and its existing subsidiaries	DPC including the acquisition of an associate interest in PPS	DPC including the acquisition of a subsidiary interest in PPS
Revenues	$60,300,000	$60,300,000	$70,500,000
Non-current assets	$50,400,000	$54,180,000	$64,220,000
Ratio	1.20	1.11	1.10

(c) **Earnings per share** will increase when DPC acquires part of PPS since the acquisition is not funded by issuing new shares and there is no increase in the number of shares.

The **non-current asset turnover ratio** measures the **efficiency** of **non-current assets**. Before any acquisition for every $1 invested in assets, DPC produces $1.20 in revenues. This falls to 1.11 when it acquires 40% of PPS because the asset base increases without a corresponding increase in revenue. The ratio falls to 1.10 when DPC acquires 60% of PPS. This fall is due to the fact that the **non-current asset turnover ratio** for PPS is much lower at $\frac{10,200}{9,800} = 1.04$, and on consolidation it affects the ratio of the combined entity.

The **gearing ratio** will increase in both cases because the acquisition in both cases is partly funded by long-term borrowing. The increase in borrowing is larger when the company acquires 60% of PPS and the impact on the **gearing ratio** is more severe.

55 FJK

REPORT

To: Kay
From: Accountant
Date: XX.XX.X8

(a) <u>Analysis and interpretation of the draft financial statements and discussion of performance and position of the FJK</u>

The purpose of the analysis is to ascertain whether it would be in Kay's interest to contribute the requested amount of $250,000. The main consideration is an examination of the performance of the last two years in order to predict both future performance and any risks that may arise from the new strategy that the company has adopted.

In order to analyse the performance of FJK from the information provided in the financial statements we shall use a number of ratios that summarise information and allow comparisons across time. The ratios we shall employ measure the **profitability** of the operation and the **efficiency**, **liquidity** and **solvency** of the company.

<u>Profitability Analysis</u>

Both **revenues** and **costs** have increased between 20X7 and 20X8. Revenue has increased by around 54% and profit before tax by over 44%. On the face of this, the strategy of expansion may appear successful in terms of increased profitability. However, it is helpful to look at **profitability** in terms of **returns** rather than in absolute terms and to this end the following ratios have been calculated:

Gross profit margin: $\frac{\text{Gross profit}}{\text{Revenue}} \times 100$

Distribution costs as % of revenues: $\frac{\text{Distribution}}{\text{Costs}} \times 100$

Administrative costs as % of revenue: $\frac{\text{Administrative expenses}}{\text{Revenue}} \times 100$

Net profit as % of revenue: $\frac{\text{Profit before finance costs}}{\text{Revenue}} \times 100$

Return on assets: $\frac{\text{Profit before finance costs}}{\text{Total assets}} \times 100$

The net profit margin has been reduced from 18.3% in 20X7 to 17.8% in 20X8. On the other hand the gross profit margin defined as gross profit over revenue has increased slightly from 26.2 % in 20X7 to 27.7% in 20X8.

Contrasting the marginal expenses increase in the **gross profit margin** with the decrease in the **net profit margin** implies that administrative and distribution costs as percentages of revenue must have increased at the same time. The table below summarises the movement of the profit and cost ratios from 20X7 to 20X8.

	20X8	*20X7*
Gross profit margin	$\frac{1,655}{5,973} \times 100 = 27.7\%$	$\frac{1,018}{3,886} \times 100 = 26.2\%$
Distribution costs as % of revenue	$\frac{270}{5,973} \times 100 = 4.5\%$	$\frac{106}{3,886} \times 100 = 2.7\%$
Administrative expense as % of revenue	$\frac{320}{5,973} \times 100 = 5.4\%$	$\frac{201}{3,886} \times 100 = 5.2\%$
Net profit as % of revenue	$\frac{968+97}{5,973} \times 100 = 17.8\%$	$\frac{671+40}{3,886} \times 100 = 18.3\%$
Return on assets	$\frac{968+97}{4,815-167} \times 100 = 22.9$	$\frac{671+40}{2,661} \times 100 = 26.7\%$
Total asset turnover	$\frac{5,973}{4,815-167} = 1.29$	$\frac{3,886}{2,661} = 1.46\%$

The increase in both distribution and administrative costs relative to revenues may be due to the new markets in which the company has expanded and the presence of teething problems in establishing new distribution channels. On the other hand it may show inability to control administrative expenses arising in new operations due to the managerial model employed. Both types of expenses therefore need further analysis in order to understand the reasons for the increase.

Another indicator of profitability, the **return on assets** (ROA) also shows a decrease, falling from 26.7% in 20X7 to 22.9% in 20X8. The ROA is the product of **net profit margin** and **total asset turnover** as given below.

$$ROA = \frac{\text{Profit before finance costs}}{\text{Total assets}} = \frac{\text{Profit before finance costs}}{\text{Revenue}} \times \frac{\text{Revenue}}{\text{Total assets}}$$

Therefore, the **return on assets** is affected by both profitability and the efficiency with which the assets are used which is measured by the **total asset turnover**. However, like net profits **total asset turnover** has also fallen from 1.46 to 1.29 so the **return on assets** was reduced both as a result of less efficient use of the assets as well as due to falling profit margins.

Property, plant and equipment has increased significantly over the two years. At the end of 20X8 property plant and equipment at $3,413,000 is more than double the figure of $1,586,000 at the end of 20X7. Even after removing the effect of revaluation it appears that a significant investment in non-current assets has been made. It may be reasonable to assume that the benefits of this investment will be apparent in 20X8/X9 and future years.

Efficiency

A number of efficiency ratios can be used to analyse performance, in addition to the **total asset turnover** used before and the ones employed are summarised below:

Non-current asset turnover: $\frac{\text{Revenue}}{\text{Non-current assets}}$

Inventory: $\frac{\text{Inventory}}{\text{Cost of sales}} \times 365$

Trade receivables: $\frac{\text{Trade receivables}}{\text{Revenues}} \times 365$

The values of the ratios are given below:

	20X8	20X7
Non-current asset turnover	$\dfrac{5,973}{3,413-167}=1.8$	$\dfrac{3,886}{1,586}=2.5$
Inventory:	$\dfrac{677}{4,318}\times 365=57.2$ days	$\dfrac{510}{2,868}\times 365=64.9$ days
Trade receivables:	$\dfrac{725}{5,973}\times 365=44.3$ days	$\dfrac{553}{3,886}\times 365=51.9$ days

The **non-current asset turnover** ratio like the **total asset turnover** ratio shows a deterioration in the efficient use of the asset of the firm. The other efficiency ratios however show some improvement. More specifically the **trade receivables** ratio shows that revenues are received within a shorter period of time whereas the **inventory ratio** shows that inventories are reduced freeing cash to meet short term liabilities. This reduction in inventory should of course been seen in terms of the requisite level of inventories for the level of business in which the company is as there is always the risk of not being able to meet customer demand if the level of inventories is too low.

Liquidity

Liquidity is measured by the **current ratio** defined as $\dfrac{\text{current assets}}{\text{current liabilities}}$ which for 20X7 was $\dfrac{1,075}{845}=1.27$

In order to calculate the **current ratio** for 20X8 we need to take into account the tax liability for 20X8.

The effective tax rate for 20X7 is $\dfrac{164}{671}=0.244$

Applying the same effective tax rate for 20X8 results in a tax liability of $0.244 \times 968 = 236$.

The additional tax liability for 20X8 should therefore be $236 - 164 = 72$.

The current ratio for 20X8 will be $\dfrac{1,402}{1,718+72}=0.78$

The **current ratio** has fallen from 1.27 in 20X7 to 0.78 in 20X8 which represents a significant worsening of the liquidity position of the company.

Solvency

Solvency is measured using the **gearing ratio** and the **interest cover** ratio. The gearing ratio is defined as $\dfrac{\text{Debt}}{\text{Equity}}$ and the interest cover as $\dfrac{\text{Profits}}{\text{Finance costs}}$. The values of the two ratios for 20X7 and 20X8 are given in the table below.

	20X8	20X7
Gearing ratio	$\dfrac{763+327}{2,334-167}=0.503$	$\dfrac{453+103}{1,363}=0.408$
Interest cover	$\dfrac{968+97}{97}=11$	$\dfrac{971+40}{40}=17.8$

The gearing ratio has increased significantly over the period as a result of increased borrowing. Total borrowings at the end of March 20X8 reached $1,090,000 (763 + 327) from $556,000 (453 + 103) at the end of March 20X7 an increase of nearly 100%. This will increase the riskiness of the company and may make the servicing of debt more difficult. The interest cover, the value of which has fallen from nearly 18 to 11 as a result of a doubling in the finance costs, is still not a cause for concern and it indicates that ability to service the debt may not have been impaired. However, since one third of the liabilities is short term (it falls due within one year) it may put pressure on profits in the short-term.

(b) Risks and problem areas revealed by the financial statements

The company has achieved in the **short-term** an impressive **increase in revenues**, but the speed with which this growth has been achieved gives cause for concern. Costs have not been able to be controlled and profitability as a result has declined. There has been a significant increase in the assets of the company but because these were funded by borrowings, both the gearing of the company and its finance costs have increased. The short-term nature of the debt will put additional pressure on the company and exacerbate the already difficult **liquidity** position of the company. The injection of **new capital** will help alleviate the liquidity problems of the company and depending on the ability of the company to increase profit margins FJK may be a reasonably good investment.

56 BHG

(a)   (i)   <u>Earnings per share</u>

Earnings per share (EPS) is defined as follows:

$$EPS = \frac{\text{Earnings attributable to ordinary shareholders}}{\text{Weighted average of the number of ordinary shares in issue}}$$

It is the only **financial ratio** that listed companies must disclose under IFRS and it is used as a measure of the **financial performance** of a company.

As an **investment appraisal tool** it is of limited use because it only looks at the current performance of a company. Comparison with earlier years may also be difficult for an investor because the ratio can be affected by both accounting policies that may affect the numerator and by the number of outstanding shares.

Finally, the ratio may be misleading because of the dilutive effect that convertible bonds or options may have on the earnings attributable to shareholders.

When EPS is used in conjunction with the price of a share to calculate the price/earnings ratio, it can be used to compare whether shares in a listed company are cheap or expensive relative to other listed companies.

(ii)   <u>Dividend yield</u>

Dividend yield is the ratio of the dividend to the market value of a share. The dividend yield is the cash component of the total return of an investment. Historically only a small proportion of the total return from equity investments is attributable to dividends, the bulk being attributed to the capital gain from the investment. For this reason, the dividend yield is not normally a good indication of the potential return from an equity investment.

A high dividend yield may be an indication that a company lacks investment opportunities and it prefers to return cash to its shareholders in the form of dividends rather than investing in new projects and returning value to its shareholders in the form of higher share prices. In some countries where the tax system is more favourable to capital gains rather than dividends, a low dividend yield may simply indicate, not the financial strength of a company but an optimal response to the tax treatment. Finally, dividend payments are sometimes perceived as signalling the financial robustness of a company (the so called **signalling effect**) and must be paid even if paying them leads to the abandonment of profitable investment opportunities.

As an investment criterion it would be of limited use to BHG in selecting a suitable target for acquisition.

(iii)   <u>Gearing</u>

Gearing measures the long-term debt liabilities of a company either in relation to the company's share capital or in comparison to the total assets of the company. Since debt holders have first claim to the earnings and the assets of a company, the higher the level of debt, the higher the uncertainty of the equity holders regarding their claim on the residual earnings or assets of the company.

Highly geared companies will be **cheaper** to acquire than **low geared** companies. However, what matters in an acquisition is not the gearing of the target entity, but the gearing of the resulting combined entity. If the resulting gearing is relatively low, the high gearing of the target company may be irrelevant. When looking at the gearing of the target company, equal attention should therefore be paid to the potential benefits that will result for the combined entity in the form of revenue or cost synergies.

(iv)   <u>Gross profit margin</u>

This ratio is defined as

$$GPM = \frac{\text{Gross profit}}{\text{Sales revenue}}$$

Gross profit margin is an indicator of a company's pricing policies and its ability to control costs. The higher a company's profit margin compared to its competitors, the better. A low profit margin indicates a low margin of safety and a higher risk that a decline in sales will erase profits and result in a net loss. Other things being equal, a company with a higher GPM is more attractive as an acquisition target compared to a low GPM company. A proper evaluation of a company on the basis of this ratio will require the calculation of the GPM for a number of years in order to see the performance of the company over time. However, like most ratios that involve profits, this may be difficult because profits are affected by both financial and accounting policies that may render comparisons across time meaningless. Similarly, the sources of revenues need to be identified and the contribution of each source of revenue properly understood in order to be able to assess the sustainability of revenue beyond the acquisition.

(v)   Asset turnover ratios

There is a variety of asset turnover ratios all of which are calculated by dividing revenue by the value of specific assets owned by the company. These ratios measure the efficiency of asset use since they compare the amount of revenues generated per unit of assets owned by the company. The ratio can be defined in terms of the total assets of a company or in terms of sub-categories, for example, non-current and current assets.

The ratio can be used as an investment criterion and a company will prefer a target with a higher asset turnover ratio to one with a low one. However, care should be taken in calculating such ratios, because the assets need to be measured at market values, which for non-current assets may be very difficult. The revenues can also be affected by revenue recognition policies that individual entities may have in place.

(b)   Accounting ratios summarise financial information and make the assessment of the historical financial performance of a company easier. However, they have several limitations that should be taken into account when accounting ratios are calculated, and some aspects that need to be taken into account are stated below.

Accounting standards

Although there is a movement towards a common set of accounting standards globally, there are still significant variations in the accounting regulations of most European countries that follow IFRS and the US where companies follow US GAAP. For example the LIFO method of valuing inventories is allowed under US GAAP whereas it is not allowed under IFRS. Even within each set of standards different treatments may be applied to different types of companies, for example listed versus unlisted companies. It is therefore important that ratios are based on comparable sets of financial statements in order to be used in investment appraisal or performance analysis.

Accounting policies

Under both IFRS and US GAPP, companies are afforded great flexibility in the selection of accounting policies in certain areas such as revenue recognition, research and development, asset valuation, depreciation and other areas that affect both the statement of financial position and the statement of comprehensive income. Although companies need to be consistent over time in terms of the accounting option they select, problems may still arise when comparing financial ratios which have been constructed under different accounting policies.

Type of business entities

Finally accounting ratios may differ because companies are in different lines of business. For example companies in the services sector have higher asset turnover ratios compared to industrial companies, since the latter require a significantly higher level of assets. Another aspect that may be important, is the different way that industries behave over the economic and business cycles. For example the construction industry may have a different cycle and therefore revenues may be affected earlier than say the pharmaceutical industry. This comment is also relevant to international comparisons when countries are subject to different economic cycles.

Even when companies operate in broadly similar lines of business, there are likely to be differences that make comparisons difficult.

			Marks
(a)	For each ratio, max 3 marks		15
(b)	Accounting standards	3	
	Accounting policies	3	
	Type of business entities	3	
	Difficulty of comparison	1	
			10
			25

57 Non-executive

Text reference. These topics are covered in Chapters 1, 2 and 14.

Top tips. It is essential that you give reasons for the conclusions you have come to. If your figures are incorrect, the examiner will be able to give you credit. It is a good idea to set our your adjustments in the form of a table, as we do.

Easy marks. These are available for re-calculating the ratios.

Examiner's comments. This question was not answered by many candidates (BPP note: in the old syllabus there was an element of choice between the 25 mark questions, if a similar question comes up now you cannot avoid attempting it.) Those who did were able to apply their knowledge of substance over form to the three transactions. The majority were able to articulate (through journals or explanation) how the treatment should be corrected. Candidates could have shown clearer workings for the adjustments to the key account headings but all managed to roll forward their adjustments and recalculate the ratios.

(a)   Transaction 1: Sale and repurchase agreement

This is a case of **inappropriate revenue recognition**.

(i)   ABC Corp **remains the owner as it retains the risks and rewards of ownership**. ABC Corp continue to insure the plant and store it on its premises.

(ii)   The transaction is **not a true sale** but a financing transaction with the asset as collateral. The transaction involves contracting to sell the financial asset with an express contract to buy it back.

As a result of (i) and (ii) above the **derecognition** criteria for an asset are **not met**.

(iii)   The **price** which ABC will be required to pay to buy the item of plant back is **equivalent to a financing cost** and appears to have no relationship to any appreciation in the value of the item.

(iv)   **XB** is an entity that provides financial services to business and **has no use for the plant**.

As a result of the above, the fundamental principle of substance over form, as identified in the IASB *Framework*, points clearly to a **financing agreement**.

(v)   Moreover, as an item of **plant** is involved, even if this was a true sale, it would **not** have been **shown in revenue**. IAS 18 *Revenue* restricts the **revenue** classification to sales of goods purchased for resale. (The question does not indicate the nature of ABC Corp's business; this answer assumes that the company has used this machine in manufacturing, and that it is not involved in selling plant as a trade.)

The **adjusting entries** should be as follows, assuming the $1,000,000 was received in cash and we need details of the accounting entries made to derecognise the asset in order to reverse these.

DEBIT	Revenue	$1,000,000
CREDIT	Short-term loan	$1,000,000

| DEBIT | Interest expense | $100,000 |
| CREDIT | Interest payable | $100,000 |

Transaction 2

This transaction does not meet the derecognition criteria for receivables as per IAS 39 *Financial instruments: recognition and measurement*, as ABC bears the risk of any uncollectible amounts. The **substance** of the transaction is a **financing agreement** with interest of 10% as the finance charge secured by ABC's receivables. The receivables must be re-instated.

The adjusting entries are:

| DEBIT | Receivables (75% × $2,000,000) | $1,500,000 |
| CREDIT | Loan | $1,500,000 |

To re-instate receivables and account for the loan.

| DEBIT | Interest expense | $150,000 |
| CREDIT | Current liabilities | $150,000 |

To account for 10% interest expense on loan.

Transaction 3

Under IAS 32 *Financial instruments: presentation*, **redeemable preference shares should be classified as debt**. The preference **dividends** payable should be **classified as interest**.

The fact that the shares are **redeemable** and the obligation to pay **dividends** indicate that the financial instrument is, in **substance, a liability** and should be classified as such.

The adjusting entries are:

| DEBIT | Interest expense | $160,000 |
| CREDIT | Statement of changes in equity | $160,000 |

To account for preference dividends

| DEBIT | Equity | $2,000,000 |
| CREDIT | Non-current liabilities (debt) | $2,000,000 |

To adjust the incorrect treatment of preference share capital as equity.

Adjustments

	As given $	Transaction 1 $	Transaction 2 $	Transaction 3 $	Adjusted figures $
Revenue	31,850,000	(1,000,000)			30,850,000
Profit before interest	2,972,000				2,972,000
Interest	1,241,000	100,000	150,000	160,000	1,651,000
Equity	22,450,800			(2,000,000)	20,450,800
Debt	18,253,500	1,000,000	1,500,000	2,000,000	22,753,500

(b) Effect of adjustments on ABC's key accounting ratios for the year ended 30 September 20X8.

$$\text{Return on capital employed} = \frac{\$2,972,000}{\$22,753,500 + \$20,450,800} \times 100$$

$$= 6.88\%$$

$$\text{Net profit margin} = \frac{\$2,972,000 - \$1,651,000}{\$30,850,000} \times 100$$

$$= 4.28\%$$

$$\text{Gearing} = \frac{\$22,753,500}{\$22,753,500 + \$20,450,800} \times 100$$

$$= 52.66\%$$

(c) The three incorrectly treated transactions resulted in **overestimating revenue, underestimating interest expense, overestimating equity and underestimating debt**.

The result is that **net profit margin and ROCE have been overstated and gearing has been understated** thus appearing to meet the targets and giving a more favourable picture of the company's **profitability** and solvency than would have been the case if the transactions had been correctly accounted for.

The transactions appear to have been incorrectly treated in a **deliberate attempt to meet the company's targets**, none of which are met when the transactions are treated correctly.

58 XYZ

> **Text reference**. This topic is covered in Chapter 14.
>
> **Top tips.** Interpretation of financial statements makes up 35% of the syllabus for paper F2. You should use part of the reading time before the exam to identify some of the key issues in the scenario, both from the numerical information and the narrative. This should help you to add some value to your comments, rather than just describing the changes in the figures.
>
> **Easy marks.** In part (a) the ratio calculations provide the easiest marks as long as you take care to select ratios that are **relevant** and show your workings clearly. Part (b) is a very common requirement in this style of question and should be quite easy if you have learned some of the basic limitations of analysis and can apply them to this particular scenario.

(a) Report to the Board of XYZ
Date: X/X/XX
Subject: Potential acquisitions

Financial analysis

Performance

B's gross profit margin of 36% is considerably higher than that of A at 29%. This implies that B has greater control over its cost of sales. However B's net profit margin is only 11% compared to A's margin of 14%. At first sight, this would seem to indicate that A's administrative and distribution costs are under tighter control than those of B. Further analysis shows that two items have inflated A's profit before tax.

A's administrative expenses have been offset by a gain on disposal of non-current assets of $350,000 following a major restructuring. Therefore this is a one-off occurrence and future administrative expenses will rise accordingly.

In addition, A's finance costs have been reduced by a gain of $20,000 on a held-for-trading investment.

After adjusting for these two items, A's net profit margin reduces to only 4%, compared to B's 11%.

B's efficiency, as revealed by the non-current asset turnover figure, is 2.93 compared to A's figure of 2.24. Therefore B seems to be making better use of its non-current assets. However, A's restructuring and reinvestment means that it has more up to date non-current assets, while B's may be older and need investment.

B's return on capital employed is 24%, while A's is only 14% after adjusting profit for the items discussed above. Once again this implies B is making better use of its assets but this may be due to older non-current assets that will need replacing shortly.

Financing

The gearing of A is 53%, compared to B's figure of 43%. A's figure could be considered too risky if we need additional funding from outside investors.

The two companies are subject to different tax regimes and A's rate is 28% compared to B's rate of 35%. However, this needs to be investigated further, as there may be opportunities to reduce B's tax rate if it invests in non-current assets.

Recommendation

Based on this initial review, I would recommend that B is the better prospect for acquisition due to its better financial performance and efficiency and its lower gearing ratio.

(b)   Limitations

Although A and B are of a similar size and operate within similar economic parameters, it is unlikely that they are exactly comparable. Different investment strategies have already been identified with A's restructuring and reinvestment in non-current assets. In addition, A has invested in held-for-trading investments and, on current information, is making gains that are not available to B.

The financial statements are for one period only and may not be representative of trends over a longer period. It would be better to compare their results over a longer period of time.

A and B may have different accounting policies. Financial reporting standards still allow some element of choice and it would be necessary to investigate this further, as it could affect ratios such as ROCE and non-current asset turnover. If one of the companies uses the fair value model for non-current assets, and the other uses the historical cost model, many of the comparisons made above may be spurious.

Finally the financial statements only reflect financial factors. There may be social and environmental considerations. For example, one of the entities may have polluted premises, which would need a clean up.

Appendix: Financial ratios

	A	B
Gross profit percentage		
$\dfrac{\text{Gross profit}}{\text{Revenue}}$	$\dfrac{1,100}{3,800} \times 100 = 29\%$	$\dfrac{1,580}{4,400} \times 100 = 36\%$
Profit margin		
Before adjustments	$\dfrac{532}{3,800} \times 100 = 14\%$	$\dfrac{484}{4,400} \times 100 = 11\%$
After adjustments	$\dfrac{(532 - 350 - 20)}{3,800} \times 100 = 4\%$	
ROCE		
$\dfrac{\text{Profit before interest and tax}}{\text{Equity + borrowings}}$		
Before adjustments	$\dfrac{(532 + 25)}{(950 + 500)} \times 100 = 38\%$	$\dfrac{(484 + 32)}{(1,500 + 650)} \times 100 = 24\%$
After adjustments	$\dfrac{(532 + 25 - 350)}{1,450} \times 100 = 14\%$	

Note: no adjustment is needed here for the gain on the held for trading investment as this ratio uses profit before interest and the investment gain was reflected in the finance costs figure.

	A	B
Non-current asset turnover		
$\dfrac{\text{Revenue}}{\text{Non-current assets}}$	$\dfrac{3,800}{1,700} = 2.24$	$\dfrac{4,400}{1,500} = 2.93$
Gearing		
$\dfrac{\text{Borrowings}}{\text{Equity}}$	$\dfrac{500}{950} \times 100 = 53\%$	$\dfrac{650}{1,500} \times 100 = 43\%$
Tax rates		
$\dfrac{\text{Tax expense}}{\text{Profit before tax}}$	$\dfrac{148}{532} \times 100 = 28\%$	$\dfrac{170}{484} \times 100 = 35\%$

59 KER

Text reference. This topic is covered in Chapter 14.

Top tips. Interpretation of financial statements makes up 35% of the syllabus for paper F2. You should use part of the reading time before the exam to identify some of the key issues in the scenario, both from the numerical information and the narrative. This should help you to add some value to your comments, rather than just describing the changes in the figures.

Easy marks. As is usual in this type of question, 8 marks are available for ratio calculations. As long as you take care to select ratios that are **relevant** and show your workings clearly, these should be the easiest marks to obtain.

Examiner's comments. I would again urge candidates to think carefully about the ratios that they calculate and remember that the calculation of ratios is a means to an end – you then need to consider the rations in the context of the business scenario that has been provided in the question. This will enable you to draw conclusions about the cause and effect of business decisions, the impact on the financials and actions that need to be taken in the future. Candidates must avoid a report that describes the ratio that has been calculated and gives in generic terms what the ratio potentially shows.

(a) Financial performance and financial position of KER

Profitability

The increase in revenue highlighted by the chairman, an increase of 40% over 20X8, presumably results from the expansion into new markets. However, this seems to have been at the expense of increased costs resulting in reduced profit margins. The gross profit margin has fallen from 31% to 26%, due to an increase in cost of sales of 50%. This may well indicate that KER has been forced to reduce prices in order to break into the new markets and increase sales.

The chairman's announcement of increased profit is based on figures including the share of the profits of an associate acquired during the year. A better analysis of the trend in profits would ignore this. Excluding the results of the associate, the profit before tax has decreased year on year from $125 million to $80 million and the net profit margin has decreased from 9% to only 2.8%. This is due in part to an increase in distribution costs of 58% and a doubling of finance costs. While we would expect the market expansion plan to result in increased distribution costs, the increase is significantly higher than the increase in revenue. It may well be that the new markets are well away from the factory, resulting in greater distances travelled.

Efficiency

The ROCE has been maintained, but examining the statement of financial position shows that a significant part ($42m) of the increase in capital is a result of the revaluation of property, plant and equipment which is unlikely to generate future revenue.

Non-current asset turnover has increased from 2.5 to 3.0 and this suggests that the company is making effective use of the new non-current assets to generate increased revenue.

Gearing

The company is becoming much more heavily reliant on borrowings. Loans have nearly doubled and KER now has an overdraft. The gearing ratio has increased from 43% to 60% as a result of this increased borrowing.

The resulting increase in finance costs has had a significant impact on profits, as mentioned above.

Interest cover has dropped from 5.2 times to 3.7 times. Although there is still a good coverage, KER would be vulnerable to any increase in interest rates. These points combined could mean that KER is a much more risky investment now than when you originally made your investment.

Working capital

The working capital situation has deteriorated as a result of the expansion. A positive cash balance of $22m has been turned into an overdraft of $37m. Inventory days have increased from 34 to 50 days, which is tying up cash. Receivables days have increased from 48 to 63 days, indicating a need to tighten up credit control unless new customers are being allowed generous terms, while payables days are static. This all indicates a shortage of cash in the short term.

Conclusion

The Chairman's comments cite increased revenues and profits. However, the net profit after removing the associate's results has in fact decreased quite considerably and the expansion has put a strain on working capital, particularly regarding receivables. The increase in non-current assets appears to have occurred mainly as a result of a revaluation rather than any genuine reinvestment and this is unlikely to generate future revenues. The profit share from the associate has supported KER this year but has masked the increased borrowings and KER's vulnerability to interest changes.

(b) Differences in accounting policies

The element of choice in IFRSs has gradually been reduced. However, there are still areas where an entity can make a perfectly legitimate choice of accounting policy which could affect comparability with other entities in a similar trade.

IAS 16 *Property, plant and equipment* still allows entities to use cost or valuation. Therefore one business may show its PPE at cost while its competitor revalues every year. This will affect total non-current assets, depreciation (and so profit), as well as total equity; which in turn will affect a number of ratios such as profitability, gearing and ROCE.

Inventory valuation can be done using FIFO or weighted average cost. This will affect cost of sales and so profitability, as well as working capital ratios. Similarly, decisions on the recoverability of receivables will affect profitability and working capital ratios.

Classification of certain expenses between cost of sales and admin expenses would affect gross profit margins. For example, one entity may include depreciation in cost of sales, while another includes it in admin expenses. So the first will have a lower gross profit margin than the second.

Appendix – relevant ratios that could be selected (up to a maximum of 8 marks)

Note: *8 pairs of ratios would be sufficient for 8 marks, any of the following would be acceptable, providing they were relevant to the comments you make in the written answer.*

	20X9	20X8
Profitability		
Increase in revenue	(1.430 – 1,022)/1,022 = 40%	
Increase in COS	(1,058 – 705)/705 = 50%	
Increase in distribution costs	(158 – 100)/100 = 58%	
Gross profit margin GP/ Revenue	372/1,430 x 100% = 26%	317/1,022 x 100% = 31%
Profit for the year Profit/revenue	120/1,430 x 100% = 8.4%	92/1,022 x 100% = 9%
Profit for the year, excluding the share of associate	(120 – 80)/1,430 x 100% = 2.8%	92/1,022 x 100% = 9%
Efficiency		
ROCE Profit before finance costs/capital employed	(160 + 60)/(663 + 400) x 100% = 21%	(125 + 30)/(487 + 210) x 100% = 22%
Non-current asset turnover Revenue/ non-current assets	1,430/480 = 3.0 times	1,022/404 = 2.5 times
Gearing		
Interest cover Profit before interest/interest	220/60 = 3.7 times	155/30 = 5.2 times

Gearing Debt/equity	400/663 x 100% = 60%	210/487 x 100% = 43%

Working capital

Current ratio CA/CL	392/136 = 2.9	221/68 = 3.25
Quick ratio CA less inventories/CL	247/136 = 1.8	(221 − 65)/68 = 2.3
Inventory days Inventory/ COS x 365 days	(145/1058) x 365 days = 50 days	(65/705) x 365 days = 34 days
Receivables days Receivables/revenue x 365 days	(247/1,430) x 365 days = 63 days	(134/1,022) x 365 days = 48 days
Payable days Payables/COS x 365 days	(99/1,058) x 365 days = 34 days	(68/705) x 365 days = 35 days

Marking scheme

	Marks
Part (a)	
Calculation of relevant ratios	
1 mark per pair of ratios, to a maximum of	8
Analysis of performance	
1 mark per well-explained point, to a maximum of	12
Part (b)	
1 mark per relevant point, including comment on impact on comparability	5
	25

60 GD

Text reference. Ratio and trend analysis is covered in Chapter 14 of the text.

Top tips. Section B analysis questions are full of detail, both numerical and narrative. You should use part of the reading time before the start of the exam to familiarise yourself with it. You cannot use your calculator during that time but you can read the scenario, identify the key facts, and read the numerical information to spot the key changes. This will make sure that you spot the main points of the question and when you write your answer, you will be able to select and calculate the ratios that are most relevant.

Easy marks. The 8 marks for calculating ratios should be easy, providing you are confident of the formulae for the ratios, and you set out your workings clearly. Part (b) should also be easy, as there are a number of fairly 'standard' points that you could make.

(a) Analysis

Financial performance

Revenue trend

The new competitor in one of GD's markets appears to have stolen market share from GD with its aggressive pricing strategy. This has resulted in a year on year reduction in revenue of 14%.

Even the acquisition of a new subsidiary during the year has not been enough to counteract this effect. If it was acquired towards the end of the year the full impact of the acquisition may not yet have been seen and the subsidiary may contribute more to group revenue in future years.

Profitability

GD's gross profit margin has **deteriorated**, so as well as a decline in volume, there has been a decline in the profitability.

This could be due to increases in the purchase prices of inventories and profitability may improve in future if GD is successful in its negotiations over bulk buying discounts with its suppliers. Although this may improve the gross margin, there is a risk that carrying excessive levels of inventory could place further stress on GD's cashflow and incur increased holding costs.

The **operating margin has also decreased** mainly due to an 8% increase in administration costs (a 15% increase if the gains on held for trading investments are ignored) despite the 14% decline in sales.

This may indicate that GD is not controlling costs effectively, but part of the increase may be due to higher depreciation charges as a result of the revaluation during the year.

Financial position

Liquidity

GD's liquidity has deteriorated during the year, as illustrated by the current ratio falling from 1.22 to 1.03 and the quick ratio falling from 0.74 to 0.52.

GD's cash position has deteriorated, going from a cash balance of $41 million in 20X7 to an overdraft of $50 million in 20X8. An overdraft is a expensive and risky form of finance as it can be recalled at any time.

The reasons for the decline in liquidity are:

- Purchases of property, plant and equipment during the year
- Acquisition of a subsidiary during the year
- Repayment of long-term loans
- Poor working capital management (see below).

Working capital management

There has been a **significant increase in inventory days** (from 47 to 63) which is tying up cash. This may be a result of GD selling lower volumes as a result of the competition in one its markets. This could mean that they are holding unsaleable inventories, although this is likely to be a major risk with non-perishable packaging products.

Part of GD's new strategy is to negotiate discount for bulk buying but this could result in even longer holding periods with the related adverse effect on liquidity.

GD appears to have **reasonably efficient credit control** procedures as there is only a slight increase in receivables days from 33 to 35.

However, there has been a worrying increase in the time taken to settle payables. Payables days have increased from 63 to 80 days. Along with the overdraft, this suggests that GD is **struggling to pay its liabilities as they fall due**. This may put the company at a disadvantage in its negotiations for discounts from these suppliers and could result in the suppliers withdrawing credit or even refusing to supply GD.

GD also appears to be **trading in investments**. This has generated some gains in the current year but is a risky activity and in the company's current situation the $31 million could be more effectively applied to the overdue payables or to reducing the overdraft.

Solvency

The low levels of the gearing ratio and the substantial margin of safety shown by the interest cover ratio (17.2 in 20X8 and 20.3 in 20X7) would appear to indicate that GD can easily afford to pay its interest as it falls due.

However, this does not allow us to conclude that GD's solvency is not at risk. As at the date of its last statement of financial position, if the overdraft were to be called in and suppliers to demand payment of all overdue balances, it looks as if GD **would not be in a position to pay this**.

Recommendation

The financial institution should have **serious reservations** about granting GD a loan because:

(i)   The company has been losing market share to the new competitor.

(ii)   There has been a decline in profit margins.

(iii)   GD's poor working capital management has led to deteriorating liquidity.

(iv)   It appears that the loan of $150 million would have to be applied to clearing the overdraft, the existing loan due for repayment in 20X9 and paying overdue trade payables accounts rather than in investing in new assets or further acquisitions that would improve the company's future trading prospects.

Lending to GD **should not ruled out entirely** because:

(i)   GD is still profitable.
(ii)   GD has low gearing and can easily afford to pay increased amounts of interest.
(iii)   GD has significant assets to offer as security for loans.
(iv)   GD has a new subsidiary that may well contribute increasing revenue and profits in future.

Ratios

Note: Only 8 ratios would be required to achieve 8 marks. Any 8 from the following would be relevant to the analysis in this question.

		20X8		20X7
ROCE $= $	$\dfrac{\text{PBIT}}{\text{Equity} + \text{Debt}}$	$= \dfrac{179+11}{496+90}$	$= $	$\dfrac{290+15}{364+180}$
		$= 32.4\%$	$= $	56%

Gross Margin $= $	$\dfrac{\text{Gross, Profit}}{\text{Revenue}}$	$= \dfrac{360}{1200}$	$= $	$\dfrac{470}{1400}$
		$= 30\%$	$= $	33.6%

		20X8		20X7
Operating Margin $= $	$\dfrac{\text{PBIT}}{\text{Revenue}}$	$= \dfrac{179+11}{1200}$	$= $	$\dfrac{290-15}{1400}$
		$= 15.8\%$	$= $	21.81%

Current Ratio $= $	$\dfrac{\text{CA}}{\text{CL}}$	$= \dfrac{292}{283}$	$= $	$\dfrac{304}{249}$
		$= 1.03$	$= $	1.22

Quick Ratio $= $	$\dfrac{\text{CA - Inventories}}{\text{CL}}$	$= \dfrac{292-146}{283}$	$= $	$\dfrac{304-120}{249}$
		$= 0.52$	$= $	0.74

Inventory Days $= $	$\dfrac{\text{Inventory}}{\text{Cost of sales}} \times 365$	$= \dfrac{146}{840} \times 365$	$= $	$\dfrac{120}{930} \times 365$
		$= 63\ \text{Days}$	$= $	$47\ \text{Days}$

Receivable Days $= $	$\dfrac{\text{Receivables}}{\text{Revenue}} \times 365$	$= \dfrac{115}{1200} \times 365$	$= $	$\dfrac{125}{1400} \times 365$
		$= 35\ \text{Days}$	$= $	$33\ \text{Days}$

Payable Days $= $	$\dfrac{\text{Payables}}{\text{Cost of sales}} \times 365$	$= \dfrac{185}{840} \times 365$	$= $	$\dfrac{160}{930} \times 365$
		$= 80\ \text{Days}$	$= $	$63\ \text{Days}$

Gearing =	$\dfrac{\text{Debt}}{\text{Equity}}$	=	$\dfrac{90}{496}$	=	$\dfrac{180}{364}$
		=	18%	=	49%
Interest cover =	$\dfrac{\text{PBIT}}{\text{Interest}}$	=	$\dfrac{179+11}{11}$	=	$\dfrac{290+15}{15}$
		=	17.2	=	20.3

(b)   <u>Further information required</u>

(Note: Four points would be sufficient here, our answer shows a wider range of points that would be relevant)

(i)   Details about when the new subsidiary was acquired and forecasts of how much revenue and profit it is likely to contribute to the group in future years.

(ii)   Details of any security over the existing loans and which assets are involved.

(iii)   The limit of the overdraft facility and when it is due for renegotiation.

(iv)   A consolidated statement of cash flows for the year.

(v)   Profit and loss and cash flow forecasts indicating how GD intends to repay the loan due in August 20X9.

(vi)   Segmental information allowing analysis of trends in GD's different markets and activities

(vii)   More details of the directors' new strategy to assess the reasonableness of any estimates and assumptions.

Marking scheme

			Marks
(a)	Ratios		8
	Comments		
	Performance	5	
	Position	6	
	Conclusion	2	
			13
(b)	1 mark for each relevant point to a maximum of		4
			25

61   DFG

Text reference. Ratio and trend analysis is covered in Chapter 14 of the study text.

Top tips. Don't dive straight into calculations, take time to read the financial statements, note the main changes and think about how these relate to the narrative information in the question. I fyou keep asking yourself 'why?' you should find some practical points to make. Think about the points that are most important to a prospective employee of the company.

As usual, there are only 8 marks available for ratio calculations, so you should select 8 ratios that are relevant and will help to add value to your answer, calculate them in an Appendix to your answer. Then you should be able to pull together your intial observations and the detail from the ratios to produce a focussed answer.

Easy marks. The easiest marks are for the ratio calculations and for the 'limitations' in part (b). This is a very typical part (b) requirement in this style of question.

Performance

DFG's sales performance appears fairly static year on year with only a 1.6% increase in revenue. Clearly the reasoning behind the planned new sales strategy aims to address this and bring about more rapid revenue increases in future.

Profitability shows a marked improvement from year to year with the company showing a profit for the year in 20X1 compared with a loss for the year in 20X0. The gross margin has improved significantly, presumably as a result of the new supplier relationship. This has probably reduced the unit cost of the goods being purchased by DFG.

However, the new supplier relationship may also be having a negative effect on the business. DFG is being sued by a customer over the alleged supply of faulty goods. This suggests that the new supplier may be supplying cheaper goods that are of poorer quality. The amount involved in this claim, which could be even more that the $30 million that has been disclosed, is large enough to threaten DFG's survival as a going concern if the case is lost.

Whatever the outcome of the case, any publicity that casts doubt on the quality of goods sold by DFG could have an adverse effect on its future trading.

The **other comprehensive income** shown is the result of a change in policy, as the company is now carrying its property, plant and equipment at fair value instead of historical cost. This is permitted under accounting standards but in analysing the financial postion of the company you should bear in mind that this may have been done on order to make the company's position appear stronger to potential lenders.

Position

The liquidity of the company has deteriorated from year to year, with the overall current ratio of assets to liabilities falling from 2.2 to 1.3. This ratio helps to assess how easily the company can pay its short term liabilities as they fall due.

The quick ratio excludes inventories and, having dropped to 0.5, indicates that DFG may struggle to pay its short term liabilities. The cash position has also worsened. In 20X0 there was a positive bank balance but in 20X1 this had turned to overdraft.

The inventory holding period has increased significantly to 191 days. This could be a result of the arrangement with the new supplier, with DFG possibly having to purchase larger quantities to obtain discounts, or it could also indicate that there are difficulties in selling the goods, perhaps because of adverse publicity from the legal claim against DFG.

The average time taken to collect cash from receivables has also lengthened, contributing to the poor cash and liquidity position. This could be a result of a deliberate policy of offering extended credit periods to attract new customers or it could again indicate problems such as customers withholding payment over disputes about the quality of goods.

The overall gearing level of the company, which shows the proportion of debt to equity, is not particularly high, but if the revaluation had not been carried out in 20X1 this ratio would have looked worse. Another key issue is that even if DFG can repay its trade payables and short term borrowings, the long-term borrowings are due to be repaid in two years time. It appears that DFG will have to start negotiating some new loan finance in order to secure its future.

Conclusion

Before you decide whether to accept the position of Sales Director with DFG, I advise you to look beyond the company's public messages about its future and its profits in its last financial year. There are general risks facing any business dependent on the building trade, which is very susceptible to changes in the general economic environment. In addition there are clear indications that the company may struggle to pay its liabilities and it may not be well placed to obtain new finance. The legal case also threatens the future viability of the business.

(b)   Limitations of ratio analysis

By the time that financial statements are published they are already **out of date**. For example, DFG's statement of financial position shows the situation as at one specific date. If, for example, the legal case is decided in the period after 31 December 20X1, the position will be changed completely.

Financial statements are **backward looking**. In this example the statement of comprehensive income show that it traded profitably in the year to the reporting date, but for the majority of stakeholders, such as prospective employees, this information is far less relevant than information about the company's future prospects.

Financial statements can only include information that can be expressed in **monetary terms**. The statement of comprehensive income shows improving profitability but may hide the fact that this has been achieved through a lowering of quality thresholds in purchasing.

Issues such as the change in policy for valuing property, plant and equipment can impair the **comparability** both from year to year, or between DFG and other companies in its sector.

APPENDIX

Key accounting ratios

> **Tutorial note:** Only **8 ratios** would be required for the 8 mark allocation, any selection of the following would gain credit.

		20X1	20X0
Performance			
Return on capital employed *(note 2)*	15/322	4.7%	
	1/275		0.4%
Gross profit margin	49/252	19.4%	
	25/248		10.1%
Operating profit margin *(note 1)*	15/252	6.0%	
	1/248		0.4%
Net profit margin (using profit for the year)	7/252	2.8%	
	(5)/248		(2.0)%
Non-current asset turnover	252/254	0.99	
	248/198		1.25
Position			
Current ratio	178/134	1.3	
	143/66		2.2
Quick ratio	72/134	0.5	
	54/66		0.8
Inventories holding period	106/203 × 365	191 days	
	89/223 × 365		146 days
Payables payment period	95/203 × 365	171 days	
	66/223 × 365		108 days
Receivables collection period	72/252 × 365	104 days	
	48/248 × 365		71 days
Gearing (debt/equity)	91+39/231	56.3%	
	91/184		49.5%
Interest cover	22/8	2.8 times	
	1/12		0.1 times
Average cost of borrowing	8/(91 + 39)	6.2%	
	12/91		13.2%

Notes

(1) Operating profit = profit before finance costs and share of profit/loss of associate
(2) Capital employed = total equity + long term borrowings + short term borrowings – investments

62 CVB

Text reference. Ratio and trend analysis is covered in Chapter 14 of the study text.

Top tips. Remember that the main marks here are for your written report, not for the ratio calculations. For 8 marks, the examiner expects 8 ratios (ie 8 pairs of ratios, for the two years). She will be more impressed by your ability to select **relevant** ratios that add value to the analysis, than your ability to calculate pages of extra ratios.

Easy marks. As long as you have learned the main accounting ratios, the marks for calculations in part (a) should be easy.

Examiner's comments. The quality of analysis was poor. Few candidates identified the urgency of the problems. Some ratio calculations posed problems, in particular interest cover, return on capital employed and operating profit margin. Few candidates included NCI in equity when calculating gearing and ROCE.

(a)

REPORT

To: A Friend
From: An Accountant
Date: November 20X5
Subject: Analysis of CVB

Introduction

I have been asked to examine the most recent financial statements of the fashion retailer, CVB, to assist you in making a decision about investing in the company. This report is based upon the financial statements of CVB for the year ended 30 September 20X5 together with comparative figures for the previous year. The analysis is based upon a number of relevant accounting ratios which are included in the Appendix to this report.

Financial performance

The overall trend in CVB's performance appears to be a **small increase in revenue** but with decreasing profitability.

The **operating profit margin** has decreased from 4.9% to 4.4%. The main factor behind this decline must relate to revenues and costs of sales, as sales and marketing costs have remained stable as a proportion of revenue and administrative expenses have declined in relation to revenue, so operating expenses appear to be under control.

The **gross profit margin** shows a decrease from 35% to 32.7%. It is possible that the company's **new fair trade clothing line** has affected the gross margin through the levels of prices that CVB must commit to pay its suppliers through the fair trade scheme. Also, the fashion retail sector is highly competitive so CVB may have been forced to **reduce its selling prices** to maintain or grow its market share.

As well as the pressure on the operating results, CVB's profit for the year has also suffered from a **loss in its associate** in the year to 30 September 20X1. The rationale for holding a loss-making investment is questionable but there may be a commercial reason for this, perhaps giving CVB significant influence over a company that is critical to its business, such as a supplier.

Another factor in the profit decline is the significant **increase in finance costs**, which increased by 60% year on year. This is the result of CVB's increasing reliance on short-term borrowings, which is mainly responsible for the decline in ROCE.

Financial position

The **liquidity** position of the business has **deteriorated significantly.** The current and quick ratios show that CVB is heading to a position where it may not be able to pay its liabilities as they fall due. The cash position has deteriorated, going from a positive cash balance to a position of net short term borrowings, presumably bank overdrafts, which carry high rates of interest and are normally repayable on demand.

Analysis of working capital shows that the **payables period** has increased significantly to 172 days. This appears to be unsustainable as few suppliers will be able to wait for six months to be paid. It may also be unethical, particularly in respect of the conditions attached to fair trade schemes, where companies such as CVB are expected to pay their small suppliers promptly.

The inventory holding period also shows a worrying increase. The **risk of obsolescence** of inventories is very high in the fashion retail business, with trends changing every season. If fashion goods are held for a period of 168 days, they may be unsaleable, or only saleable at significant discounts.

Looking at the company's financing structure, its **gearing ratio is comparatively low**, so there could be potential for it to raise more debt finance. However, the decline in profits has severely **reduced the interest cover**, so potential lenders may be unwilling to risk lending to CVB as any continuing decline in results would mean the company could not afford to pay its interest.

Investor sentiment

The trend in the price earnings ratio shows that the declining earnings trend has hit the share price, and it has even dipped a little further, perhaps indicating that investors see CVB as a more risky investment now than it was a year ago.

Conclusion

Based on the available information it appears that it would be unwise to invest in CVB unless it obtains new finance and starts to improve its performance. I would advise that you look into other companies within the sector to find an investment that offers better performance prospects and a more secure financial position.

APPENDIX

Key accounting ratios

> **Tutorial note:** Only **8 ratios** would be required for the 8 mark allocation, any selection of the following would gain credit.

		20X1	20X0
Performance			
Gross profit margin	148/453	32.7%	
	144/412		35.0%
Profit margin (using profit for the year)	8/453	1.8%	
	13/412		3.2%
Operating profit margin *(note 1)*	20/453	4.4%	
	20/412		4.9%
Return on capital employed *(note 2)*	20/332	6.0%	
	20/298		6.7%
Position			
Current ratio	215/162	1.3	
	159/95		1.7
Quick ratio	75/162	0.5	
	72/95		0.8
Inventories holding period	140/305 × 365	168 days	
	87/268 × 365		118 days
Payables payment period	144/305 × 365	172 days	
	95/268 × 365		129 days
Receivables collection period	75/453 × 365	60 days	
	63/412 × 365		56 days
Gearing (debt/equity)	55+18/273	26.7%	
	58/256		22.7%
Interest cover (op.profit *(note1)*/finance cost)	20/8	2.5 times	
	20/5		4 times
Average cost of borrowing	8/(55 + 18)	11%	
	5/58		8.6%
Earnings per share	7/30	$0.23	
	11/30		$0.37
P/E ratio	1.25/0.23	5.4	
	2.08*(note 3)*/0.37		5.7

Notes

(1) Operating profit = profit before finance costs and share of profit/loss of associate
(2) Capital employed = total equity + long term borrowings + short term borrowings – investments
(3) 20X0 share price $1.25 × 100/60

(b)   **Further financial information**

More recent financial information would be useful, as the financial statements are already months out of date by the time they are published. CVB may have issued interim financial statements, reviews or other announcements and these will show whether performance has improved since the last annual financial statements.

Financial statements of the associate would help in understanding the nature of its business and how it links with that of CVB. This would also help to explain whether the losses are due to a one-off event or whether they are likely to recur.

Information about dividends would be relevant to assessing the risk and return of an investment in the short term.

There may be other financial information, such as forecasts, and indications of the directors' plans for addressing risks within the management commentary.

General financial information and comparative ratios for the fashion sector would help to assess whether CVB's results reflect general conditions within the industry or are more directly the result of CVB's management's decisions.

63   JKL

Text reference. EPS is covered in Chapter 15.

Top tips. No huge complications in this basic and diluted EPS question: Start off by calculating the theoretical ex rights price to get the bonus fraction. In calculating diluted EPS, don't forget to add back the post tax interest saved. In part (b), don't just talk about EPS generally – you need to focus on diluted EPS.

Easy marks. Obviously the calculation of basic EPS is a source of easy marks. Part (b) has 3 marks – you are bound to get at least one of these if you put pen to paper and say something sensible.

(a)   Basic earnings per share $= \dfrac{\$2,763,000}{6,945,922}$ (W2)

$= 39.8\ c$

Diluted earnings per share $= \dfrac{\$2,858,200\ \text{(W3)}}{9,045,922\ \text{(W4)}}$

$= 31.6\ c$

Workings

(1)   <u>Theoretical ex rights price</u>

Theoretical ex rights price $= 141c$

		c
4 shares @ 145c		580
1 share @ 125c		125
5 shares @ 141c		705

(2)   <u>Weighted average number of shares in issue for year ending 31 August 20X4</u>

Date	Narrative	Shares	Time	Fraction	Weighted average
1.9.X3	B/F	6,000,000	$\times\ ^{5}/_{12}$	$\times\ ^{145}/_{141}$	2,570,922
1.2.X4	Rights issue				
	(6m × ¹/₄)	1,500,000			
		7,500,000	$\times\ ^{7}/_{12}$		4,375,000
					6,945,922

(3)   Diluted earnings

	$
Basic earnings	2,763,000
Add post tax interest saved (2,000,000 × 7%) × (1 − 0.32)	95,200
Diluted earnings	2,858,200

(4)   Diluted number of shares

	Number
Basic weighted average number of shares	6,945,922
Convertible loan 2,000,000/100 × 105	2,100,000
	9,045,922

(b)   **Historical information**, such as most of the contents of a set of financial statements, is **not always useful** for making economic decisions. **Forecasts** and projections for the future can be much more appropriate for **decision making**.

The **diluted** earnings per share figure is an attempt to provide **information about the future to current holders of shares**. Where financial instruments have been issued which will potentially dilute future earnings, the diluted EPS figure shows how the current earnings would be diluted, or shared out amongst the new as well as the current shareholders. This gives the current shareholders an idea of the effect that these dilutive financial instruments may have on their shareholding in future.

There are, however, **limitations** to the use of these figures. The most basic limitation is that the diluted EPS is based upon the **current earnings** figure which **may not be relevant in future years**. The calculation for **convertible loan stock** also **assumes that all holders will convert** to ordinary shares rather than having their loan stock redeemed. As the share price currently stands at significantly higher than the redemption value then this is currently a fairly safe assumption to make but it may not always be the case.

64   CB

Text reference. The topic of EPS is covered in Chapter 15.

Top tips. First calculate the theoretical ex-rights price, selecting the correct share value (for 1 mark). Then calculate, for 1 mark, the bonus fraction. Calculating the weighted average number of shares in issue will get you 2 marks as will calculation of EPS and P/E discussion of the significance of P/E ratios and of CB's P/E ratio.

Easy marks. This is a step by step question. No particular marks are any easier to gain than others.

Examiner's comment. The examiner noted that there was a high proportion of correct answers to part a) as it is a standard EPS calculation. However take care when explaining the significance of the P/E ratio. It is not enough simply to say that the P/E ratio is the price divided by the earnings and no marks were awarded for such observations.

(a)   Earnings for year ended 31 Jan 20X5 = $725,000

Weighted average number of shares:

Date	Narrative	Shares	Time	Bonus Fraction	Weighted average
1 Feb 20X4	B/F	3,000,000	× $^1/_{12}$	× $\frac{7.50}{7.30}$	256,849
1 Mar 20X4	Rights issue ($^1/_4$)	750,000			
		3,750,000	× $^{11}/_{12}$		3,437,500
					3,694,349

Earnings per share = $\dfrac{\$725,000}{3,694,349}$ = 19.6 cents

P/E ratio = $\dfrac{625c}{19.6c}$ = 31.9

Working: theoretical ex rights price

	$
4 shares @ $7.50	30.00
$\frac{1}{5}$ share @ $6.50	6.50
	36.50

Theoretical ex rights price = $36.50/5 = $7.30

Bonus fraction = $7.50/$7.30

(b) The price earnings ratio is an **indicator of the stock market's view of a share**. In general terms a high P/E ratio indicates that the stock market views this share favourably and that it is a sound and safe investment. Conversely a low P/E ratio indicates that the market views the investment as more risky and volatile.

CB's P/E ratio is **higher than the industry average**, indicating that the market views the shares in CB fairly favourably and that it is probably a less risky investment than some shares in this sector. CB's principal competitor however has a significantly higher P/E ratio than CB, indicating that the market views the competitor as a better investment than CB.

65 EPS ratio

Text reference. These topics are covered in Chapter 15.

Top tips. Make sure you answer the question asked. In part (b) you are specifically required to address the limitations of EPS for investors comparing the performance of different entities.

Easy marks. A brief explanation for part (a) and a well presented exposition of the limitations in part (b) should gain most the marks.

(a) Earnings per share (EPS) is important because it is used as a **summary measure of an entity's performance** and because it is the **denominator in the P/E ratio** which is accepted as one of the most significant indicators of an entity's prospects.

(b) EPS is calculated by dividing earnings attributable to ordinary shareholders by the number of outstanding ordinary shares.

The **numerator** in the definition of EPS is earnings attributable to shareholders which **can be manipulated** by management.

For example a company may manipulate the timing of payments and receipts and it can therefore affect the earnings figure in a particular year.

Earnings per share may also differ from company to company due to **different accounting policies** in relation to revaluation of assets and depreciation.

Earnings could also be affected by **'one-off' items** that may affect earnings for only one period.

Finally earnings are affected by the capital structure of the company and a change in the capital structure will affect funds attributable to shareholders. It is very difficult to predict future earnings unless one is able to predict the future funding policies of the firm.

The **number of shares** may also change if the company has issued convertible instruments or employee share options that may lead to future dilution of earnings and to a lower EPS.

			Marks
(a)	Performance	1	
	P/E ratio	1	
			2
(b)	Manipulation by management	2	
	Accounting policies	2	
	One-off items	2	
	Change in number of shares	2	
			8
			10

66 AGZ

Text reference. This topic is covered in Chapter 15 of the Study Text.

Top tips. Remember that the bonus shares do not affect earnings, only the number of shares. Remember to take account of the tax, when adjusting for the interest on the convertible bonds. Show full workings to make sure you get full credit for correct methods even if you have made a numerical error at some point.

Easy marks. These are available for Basic Earnings per share, and for the explanation in Part (b).

Examiner's comments. The diluted EPS calculation was reasonably well answered. The answers to the basic EPS were poor. Lack of technical knowledge resulted in candidates time weighting the shares or treating the issue as a rights issue. Even those who had correctly ealt with the bonus issue were unable to articulate why this treatment was appropriate in part (b). A number of candidates only calculated one year's figures, ignoring the request for comparatives to be shown.

(a)   <u>Basic earnings per share</u>

	20X8	20X7
Profits attributable to the ordinary shareholders for the year ending 31 August	$191,400,000	$182,700,000
Number of ordinary shares in issue at 31 August	1,000,000,000	750,000,000

Calculation of Earnings per share

$$20X7 = \frac{182.7}{1,000} = 18.27$$

$$20X8 = \frac{194.0}{1,000} = 19.14$$

In the accounts the EPS for the year ending 31 August 20X7 would have appeared as 24.36c (182.7 ÷ 750)

Diluted earnings per share

To calculate dilute earnings per share we need to adjust both earnings and the number of shares. The adjusted earnings are calculated as:

	20X8	20X7
	$	$
Profits attributable to the ordinary shareholders for the year ending 31 August	191,400,000	182,700,000
Add interest on the convertible bonds	6,300,000	6,200,000
Less tax	(2,000,000)	(1,800,000)
Adjusted earnings	195,700,000	187,100,000

The maximum number of shares that the convertible bond holders will receive is 150,000,000. The fully diluted number of shares will be 1,150,000,000 and the fully diluted EPS will be 17.02c. (20X7: 16.27c).

Basic number of shares	1,000,000,000
Additional shares on conversion	

$$75m \times \frac{200}{100} \qquad = \qquad \underline{150,000,000}$$

$$\underline{1,150,000,000}$$

Fully diluted EPS

20X8	$\dfrac{195,700,000}{1,150,000,000}$	=	17.02¢
20X7	$\dfrac{187,100,000}{1,150,000,000}$	=	16.27¢

(b) Where a company issues new shares by way of a bonus issue during the period, the effect is to increase only the number of shares outstanding. There is no effect on earnings as there is **no flow of funds** as a result of the issue. Consequently the shares are treated as outstanding as if the issue had occurred at the beginning of the earliest period reported. This means that the number of shares outstanding before the issue must be adjusted so that the effect of the bonus issue does not distort any comparison from one period to the next.

67 CSA

Text reference. Earnings per share is covered in chapter 15 of the text.

Top tips When you are asked to calculate basic EPS, the weighted number of equity shares is usually the trickiest calculation so it is important to learn a methodical layout for this so that you can deal with the numbers quickly in the exam.

When you are calculating the diluted EPS, remember to start with the figures you used for the basic version, then adjust them for the effect that the potential shares would have had if they had been converted into equity shares during the year.

Easy marks. The ability to identify the correct figure for earnings and to keep track of the number of shares in issue during the year would gain some marks even if you went wrong on some of the more difficult aspects.

Examiner's comments. Many candidates did not treat the bonus issue correctly and used incorrect fractions to restate the comparative. The diluted calculation was better dealt with and most candidates tried to revise both the numerator and the denominator.

(a) Basic EPS

Profit after tax (1,040 – 270)   770,000

Weighted average number of shares:

Date	Narrative	Shares	Time	Bonus Fraction	Weighted average
1 Jan 20X9	B/F	3,000,000	$\times \,^{4}/_{12}$	$\times \,^{4}/_{3}$	1,333,333
1 May 20X9	Bonus issue 1 for 3	1,000,000			
		4,000,000	$\times \,^{4}/_{12}$		1,333,333
1 Sept 20X9	Issue	2,000,000			
		6,000,000	$\times \,^{4}/_{12}$		2,000,000
					4,666,666

Basic EPS 20X9 (770,000/4,666,666)   16.5 cents per share

Restated basic EPS 20X8   11.6 cents per share

(15.4 × ¾)

To apply the bonus fraction retrospectively, the EPS disclosed in the prior year is multiplied by the reciprocal of the bonus fraction, ie ¾.

(b)   Diluted EPS

Diluted earnings

	$
Basic earnings	770,000
Add: post-tax savings of finance costs (70% x 7% x $4m x 2/12)	32,667
Diluted earnings	802,667

Note (1) As interest is a tax deductible expense, the saving to the company would be net of tax, so 70% of the gross amount.

Note (2) The effect of potential ordinary shares must be time-apportioned if they were issued during the current year as in this example.

Diluted no of shares

	$
Basic weighted average no of shares	4,666,666
On conversion of loan stock (2,400,000 x 2/12)	400,000
	5,066,666

Diluted EPS = $\dfrac{\$802,667}{5,066,666}$ = 15.8 cents per share

(c)   Treatments

A bonus issue **does not raise any new funds**; it is a capitalisation of existing reserves. Therefore the bonus issue has no effect on profit and it is treated as **having applied for the whole year**. The **comparative figure has to be restated** as if the bonus issue had taken effect for the whole of the previous period as well.

In contrast, the issue at full market value **has generated additional funds** which will impact on profit from the date of issue. Therefore, the **weighted average for the full year** is used to calculate basic EPS.

Marking scheme

	Marks
Part (a)	
Calculation of basic EPS	3
Restatement of prior year EPS	1
Part (b)	
Calculation of diluted EPS	3
Part (c)	
1 mark per well-explained point, to a maximum of	3
	10

68 Preparation question: Operating segments

Text reference. Segment reporting is covered in Chapter 16.

Top tips. Segment analysis is very important as it is such a practical skill. The hardest part (usually) is deciding what segments to use.

IFRS 8 requires operating segments to be identified on the basis of internal reports about components of the entity that are regularly reviewed by the chief operating decision maker in order to allocate resources to the segment and assess its performance.

(a)   Ignoring comparative figures, Multitrade group's segment report would look like this.

CLASSES OF BUSINESS

	Group $'000	Division A $'000	Division B $'000	Division C $'000
Revenue				
Total sales	1,200,023	846,071	226,949	127,003
Inter-segment sales	335,962	304,928	31,034	–
Sales to third parties*	864,061	541,143	195,915	127,003
Result				
Segment profit/(loss)	172,818	162,367	18,754	(8,303)
Unallocated corporate expenses**	96,724			
	76,094			
Net interest	10,028			
Profit	66,066			
Assets				
Segment assets	608,823	322,753	80,656	205,414
Unallocated corporate assets	96,871			
Consolidated assets	705,694			

GEOGRAPHICAL SEGMENTS

	Group $'000	Home $'000	Middle East $'000	Pacific fringe $'000	Europe $'000	North America $'000
Revenue						
Sales to third parties*	864,061	57,223	406,082	77,838	195,915	127,003

*   Revenue, profit, net interest and assets should be the same as those shown in the consolidated accounts.

**   Unallocated corporate expenses are those items in the consolidated accounts which cannot reasonably be allocated to any one segment nor does the group wish to apportion them between segments. An example of a common cost is the cost of maintaining the holding company share register, and an example of an unallocated asset might be the head office building.

(b)   **What do we learn** from Multitrade's segment report?

(i)   The relative sizes of each division. Here, A is obviously the most important.

(ii)   The profitability of each division. A has the highest net profit margin and return on capital employed. C is a loss maker.

(iii)   A depends most heavily on inter-segment sales.

(iv)   A high proportion of the group's sales are to areas with a high political risk and nearly 95% are export, exposing it to considerable exchange risks.

What *don't* we learn from the report?

(i) Which division trades in the riskiest areas?

(ii) How old are each division's assets?

(iii) How many staff does each division employ?

(iv) How much of a mark-up do A and B earn on their sales to other divisions?

(v) Which divisions are benefiting from inter-segment purchases at potentially advantageous prices?

As usual with ratio analysis, the information provided in segment reports can only suggest further avenues of enquiry. However, such reports are useful in indicating **which parts of a business are out of step** with the rest in terms of:

(i) Profitability

(ii) Potential for future growth

(iii) Rate of past growth

(iv) Degree of business or economic risk

69 STV

Text references. Segment reporting is covered in Chapter 16 and financial analysis in Chapter 14.

Top tips. You were presented with a segment report on a company that provides haulage and freight services in several countries and required to comment on various aspects of it. Part (a) required a discussion of the reasons for including segment information. Part (b) required an analysis of the company's segment report and Part (c) asked you to bring this into a general discussion of the limitations of segment reporting.

Easy marks. There was plenty of scope for gaining easy marks. Part (a) was straightforward memory work, as, to a less extent, was Part (c). And with the analysis, in Part (b) you can always say something.

Examiner's comment. This was not a popular question. Some candidates produced very good, well-considered and articulate answers. However, many did not allow themselves enough time. Some of the comments were sketchy and unsupported by ratio calculations.

(a) Many entities carry on several classes or different types of business or operate in several geographical areas. Although the purpose of consolidated financial statement is to aggregate all of the information about a group into an understandable form from the perspective of the entire entity, if the financial statements are for a diverse group it is also useful to have disaggregated information in the notes about these different businesses or geographical areas.

To assess risks and returns

In an entity with different products or different geographical areas of operation it is likely that each business or area will have different rates of profitability, different opportunities for growth, different future prospects and different degrees of risk. The overall risks and returns of the entity can only be fully assessed by looking at the individual risks and returns attached to each of these businesses or geographical areas.

To assess past performance and future prospects

Segment reporting should help investors to appreciate the results and financial position of the entity by permitting better understanding of past performance and thus a better assessment of its future prospects. It should also help investors to be aware of the impact that changes in significant components of a business may have on the business as a whole and to assess the risks and returns of the business.

(b)

REPORT

To:	Investor
From:	Accountant
Date:	November 20X5
Subject:	Segment analysis of STV

I have looked at the segment analysis note from STV's financial statements and have made the following analysis of the figures shown which may be of use to you. The detailed calculations upon which this analysis has been based are included in the appendix to this report.

From the segment analysis we can add more information to our overview of the results of the organisation.

Profit margin

The **overall profit margin of the group has increased slightly** from 24% in 20X4 to 25% in 20X5. We can also see that this is **nothing to do with road haulage** as its profit margin has stayed the same but is in fact due to a 2% increase from 31% to 33% for airfreight and the change from an operating loss in 20X4 of 25% for the new secure transport business to an operating profit in 20X5 of 6%.

ROCE

Similarly with return on **capital employed** the overall figure is an increase from 27% in 20X4 in 29% in 20X5. However, this is **solely** due to the performance of the **secure transport activities**. Road haulage shows a slight decrease in ROCE but air freight shows a decrease from 57% to 52%.

Summary

Although the figures for the secure transport business are still small with low profit margins it is clearly improving as the investment in the infrastructure starts to feed through to the profits. However for the other two divisions the position is either only slightly better than last year or worse.

I hope that this additional information has been of use to you.

APPENDIX

Key Ratios

		20X5	*20X4*
Profit margin			
Road haulage	169/653	26%	
	168/642		26%
Air freight	68/208	33%	
	62/199		31%
Secure transport	6/98	6%	
	(16)/63		-25%
Group	243/959	25%	
	214/904		24%
Return on capital employed			
Road haulage	169/(805 – 345)	37%	
	168/(796 – 349)		38%
Air freight	68/(306 – 176)	52%	
	62/(287 – 178)		57%
Secure transport	6/(437 – 197)	2.5%	
	(16)/(422 – 184)		-6.7%
Group	243/(1,548 – 718)	29%	
	214/(1,505 – 711)		27%

Note to appendix. When the group ratios were calculated the figures did not include unallocated expenses or assets/liabilities in order to be able to compare directly with the segmental figures.

(c) Even though segment reporting can be very useful to investors it does also have some limitations.

<u>Defining segments</u>

IFRS 8 *Operating segments,* which replaced IAS 14 *Segmental reporting* with effect from 1 January 2009, does not define segment revenue and expense, segment results or segment assets and liabilities. It does, however, require an explanation of how segment profit or loss, segment assets and segment liabilities are measured for each operating segment.

IFRS 8 requires operating segments to be identified on the basis of internal reports about components of the entity that are regularly reviewed by the chief operating decision maker in order to allocate resources to the segment or assess performance.

Consequently, entities have discretion in determining what is included under segment results, which is limited only by their reporting practices.

Although this should mean that the analysis is comparable over time, it is unlikely to be comparable with that of another business.

<u>Common costs</u>

In many cases it will not be possible to allocate an expense to a segment and therefore they will be shown as unallocated expenses as in STV's segmental analysis. If these unallocated costs are material it can distort the segment results and make comparison with the overall group results misleading. Also if costs are allocated to segments on an arbitrary basis then this can distort the segment results.

<u>Unallocated assets/liabilities</u>

In a similar way to common costs it may be that some of the entity's assets and/or liabilities cannot be allocated to a particular segment and must be shown as unallocated assets/liabilities as in STV. Again this can make the results and comparisons misleading.

<u>Finance costs</u>

Finance is normally raised centrally and allocated to divisions etc as required therefore the normal treatment for finance costs is to show them as an unallocated expense. However if some areas of the business rely more heavily on debt finance than others then this exclusion of finance costs could be misleading.

<u>Tax costs</u>

As with finance costs the effects of tax are normally shown as a total rather than split between the segments. If however a segment had a significantly different tax profile to other segments again this information would be lost.

70 RG

Text reference. This topic is dealt with in Chapter 14 of the text.

Top tips. You could make good use of the reading and planning time here, identifying some of the key points in the scenario and financial statements.

Easy marks. The ratio calculations provide the easiest marks here, as long as you remember to select **relevant** ratios and don't waste too much time over the calculations.

Examiner's comments. Candidates should note that there are no marks for describing what a ratio tells us, eg gearing ratio tells us how reliant the entity is on debt finance – clients are not interested in the ratio definition but what the ratio tells us in the context of the scenario.

(a) Report: To: A. Friend
From: AN. Accountant
Subject: Financial Statements of RG
Date: 10 October 20X9

I have reviewed the financial statements of RG for the financial years 20X8 and 20X9 and the following points cover the key issues relevant to yours the company's performance and position and your decisions in respect of your investment. My comments are supported by a schedule of accounting ratios in Appendix A.

Performance

The year on year decrease in profitability should be considered in the light of RG's particular circumstances.

The overall return on capital employed (ROCE) has decreased from 12.2% to 9.1%. The turnover is virtually unchanged from year to year. But this may not indicate an ongoing trend. The company's current strategies are directed at increasing market share but the results of this strategy were only felt in the last month of the year. If the strategy is successful revenues may increase in future years.

ROCE is the product of asset turnover and the operating profit margin. Part of the strategy has been to invest in new assets so it is worth reviewing the asset turnover ratio to assess how efficiently the company's capital is being used to generate turnover. This shows hardly any change from year to year. Again, if the strategy succeeds, this ratio would be likely to increase and contribute to an improving ROCE in future.

The main reason for the decline in the ROCE is the significant decrease in the operating margin from 14.5% to 10.6%. Clearly, costs have risen in relation to the static turnover, which indicates that some costs may be out of control. This cannot be cost of sales as the gross profit margin has increased slightly. The main increase appears to be in distribution costs as these now represent 9.7 % of turnover, compared with 6.9% in the previous year. The increase may well relate to one-off costs incurred in setting up the new distribution network, so again there is a prospect of improvement in future.

Dividends

RG is currently continuing to pay a substantial dividend, even in its latest financial year when profits are not sufficient to cover the dividend. This could be taken as an indication of the directors' confidence in an upturn in profitability in the next few years but, in any case, RG has substantial distributable reserves so there is a strong likelihood of the generous dividend payout continuing.

Position

It is also worth assessing RG's financial position to determine whether there are any financial pressures that could cast doubt on the company's ability to continue trading.

Looking first at its short-term liquidity, the current ratio shows a small decrease but still appears healthy at 2.4:.1 However, inventory has increased significantly, probably a deliberate strategy as the company gets ready to supply an increasing number of new customers, so the quick ratio (ignoring inventory) maybe more meaningful here. The quick ratio shows a dramatic decrease from 2.11 to 1.14, indicating that RG has very little margin of safety in meeting its short-term liabilities as they fall due. Its working capital ratios show that as well as the current apparent slow movement of inventory, the main problem seems to relate to the time taken to collect trade receivables. Part of the increase in receivables days may relate to the actions being taken to win new customers. Extended credit periods may be used as an incentive to buy from RG. This area needs some attention as RG has very little cash at present to use to settle its payables.

The longer term capital structure of the company could also introduce risks, but the gearing ratio here has decreased to 30%, which would be considered low, and this is backed up by the interest cover ratio sharing that even with declining profitability, RG was easily able to afford its interest commitments. The company has repaid some borrowings during the year. All of this would seem to indicate that RG would be well-placed to raise new barrowings, if this was necessary. The statement of changes in equity also shows that RG raised new equity capital in the year which indicates a level of confidence in its future prospects.

Conclusion

It is important that you do not base any decisions about your investment in RG solely on a year on year decrease in profits. It will be important to consider the future prospects of the business, using information that would appear in narrative reports such as the Operating and Financial Review.

(b)   Segmental information

The aim of segmental information, as required by IFRS 8, is to allow users of financial statements to understand the different business activities carried out by the company. The rates of profit, and risks faced by different activities may be very different.

In the case of RG, the segmental information would let you:

- Identify what proportion of the company is made up by the segment that has received the new investment and the overall impact of the new strategy introduced in that segment

- Calculate ratios such as ROCE and margins by segment

The overall profit may be the net result of some profitable segments plus some loss-making ones. Also, when the different business activities are identified, it is easier to form a judgement as to how the company may be affected by external economic circumstances.

Appendix 1: Ratio calculations

Performance		*20X9*		*20X8*
ROCE		$\dfrac{60-5+6}{515+154} = 9.1\%$		$\dfrac{75+8}{475+205} = 12.2\%$
Operating profit margin		$\dfrac{60-5+6}{576} = 10.6\%$		$\dfrac{75+8}{573} = 14.5\%$
Asset turnover		$\dfrac{576}{515+154} = 0.86$		$\dfrac{573}{475+205} = 0.84$
Gross profit margin		$\dfrac{154}{576} = 26.7\%$		$\dfrac{145}{573} = 25.3\%$
Distribution costs as a percentage of revenue		$\dfrac{56}{576} = 9.7\%$		$\dfrac{40}{573} = 6.9\%$
Liquidity				
Current ratio		$\dfrac{254}{106} = 2.4$		$\dfrac{295}{101} = 2.9$
Quick ratio		$\dfrac{254-133}{106} = 1.14$		$\dfrac{295-82}{101} = 2.11$
Receivables days		$\dfrac{109}{576} \times 365 = 69$ days		$\dfrac{76}{573} \times 365 = 48$ days
Payables days		$\dfrac{91}{422} \times 365 = 79$ days		$\dfrac{87}{428} \times 365 = 74$ days
Inventory days		$\dfrac{133}{422} \times 365 = 115$ days		$\dfrac{82}{428} \times 365 = 70$ days
Gearing (Debt to equity)		$\dfrac{154}{515} = 30\%$		$\dfrac{205}{475} = 43\%$
Interest cover		$\dfrac{60-5+6}{6} = 10.2$ times		$\dfrac{75+8}{8} = 10.4$ times

71 FGH

> **Text reference**. Segment reporting is covered in Chapter 16 of the study text.
>
> **Top tips.** You must read the requirements carefully here and make sure that you answer the specific questions that are asked. This question does not ask you to write out all you know about IFRS 8, or to list out all of its detailed disclosure requirements.
>
> **Easy marks.** If you have a reasonable basic knowledge of IFRS 8, you should be able to make a few obvious points in both parts of this question.
>
> **Examiner's comments.** Part (a) was poorly answered. Few candidates realised that IFRS 8 aims to minimise costs by using information that is already produced for internal purposes. Many candidates ignored the requirement and provided a list of the thresholds and percentages from the standard.
>
> Part (b) was answered well but in part (ii) many candidates again failed to address the specific requirement and wrote about general limitations of financial analysis rather than limitations specific to segment analysis.

(a)

IFRS 8 *Operating Segments* applies to listed entities and does require detailed disclosures of segmental information. The managing director's comment is accurate in that there will be time and cost implications involved in **gaining familiarity with the requirements of the standard** and in preparing the **extra disclosure notes**.

The requirements may be less onerous than the managing director imagines them to be, for a number of reasons:

1. The standard does not prescribe in detail how the segment information is measured, so the directors have some **choice**.

2. The standard defines an operating segment as a component of the entity that engages in business activities and whose operating results are **regularly reviewed by the chief operating decision maker**. Assuming that FGH already prepares information for internal purposes that splits out results and resources between different areas of the business it is likely that the basic information for the IFRS 8 disclosures can be obtained without setting up any new systems.

3. Disclosures are not required for every individual operating segment. The standard sets out **quantitative thresholds** that mean that some smaller segments may be aggregated, so the level of detail required may be less that the managing director expects.

(b)

(i) Relevance to investors

Many large businesses operate in a range of different business sectors and geographical areas. The different activities may produce very different results and the different areas may be subject to very different risks and opportunities. If investors only see the total figures in the financial statements, it is impossible to understand how the different parts of the business are performing.

Information about revenue, expenses, profits or losses, assets and liabilities must be disclosed separately for each segment above the size threshold set out in IFRS 8 (10% or more of total revenue, profit, of all segments not reporting a loss, or assets). At least 75% of total external revenue must be reported by operating segments. Other segments may be aggregated together.

This means that investors will have segment information covering most of the results split out by segment, so they can assess performance using ratios calculated for a specific segment rather than the business as a whole. In this way they can assess the decisions made by management in terms of how resources are allocated to the various activities and obtain a better basis for assessing the future prospects of the business.

(ii) Limitations of operating segment analysis

The main limitation of operating segment analysis when comparing different entities relates to the **comparability** of the information. IFRS 8 gives the directors freedom to **define segments** based on how information is prepared for review by the chief operating decision maker. Different companies operating in similar business sectors could split results in different ways. There is also freedom in terms of how smaller segments could be aggregated together if they are individually below the 10% thresholds.

72 MNO

Briefing paper to the directors of MNO: Operating and Financial Review (OFR)

(a)   Relevant regulatory requirements of an OFR

Increasingly international companies are including a form of Operating and Financial Review (OFR) within their annual financial statements. However, there is currently **no formal regulatory requirement**, either internationally or nationally, to prepare an OFR.

IAS 1 *Presentation of financial statements* encourages the preparation and presentation of a management review in the financial statements that would be likely to cover many of the areas typically covered by an OFR. However, this is not mandatory therefore any disclosure is voluntary. In June 2009 the IASB issued an **exposure draft** on 'Management Commentary' but as yet no standard has been published on the topic.

In the UK there is **no legal requirement** for companies to produce an OFR but for those that do the ASB issued in January 2006 a *Reporting Statement: Operating and Financial Review* but this has no status except as **a source of guidance**.

(b)   Purpose and typical content of an OFR

The overall purpose of an OFR is that it is to provide **forward-looking information**, addressed to and aimed at shareholders in the company, in order to help them to assess the strategies adopted by the company and the potential for those strategies to succeed. The OFR should both **complement and supplement the financial statements**, it should be comprehensive and understandable, balanced and neutral and comparable over time.

The **key elements** of an OFR will tend to be:

(i)   The nature of the business, including a description of the market, competitive and regulatory environment in which the business operates

(ii)   The business's objectives and strategies

(iii) The development and performance of the business both in the current financial year and in the future

(iv)   The resources, principal risks and uncertainties and relationships that may affect the business's long-term value

(v)   The position of the business including a description of the capital structure, treasury policies and objectives and liquidity of the business both currently and in the future

The OFR should also **include information** about:

(i)   Environmental matters

(ii)   The employees

(iii) Social and community issues

(iv)   Details of persons with which the business has contractual arrangements which are essential to the business

(v)   Receipts from and returns to shareholders

(c) Advantages and drawbacks of an OFR

There are a number of **advantages** to MNO of producing an OFR:

(i) The production of an OFR is often viewed favourably by shareholders as a further means of communication and transparency.

(ii) The investment community could perceive MNO as a progressive and forward looking company.

(iii) If a compulsory OFR were to be introduced at some future date by the IASB then MNO would already have the structures and systems in place to report the necessary information.

There are, however, **drawbacks** to producing an OFR.

(i) If a genuinely useful OFR is to be produced then it is likely to require a large amount of management time and therefore be costly to the business.

(ii) There is a risk that users of the financial statements may concentrate only on the rather more user-friendly OFR in preference to the financial statements themselves and therefore not have a clear picture of the position and results of the business.

73 NGO

Text reference. These topics are covered in Chapters 6, 14 and 17 of the text.

Top tips. This question covers a wide range of topics and techniques. You need to read it carefully to identify the most logical approach. Time management is also tested here. Make sure you spread your time over all of the requirements.

Easy marks. Only two marks were available for calculating the revised ratios but logical comments **with reasons** would earn a further three marks in part (b). Part (c) should have been the most straightforward. The convergence project is a regular feature in this exam so you must go into the exam ready to explain some of the key developments there.

Examiner's comments. This question was attempted by so few candidates that it was difficult to observe a pattern. (*BPP note: in the previous syllabus there was an element of choice in the 25 mark questions. If the same style of question came up now you could not avoid it.*) Those that attempted it did in fact answer it very well. The accounting adjustments proved no problem and many were able to display an excellent knowledge of the progress on convergence.

(a) (i) The convertible bonds would be treated as a **compound financial instrument** under IAS 32 *Financial Instruments: Presentation*. It should be separated into its **debt** and **equity** components.

The debt element is recognised as a **liability** and this is measured as the fair value of a similar liability that does not have an associated equity element (such as the right to convert into equity shares). This is done by discounting the cash flows related to the bond to their present value using the market rate of interest (for a similar liability that does not have an associated equity element). This is then deducted from the proceeds and the remaining amount is treated as equity.

Applying this principle to the convertible bond in TRP:

Fair value of equivalent non-convertible debt

	$'000
Present value of principal payable at end of 7 years ($6m × 0.665*)	3,990
Present value of interest annuity payable annually in arrears for 7 years [(4% × $6m) × 5.582*]	1,340
	5,330

* using discount factors from tables

Equity $6m − $5.33m = $0.670m

(ii)   <u>Revised statement of financial position</u>

TRP
STATEMENT OF FINANCIAL POSITION AS AT 31 DECEMBER 20X8

	Original $'000	Adjustment $'000	Revised $'000
Assets			
Non-current assets			
Property, plant and equipment (W1)	8,600	+1,400	10,000
Investment in associate	4,200		4,200
	12,800		14,200
Current assets			
Inventories (W2)	3,300	+300	3,600
Trade receivables	3,100		3,100
Cash at bank	1,200		1,200
	20,400	+1,700	22,100
Equity and liabilities			
Equity			
Share capital ($1 ordinary shares)	8,000		8,000
Other reserves (W3)	500	+670	1,170
Revaluation surplus (W1)	–	+1,400	1,400
Retained earnings (W2)	2,500	+300	2,800
	11,000		13,370
Non-current liabilities			
4% convertible bonds 20Y5 (W3)	6,000	–670	5,330
Current liabilities			
Trade and other payables	3,400		3,400
	20,400	+1,700	22,100

Workings

1   <u>Property, plant and equipment</u>

Group policy is to revalue under IAS 16. Therefore land needs to be increased in value by $1.4m (5.4m – 4.0m). Land is not depreciated, so the only adjustment is:

| DEBIT | Property, plant and equipment | $1,400,000 | |
| CREDIT | Revaluation surplus | | $1,400,000 |

2   <u>Inventories</u>

Under FIFO, inventory valuation would be $3.6m. In the financial statements, inventory is valued at $3.3m under LIFO. Inventories, therefore, need to be increased by $0.3m (3.6 – 3.3), and cost of sales adjusted in the income statement. Closing inventory will increase by $0.3m, so cost of sales will decrease by $0.3m and profit will increase by $0.3m.

The adjustments are:

| DEBIT | Inventory | $300,000 | |
| CREDIT | Retained earnings | | $300,000 |

3   <u>4% Convertible Bonds 20Y5</u>

As calculated in part (a) (i) the equity component is (6,000 – 5,330) = $670,000.

The adjustments are:

| Dr | 4% Convertible bonds 20Y5 | $670,000 | |
| Cr | Other reserves | | $670,000 |

(b) Recalculated ratios

	Previously	Recalculated
Gearing		
$\dfrac{\text{Debt}}{\text{Equity}} = \dfrac{5,330}{13,370}$	54.5%	39.9%
Return on assets		
$\dfrac{\text{PBIT}}{\text{Total assets}} = \dfrac{(1,848 + 300)}{22,100}$	9.1%	9.7%
Basic EPS		
$\dfrac{\text{Profit for year}}{\text{No. of equity shares}} = \dfrac{(1,650 + 300)}{8,000}$	20.6c	24.4c
Current ratio		
$\dfrac{\text{Current assets}}{\text{Current liabilities}} = \dfrac{7,900}{3,400}$	2.2:1	2.3:1

The recalculated ratios show that TRP is doing better than NGO in the following areas:

(i)   Gearing is considerably lower than NGO (39.9% compared to 52.6%). This is due to part of the debt being reclassified as equity.

(ii) Return on assets at 9.7% is better than NGO's 7.9%.

(iii) Current ratio of 2.3:1 is better than NGO's 1.2:1. This is due to the large amount of cash at bank.

The only area where TRP is worse than NGO is earnings per share, where TRP is 24.4c/share compared to NGO's 102.6c/share. We do not have enough information to compare these further.

On the basis of this limited initial review, TRP seems to be a suitable target for acquisition by NGO.

(c)   In October 2002, the IASB reached an agreement with the US's FASB (Financial Accounting Standards Board) (the **'Norwalk' agreement**) to undertake a short-term convergence project aimed at removing a variety of individual differences between US GAAP and International standards.

In March 2003, an 'identical style and wording' approach was agreed for standards issued by FASB and the IASB on joint projects.

FASB also recognised the need to follow a **'principles-based' approach** to standard-setting (as the IASB has always done) in the light of recent corporate failures and scandals which have led to criticism of the 'rules-based' approach.

In October 2004 the IASB and FASB agreed to develop a **common conceptual framework** which would be a significant step towards harmonisation of future standards.

In February 2006, the two Boards signed a **'Memorandum of Understanding'**. This laid down a 'roadmap of convergence' between IFRSs and US GAAP in the period 2006-2008.

The aim was to remove by 2009 the requirement for foreign companies reporting under IFRSs listed on a US stock exchange to have to prepare a reconciliation to US GAAP.

Events moved faster than expected, and in November 2007 the US Securities and Exchange Commission (SEC) decided to allow non-US filers to report under IFRSs for years ended after 15 November 2007 with no reconciliation to US GAAP.

Consultation is also underway on the possibility of the use of IFRSs by US filers. In November 2008, the SEC published a proposal, titled *Roadmap for the Potential Use of Financial Statements Prepared in accordance with International Financial Reporting Standards by U.S. Issuers*. The proposed roadmap sets out milestones that, if achieved, could lead to the adoption of IFRSs in the US in 2014. It also proposes to permit the early adoption of IFRSs from 2010 for some US entities.

Progress has been achieved in the following areas:

(a)   The reconciliation between IFRS and US GAAP for non-US companies listed on the US Stock Exchange is no longer needed. Companies can now file using just IFRS.

(b)   Business combinations are now in line, with the issue of the revised IFRS 3 *Business Combinations* in January 2008.

(c)   The first standard issued as a result of the IASB/FASB project was IFRS 5 *Non-current Assets Held for Sale and Discontinued Operations* (published March 2004).

(d)   IFRS 8 *Operating segments* was issued following a joint project.

> **Top tip**. You were only asked to comment on four areas of convergence. You could also have commented on other areas such as financial instruments, retirement benefits or revenue recognition.

74 Environmental disclosure

> **Text reference.** These topics are covered in Chapter 18.
>
> **Top tips.** Note that the question is asking you to explain the principal arguments *against* voluntary disclosures of their environmental policies, impacts and practices.
>
> **Easy marks**. Identifying and clearly explaining at least four principal arguments should gain you virtually full marks.

The **voluntary** as opposed to the **statutory nature** of **environmental disclosures** presents a number of problems such as:

(a)   Not all entities report **environmental information** which makes the evaluation of their **environmental policies** and impacts difficult

(b)   There is **no consistency** in **reporting practice** and companies may report in a way that shows their environmental policies in a more flattering way.

(c)   The information provided may be unreliable, as environment statements **do not need** to be **audited**.

(d)   There is no provision for companies in more **environmentally damaging industries** to provide more information on their impact on the environment.

(e)   Those companies who in fact **care most** about environmental reporting are likely to **give more details** than those for whom it is not a priority.

(f)   **Competitors** may **exploit honesty** and full disclosure by companies that do report openly on environmental matters.

(g)   Conversely, it may be **assumed** that the companies that give the **most information** on environmental matters are the **most responsible**. This **does not follow**.

Marking scheme

	Marks
For each point raised, 2 marks	10

75 FW

(a)   Briefing paper

From: Assistant to CFO

This briefing paper considers the effect on our key financial ratios of including a provision for $500 million for potential legal costs, fines and compensation. The key ratios for 20X5 both before any provision and after the provision together with the ratios for 20X4 are included as an appendix to this paper.

The effect of making the provision is seen in all of the key financial ratios and **each one shows a poorer position once the provision has been made**. However, in comparison to the 20X4 ratios the return on equity, and return on net assets are only marginally lower than the 20X4 ratios once the provision is made and the level of gearing is only marginally higher than 20X4.

The **main area of damage** to the key financial ratios is in the **operating profit margin** and earnings per share. If the provision is made the operating profit margin falls to 7.7% from 10.1% in 20X4 and earnings per share is just 8.4 cents compared to 12.2 cents in 20X4.

If all the ratios are considered together, **even after making the provision**, it would be clear that **the business is sound and profitable**, particularly if the analysts take into account the reasons for the provision. In fact they may well feel that it is better to be aware of the worst case scenario. However the concern with the public and market perception of the company is that earnings per share in particular is often looked at by investors in isolation and this shows a marked drop of over 31%. When this is taken together with a 24% drop in operating profitability then there is concern that this could have an adverse effect on the market perception of the company.

APPENDIX

Key financial ratios

	20X5 before provision (W)	20X5 after provision (W)	20X4
Return on equity	18.8%	9.9%	24.7%
Return on net assets	21.8%	17.0%	17.7%
Gearing	78.0%	85.5%	82.0%
Operating profit margin	10.2%	7.7%	10.1%
Earnings per share	16.7 cents	8.4 cents	12.2 cents

Workings

	20X5 before provision	20X5 after provision

Return on equity

$$\frac{\text{Profit after tax}}{\text{Average share capital} + \text{reserves}} \times 100$$

$$\frac{1,002}{(4,954 + 5,656)/2} \times 100 \qquad\qquad 18.9\%$$

	20X5 before provision	20X5 after provision

$$\frac{1,002 - 500}{(4,954 + (5,656 - 500))/2} \times 100 \qquad\qquad 9.9\%$$

Return on net assets

$$\frac{\text{Operating profit}}{\text{Average net assets}} \times 100$$

$$\frac{2,080}{(9,016 + 10,066)/2} \times 100 \qquad\qquad 21.8\%$$

$$\frac{2,080 - 500}{(9,016 + (10,066 - 500))/2} \times 100 \qquad\qquad 17.0\%$$

Gearing

$$\frac{\text{Long term loans}}{\text{Share capital} + \text{reserves}} \times 100$$

$$\frac{4,410}{5,656} \times 100 \qquad\qquad 78.0\%$$

$$\frac{4,410}{5,656 - 500} \times 100 \qquad\qquad 85.5\%$$

Operating profit margin

$$\frac{\text{Operating profit}}{\text{Revenue}} \times 100$$

$$\frac{2,080}{20,392} \times 100 \qquad\qquad 10.2\%$$

$$\frac{2,080 - 500}{20,392} \times 100 \qquad\qquad 7.7\%$$

Earnings per share

$$\frac{\text{Profit for the year}}{\text{Number of shares}}$$

$$\frac{1,002}{6,000} \qquad\qquad 16.7 \text{ cents}$$

$$\frac{1,002 - 500}{6,000} \qquad\qquad 8.4 \text{ cents}$$

(b) Advantages of publishing an environmental and social report

Many businesses are reacting to stakeholder information requirements and now providing **additional reporting** within the annual financial statements, in particular in the area of **environmental and social reporting**. The production of such a report would most probably **enhance the reputation** of FW as a good corporate citizen and we would appear to be responding to the needs of our stakeholders. If there is genuine information about our corporate achievements, environmentally and socially, then an environmental and social report would appear to an appropriate document for FW to prepare.

Disadvantages of publishing an environmental and social report

However, there are also **disadvantages** in providing this information and preparing an environmental and social report. Such a report will be a **costly** exercise. It is not something that we are likely to be able to 'pull together' and may not be able to produce it in time to go out with the annual report. The form of the report must be considered and the key performance indicators that would be reported. We may then need to consider our accounting system which may not currently be able to easily produce the figures we need for these performance indicators.

For an environmental and social report to be taken seriously and to reflect well upon the company then it must not be perceived as simply a public relations exercise but a **genuine attempt to provide additional information to users of the reports**. Such a report must also be at least as good as those of our competitors as if it is not then this will disadvantage FW rather than enhancing the company.

In deciding which performance indicators to report regarding environmental and social issues, it must be considered that once reported there will be **expectations** that they will continue to be reported even if the performance indicator in that area declines.

(c)   The three principal sustainability dimensions covered by the GRI's framework of performance indicators are:

(i)   **Economic.** This should include performance indicators to reflect the direct economic impacts of the entity on those with which it deals such as customers and suppliers

(ii)   **Environmental.** This should include performance indicators relating to the environmental impact of the company's operations such as those concerned with emissions, effluents and waste

(iii)   **Social.** This should include performance indicators relating to labour practises, human rights and product responsibility

76 Intellectual capital

Text references. This topic is covered in Chapter 18 of the Study Text, but also draws on your F1 knowledge of intangible assets.

Top tips. This question is fairly open-ended, so you can make a lot of points, provided you back up your arguments. The key point to note is that intellectual assets – in the form of employees – are difficult to control.

Easy marks. This question allows you to earn marks for common sense, as well as technical knowledge.

(a)   A frequent criticism that is levelled against conventional accounting is that the statement of financial position **does not reflect the true value of a business** as it fails to recognise the value of intellectual capital, a wide term which includes a range of intellectual assets such as copyrights, patents, the brain power of a company's workforce, customer relationships, information technology networks and management skills.

The criticism that traditional accounting measures fail to account for the intellectual capital and hence the true value of companies, is evidenced by the growing gap between a company's market value and the value of all its tangible assets which has widened significantly over the last two decades.

Most rapidly growing companies tend to be **knowledge intensive** in the fields of microelectronics, biotechnology, new materials industries and telecommunications.

There are several **potential advantages** to be gained by the recognition of intellectual assets.

(i)   **Improved information to investors and potential investors.** Investors as a stakeholder group comprise both shareholders and other capital contributors such as bondholders. Under the existing reporting system, a typical investor does not receive an accurate picture of a company's true value or the sources of value since a company's investment in intellectual capital such as employee training does not appear in the statement of financial position. Indeed a company that invests in its future may appear undercapitalised.

(ii)   **Improve profitability through better identification of the company's hidden resources** and better management of investment in the company's intellectual capital. Evaluating intellectual capital can help make a company more efficient, profitable and competitive. By identifying and evaluating intellectual capital a company is better able to:

(1)   Asses its ability to achieve its goals
(2)   Plan and fund research and development
(3)   Plan and fund education and training

(iii)   Provide useful information to **employees and future employees.** Better information about skills and human capital would help recruit and retain motivated staff.

(iv)   Provide useful information to **the local community.** The positive contribution made to the economy by a company that invests in intellectual capital would be apparent.

(b)   The principal reasons why IFRS do not currently permit the recognition of intellectual assets on the statement of financial position relate to **proper definition and measurement** of such assets. Defining as well as measuring intellectual capital is fraught with difficulties . A range of intellectual assets such as know-how, the value of the workforce and employee skills are not recognised by IFRS.

The IASB's Framework and IAS 38 *Intangible assets* define an asset as a 'resource controlled by an entity as a result of past events from which future economic benefits will flow to the entity'. IAS 38 *Intangible assets* further defines intangible assets a subset of this group as 'identifiable non-monetary assets without physical substance'.

Not all types of intellectual assets meet the definition of an intangible asset under IAS 38. The three key aspects of the definition are:

(i)   **Identifiability**
(ii) **Control**
(iii) The existence of future **economic benefits**

Even if the above three criteria are met, a further criterion for recognition requires that the cost of the asset can be measured reliably.

The main difficulty with treating know-how and intellectual capital such as employee skills as intangibles is the **uncertainty as to whether the entity can control the benefits**. The problem with recognising human resource related assets in the statement of financial position is that the **employer cannot normally prevent the employee from changing employment** and from other entities obtaining the future benefits. Moreover, even if the employee was bound to stay with the company, the benefit of know-how and skills would be difficult to quantify.

IAS 38 specifically prohibits the recognition of either a highly skilled workforce or specific management know-how to be recognised as an intangible unless it is protected by legal rights and the entity has control over the expected future economic benefits.

In practice, an example of an intangible skill that is recognised, is in football clubs. In a form of human resource accounting, fees paid for the transfer of players are capitalised and amortised over the players' estimated period of service to the club. This is an example where the criteria of **identifiability**, **control**, **future economic benefits** and **reliable measurement** are met.

77 Staff resource

> **Text reference**. This topic is dealt with in Chapter 18 of the text.
>
> **Top tips**. You must take time to read the requirement carefully to identify the tasks you are being set. You should plan your answer using words from the requirement in your headings. This will make sure that your answer is relevant.
>
> **Easy marks**. As long as you had covered this topic in your revision, there were some fairly easy marks available for applying your knowledge of the basic issues, as well as for applying some basic definitions and criteria from the *Framework* that you will have seen in your earlier studies.

Why narrative elements of financial statements are likely to include comments about staff resources being a key asset

In many modern businesses, especially in the services sector, **success is far more dependent on the qualities of the staff resources**, rather than on the amounts invested in property, plant and equipment and inventories that appear on the statement of financial position. As explained below, accounting principles do not allow the recognition of staff resources within the financial statements, so the narrative reports have to be used to inform users of the financial statements about the staff resources of the entity.

Disclosing information about staff resources and related company policies in the areas of recruitment, training and staff welfare in narrative statements such as the management commentary is likely to assist the entity to:

(a) **Motivate employees** as they will feel valued due to their public recognition

(b) **Attract high quality employees** to join an entity where staff feel valued

(c) **Encourage staff retention** and efficient working practices resulting in increased profitability see what the entity is giving back to the local community

(d) **Attract new customers** with a social conscience who value how an entity treats its employees, or who are keen to purchase from a business that has committed and well-trained staff

(e) Allow ethically minded investors to **compare working practices** between different entities

(f) **Improve public relations** with the local community as they will clearly see what the entity is giving back to the local community

(g) **Gain access to preferred suppliers lists**

Issues of recognition preventing assets being recognised in the statement of financial position

In everyday language, employees are often described as being 'assets' of a business. However, the IASB *Framework for the Preparation and Presentation of Financial Statements* has a precise definition of an asset and sets very specific criteria that must be met for an asset to be recognised in the statement of financial position.

The definition of an asset in the *Framework* is:

'A resource controlled by an entity as a result of past events and from which future economic benefits are expected to flow to an entity.'

It can be argued that:

• Staff are a resource

• There has been a past event – the staff were recruited under an employment contract

• Future benefits are expected to flow – staff are expected to generate revenue for the entity either directly or indirectly

But:

• **Control is very hard to prove.** Even though a contract exists, an employee can leave, take time off sick, or not work to the best of their ability.

Also, the recognition criteria from the *Framework* must be met:

• **There must be probable economic benefits** – it is very hard to guarantee benefits from an employee

The asset must be able to be reliably measured – it is very difficult to put an objective value on staff skills.

Therefore as staff skills neither fully meet the definition of an asset nor the *Framework's* recognition criteria, they **should not be recognised as an asset** in the statement of financial position.

Marking scheme

	Marks
1 mark for each relevant point	
Explanation of why the narrative elements include comments about staff resource being a key asset to a maximum of -	6
Issues of recognition	4
	10

78 Service and knowledge

(a)

There are a number of reasons why investors may find that financial statements of entities in the service and knowledge-based sectors are less useful than the financial statements of entities in more traditional areas of business.

(1)   Valuation

In a traditional manufacturing or retail business, investors are used to seeing significant assets in the statement of financial position in the form of **property, plant and equipment and inventories**. This would not equate to the market value of the business but would give some meaningful indication of the worth of the business. In a service or knowledge-based company, there may be very few such assets in the statement of financial position.

(2)   Analysis

Investors are familiar with traditional **profitability and efficiency ratios** such as Return on Assets and Asset Turnover. In a business where the main profit and revenue-generating assets, such as intellectual capital and other intangibles are unlikely to be recognised, these ratios can be meaningless.

(3)   Predictive value

Investors are generally interested in using financial statements as a basis for predictions of the future performance and position of the entity. The incomplete information about assets and the lack of relevance of the main accounting ratios mean that it is more difficult to form these predictions.

It could be argued that most of the same issues arise in using financial statements of any company, given the limitations of historical cost information and traditional ratio analysis. Investors should always read the additional narrative information provided within a company's annual report in order to gain a fuller understanding of its performance and position.

(b)

It is common for company directors to state that the entity regards its human resources as 'assets'. However, for any asset to be recognised in financial statements, it must meet certain criteria laid down in the *Framework for the Preparation and Presentation of Financial Statements.*

The *Framework* defines an **asset** as: a resource **controlled** by an entity as a result of **past events** and from which **future economic benefits** are expected to flow to the entity.

Also, in order to recognise an asset, it must have a cost or value that can be **measured with reliability**.

Applying these criteria to human capital:

Past events can be identified. These could be the recruitment of new staff, or an investment in training existing staff.

Human capital is not **controlled** by an entity. No matter how much an entity may have invested in recruiting and training its employees, they are free to leave.

It is not always clear that there is a direct link between the past events and probable **future benefits.** For example, extra training provided to the salesforce will not necessarily increase future revenue.

It is also not clear how the asset would be **measured**. The amounts paid to employees as salaries are costs that relate to a specific period and must be written of to profit or loss. Other one-off costs, such as training expenses, are unlikely to meet the criteria to be carried as assets. There is no reliable way of estimating future cash flows arising from human capital, so it would not be possible to arrive at a reliable fair value for the assets through the use of discounted cash flows.

The *Framework* criteria make it impossible to recognise human capital as an asset in the statement of financial position.

MOCK EXAMS

220

CIMA – Management Level
Paper F2
Financial Management

Mock Examination 1

Instructions to candidates:

You are allowed three hours to answer this question paper.
In the real exam, you are allowed 20 minutes reading time before the examination begins during which you should read the question paper, and if you wish, highlight and/or make notes on the question paper. However, you will **not** be allowed, **under any circumstances**, to open the answer book and start writing or use your calculator during this reading time.
You are strongly advised to carefully read ALL the question requirements before attempting the question concerned (including all parts and/or sub-questions).
Answer ALL FIVE questions in Section A.
Answer BOTH questions in Section B.

DO NOT OPEN THIS PAPER UNTIL YOU ARE READY TO START UNDER EXAMINATION CONDITIONS

SECTION A – 50 marks

(The indicative time for answering this Section is 90 minutes.)

Answer ALL FIVE questions. You should show your workings as marks are available for the method you use.

---

1 SGB   5/09, amended

SGB prepares its accounts to 31 December. The entity acquired 1,600,000 of the 2,000,000 $1 ordinary shares of FMA in 20X6 for $2,800,000. The retained earnings at the date of acquisition were $1,000,000.

It is group policy to measure non-controlling interests at acquisition at the proportionate share of the fair value of net assets.

The goodwill arising on acquisition suffered impairment in 20X7 and was written down by 20%.

SGB sold 1,000,000 of the shares in FMA for $2,200,000 on 1 October 20X8. The fair value of the remaining shares held by SGB was $1.2m at that date.

The profits of both entities accrue evenly throughout the year. The retained earnings of FMA at 31 December 20X7 were $1,150,000. SGB is charged tax at 30% on profits earned in the period.

The income statements for both entities for the year ended 31 December 20X8 are presented below:

	SGB	FMA
	$'000	£'000
Revenue	8,200	3,600
Cost of sales	(4,300)	(1,900)
Gross profit	3,900	1,700
Distribution costs	(1,200)	(800)
Administrative expenses	(800)	(600)
Profit before tax	1,900	300
Income tax expense	(600)	(100)
Profit for the year	1,300	200

Required

Prepare the consolidated income statement in accordance with IAS 1 (revised) *Presentation of Financial Statements* for the SGB group for the year ended 31 December 20X8.

(Total for Question One = 10 marks)

---

2 GHK   5/09

GHK is preparing its financial statements to 31 January 20X9 in accordance with International Financial Reporting Standards (IFRS). The financial director is querying the treatment of two transactions that occurred during the year.

Property sale

On 1 February 20X8, GHK sold a property to a financial institution for $65 million. The property had originally been purchased in August 20W8 for $60 million and was depreciated at 2% per annum straight line, with a full year's depreciation charge being recorded in the year of purchase and none in the year of sale. The financial accountant has derecognised the property and recorded the subsequent gain on disposal in the income statement for the year ended 31 January 20X9.

Under the terms of the sale agreement GHK has a call option to repurchase the property at any time in the next five years. The repurchase price of $65 million set at the start of the agreement will increase by $2·5 million after the first year and $3 million in the following year. The financial institution can require GHK to repurchase the property on 1 February 20Y1 for $74 million, if GHK fails to exercise the option before that date.

Share issue

GHK issued 10 million $1 cumulative non-redeemable 6% preference shares during the year. The proceeds of the issue were debited to cash and credited to equity. Issue costs paid of $50,000 were debited to share premium and the dividend paid shortly before the year end was debited to retained earnings.

Required

(a) Explain how the sale of property transaction should be treated in accordance with IFRS. Prepare any correcting journal entries that are required to be made to the financial statements for the year to 31 January 20X9 in respect of this sale of property transaction. **(6 marks)**

(b) Explain how the share issue should have been classified in accordance with IAS 32 *Financial instruments: presentation*, and prepare any correcting journal entries that are required to be made to the financial statements for the year to 31 January 20X9 in respect of this share issue transaction.

(4 marks)

(Total for Question Two = 10 marks)

3 FDE
5/09, amended

FDE is finalising its accounts for the year ended 31 March 20X9. FDE operates a defined benefit pension scheme for all its eligible employees. The current service cost of operating the scheme was $7·8 million for the year ended 31 March 20X9. At 31 March 20X8, the fair value of the pension scheme assets was $73 million and the present value of the pension scheme liabilities was $80 million. $8·8 million of unrecognised actuarial losses were brought forward at 1 April 20X8.

FDE made contributions to the scheme in the year of $8·8 million. The expected return on the pension scheme assets is 8·219% and the interest cost for the year is $10·2 million. The pension scheme paid out $4 million in benefits in the year to 31 March 20X9.

FDE adopts IAS 19 *Employee Benefits* and follows the corridor approach in recognising actuarial gains and losses. As at 31 March 20X9, the fair value of pension scheme assets was $84 million and the present value of pension scheme liabilities was $95 million. The average remaining service lives of employees who participate in the scheme is 10 years.

Required

(a) Calculate the expense, in respect of the pension scheme, that FDE will include in its statement of comprehensive income for the year ended 31 March 20X9. **(3 marks)**

(b) Calculate the net pension asset or liability that will appear in the statement of financial position of FDE as at 31 March 20X9. **(5 marks)**

(c) IAS 19 currently permits alternative treatments for actuarial gains or losses. Briefly explain the impact of adopting ONE of these alternative treatments on the financial statements of FDE. **(2 marks)**

(Total for Question Three = 10 marks)

4   JK   5/10

JK is a motor dealership which prepares its financial statements to 30 November. In the year to 30 November 20X9, transactions included the following:

(a)   JK had motor vehicles on its premises that were supplied by a car manufacturer, SB. Trading between JK and SB was subject to a contractual agreement. This agreement stated that JK could hold up to 100 vehicles on its premises although the legal title of the vehicles remained with SB until they were sold by JK to a third party. JK was required to inform SB within 5 working days of any sale, at which time SB would raise an invoice at the price agreed at the original date of delivery. JK had the right to return any vehicle at any time without incurring a penalty. JK was responsible for insuring all the vehicles on its property.

Required

Briefly discuss the economic substance of JK's contractual agreement with SB and explain which entity should recognise the vehicles in inventory during the period that they were held at JK's premises.   **(5 marks)**

(b)   JK granted 1,000 share appreciation rights (SARs) to its 120 employees on 1 December 20X7. To be eligible, employees must remain employed for 3 years from the grant date. The rights must be exercised in December 20Y0. In the year to 30 November 20X8, 12 staff left and a further 15 were expected to leave over the following two years. In the year to 30 November 20X9 8 staff left and a further 10 were expected to leave in the following year. The fair value of each SAR was $15 at 30 November 20X8 and $17 at 30 November 20X9.

Required

Prepare the accounting entries to record, for the year to 30 November 20X9, the expense associated with the SARs.   **(5 marks)**

(Total for Question Four = 10 marks)

5   Convergence update   5/10

You are a trainee accountant with a large accountancy firm and a training day has been organised to update all technical staff on a range of topics across various technical disciplines.

You have been asked to prepare a brief report for inclusion in the course notes which will be distributed to all staff attending the training day. The report is to cover the recent attempts at convergence between IFRS and US GAAP.

Required

Prepare the report, explaining the progress to date of the convergence project. Include four examples of areas of accounting where convergence has been achieved.   **(Total for Question Five = 10 marks)**

SECTION B – 50 marks

(The indicative time for answering this Section is 90 minutes.)

Answer BOTH questions.

| 6 | ELB | 5/09 |

ELB is an entity that manufactures and sells paper and packaging. For the last two years, the directors have pursued an aggressive policy of expansion. They have developed several new products and market share has increased.

ELB is finalising its financial statements for the year ended 31 December 20X8. These will be presented to the Board of Directors at its next meeting, where the results for the year will be reviewed.

The statement of financial position at the year end and its comparative for last year are presented below:

STATEMENT OF FINANCIAL POSITION	20X8		20X7	
	$'000	$'000	$'000	$'000
Assets				
Non-current assets				
Property, plant and equipment	25,930		17,880	
Investments – available for sale	6,200		5,400	
		32,130		23,280
Current assets				
Inventories	4,500		3,600	
Trade receivables	4,300		5,200	
Cash and cash equivalents	–		120	
		8,800		8,920
Total assets		40,930		32,200
Equity and liabilities				
Equity				
Share capital ($1 ordinary shares)	10,000		10,000	
Revaluation reserve (Note 1)	4,200		1,100	
Other reserves (Note 2)	1,800		1,000	
Retained earnings	7,460		4,200	
		23,460		16,300
Non-current liabilities				
Term loan	6,000		6,000	
6% bonds 20Y0 (Note 3)	5,400		5,200	
		11,400		11,200
Current liabilities				
Trade and other payables	5,800		4,700	
Short term borrowings	270		–	
		6,070		4,700
Total equity and liabilities		40,930		32,200

INCOME STATEMENT FOR THE YEAR ENDED 31 DECEMBER	20X8	20X7
	$'000	$'000
Revenue	34,200	28,900
Cost of sales	(24,000)	(20,250)
Gross profit	10,200	8,650
Distribution costs and administrative expenses	(5,120)	(3,300)
Finance costs	(520)	(450)
Profit before tax	4,560	4,900
Income tax expense	(1,300)	(1,400)
Profit for the year	3,260	3,500

Note 1

The movement on the revaluation reserve relates to property, plant and equipment that was revalued in the year.

Note 2

The movement on other reserves relates to the gains made on the available for sale investments.

Note 3

The bonds are repayable on 1 July 20Y0.

As part of their review, the directors will discuss certain key ratios that form part of the banking covenants in respect of the borrowing facilities as well as reviewing the performance in the year. The key ratios for the covenants include:

• Gearing (debt/equity)	target is 50%
• Interest cover	target is 9·5 times
• Current ratio	target is 1·5 : 1
• Quick ratio	target is 1·1 : 1

You are the assistant to the Chief Financial Officer of ELB and you have been asked to perform a preliminary review of, and prepare a commentary on, the year end figures. These comments will form part of the financial presentation to the board.

Required

(a) Calculate the ratios required as part of the review of covenants and any other ratios that are relevant to assess the financial performance and position of ELB. **(8 marks)**

(b) Prepare a report that explains the financial performance and position of ELB for presentation to the Board of Directors, including reference to the banking covenants. **(12 marks)**

(c) Identify, and briefly describe, any other points that should be added to the meeting agenda for the Board of Directors to discuss in respect of the future financing of ELB. **(5 marks)**

(Total for Question Six = 25 marks)

---

7 AC   5/09, amended

AC is a listed entity that has made several investments in recent years, including investments in BD and CF. The financial assistant of AC has prepared the accounts of AC for the year ended 31 December 20X8. The financial assistant is unsure of how the investments should be accounted for and is not sufficiently experienced to prepare the consolidated financial statements for the AC group.

The summarised statements of financial position of AC, BD and CF are given below.

SUMMARISED STATEMENTS OF FINANCIAL POSITION

	AC $'000	BD $'000	CF $'000
Assets			
Non-current assets			
Property, plant and equipment	25,700	28,000	15,000
Investments	34,300	–	–
Current assets	17,000	14,000	6,000
	77,000	42,000	21,000
Equity and liabilities			
Equity			
Share capital ($1 ordinary shares)	30,000	20,000	8,000
Revaluation reserve	3,000	1,000	1,000
Other reserves	1,000	–	–
Retained earnings	22,000	9,000	9,000
	56,000	30,000	18,000
Non-current liabilities	6,000	4,000	–
Current liabilities	15,000	8,000	3,000
	77,000	42,000	21,000

Additional information

1 Investments

AC acquired 14 million $1 ordinary shares in BD on 1 March 20X3 for $18 million. At the date of acquisition BD had retained earnings of $3 million and a balance of $1 million on revaluation reserve.

On 1 July 20X8, AC acquired a further 20% stake in BD for $7 million. BD made profit of $1·6 million in the year to 31 December 20X8 and profits are assumed to accrue evenly throughout the year.

AC acquired 40% of the $1 ordinary share capital of CF on 1 February 20X5 at a cost of $7 million. The retained earnings of CF at the date of acquisition totalled $6 million.

The remaining investment relates to an available for sale investment. The investment has a market value of $2·6 million at 31 December 20X8. The financial assistant was unsure of how this investment should be treated, so the investment is included at its original cost.

2 CF revalued a property during the year resulting in a revaluation gain of $1 million. There were no other revaluations of property, plant and equipment in the year for the other entities in the group. All revaluations to date relate to land, which is not depreciated in accordance with group policy.

3 During the period, AC sold goods to CF with a sales value of $800,000. Half of the goods remain in inventories at the year end. AC made 25% profit margin on all sales to CF.

4 An impairment review was performed on 31 December 20X8 and it was estimated that the investment in the associate (CF) was impaired by 30%.

5 It is group policy to measure non-controlling interests at acquisition at the proportionate share of the fair value of net assets.

Required

(a) Explain how each of the three investments held by AC should be accounted for in the consolidated financial statements. **(5 marks)**

(b) Prepare the consolidated statement of financial position of the AC group as at 31 December 20X8. **(20 marks)**

(Total for Question Seven = 25 marks)

Answers

**DO NOT TURN THIS PAGE UNTIL YOU HAVE
COMPLETED THE MOCK EXAM**

A plan of attack

The exam may look daunting at first. You need to adopt a calm approach. The following plan of attack is just a suggestion.

Part A

Part A is compulsory so you may as well deal with these five ten-mark questions first. This section, in keeping with the style of the real exam, is a combination of discursive and numerical questions. Do not get bogged down in the detail and remember to allow yourself only **90 minutes**, allocating equal time to each question. The first question requires the calculation of the consolidated income statement following a partial disposal. It needed you to time apportion the results prior to and following the change. Question 2 was a straightforward question requiring knowledge of the substance over form and IAS 32 requirements. The third question tested your knowledge of pension accounting. Part (c) was only worth 2 marks, so you could have obtained easy marks here. Question 4 involved two topics. The first was consignment inventory, where the majority of marks could be gained for discussing relevant risks and rewards. The second part required calculations and journal entries for a cash-settled share-based payment. Finally Question 5 was a straightforward question on convergence between IFRS and US GAAP.

Part B

Part B has **two compulsory questions**.

Question 6. This is a good question involving ratios and report writing.

Question 7. This had an easy five marks for knowledge of accounting for investments. The consolidated statement of financial position was fairly straightforward if you worked logically through the information given.

Remember

Always – well nearly always – **allocate your time** according to the marks for the question in total and then according to the parts of the question. The only exception is if the question is compulsory, say in Section A, and you really know nothing about it. You may as well try to pick up marks elsewhere. And **always, always follow the requirements** exactly.

You've got spare time at the end of the exam … ?

If you have allocated your time properly then you **shouldn't have time on your hands** at the end of the exam. But if you find yourself with five or ten minutes to spare, **go back to the questions** that you couldn't do or to **any parts of questions that you didn't finish** because you ran out of time.

Forget about it!

And don't worry if you found the paper difficult. More than likely other candidates will too. If this were the real thing you would need to **forget** the exam the minute you leave the exam hall and **think about the next one**. Or, if it's the last one, **celebrate**!

SECTION A

Question 1

> **Text reference**. This topic is dealt with in Chapter 10 of the text.
>
> **Top tips**. You needed to remember to time apportion the results up to the change in the investment.
>
> **Easy marks**. If you remembered to time apportion the results of the subsidiary, then you could obtain easy marks just by getting the correct figures into the income statement.
>
> **Examiner's comments**. The part disposal was generally well handled. However, some students became confused when calculating the gain for the group and the individual company.

SGB GROUP
CONSOLIDATED INCOME STATEMENT FOR THE YEAR ENDED 31 DECEMBER 20X8

	$'000
Revenue (8,200 + 9/12 × 3,600)	10,900
Cost of sales (4,300 + 9/12 × 1,900)	(5,725)
Gross profit	5,175
Distribution costs (1,200 + 9/12 × 800)	(1,800)
Administrative expenses (800 + 9/12 × 600)	(1,250)
Gain on disposal (W5)	440
Share of profit of associate (W3)	15
Profit before tax	2,580
Income tax expense (W7)	(810)
Profit for the year	1,770
Profit attributable to:	
Owners of the parent (balance)	1,740
Non-controlling interest (W8)	30
	1,770

Workings

1   Timeline

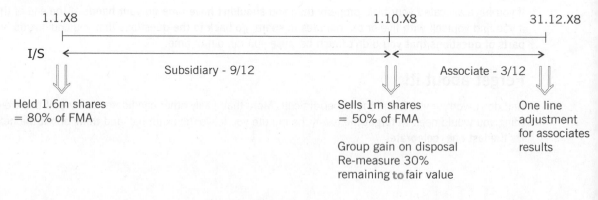

2   Goodwill

	$'000	$'000
Consideration transferred		2,800
Non-controlling interest (20% × 3,000)		600
Net assets acquired:		
Share capital	2,000	
Retained earnings	1,000	
		(3,000)
		400
Impairment written down in 20X7 (20%)		(80)
		320

3 <u>Share of profit of associate</u>

	$'000
FMA's profit after tax (3/12 × 200)	50
Group share (30%)	15

4 <u>FMA's retained earnings at 1.10.X8</u>

	$'000
Retained earnings at 31.12.X7	1,150
Profit to 1.10.X8 (200 × 9/12)	150
Total as at 1.10.X8	1,300

5 <u>Group profit on disposal of FMA</u>

	$'000
Fair value of consideration received	2,200
Fair value of 30% investment retained	1,200
Share of consolidated carrying value when control lost:	
Net assets ((2m + 1.3m (W4)) × 80%)	(2,640)
Goodwill (W2)	(320)
Gain on disposal	440

6 <u>Gain on disposal of shares in SBG's individual statements</u>

	$'000
Fair value of consideration received	2,200
Cost of shares disposed of (50/80 × 2,800)	(1,750)
Gain	450
Tax thereon @ 30%	135

Note: the purpose of this working is to calculate the tax on the gain on disposal as this is always based on **individual company** profits.

7 <u>Income tax expense</u>

	$'000
SBG (600 + 135 (W6))	735
FMA's charge (100 × 9/12)	75
	810

8 <u>Non-controlling interest</u>

	$'000
Profit after tax of subsidiary (9/12 × 200)	150
NCI share (20%)	30

Question 2

Text reference. Substance over form is dealt with in Chapter 1 and financial instruments in Chapter 2 of the text.

Top tips. Both transactions also required the correcting journal entries. So it was essential to know how to apply the theory in practice.

Easy marks. Knowledge of the standards would have enabled you to write something on substance over form and financial instruments in order to pick up some marks. However the majority of the marks were for the journal entries.

Examiner's comments. Although students answered the theory parts extremely well, very few knew how to apply the theory in practice. It is essential to know the correcting journal entries.

(a)   Property sale

The financial institution can **require GHK to repurchase** the property on 1 February 20Y1, **at a set price which may not reflect market value** on that date. Therefore GHK continues to run the risks or gain the rewards of owning the property. So a genuine sale has not taken place.

The substance of the transaction is a **refinancing deal**. In effect, the finance institution has lent GHK $65m. The sale transaction needs to be **reversed** and the **property reinstated** in the books. The $65m needs to be entered in the books as a **liability**. **Depreciation** will need to be charged and the increase in the repurchase price of $2.5m in the first year will need to be recorded as a **finance cost**.

Journal entries required:

(i)   *Reversal of sale*

		$m	$m
Dr	Gain on sale (W1)	17	
Dr	Property, plant and equipment – cost	60	
Cr	Property, plant and equipment – acc depreciation (W1)		12
Cr	Loan liability		65

Working

1   *Gain on sale*

	$m	$m
Sale proceeds		65
Cost of asset	60	
Depreciation to sale (10 × 2% × 60)	(12)	
		(48)
Gain on sale		17

(ii)   *Depreciation charge for year to 31.1.X9*

		$m	$m
Dr	Depreciation charge (60 × 2%)	1.2	
Cr	Property, plant and equipment – accum depreciation		1.2

(iii)   *Finance cost for year to 31.1.X9*

		$m	$m
Dr	Finance cost	2.5	
Cr	Loan liability		2.5

(b)   <u>Share issue</u>

According to IAS 32, the preference shares should be **treated as a loan liability**, not equity. The shares are cumulative so if reserves are insufficient to pay the set dividend in the current year it must be paid in future. In substance the shares behave like debt. The terms of the shares require a set dividend to be paid, which needs to be treated as a **finance cost**. The issue costs must be **deducted from the issue proceeds** and the net amount included as a non-current liability.

(i)   *Issue of preference shares*

		$m	$m
Dr	Share capital	10	
Cr	Share premium		0.05
Cr	Long-term liability (10m – 50k)		9.95

(ii)   *Non-equity dividend*

		$m	$m
Dr	Finance costs (10m × 6%)	0.6	
Cr	Retained earnings		0.6

Question 3

(a)   Charge to statement of comprehensive income

	$m
Service cost	7.8
Interest cost	10.2
Expected return (W3)	(6.0)
	12.0
Actuarial loss (W1)	0.08
	12.08

(b)   Statement of financial position

	$m
PV of defined benefit plan liabilities	95.0
Less FV of defined benefit plan assets	(84.0)
	11.0
Unrecognised actuarial losses (W2)	(9.52)
Net pensions liability	1.48

Workings

1   *Actuarial loss*

The corridor is 10% of the higher of opening plan assets or liabilities.

10% × 80m = $8m

Unrecognised actuarial losses brought forward are $8.8m. So FDE needs to recognise part of the loss.

$$\text{Amount to be recognised} = (8.8 - 8.0)/10$$
$$= 0.08$$

2   *Unrecognised actuarial losses*

	$m
Unrecognised actuarial losses b/f	(8.8)
Actuarial loss on plan liabilities (W3)	(1.0)
Actuarial gain on plan assts (W3)	0.2
Recognised in the period (corridor approach) (W1)	0.08
Unrecognised actuarial losses at 31.03.X9	9.52

3   *Actuarial gains/losses in period*

	Assets $m	Liabilities $m
PV of plan liabilities b/f		(80.0)
FV of plan assets b/f	73.0	
Current service cost		(7.8)
Interest cost		(10.2)
Expected return on plan assets (8.219% × 73)	6.0	
Contributions	8.8	
Benefits paid	(4.0)	4.0
Actuarial gain on plan assets (balance)	0.2	
Actuarial loss on plan liabilities (balance)		(1.0)
Value of assets/liabilities at 31.03.X9	84.00	(95.0)

(c)   IAS 19 treatments

IAS 19 allows **any systematic method** to be adopted if it results in **faster recognition** of actuarial gains and losses. The **same basis** must be applied to **both gains and losses** and **applied consistently** between periods.

The entity can recognise actuarial gains and losses **immediately** in the period in which they arise. The gain or loss does not go through profit or loss but instead is recognised in other comprehensive income.

Question 4

Text reference. Substance over form covered in Chapter 1 of the study text and share-based payment is covered in Chapter 4.

Top tips. When you identify that the scenario involves substance over form, make sure that you use the detail in the scenario and apply your knowledge, rather than repeating general points that you may have learned.

Easy marks. In both parts of this question some easy marks were available for demonstrating that you have some basic knowledge of the relevant accounting standards.

Examiner's comments. Both parts of this question were answered very well. Poorer answers to part (a) repeated the question without relating the points to which party held the risks and rewards. The most common errors in part (b) were not allocating the liability over three years and crediting equity rather than a liability.

(a)   Agreement with SB

The question of whether JK or SB should recognise the inventory depends on which party holds the main **risks and benefits** relating to holding the vehicles.

The **benefits** controlled by JK are:

- The vehicles are stored at its premises and it does not appear that JK can be compelled to return them to SB

- The price charged by the manufacturer is determined at the original delivery date, so JK is **protected from price increases**. It can **return the vehicles at any time**. In addition, JK is only invoiced for the vehicles **once they have been sold**

The **risks** that have been transferred to JK are:

- The cost of **insuring** the vehicles whilst on its property
- Paying the **costs of storage** as it has to keep space available for up to 100 vehicles

JK appears to have many of the risks and benefits of holding inventory but the most significant risk of holding inventory is the risk of **obsolescence or unsaleability**. The fact that this agreement allows JK to return a vehicle at any time without incurring a penalty means that this major risk remains with SB.

SB runs the **major risk of obsolescence** and so the vehicles should be **recognised in SB's inventory** until sale.

(b)   SARs

Under IFRS 2 *Share based payments*, share appreciation rights are initially measured at fair value at the date of the grant and **remeasured to fair value** at the end of each subsequent accounting period. The increase in the **liability** at the end of each period is treated as an **expense** charged to profit or loss. The expense is **spread over the vesting period**.

	$
Year ended 31 December 20X8	
Liability c/d and P/L expense $((120 - 12 - 15) \times 1,000 \times \$15 \times 1/3)$	465,000

	$
Year ended 31 December 20X9	
Liability b/d	465,000
∴ Profit or loss expense	555,000
Liability c/d $((120 - 12 - 8 - 10) \times 1,000 \times \$17 \times 2/3)$	1,020,000

So the expense for the year ended 30 November 20X9 will be $555,000. The accounting entries are:

Dr Income statement	$555,000	
Cr SARs liability (SOFP)		$555,000

Question 5

Text reference. This topic is covered in chapter 17 of the text.

Top tips The convergence project between the IASB and FASB is one of the most commonly tested discussion topics. It is important to learn the basic facts.

Easy marks. This is a very straightforward knowledge-based question, so as long as you had studied the topic, a pass mark should have easily obtainable.

Examiner's comments. Developments in accounting should be easy to study as there are no technical calculations or detailed rules to apply. Prepared candidates sailed through this. Others stumbled, often highlighting the areas that are not yet converged, the opposite of what was required.

Convergence between IFRS and UK GAAP

In October 2002, the IASB reached an agreement with the US's FASB (Financial Accounting Standards Board) (the **'Norwalk' agreement**) to undertake a short-term convergence project aimed at removing a variety of individual differences between US GAAP and International standards.

In March 2003, an 'identical style and wording' approach was agreed for standards issued by FASB and the IASB on joint projects.

FASB also recognised the need to follow a **'principles-based' approach** to standard-setting (as the IASB has always done) in the light of recent corporate failures and scandals which have led to criticism of the 'rules-based' approach.

In October 2004 the IASB and FASB agreed to develop a **common conceptual framework** which would be a significant step towards harmonisation of future standards.

In February 2006, the two Boards signed a **'Memorandum of Understanding'**. This laid down a 'roadmap of convergence' between IFRSs and US GAAP in the period 2006-2008.

The aim was to remove by 2009 the requirement for foreign companies reporting under IFRSs listed on a US stock exchange to have to prepare a reconciliation to US GAAP.

Events moved faster than expected, and in November 2007 the US Securities and Exchange Commission (SEC) decided to allow non-US filers to report under IFRSs for years ended after 15 November 2007 with no reconciliation to US GAAP.

Consultation is also underway on the possibility of the use of IFRSs by US filers. In November 2008, the SEC published a proposal, titled *Roadmap for the Potential Use of Financial Statements Prepared in accordance with International Financial Reporting Standards by U.S. Issuers*. The proposed roadmap sets out milestones that, if achieved, could lead to the adoption of IFRSs in the US in 2014. It also proposes to permit the early adoption of IFRSs from 2010 for some US entities.

Progress has been achieved in the following areas:

(a) The reconciliation between IFRS and US GAAP for non-US companies listed on the US Stock Exchange is no longer needed. Companies can now file using just IFRS.

(b) Business combinations are now in line, with the issue of the revised IFRS 3 *Business Combinations* in January 2008.

(c) The first standard issued as a result of the IASB/FASB project was IFRS 5 *Non-current Assets Held for Sale and Discontinued Operations* (published March 2004).

(d) IFRS 8 *Operating segments* was issued following a joint project.

(Note: you were asked for four areas. You could also have mentioned the revision to IAS 1 *Presentation of financial statements,* the agreement to use common terminology in accounting standards and the joint project to improve the conceptual framework.)

SECTION B

Question 6

Text reference. This topic is covered in chapter 14 of the text.

Top tips. In reports, remember to analyse the data and offer reasoned opinions why the ratios differ from the banking covenants.

Easy marks. Eight marks are available just for calculating the ratios, but remember that the question asks for 'other relevant ratios'. Therefore at last four others are required.

Examiner's comments. Candidates should have highlighted points **relevant to the scenario** (debentures, sales of investments) instead of just making general comments.

(a)   Ratio analysis (Appendix A)

	20X8	20X7
Gearing		
$\dfrac{\text{Debt}}{\text{Equity}}$	$\dfrac{11,400}{23,460} = 48.6\%$	$\dfrac{11,200}{16,300} = 68.7\%$
Interest cover		
$\dfrac{\text{PBIT}}{\text{Interest}}$	$\dfrac{(4,560 + 520)}{520} = 9.8$ times	$\dfrac{(4,900 + 450)}{450} = 11.9$ times
Current ratio		
$\dfrac{\text{Current assets}}{\text{Current liabilities}}$	$\dfrac{8,800}{6,070} = 1.45:1$	$\dfrac{8,920}{4,700} = 1.90:1$
Quick ratio		
$\dfrac{\text{Current assets} - \text{inventories}}{\text{Current liabilities}}$	$\dfrac{4,300}{6,070} = 0.71:1$	$\dfrac{5,320}{4,700} = 1.13:1$
Gross profit margin		
$\dfrac{\text{Gross profit}}{\text{Revenue}}$	$\dfrac{10,200}{34,200} = 29.8\%$	$\dfrac{8,650}{28,900} = 29.9\%$
Profitability		
$\dfrac{\text{Profit for year}}{\text{Revenue}}$	$\dfrac{3,260}{34,200} = 9.5\%$	$\dfrac{3,500}{28,900} = 12.1\%$
Receivables turnover period		
$\dfrac{\text{Receivables}}{\text{Revenue}} \times 365$	$\dfrac{4,300}{34,200} \times 365 = 46$ days	$\dfrac{5,200}{28,900} \times 365 = 66$ days
ROCE		
$\dfrac{\text{PBIT}}{(\text{Equity} + \text{long term debt})}$	$\dfrac{(4,560 + 520)}{(23,460 + 11,400)} = 14.6\%$	$\dfrac{(4,900 + 450)}{(16,300 + 11,200)} = 19.5\%$

(b)   Report to the Board of Directors

This report reviews the financial performance and position of ELB based on the financial statements for the year ended 31 December 20X8 and the ratios included in Appendix A to this report.

Financial performance

Revenue has increased by 18.3% over 20X7 and the gross profit margin has been maintained at 29.8% (29.9% in 20X7). This increase in turnover reflects the aggressive policy of expansion and the fact that the gross profit margin has been maintained means that costs of sales have been closely controlled.

Unfortunately distribution and administrative expenses have increased by 55% over 20X7 and finance costs have increased by 15.6%. This has had an adverse effect on net profit, with profitability dropping from 12.1% in 20X7 to 9.5% in 20X8. It is likely that distribution and administrative expenses have increased so much as part of the expansion policy, with increased need for marketing and new distribution channels to cover increased demand.

Return on capital employed has decreased from 19.5% in 20X7 to 14.6% in 20X8. Once again this is due to decreased net profit and increased capital employed. This ratio will have been affected by the revaluation of property, plant and equipment during the year which accounts for $3.1m of the increase in capital employed.

Interest cover has dropped from 11.9 times in 20X7 to 9.8 times in 20X8. The banking covenants require 9.5 times cover and, although we are still above this figure, the big drop this year is worrying. The bank will be concerned by this together with the falling profitability. Distribution and administrative expenses will need to be kept under strict control in the coming year .

Financial position

Gearing has decreased from 68.7% in 20X7 to 48.6% in 20X8. This means that we are below the 50% target set by the bank. However this ratio is misleading as long-term liabilities have not decreased. The fall in the ratio is due to increased equity, which includes the revaluation of non-current assets. If this increase of $3.1m is removed, the gearing ratio for 20X8 is 56%, which exceeds the banking covenant figure.

The current ratio has dropped from 1.90 to 1.45 this year and the quick ratio from 1.13 to 0.71. This reflects a decrease in cash of $390,000 over the year (with the bank balance going from $120k to an overdraft of $270k). Taken with the fact that the receivables turnover period has decreased from 66 days to 46 days, this implies that customers are being pressed to pay earlier. In contrast, our suppliers are being asked to wait longer to be paid. All this reflects a serious shortage of cash and implies that ELB may be overtrading. As the current and quick ratios are below the banking covenants, it may be that the bank will be unwilling to support us unless prompt action is taken to deal with this.

(c) Agenda points

The following points should be added to the meeting agenda in respect of the future financing of ELB.

- The bonds are repayable in July 20Y0. This is within 2 years from now. We do not have the funds to repay them and we urgently need to secure longer term funding to replace these bonds.

- Working capital. We need to improve working capital in order to continue with the expansion strategy. The bank will be paying particular attention to this. We also need to control receivables and payables better before ELB loses its reputation and damages relationships with customers and suppliers.

- Sell investments. The available for sale investments showed growth of 14.8% over the year. We urgently need to realise this investment to provide an immediate injection of funds.

Question 7

Text reference. This topic is covered in chapters 6 to 10 of the text.

Top tips. Watch out for the increase in investment in BD during the period.

Easy marks. Part (a) on the treatment of the investments represents five easy marks. There were a further seven marks for correctly preparing the basics of the statement of financial position.

Examiner's comments. The biggest challenge was the piecemeal acquisition. Many students wasted time preparing calculations not needed in the answer.

(a)   Investments

    (i)   **BD**

        AC acquired 70% of BD on 1 March 20X3 giving AC control, therefore it needs to be consolidated as a subsidiary. The acquisition of a further 20% during the year does not result in the control boundary being crossed and so this should be treated as a transaction between group shareholders and adjusted in equity.

    (ii)   **CF**

        The 40% investment in CF gives AC significant influence and so CF should be treated as an associate. Its results will be included in the group using equity accounting.

    (iii)   **Remaining investment**

        The remaining investment is an available-for-sale investment and needs to be accounted for under IAS 39. It will be included at fair value in the statement of financial position at the year end, with the gain taken to reserves. (The gain would be recognised in other comprehensive income in the statement of comprehensive income.)

(b)   AC GROUP
    CONSOLIDATED STATEMENT OF FINANCIAL POSITION AS AT 31 DECEMBER 20X8

	$'000	$'000
Non-current assets		
Property, plant and equipment (25,700 + 28,000)		53,700
Goodwill on acquisition (W1)		1,200
Investment in associate (W7)		5,992
Available-for-sale investments (W3)		2,600
		63,492
Current assets (17,000 + 14,000)		31,000
		94,492
Equity and liabilities		
Equity		
Share capital	30,000	
Revaluation surplus (W5)	3,400	
Other reserves (W9)	1,300	
Retained earnings (W4)	23,792	
		58,492
Non-controlling interests (W6)		3,000
Non-current liabilities (6,000 + 4,000)		10,000
Current liabilities (15,000 + 8,000)		23,000
		94,492

Workings

1   Goodwill in BD

	$'000	$'000
Consideration transferred		18,000
Non-controlling interest (30% × 24,000)		7,200
Net assets acquired:		
Share capital	20,000	
Revaluation surplus	1,000	
Retained earnings	3,000	
		(24,000)
		1,200

2   Retained earnings at 1 July 20X8 (BD)

	$'000
Retained earnings at 31 December 20X8	9,000
Less: profit earned for the period 1 July to 31 December 20X8 ($^6/_{12}$ × 1.6m)	(800)
	8,200

3   Investments

	$'000
Investment in BD at cost (18m + 7m)	25,000
Investment in CF at cost	7,000
	32,000
Available-for-sale investments (balance)	2,300
Balance per SOFP	34,300
Market value at 31 December 20X8	2,600
Cost (as above)	(2,300)
Increase credited to other reserves (W9)	300

4   Consolidated retained earnings

	AC $'000	BD 70% $'000	BD 90% $'000	CF $'000
Per question/date of increase in shareholding (W2)	22,000	8,200	9,000	9,000
PUP (W8)	(40)			
Adjustment to equity (W10)	(1,160)			
Pre-acquisition		(3,000)	(8,200)	(6,000)
		5,200	800	3,000

Share of post acquisition reserves:

	$'000
BD (70% × 5,200)	3,640
(90% × 800)	720
CF (40% × 3,000)	1,200
Impairment of associate (W7)	(2,568)
	23,792

5   Revaluation surplus

	AC $'000	BD $'000	CF $'000
Per question	3,000	1,000	1,000
Pre-acquisition		(1,000)	–
		–	1,000
Share of post-acquisition reserve (40% × 1,000)	400		
	3,400		

6   Non-controlling interests (BD)

	$'000
NCI on acquisition (W1)	7,200
NCI share of post-acquisition reserves to 1 July 20X8 (30% × 5,200 (W4))	1,560
	8,760
Decrease in NCI on acquisition of 20% on 1 July 20X8 (8,760 × 20/30)	(5,840)
NCI share of post-acquisition reserves from 1 July to 31 December 20X8 (10% × 800 (W4))	80
	3,000

7   Investment in associate (CF)

	$'000
Consideration transferred	7,000
Share of post-acquisition retained earnings (W4)	1,200
PUP (W8)	(40)
Share of post-acquisition revaluation surplus (W5)	400
	8,560
Impairment (30% × 8,560)	(2,568)
	5,992

8   PUP on sales to associate

		$'000
Profit on goods transferred (800 × 25%)		200
Unrealised (50%)		100
Group share – 40%		40

9   Other reserves

	$'000
AC	1,000
Gain on available-for-sale investment (W3)	300
	1,300

10   Adjustment to equity on acquisition of further stake in BD

	$'000
Consideration paid	(7,000)
Decrease in NCI (W6)	5,840
	(1,160)

CIMA – Management Level
Paper F2
Financial Management

Mock Examination 2

Instructions to candidates:

You are allowed three hours to answer this question paper.
In the real exam, you are allowed 20 minutes reading time before the examination begins during which you should read the question paper, and if you wish, highlight and/or make notes on the question paper. However, you will **not** be allowed, **under any circumstances**, to open the answer book and start writing or use your calculator during this reading time.
You are strongly advised to carefully read ALL the question requirements before attempting the question concerned (including all parts and/or sub-questions).
Answer ALL FIVE questions in Section A.
Answer BOTH questions in Section B.

DO NOT OPEN THIS PAPER UNTIL YOU ARE READY TO START UNDER EXAMINATION CONDITIONS

SECTION A – 50 marks

[Indicative time for answering this Section is 90 minutes]

Answer ALL FIVE questions

---

1 SD   9/11

SD acquired 60% of the 1 million $1 ordinary shares of KL on 1 July 20X0 for $3,250,000 when KL's retained earnings were $2,760,000. The group policy is to measure non-controlling interests at fair value at the date of acquisition. The fair value of non-controlling interests at 1 July 20X0 was $1,960,000. There has been no impairment of goodwill since the date of acquisition.

SD acquired a further 20% of KL's share capital on 1 March 20X1 for $1,000,000.

The retained earnings reported in the financial statements of SD and KL as at 30 June 20X1 are $9,400,000 and $3,400,000 respectively.

KL sold goods for resale to SD with a sales value of $750,000 during the period from 1 March 20X1 to 30 June 20X1. 40% of these goods remain in SD's inventories at the year-end. KL applies a mark-up of 25% on all goods sold.

Profits of both entities can be assumed to accrue evenly throughout the year.

Required:

Calculate the amounts that will appear in the consolidated statement of financial position of the SD Group as at 30 June 20X1 for:

(i)   Goodwill;
(ii)   Consolidated retained earnings; and
(iii)   Non-controlling interests.

(Total = 10 marks)

---

2 VB   9/11

(a)   <u>Financial instruments</u>

VB acquired 40,000 shares in another entity, JK, in March 20X3 for $2.68 per share. The investment was classified as available for sale on initial recognition. The shares were trading at $2.96 per share on 31 July 20X3. Commission of 5% of the value of the transaction is payable on all purchases and disposals of shares.

Required:

(i)   **Prepare** the journal entries to record the initial recognition of this financial asset and its subsequent measurement at 31 July 20X3 in accordance with IAS 39 *Financial Instruments: Recognition and Measurement*.   **(3 marks)**

The directors of VB are concerned about the value of VB's investment in JK and in an attempt to hedge against the risk of a fall in its value, are considering acquiring a derivative contract. The directors wish to use hedge accounting in accordance with IAS 39.

Required:

(ii)   **Discuss** how both the available for sale investment and any associated derivative contract would be subsequently accounted for, assuming that the criteria for hedge accounting were met, in accordance with IAS 39.   **(3 marks)**

(b)   Share options

VB granted share options to its 500 employees on 1 August 20X1. Each employee will receive 1,000 share options provided they continue to work for VB for the four years following the grant date. The fair value of the options at the grant date was $1.30 each. In the year ended 31 July 20X2, 20 employees left and another 50 were expected to leave in the following three years. In the year ended 31 July 20X3, 18 employees left and a further 30 were expected to leave during the next two years.

Required:

Prepare the journal entry to record the charge to VB's income statement for the year ended 31 July 20X3 in respect of the share options, in accordance with IFRS 2 *Share-based Payments*.   **(4 marks)**

(Total = 10 marks)

3   SRT   9/11

SRT is an entity quoted on its local stock exchange which is engaged in environmentally sensitive operations. A number of its competitors provide extensive disclosures in their external reports about their environmental policies, impacts and practices, albeit on a voluntary basis.

Required:

(a)   **Discuss** the pressures for extending the scope of external reports prepared by entities to include voluntary disclosures about their environmental policies, impacts and practices.   **(4 marks)**

(b)   **Discuss** the potential advantages AND disadvantages **to SRT** of providing voluntary environmental disclosures.   **(6 marks)**

(Total = 10 marks)

4   BAQ   9/11

(a)   OVS is a car dealership and prepares its financial statements to 30 June. In the year to 30 June 20X1, it held a number of vehicles at a number of different sites. The vehicles were supplied by GH, a car manufacturer, which is OVS's main supplier. Under the trading terms agreed with GH, OVS is entitled to hold up to a maximum of 1,000 vehicles although legal title remains with GH until the vehicle is sold to a third party. OVS is able to use the cars for demonstration purposes and can relocate the vehicles between sites, provided the mileage on any individual vehicle does not exceed 1,500 miles. Breach of this mileage limit would result in OVS incurring a penalty. OVS has the right to return vehicles at any time within six months of delivery, with no charge. OVS is responsible for insuring all the vehicles on its premises.

Required:

Discuss the economic substance of OVS's trading agreement with GH in respect of the vehicles, concluding which entity should recognise the vehicles as inventory for the period that they are held by OVS.   **(6 marks)**

(b)   OVS is considering acquiring an entity called RT which is based overseas. RT operates car dealerships throughout Eastern Europe and the directors view this entity as an excellent strategic fit with the OVS business model. They are reviewing the financial statements of RT (which are prepared on a historic cost accounting basis), but are aware that RT is currently operating in an economic environment that is subject to high inflation.

Required:

Discuss the potential drawbacks of using RT's financial statements as a basis for making business decisions in times of high inflation.   **(4 marks)**

(Total = 10 marks)

5 Bob

9/11

Bob is a financial analyst whose job is to compare the financial performance of different entities which operate in the same sector, but which may be located at home or overseas. He uses the following four key performance indicators when undertaking this comparison:

- Gross margin
- Profit margin (profit for the year/ revenue)
- P/E ratio
- Return on capital employed

Required:

Discuss, with specific reference to the four ratios above, the extent to which entities within the same business sector can be validly compared with each other. Include in your discussion the limitations of both, same sector and international comparison.

(Total = 10 marks)

SECTION B – 50 marks

[Indicative time for answering this Section is 90 minutes]
Answer BOTH questions

6 AB   9/11

The statement of financial position for the AB Group as at 30 June 20X1 and its comparative for 20X0 are shown below:

	20X1 $000	20X0 $000
ASSETS		
Non-current assets		
Property, plant and equipment	51,100	44,400
Goodwill	8,000	7,200
Investment in associate	24,400	23,400
Held to maturity asset	6,200	6,000
	89,700	81,000
Current assets		
Inventories	34,800	36,000
Receivables	28,200	26,400
Cash and cash equivalents	10,200	12,300
	73,200	74,700
Total assets	162,900	155,700
EQUITY AND LIABILITIES		
Equity attributable to owners of the parent		
Share capital ($1 ordinary shares)	36,000	30,000
Share premium	8,400	-
Revaluation reserve (Note 3)	1,250	-
Retained earnings	21,850	20,100
	67,500	50,100
Non-controlling interests	19,500	18,300
Total equity	87,000	68,400
Non-current liabilities		
Long-term borrowings	41,100	53,400
Provision for deferred tax	900	600
	42,000	54,000
Current liabilities		
Payables	32,100	30,600
Income tax	1,800	2,700
	33,900	33,300
Total liabilities	75,900	87,300
Total equity and liabilities	162,900	155,700

The statement of total comprehensive income for the AB Group for the year ended 30 June 20X1 is shown below:

	$000
Revenue	36,000
Cost of sales	(25,200)
Gross profit	10,800
Distribution costs	(1,200)
Administrative expenses	(3,780)
Investment income (note 4)	320
Finance costs (note 5)	(1,350)
Share of profit of associate	1,500
Profit before tax	6,290
Income tax expense	(1,800)
Profit for the year	4,490

Other comprehensive income:	
Revaluation gain on PPE	1,450
Share of associate's OCI (net of tax)	120
Tax on OCI	(250)
Other comprehensive income for the year	1,320
Total comprehensive income	5,810
Profit for the year attributable to:	
Owners of the parent	3,880
Non-controlling interests	610
	4,490
Total comprehensive income attributable to:	
Owners of the parent	5,130
Non-controlling interests	680
	5,810

Additional information

1.   There were no disposals of property, plant and equipment in the year. Depreciation charged in arriving at profit was $3,100,000.

2.   AB acquired 70% of the ordinary share capital of XY on 1 January 20X1 for a cash consideration of $500,000 plus the issue of 1 million $1 ordinary shares in AB, which had a deemed value of $3.95 per share at the date of acquisition. The fair values of the net assets acquired on 1 January 20X1 were as follows:

	$000
Property, plant and equipment	2,400
Inventories	3,600
Receivables	2,000
Cash and cash equivalents	200
Payables	(3,800)
	4,400

AB made no other purchases or sales of investments in the year. The group policy is to value non-controlling interests at acquisition at its proportionate share of the fair value of the net assets.

3.   The revaluation reserve consists of the revaluation gains of the parent plus the parent's share of its subsidiaries' and associates' revaluation gains, all net of relevant tax.

4.   The held to maturity investment is measured at amortised cost. The investment income included in profit for the year was $320,000. The actual interest received based upon the coupon rate was $120,000.

5.   Finance costs include interest on long-term borrowings. The effective rate equated to the coupon rate and all interest due was paid in the year.

Required:

Prepare the consolidated statement of cash flows for the AB Group for the year ended 30 June 20X1 in accordance with IAS 7 Statement of *Cash Flows*. Use the indirect method for calculating cash flows from operating activities.

(Total = 25 marks)

7 LKJ

LKJ has expanded during the last year and from 1 October 20X0 has been supplying a new range of products, some of which are simply cheaper versions of existing products and some of which are completely new. This has resulted in LKJ increasing its market share and creating a more mixed customer base. The directors have been looking at ways that fixed overheads can be cut and following a review last year, outsourced its payroll requirements, which led to a significant drop in administrative expenses.

In the past, LKJ has been known as a cash-rich business and a regular payer of dividends. However a recent cash shortage meant that a cash dividend was not possible in the year ended 30 April 20X1. Therefore, in lieu of paying a dividend, LKJ made a 1 for 2 bonus issue on 1 January 20X1.

The financial statements of LKJ are provided below:

	20X1 $m	20X0 $m
ASSETS		
Non-current assets		
Property, plant and equipment (Note 1)	554	418
Investment in associate	140	-
Available for sale investments	300	280
	994	698
Current assets		
Inventories	290	130
Receivables	468	263
Cash and cash equivalents	-	144
	758	537
Total assets	1,752	1,235
EQUITY AND LIABILITIES		
Equity		
Share capital ($1 ordinary shares)	300	200
Revaluation reserve	130	64
Other reserves	66	44
Retained earnings	799	739
Total equity	1,295	1,047
Non-current liabilities		
Long term borrowing	200	60
Current liabilities		
Payables	199	128
Short-term borrowings (overdraft)	58	-
	257	128
Total equities		
Total equities and liabilities	457	188
	1,752	1,235

Statement of comprehensive income for the year ended 30 April

	20X1 $m	20X0 $m
Revenue	2,630	2,022
Cost of sales	(2,058)	(1,505)
Gross profit	572	517
Distribution costs	(114)	(163)
Administrative expenses (Note 2)	(288)	(203)
Finance costs	(20)	(6)
Share of profit of associate	80	-
Profit before tax	230	145
Income tax expense	(70)	(63)
Profit for the year	160	82
Other comprehensive income		
Revaluation gain on property, plant and equipment	80	25
Gains on available for sale investments	32	12
Tax effects of other comprehensive income	(24)	(15)
Other comprehensive income for the year, net of tax	88	22
Total comprehensive income	248	104

LKJ has submitted an application for long-term borrowing to the finance company that you work with. You are to prepare a report that analyses the financial performance and position of LKJ for review by your supervisor. Your supervisor encourages his employees to make an initial recommendation as to whether or not the application should be given further consideration.

Required

(a) **Prepare** a report that analyses the financial performance of LKJ for the year ended 30 April 20X1 and its financial position at that date.

(8 marks are available for the calculation of relevant ratios)   **(20 marks)**

(b) (i) **Explain** how the bonus issue in the year will impact the calculation of the earnings per share of LKJ for inclusion in its financial statements for the year ended 30 April 20X1.

(ii) **Calculate** the basic earnings per share for LKJ for the year ended 30 April 20X1 and the comparative figure for 20X0 that would appear in the 20X1 financial statements.

(5 marks)

(Total = 25 marks)

Answers

DO NOT TURN THIS PAGE UNTIL YOU HAVE
COMPLETED THE MOCK EXAM

254

A plan of attack

The exam may look daunting at first. You need to adopt a calm approach. The following plan of attack is just a suggestion.

Part A

Part A is compulsory so you may as well deal with these five first. Do not get bogged down in the detail and remember to allow yourself only **90 minutes**, allocating equal time to each question.

Part B

Part B has **two compulsory questions**. Choose the question that you know most about to answer first.

Question 6. The question required the preparation of a consolidated statement of cash flows. The key to success here is working methodically through the question, and showing clear workings.

Question 7. A financial analysis question which requires both calculations and commentary. You need to use **all** of the information, narrative and numerical, in your analysis. Ratios should be selected carefully to be relevant to your answer. The examiner wants to see that you can explain **why** changes have happened, not just state what has increased or decreased. In part (b) you need to be able to explain the treatment of a bonus issue in an earnings per share calculation and to perform the calculations.

Remember

Always – well nearly always – **allocate your time** according to the marks for the question in total and then according to the parts of the question. The only exception is if the question is compulsory, say in Section A, and you really know nothing about it. You may as well try to pick up marks elsewhere. And **always, always follow the requirements** exactly.

You've got spare time at the end of the exam ... ?

If you have allocated your time properly then you **shouldn't have time on your hands** at the end of the exam. But if you find yourself with five or ten minutes to spare, **go back to the questions** that you couldn't do or to **any parts of questions that you didn't finish** because you ran out of time.

Forget about it!

And don't worry if you found the paper difficult. More than likely other candidates will too. If this were the real thing you would need to **forget** the exam the minute you leave the exam hall and **think about the next one**. Or, if it's the last one, **celebrate**!

SECTION A

Question 1

Text reference. The consolidated statement of financial position is covered in Chapter 7 of the study text and piecemeal acquisitions are covered in Chapter 10.

Top tips. The most important stage in this question is the identification of the group structure and the fact that it changes during the year. You should always take time to draw up a group structure diagram and a timeline. Although the question does not require the complete statement of financial position, you should use the same basic workings and step by step method to arrive at the specific figures required.

Easy marks. Easy marks are available for dealing with the main components of each of the workings.

(i)   Goodwill $1,450,000 (W2)

(ii) Group retained earnings $9,843,999 (W3)

(iii) Non-controlling interests $1,095,999 (W4)

Workings

1   *Group structure*

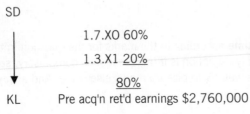

SD

1.7.XO 60%

1.3.X1 <u>20%</u>

<u>80%</u>

KL   Pre acq'n ret'd earnings $2,760,000

Timeline

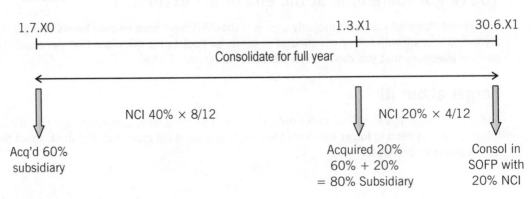

| 1.7.XO | 1.3.X1 | 30.6.X1 |

Consolidate for full year

NCI 40% × 8/12   NCI 20% × 4/12

Acq'd 60%   Acquired 20%   Consol in
subsidiary   60% + 20%   SOFP with
                   = 80% Subsidiary   20% NCI

2   *Goodwill (calculated at date when control was originally obtained)*

	$	$
Consideration transferred		3,250,000
NCI at fair value		1,960,000
Less net assets acquired:		
Share capital	1,000,000	
Pre-acquisition retained earnings	2,760,000	
		(3,760,000)
Goodwill		1,450,000

3   *Consolidated retained earnings*

	SD	KL 60%	KL 80%
	$	$	$
Per question/date of further acquisition	9,400,000	3,186,667	3,400,000
Unrealised profit (W5)			(60,000)
Pre-acq'n/further acquisition retained earnings		(2,760,000)	(3,186,667)
		426,667	153,333
Group share (60% × 426,667)	256,000		
(80%× 153,333)	122,666		
Adjustment to parent's equity (W6)	65,333		
	9,843,999		

KL's retained earnings for the year to 30 June 20X1 (3,400,000 – 2,760,000) = $640,000

KL' retained earnings for the 8 months to 28 February 20X2 (640,000 × 8/12) = $426,667

KL's retained earnings as at 28 February 20X2 (2,760,000 + 426,667 = $3,186,667

4   *Non-controlling interest*

		$
At acquisition		1,960,000
NCI share of post-acq retained earnings to 28 February 20X1	(40% x 426,667 (W3))	170,666
		2,130,666
Decrease in NCI on further acquisition	(20/40 x 2,130,000)	(1,065,333)
NCI share of post-acq retained earnings to 28 February 20X1	(20% x 153,333 (W3))	30,666
		1,095,999

5   *Provision for unrealised profit*

Intragroup sales by KL $750,000

Mark-up $(750,000 \times \dfrac{25}{125}) \times 40\% = \$60,000$ (adjust in KL's retained earnings for the period **after** 1 March 20X1)

6   *Adjustment to parent's equity on acquisition of further 20% of KL*

	$
Fair value of consideration transferred	1,000,000
Decrease in NCI (W4)	(1,065,333)
	(65,333)

Adjustment would be:

	$	$
DR Non-controlling interest	1,065,333	
CR Parent's equity		65,333
CR Cash (consideration)		1,000,000

Question 2

> **Text reference**. Financial instruments are covered in Chapter 2 of the study text and share-based payment is covered in Chapter 4.
>
> **Top tips.** Read the question carefully to make sure the answer the specific requirements Part (a) (i) requires journal entries and part (ii) requires a written explanation. In part (b), only journal entries are required so you should not waste time writing a detailed explanation of the treatment.
>
> **Easy marks.** This is a fairly detailed question but there are some marks available for demonstrating a knowledge of the basics of each of the topics covered.

(a)   (i)   <u>Initial recognition</u>

| DEBIT | Available for sale financial asset | $112,560 | |
| CREDIT | Bank | | $112,560 |

Being the initial recognition of available for sale asset (at fair value, including transaction costs)(W1)

Measurement at 31 July 20X3

| DEBIT | Available for sale financial asset | $5,840 | |
| CREDIT | Other comprehensive income | | $5,840 |

Being the gain on remeasurement of the available for sale financial asset. (The gain will be recognised on other components of equity).

Workings

1   *Fair value March 20X3*

	$
Fair value	
40,000 shares @ $2.68	107,200
Commission (5% × 107,200)	5,360
	112,560

2   *Gain to 31 July 20X3*

	$
Fair value	
40,000 shares @ $2.96	118,400
Previous value	(112,560)
	5,840

(ii)   <u>Fair value hedge</u>

Under the normal rules of IAS 39, the gain or loss on an available for sale financial asset is recognised in **other comprehensive income** and the gain or loss on a derivative is recognised in **profit or loss**.

However, assuming that the derivative meets the criteria to be treated as a hedging instrument, it would be treated as a **fair value hedge**. This means that:

- The gain or loss on the financial asset (the 'hedged item') would be taken to **profit or loss**
- This would be offset by the corresponding loss or gain on the derivative.

This treatment is a fair reflection of the economic substance of the hedging arrangement, where the intention is that the changes in value of the derivative will cancel out the changes in value of the hedged item.

(b)   **Share options**

Journal entries for the year ended 31 July 20X3 are:

| DEBIT | Staff costs | $141,050 | |
| CREDIT | Equity (other reserves) | | $141,050 |

Being the expense for employee share options for the year ended 31 July 20X3.

20X2	$
Equity c/d and P/L expense	
$((500 - 20 - 50) \times 1{,}000 \times \$1.30 \times 1/4)$	139,750

20X3	$
Equity b/d	139,750
∴ Profit or loss expense	141,050
Equity c/d $((500 - 20 - 18 - 30) \times 1{,}000 \times \$1.30 \times 2/4)$	280,800

Question 3

Text reference. Developments in non-financial reporting are covered in Chapter 18 of the study text.

Top tips. A common mistake in this type of question is to rush into writing an answer without analysing the requirements. This topic area is tested regularly but the requirements will vary and only answers that address the specific requirements will score well. Take time to read all of the requirements carefully and plan the points you want to make in each part of the requirements before you start writing.

Easy marks. There are some fairly easy marks available for applying basic knowledge about environmental reporting, as long as you make this relevant to the requirements.

(a)   Pressures to extend the scope of external reports

The annual report produced by an entity is expected to provide useful information for decision making by a wide range of stakeholders. The information within financial statements has a number of **limitations**. It can only include information that can be expressed in **monetary terms**, and its focus is historical and **backward-looking**.

In recent years, the general awareness of the importance of environmental issues and other matters that affect the **sustainability** of businesses has grown. Campaigns by pressure groups have raised the profile of environmental matters in the media and any **publicity** about adverse environmental impacts can have a massively detrimental effect on the **reputation** and **share price** of an entity. Many potential investors now look for entities that appear to have sound environmental and ethical policies, as well as healthy reported profits.

As a result, an increasing number of entities produce reports on their environmental policies, impacts and practices in order to explain to stakeholders the risks that are faced by the business as a result of environmental issues and the policies and actions that are being taken to minimise these. There is no specific accounting standard that requires such a report, so the content and level of detail can be **chosen** by the entity.

As the level of voluntary disclosures increases amongst entities within a particular sector, it can be difficult for an entity to avoid providing this additional information if it wants to maintain its reputation in comparison with its competitors.

(b)   Advantages and disadvantages to SRT

SRT may be more attractive to a wider range of **investors** if it provides voluntary environmental disclosures as investors who follow ethical investment policies may be more inclined to include SRT in their portfolios. This could widen the investor base and help to **sustain the share price** of SRT.

The additional disclosures may also help SRT to gain new **customers**, as many businesses now follow ethical procurement policies and would be more likely to buy from SRT if more information was available about the entity's environmental practices.

The disadvantage of producing this information is that it will require additional staff resource and extra **costs** will be incurred.

An advantage of the disclosures being voluntary is that SRT can select the **level of detail** and the aspects to include in the report.

One disadvantage of this that a report that includes only statements of policies and aims may be seen as being too **superficial**. This could even be seen as detrimental to the reputation of the entity of readers of the information consider it to be little more than a public relations exercise, and may even question whether the entity has something to hide.

If SRT selects issues to include that currently show the entity in a positive light, there will be an expectation that the same issues will be highlighted every year, even when performance in that area has been poor.

Question 4

Text reference. Substance over form is covered in Chapter 1 of the Study Text and issues relating to high inflation are dealt with in Chapter 5.

Top tips. In part (a) you should read the scenario carefully and try to discuss how each fact influences which party holds the benefits and risks. The more of the points you can use in your answer, the better your mark will be, irrespective of your final conclusion on who should recognise the inventories.

Easy marks. In part (a) you can get some easy marks by demonstrating some basic knowledge of issues relevant to a consignment inventory arrangement, but you must relate these to the scenario. In part (b) the marks are easy as long as you have studied this topic.

(a)   Substance of consignment inventory arrangement

The decision as to which party should recognise the inventory depends on the substance of the arrangement, and this in turn depends on which party to the arrangement controls the main **benefits** and is exposed to the main **risks** of the inventory.

The terms of the arrangement suggest that once the vehicles are delivered to OVS, the dealership controls many of the benefits inherent in holding inventory. It can **sell** the vehicles, and is free to **relocate** the vehicles to any of its outlets where the vehicle is most likely to be sold. OVS can also use the vehicles as **demonstrators**, to help persuade customers to purchase the vehicles but there is a **restriction** to this right, as a penalty has to be paid if the mileage limit is exceeded.

The main risks attached to holding inventory are **obsolescence** and costs arising from slow-moving inventories. The main element of this risk appears to remain with GH, as OVS has a **right to return** the vehicles within six months of delivery, so it seems that any vehicles that are hard to sell are likely to be returned to the manufacturer. OVS does suffer part of the risk of **slow-moving inventory** as it is responsible for the **costs of insuring** the vehicles for the time they are held on its premises.

Conclusion

As with many such arrangements, **the risks and benefits do not all rest with one of the parties**. In this case, the key factors seem to be that GH still bears the main risk of obsolescence through the right to return, and that OVS does not have full access to the benefits of the inventory as there is a restriction on the usage of the vehicles. **The most appropriate treatment is for GH to recognise the inventory.**

(b)   Drawbacks of historical cost accounting in high inflation environment

In environments where inflation is high, such as that experienced by RT, historical cost accounting has a number of **weaknesses** that could impair its usefulness for decision making:

(i)   **Mismatch between revenues and costs**

Revenues are stated in **current** terms but costs of goods sold are stated at **historical** amounts. This means that profits are overstated.

(ii)   **Out of date values**

Asset valuations on the statement of financial position will be out of date and **understated**. This means that the statement of financial position does not give a meaningful valuation of the business. The other related effect is that depreciation will be charged only on the historical cost of property, plant and equipment, again resulting in profits being overstated.

The combination of these effects mean that **many key ratios**, which OVS might want to employ in evaluating RT as an acquisition, will be **distorted.** For example, the return on capital employed is likely to be overstated, taking the overstated historical cost profit figure over the understated total capital from the statement of financial position.

Question 5

> **Text reference.** Ratio and trend analysis is covered in Chapter 14 of the study text.
>
> **Top tips.** Analyse the requirement carefully. Once you identify that there are **two** issues to discuss, namely sector comparison and international comparison, and **four** ratios to mention, you should find find it much easier to identify enough points to gain well over the pass mark. In a question like this you must aim to cover a good range of separate points, rather than going into great detail on just one or two points.
>
> **Easy marks.** There are no marks here for calculating or defining ratios, so there are few really straightforward marks to gain. However, if you know the basic ratio calculations and think about any issues that could affect the comparability of the components of the ratios, you should be able to find some ideas.

Limitations of same sector comparison

When analysts compare entities within a sector, there is an assumption that all of the entities share many similarities, but this could be inappropriate. For example, within the clothes retail sector, entities may specialise in a particular area of the market and this will affect ratios such as the **gross profit margin.** A retailer of luxury, designer fashion goods would be expected to have a lower volume of business but to achieve significantly higher gross margins than a high volume, discount clothing retailer. Also, many large entities now operate in a range of business sectors, so a comparison of, say, supermarkets, could risk ignoring facts such as the differing proportions of food sales versus perhaps electrical goods sales within the different entities.

Within the same sector, differences in gross margin may result from the different **sizes** and purchasing power of different companies. Larger companies can benefit from **economies of scale** which can improve their gross margin.

There are features of accounting that can distort comparisons within a sector. Even if all the entities under comparison use IFRS, there are still areas where the standards **permit a choice** of policy or method. If one entity chooses to adopt the **fair value model of IAS 16** and revalues its property, plant and equipment, its profit margin will be lower than that of its competitors who use the historical cost model as its depreciation expense will be higher. Revaluation will also increase the equity total so the **ROCE** of the entity using the fair value model will also be lower.

In addition, IFRS leaves many choices in how costs are classified in the statement of comprehensive income. Different entities may follow different polices in classifying costs into *cost of sales* or *operating expenses* and this could lead to a lack of comparability of **gross profit margins.**

Some of the criteria in IFRS, such as the distinction between operating leases and finance leases mean that entities that lease and use very similar assets could show very different **ROCE** ratios if the leases in one entity fall to be treated as operating leases and in the other as finance leases. Under a finance lease, the asset and corresponding liability are recognised and would increase the total capital employed.

The **profit margin,** using profit for the year, will be affected by finance costs. This could mean that an entity might show a lower ratio than others in its sector purely because it had more debt in its financing structure.

The **P/E ratio** is often viewed as a reliable comparison between companies in a sector. This could also be misleading. The factors already mentioned above could lead to a lack of comparability in the earnings figure taken into the earnings per share calculation, and into the P/E ratio. But the market price that forms part of the ratio will reflect market sentiment about particular companies rather than their actual performance. In general, smaller and newer entities are seen as riskier investments and this may lead to lower P/E ratios.

Limitations of international comparisons

When comparisons involve financial statements prepared in a range of different countries, there are more possible distortions that need to be considered in the analysis. One key issue is that **a significant number of countries have still not adopted IFRS** so it may not be appropriate to assume that accounting policies are similar. Different policies for issues such as **revenue recognition**, **asset valuation**, **share-based payment** etc could make comparisons meaningless for **profit margins and ROCE.**

Different frameworks for tax and other legal matters can have a significant effect on ratios. The **profit margin** using the profit for the year takes an after tax profit figure, where the **rate of tax charged** is likely to have a significant effect. The **profit margin** may also be hit by laws such as a minimum wage.

Different local economic conditions may also affect interest rates, which will also be reflected in the **profit margin**.

The **P/E ratios** based on information from different stock markets may not be comparable. The share prices in smaller, less liquid markets are likely to be lower than those is larger, high-volume markets.

SECTION B

Question 6

> **Text reference.** Consolidated statements of cash flows are covered in Chapter 13 of the study text.
>
> **Top tips.** Statements of cash flows lend themselves to a very methodical technique. You should set up a proforma for your answer then work line by line down the statements of financial position. If the change over the year is clearly a cash flow, then take it straight onto your answer, otherwise open up a working with the opening and closing balances. Do the same with the statement of comprehensive income, then work through the extra information. If anything seems complicated, leave it until the end, and make sure that you get credit for all of the easier parts of the question.
>
> **Easy marks.** Certain aspects appear in every question of this type. If you stick to your methodical technique, you should be able to deal with the common items like the changes in working capital, property, plant and equipment and the main components of other workings like income tax.

AB GROUP CONSOLIDATED STATEMENT OF CASH FLOWS FOR THE YEAR ENDED 30 JUNE 20X1

	$'000	$'000
Cash flows from operating activities		
Profit before taxation	6,290	
Adjustment for		
Depreciation	3,100	
Impairment of goodwill (W2)	570	
Investment income	(320)	
Finance costs	1,350	
Share of associate's profit	(1,500)	
Decrease in trade receivables (W4)	4,800	
Increase in inventories (W4)	200	
Decrease in trade payables (W4)	(2,300)	
Cash generated from operations	12,190	
Interest paid	(1,350)	
Income taxes paid (W9)	(2,650)	
Net cash from operating activities		8,190
Cash flows from investing activities		
Acquisition of subsidiary, net of cash acquired (500 – 200)	(300)	
Purchase of property, plant and equipment (W1)	(5,950)	
Interest received on held to maturity asset	120	
Dividend received from associate (W3)	620	
Net cash used in investing activities		(5,510)
Cash flows from financing activities		
Repayment of interest-bearing borrowings (53,400 – 41,100)	(12,300)	
Proceeds of share issue (W5)	10,450	
Dividends paid to shareholders of the parent (W7)	(2,130)	
Dividends paid to non-controlling interests (W8)	(800)	
Net cash used in financing activities		(4,780)
Net decrease in cash and cash equivalents		(2,100)
Cash and cash equivalents at beginning of period		12,300
Cash and cash equivalents at end of period		10,200

Note. Dividends paid could also be shown under financing activities and dividends paid to non-controlling interest could also be shown under either operating activities or under financing activities.

Workings

1   *Property, plant and equipment*

	$'000
B/f	44,400
Depreciation	(3,100)
Acquisition of subsidiary	2,400
Revaluation	1,450
	45,150
Additions (balancing figure)	5,950
C/f	51,100

PROPERTY, PLANT AND EQUIPMENT

	$'000		$'000
Opening balance	44,400	Depreciation	3,100
Acquisition of subsidiary	2,400		
Revaluation	1,450		
Additions (bal fig)	5,950	Closing balance	51,100
	54,200		54,200

2   *Goodwill*

	$'000
B/f	7,200
Acquisition of subsidiary	1,370
	8,570
Impairment (balancing figure)	(570)
C/f	8,000

GOODWILL

	$'000		$'000
Opening balance	7,200	Impairment (balancing figure)	570
Acquisition of subsidiary	1,370	Closing balance	8,000
	8,570		8,570

Goodwill on acquisition

	$'000	$'000
Consideration transferred		
Cash	500	
Shares (1m × $3.95)	3,950	
		4,450
NCI (30% × 4,400)		1,320
		5,770
Less: fair value of net assets acquired		(4,400)
Goodwill		1,370

3   *Dividends received from associate*

	$'000
B/f	23,400
Share of associate's profit	1,500
Share of associate's other comprehensive income	120
	25,020
Dividends received (balancing figure)	(620)
C/f	24,400

INVESTMENT IN ASSOCIATE

	$'000		$'000
Opening balance	23,400		
Share of associate's profit	1,500	Dividends received (bal. figure)	620
Share of associate's OCI	120	Closing balance	24,400
	25,020		25,020

4   *Inventories, trade receivables and trade payables*

	Inventories	Trade receivables	Trade payables
	$'000	$'000	$'000
B/f	36,000	26,400	30,600
Acquisition of subsidiary	3,600	2,000	3,800
	39,600	28,400	34,400
Increase/(decrease)(balancing figure)	(4,800)	(200)	(2,300)
C/f	34,800	28,200	32,100

5   *Share capital (including share premium)*

	$'000
B/f	30,000
Acquisition of subsidiary (1m × $3.95)	3,950
	33,950
Additions (balancing figure)	10,450
C/f (36,000 + 8,400)	44,400

SHARE CAPITAL (INCLUDING PREMIUM)

	$'000		$'000
		Opening balance	30,000
		Acquisition of subsidiary	3,950
Closing balance (36,000 + 8,400)	44,400	Proceeds of issue for cash (balancing figure)	10,450
	44,400		44,400

6   *Revaluation reserve*

	$'000
B/f	-
Revaluation gain in OCI	1,450
Tax on OCI	(250)
Share of associate's OCI (net of tax)	120
	1,320
NCI share of OCI (balancing figure)*	(70)
C/f	1,250

REVALUATION RESERVE

	$'000		$'000
Tax on OCI	250	Opening balance	-
NCI share of OCI (balancing figure)*	70	Revaluation gain in OCI	1,450
Closing balance	1,250	Share of associate's OCI (net of tax)	120
	1,570		1,570

* The NCI share of the subsidiaries' revaluation gain could also be calculated by comparing the NCI share of total comprehensive income with the NCI share of profit for the year (680 – 610).

7 *Retained earnings*

	$'000
B/f	20,100
Profit attributable to parent	3,880
	23,980
Dividends paid (balancing figure)	(2,130)
C/f	21,850

RETAINED EARNINGS

	$'000		$'000
Dividends paid (balancing figure)	2,130	Opening balance	20,100
Closing balance	21,850	Profit attributable to parent	3,880
	23,980		23,980

8 *Dividends paid to non-controlling interests*

	$'000
B/f	18,300
Total comprehensive income attributable to NCI	680
Acquisition of subsidiary (W2)	1,320
	20,300
Dividends paid (balancing figure)	(800)
C/f	19,500

NON-CONTROLLING INTEREST

	$'000		$'000
Cash paid (bal fig)	800	Opening balance	18,300
		Acquisition of subsidiary (W2)	1,320
Closing balance	19,500	NCI share of TCI	680
	20,300		20,300

9 *Income taxes paid*

	$'000
B/f (600 + 2,700)	3,300
IT expense – P/L	1,800
Tax on OCI	250
	5,350
Tax paid (balancing figure)	(2,650)
C/f (900 + 1,800)	2,700

INCOME TAXES PAYABLE

	$'000		$'000
Cash paid (bal fig)	2,650	Opening balance – deferred tax	600
		– current tax	2,700
Closing balance – deferred tax	900	IT expense – P/L	1,800
– current tax	1,800	Tax on OCI	250
	5,350		5,350

Question 7

(a)   Report to: Supervisor

Date: X/X/XX

Subject: Analysis of LKJ

Financial analysis

<u>Performance</u>

The overall **return on capital employed** has fallen from 13.6% to 12.0% from year to year. This needs to be considered in the light of LKJ's policy of revaluing its property, plant and equipment, which is likely to keep increasing the capital figure each year, and increasing the depreciation expense, and both of these effects will tend to depress the ROCE.

Another factor relevant to this is that the new investments in non-current assets and inventories related to the expansion of the business may not have been made until part way through the year to 30 April 20X1 so the return generated on these assets may improve in future years.

A closer analysis of LKJ's performance gives a more positive picture of the entity's performance and the management decisions that influenced it.

The **expansion** strategy followed by management during the year has succeeded in increasing revenues. The increased market share that has been achieved by moving into cheaper products has decreased the rate of gross profit margin achieved from 25.6% to 21.7% but the increased sales volumes mean that the absolute amount of gross profit achieved has improved.

As well as the efforts to gain market share, management has also focused on **controlling costs**. The decision to outsource the payroll function has contributed to administrative expenses being only 4.1% of revenue, compared to 8.1% in the previous year. Distribution costs show a slight increase in proportion to sales but this is unlikely to be a result of poor cost control. It is more likely to be the result of a change in the customer base, or to outside factors such as fuel costs.

LKJ made **an investment in an associate** during the year. This has already contributed a substantial **return**. The investment may also have been made in order to give LKJ significant **influence** over another entity that is critical to its operations, perhaps a supplier of some of its inventories.

LKJ has a policy of carrying its property, plant and equipment at **fair value** and this has produced a gain in the current year. It also owns some available for sale investments, which have also produced gains in the year. These gains help to strengthen the entity's financial position and give a better indication of the value of assets that could provide security for any further borrowings.

<u>Position</u>

LKJ is clearly facing pressures in the area of **short-term liquidity**. From being a cash-rich business, it now finds itself with a substantial overdraft and has had to substitute a bonus issue for the usual dividend payment.

The overall **current ratio** has deteriorated from 4.2 to 2.9, and the quick ratio also shows a similar deterioration. The ratios for 20X1 still show that the company has some margin of safety before it reaches the point of being unable to meet its liabilities.

The average **inventory holding period** has increased significantly, although the period for 20X1, of 51 days, does not appear to be excessive. This may well be related to the change of product mix and the expansion and simply indicate that LKJ has invested in large quantities of the new product lines. Alternatively, the company may still be holding quantities of its older products that cannot be sold easily and these may be overvalued.

The **receivables collection period** has also increased from 47 days to 65 days. The new customer base could be the reason for this. There is a risk that the customers now buying the new, cheaper products, are potentially less credit-worthy. It may be that LKJ has offered extended credit terms in order to win new customers and if this is the case, the policy may need to be reviewed if there appears to be difficulty in collecting receivables.

Despite the pressure on its cash flow, LKJ is continuing to pay its suppliers reasonably promptly, although the payment period has increased slightly from the previous year.

In terms of its long term **gearing**, new borrowings were raised in the current year in order to invest in property, plant and equipment and inventories as part of the expansion of the business. Despite this, the debt/equity ratio is still fairly low at 19.9%, even though this is a significant increase over the previous year. It appears that the entity could support additional borrowings and this is backed up by the interest cover ratio. The interest cover ratio of 8.5 in 20X1 shows a significant decrease over the previous year, but assuming that its overall profitability can be maintained, LKJ could afford to pay the additional interest on a higher level of borrowings.

<u>Recommendation</u>

Based on this initial review, I would recommend that LKJ's application for long-term borrowing should be given further consideration as it appears to be a well-managed business that is putting into place an expansion plan that already appears to be producing positive results. Management appear to take a responsible view, paying suppliers promptly, and making the wise decision to avoid paying a cash dividend when the cash flow is under pressure.

<u>Appendix: Financial ratios</u>

(**Note:** only 8 ratios should be calculated for the mark allocation, more are illustrated in this answer.)

		20X1	20X0
Performance			
Gross profit margin	572/2,630	21.7%	
	517/2,022		25.6%
Profit margin (using profit for the year)	160/2,630	6.1%	
	82/2,022		4.1%
Operating profit margin *(note 1)*	170/2,630	6.5%	
	151/2,022		7.5%
Return on capital employed *(note 2)*	170/1,413	12.0%	
	151/1,107		13.6%
Administrative expenses/revenue	114/2,630	4.3%	
	163/2,022		8.1%
Distribution costs/revenue	288/2,630	11%	
	203/2,022		10%
Position			
Current ratio	758/257	2.9	
	537/128		4.2
Quick ratio	468/257	1.8	
	407/128		3.2

Inventories holding period	290/2,058 × 365	51 days	
	130/1,505 × 365		32 days
Payables payment period	199/2,058 × 365	35 days	
	128/1,505 × 365		31 days
Receivables collection period	468/2,630 × 365	65 days	
	263/2,022 × 365		47 days
Gearing (debt/equity)	(58+200)/1,295	19.9%	
	60/1,047		5.7%
Interest cover (op.profit *(note1)*/finance cost)	170/20	8.5 times	
	151/6		25.2 times

Notes

(1) Operating profit is taken as profit before interest and the share of the associate's profit.

(2) Capital employed is the total of equity plus long and short-term borrowings net of investments.

(b)   (i) Bonus issue and EPS

A bonus issue is a change in share capital that does not bring any extra resources into the company. If no adjustments were made, any comparison of EPS before and after the bonus issue would be misleading. In order to produce a meaningful comparison, the effect of the bonus issue is applied retrospectively. The increase in the number of shares as a result of the bonus issue will be treated as if it had occurred at the start of the year to 30 April 20X1. The comparative shown for the year to 30 April 20X0 will also be restated for the effect of the bonus issue.

(ii) Basic EPS for the year to 30 April 20X1

$$\frac{\$160,000,000}{300,000,000} = 53.3 \text{ cents}$$

Comparative for the year to 30 April 20X0

Originally $\dfrac{\$82,000,000}{200,000,000} = 41.0$ cents

Restated as (multiplied by the inverse of the bonus fraction) 41.0 × 2/3 = 27.3 cents

CIMA – Management Level
Paper F2
Financial Management

Mock Examination 3

Instructions to candidates:

You are allowed three hours to answer this question paper.
In the real exam, you are allowed 20 minutes reading time before the examination begins during which you should read the question paper, and if you wish, highlight and/or make notes on the question paper. However, you will **not** be allowed, **under any circumstances**, to open the answer book and start writing or use your calculator during this reading time.
You are strongly advised to carefully read ALL the question requirements before attempting the question concerned (including all parts and/or sub-questions).
Answer ALL FIVE questions in Section A.
Answer BOTH questions in Section B.

DO NOT OPEN THIS PAPER UNTIL YOU ARE READY TO START UNDER EXAMINATION CONDITIONS

SECTION A – 50 MARKS

[You are advised to spend no longer than 18 minutes on each question in this section.]

ANSWER *ALL* FIVE QUESTIONS IN THIS SECTION

Question One

BG acquired 25% of the equity share capital of JV several years ago when the retained earnings of JV were $40,000. JV operates as a separate entity under a contractual agreement between BG and 3 other parties, each party holding an equal proportion of the equity share capital. The investment in JV is held at cost in BG's individual financial statements, and has been correctly classified as a joint venture.

Statement of financial position as at 31 March 2011	BG $000	JV $000
ASSETS		
Non-current assets		
Property, plant and equipment	322	280
Investment in JV	70	-
	392	280
Current assets		
Inventories	111	120
Receivables	115	132
Held for trading investment	35	-
Cash and cash equivalents	21	40
	282	292
Total assets	674	572
EQUITY AND LIABILITIES		
Equity attributable to owners of the parent		
Share capital ($1 shares)	120	200
Revaluation reserve	18	-
Retained earnings	213	120
Total equity	351	320
Non-current liabilities		
Long term borrowings	90	-
Current liabilities		
Payables	185	160
Income tax payable	48	92
	233	252
Total liabilities	323	252
Total equity and liabilities	674	572

Additional information:

1. During the year JV sold goods to BG for $200,000. Half of these goods remain in BG's inventories at 31 March 2011. JV makes a 20% margin on all sales. The most recent invoice for $24,000 sent from JV to BG in respect of these sales remains outstanding at the year end.

2. BG holds another investment, which it has correctly classified as held for trading. The fair value of this investment at 31 March 2011 was $42,000, although this has not yet been reflected in the financial statements.

Required:

(a) **Prepare** the consolidated statement of financial position for the BG group as at 31 March 2011, assuming BG group adopts proportionate consolidation in accounting for joint ventures.

(7 marks)

(b) **Explain** the alternative accounting treatment permitted by IAS 31 *Interests in Joint Ventures* in accounting for joint venture entities AND how adopting this policy would change the BG group's statement of financial position (no further calculations are required).

(3 marks)

(Total for Question One = 10 marks)

Question Two

DRT has entered into the following agreements in the year to 31 May 2011:

Sale of land

On 31 May 2011 DRT sold land to NKL, an entity that provides DRT with long-term finance. The sale price was $1,600,000 and the carrying value of the land on the date of the sale was $1,310,000 (the original cost of the asset). Under the terms of the sale agreement DRT has the option to repurchase the land within the next four years for between $1,660,000 and $1,800,000 depending on the date of repurchase. NKL cannot use the land for any purpose without the prior consent of DRT. The land must be repurchased for $1,800,000 at the end of the four year period if the option is not exercised before that time.

DRT has derecognised the land and recorded the subsequent gain within profit for the year ended 31 May 2011.

Required:

(a) **Discuss** how the sale of the land should be accounted for in accordance with the principles of IAS 18 *Revenue* and the *Framework for Preparation and Presentation of Financial Statements* AND prepare any accounting adjustments required to DRT's financial statements for the year to 31 May 2011.

(5 marks)

Set-up of payroll services entity, GHJ

Until 1 January 2011, DRT operated a payroll services division providing payroll services for itself and also for a number of external customers. On 1 January 2011 the business of the division and assets with a value of $300,000 were transferred into a separate entity called GHJ, which was set up by DRT. The sales director of GHJ owns 100% of its equity share capital. A contractual agreement signed by both the sales director of GHJ and a director of DRT, states that the operating and financial policies of GHJ will be made by the board of DRT. GHJ has acquired a long-term loan of $1 million with DRT acting as guarantor. Profits and losses of GHJ, after deduction of the sales director's salary, flow to DRT. The directors of DRT wish to avoid consolidating GHJ as the additional borrowings of GHJ would negatively impact DRT's gearing ratio.

Required:

(b) **Discuss** how the relationship with GHJ should be reflected in the financial statements of the DRT group. Your answer should make reference to any relevant international accounting standards.

(5 marks)

(Total for Question Two = 10 marks)

Question Three

On 1 July 2010 BNM, a listed entity, had 5,000,000 $1 ordinary shares in issue. On 1 September 2010, BNM made a 1 for 2 bonus issue from retained earnings. On 1 February 2011 BNM issued 3,000,000 $1 ordinary shares for $4.10 each, which was their full market price.

BNM generated profit after tax of $3.8m for the year ended 30 June 2011.

The basic earnings per share for the year ended 30 June 2010 was 48.2 cents.

At 1 July 2010 the ordinary shareholders of BNM held options to purchase 1,000,000 $1 ordinary shares at $3.10 per share. The options are exercisable between 1 July 2012 and 30 June 2014. No further options were issued in the year. The average market value of one $1 ordinary share of BNM during the year ended 30 June 2011 was $4.00.

Required:

(a) **Calculate** the basic earnings per share to be reported in the financial statements of BNM for the year ended 30 June 2011, including the comparative figure, in accordance with the requirements of IAS 33 *Earnings Per Share*.

(5 marks)

(b) **Calculate** the diluted earnings per share for the year ended 30 June 2011, in accordance with the requirements of IAS 33 *Earnings Per Share*. (A comparative figure is NOT required).

(3 marks)

(c) **Explain** why it is important for users to have diluted earnings per share presented in the financial statements.

(2 marks)

(Total for Question Three = 10 marks)

Question Four

Financial Instrument

QWS issued a redeemable debt instrument on 1 July 2009 at its par value of $6 million. The instrument carries a fixed coupon interest rate of 6%, which is payable annually in arrears. The debt instrument will be redeemed for $6.02 million on 30 June 2013. Transaction costs associated with the issue were $200,000 and were paid at the time of issue. The effective interest rate applicable to this liability is approximately 7.06%.

> *Required:*
>
> (i) **Explain** how this instrument will be initially and subsequently measured.
>
> (ii) **Calculate** the carrying value of the liability to be included in QWS's statement of financial position as at 30 June 2011. (Round all workings to the nearest $000)
>
> *(5 marks)*

Pension plan

QWS operates a defined benefit pension plan for its employees. At 1 July 2010 the fair value of the pension plan assets was $1,200,000 and the present value of the plan liabilities was $1,400,000. The interest cost on the plan liabilities was estimated at 7% and the expected return on plan assets at 4%.

The actuary estimates that the current service cost for the year ended 30 June 2011 is $300,000. QWS made contributions into the pension plan of $400,000 in the year.

The pension plan paid $220,000 to retired members in the year to 30 June 2011.

At 30 June 2011 the fair value of the pension plan assets was $1,400,000 and the present value of the plan liabilities was $1,600,000.

In accordance with the amendment to IAS 19 *Employee Benefits*, QWS recognises actuarial gains and losses in other comprehensive income in the period in which they occur.

> *Required:*
>
> **Calculate** the net expense that will be included in QWS's profit or loss AND the amounts that would be included in other comprehensive income in respect of actuarial gains or losses for the year ended 30 June 2011. (Round all workings to the nearest $000)
>
> *(5 marks)*
>
> *(Total for Question Four = 10 marks)*

Question Five

The Financial Accounting Standards Board, the main standard-setting body in the USA, and the International Accounting Standards Board agreed, at their Norwalk meeting in 2002, to work towards making their existing and future financial reporting standards fully compatible.

Required:

(a) **Discuss** the progress made towards convergence, including how this has been achieved.

(6 marks)

(b) **Discuss** the benefits of convergence to BOTH investors and accounting students.

(4 marks)

(Total for Question Five = 10 marks)

(Total for Section A = 50 marks)

SECTION B – 50 MARKS

[You are advised to spend no longer than 45 minutes on each question in this section.]

ANSWER BOTH QUESTIONS IN THIS SECTION – 25 MARKS EACH

Question Six

The statements of comprehensive income for three entities for the year ended 31 March 2011 are presented below:

	BH $000	NJ $000	MK $000
Revenue	3,360	3,240	2,390
Cost of sales	(1,800)	(1,860)	(1,380)
Gross profit	1,560	1,380	1,010
Administrative expenses	(380)	(340)	(250)
Distribution costs	(400)	(300)	(150)
Investment income	80	-	-
Finance costs	(180)	(140)	(110)
Profit before tax	680	600	500
Income tax expense	(200)	(160)	(150)
Profit for the year	480	440	350
Other comprehensive income			
Revaluation of property, plant and equipment	70	40	30
Gains on investments in NJ and MK	96	-	-
Tax effect of OCI	(50)	(16)	(10)
Other comprehensive income for the year, net of tax	116	24	20
Total comprehensive income for the year	596	464	370

Additional information:

1. BH acquired a 25% investment in NJ on 1 September 2002 for $300,000. The investment was classified as available for sale and the gains earned on it have been recorded within other comprehensive income in BH's individual financial statements. The fair value of the 25% investment at 31 March 2010 was $400,000 and at 1 January 2011 was $425,000. BH was not able to exercise significant influence over the financial and operating policies of NJ.

    On 1 January 2011, BH acquired an additional 40% of the 1 million $1 equity shares of NJ for $680,000. The retained reserves of NJ at that date were $526,000. The group policy is to value the non-controlling interest at its fair value at the date of acquisition. The non-controlling interest had a fair value of $581,000 at 1 January 2011. NJ lost a key customer in February and BH's directors have decided that goodwill on acquisition is impaired by 10% at 31 March 2011. Impairment losses are charged to group administrative expenses.

    The investment in NJ continues to be held as an available for sale asset in BH's individual financial statements and recorded at its fair value of $1,170,000 at 31 March 2011. The total gains recorded to date in respect of NJ are $190,000, of which $90,000 occurred in the year and are included in the other comprehensive income of BH.

2.   BH acquired 40% of the equity share capital of MK for $334,000 on 1 October 2010. The investment was classified as available for sale and the gains earned on it since its acquisition have been recorded within other comprehensive income in the year in BH's individual financial statements. The fair value of this available for sale asset at 31 March 2011 was $340,000. BH exercises significant influence over the financial and operating policies of MK.

A new competitor has recently entered the market in which MK operates and it is likely that this will have an immediate impact on MK's profits in the coming period. As a result, the directors of BH have decided that the investment in MK should be subject to 10% impairment at 31 March 2011.

3.   NJ sold goods to BH in January 2011 for $200,000. Half of these items remain in BH's inventories at the year end. NJ earns a 20% gross margin on all sales.

4.   The profits of all three entities can be assumed to accrue evenly throughout the year. Assume there is no further impact to income tax figures.

5.   MK paid a dividend of $80,000 to its equity shareholders on 31 March 2011. BH included its share of the dividend in investment income.

Required:

Prepare the consolidated statement of comprehensive income for the BH Group for the year ended 31 March 2011. (Round all figures to the nearest $000.)

(18 marks)

The directors of BH, with the backing of the non-controlling shareholders of NJ, are considering moving NJ to a new facility overseas. NJ would then source all raw materials locally, recruit a local workforce and would be subject to local taxes and corporate regulations. The facility identified is in a country that uses the KRON as its currency, whilst BH and the rest of the group use the $. Since acquisition, NJ has operated relatively autonomously within the group and this is expected to continue if the move takes place.

The directors are unsure about the currency that would be used to prepare the financial statements of NJ if the relocation was to go ahead and what implication this might have for the group financial statements.

Required:

Apply the principles of IAS 21 *The Effects of Changes in Foreign Exchange Rates*, to establish which currency should be used to prepare the financial statements of NJ, assuming that NJ moves to the overseas facility identified above.

(7 marks)

(Total for Question Six = 25 marks)

Question Seven

Mr X owned a highly successful technology business which he sold five years ago for $20 million. He then set up an investment entity that invests, primarily in smaller private businesses in need of short to medium term funding. Mr X sits on the board as a non-executive director of a number of the entities that his business has invested in and is often able to offer valuable business advice to these entities, especially in the area of research and development activities.

Mr X has been approached by the managing director of ABC, a small private entity looking for investment. ABC has been trading for more than 10 years manufacturing and selling its own branded perfumes, lotions and candles to the public in its 15 retail stores and to other larger retailing entities. Revenues and profits have been steady over the last 10 years. However 18 months ago, the newly appointed sales director saw an opportunity to sell the products on-line. Using long term funding, he therefore set up an online shop. The online shop has been operating successfully for the last 14 months. The sales director also used his prior contacts to secure a lucrative deal with a boutique hotel chain for ABC to manufacture products for the hotel, carrying the hotel chain name and logo.

The managing director of ABC now believes that the business has further opportunities and does not wish to lose the momentum created by the sales director. The bank that currently provides both a long-term loan and an overdraft facility has rejected ABC's request for additional funds on the basis that there are insufficient assets to offer for security (the existing funding is secured on ABC's property, plant and equipment).

Extracts from the financial statements for ABC are provided below:

Statement of comprehensive income for the year ended 30 June	2011	2010
	$'000	$'000
Revenue	6,000	3,700
Cost of sales	(4,083)	(2,590)
Gross profit	1,917	1,110
Administrative expenses	(870)	(413)
Distribution costs	(464)	(356)
Finance costs	(43)	(34)
Profit before tax	540	307
Income tax expense	(135)	(80)
Profit for the year	405	227

The revenues and profits of the three business segments for the year ended 30 June 2011 were:

	Retail operations	Online store	Hotel contract
	$'000	$'000	$'000
Revenues	4,004	1,096	900
Gross profit	1,200	330	387
Profit before tax	320	138	82

The online store earned a negligible amount of revenue and profit in the year ended 30 June 2010.

Statement of financial position as at 30 June	2011 $'000	2010 $'000
ASSETS		
Non-current assets		
Property, plant and equipment	380	400
Intangible assets – development costs	20	10
	400	410
Current assets		
Inventories	1,260	1,180
Receivables	455	310
Cash and cash equivalents	-	42
	1,715	1,532
Total assets	2,115	1,942
EQUITY AND LIABILITIES		
Equity		
Share capital ($1 equity shares)	550	550
Retained earnings	722	610
Total equity	1,272	1,160
Non-current liabilities		
Long-term borrowings	412	404
Current liabilities		
Payables	363	378
Short-term borrowings (overdraft)	68	-
	431	378
Total liabilities	843	782
Total equity and liabilities	2,115	1,942

As a member of Mr X's investment management team, you have been asked to analyse the financial performance and position of ABC and make a recommendation as to whether this request for investment should be considered further by Mr X.

Required:

(a) **Prepare** a report that analyses the financial performance of ABC for the year ended 30 June 2011 and its financial position at that date, and makes a recommendation as to whether the investment should be considered further. (8 marks are available for the calculation of relevant ratios)

(20 marks)

(b) **Discuss** the benefits and limitations to Mr X of relying on traditional ratio analysis when deciding whether or not to invest in ABC.

(5 marks)

(Total for Question Seven = 25 marks)

(Total for Section B = 50 marks)

Answers

**DO NOT TURN THIS PAGE UNTIL YOU HAVE
COMPLETED THE MOCK EXAM**

A plan of attack

The exam may look daunting at first. You need to adopt a calm approach. The following plan of attack is just a suggestion.

Part A

Part A is compulsory so you may as well deal with these five first. Do not get bogged down in the detail and remember to allow yourself only **90 minutes**, allocating equal time to each question. **Question 1** requires the preparation of a consolidated statement of financial position. There is also a discussion on IAS 31. **Question 2** is a discussion on the sale and repurchase of land and narrative reporting of staff resources; read the requirement carefully and avoid the temptation just to start writing all you can remember about the topic. **Question 3** requires various calculations of earnings per share. **Question 4** is on financial instruments and employee benefits. **Question 5** is a question on convergence.

Part B

Part B has **two compulsory questions**. Choose the question that you know most about to answer first but remember to give each question its full 45 minute time allocation.

Question 6. A consolidated statement of comprehensive income, including a discussion of IAS 21. As always, the key here is to use the methodical techniques you have studied. There are quite a number of adjustments in this question. Never get bogged down in any one adjustment if you realise that you are struggling. The best strategy is to make sure that you work through all the steps that you are confident about.

Question 7. A financial analysis question which requires both calculations and commentary. You need to use **all** of the information, narrative and numerical, in your analysis. Ratios should be selected carefully to be relevant to alculations of earnings your answer. Your analysis must be targeted towards what a **prospective lender** would want to know.

Remember

Always – well nearly always – **allocate your time** according to the marks for the question in total and then according to the parts of the question. The only exception is if the question is compulsory, say in Section A, and you really know nothing about it. You may as well try to pick up marks elsewhere. And **always, always follow the requirements** exactly.

You've got spare time at the end of the exam ... ?

If you have allocated your time properly then you **shouldn't have time on your hands** at the end of the exam. But if you find yourself with five or ten minutes to spare, **go back to the questions** that you couldn't do or to **any parts of questions that you didn't finish** because you ran out of time.

Forget about it!

And don't worry if you found the paper difficult. More than likely other candidates will too. If this were the real thing you would need to **forget** the exam the minute you leave the exam hall and **think about the next one**. Or, if it's the last one, **celebrate**!

Question 1

Text reference. Joint ventures are covered in Chapter 9 of the Study Text.

Top tips. Part (a) of the question tells you to use proportionate consolidation to consolidate the joint venture, so it would be throwing marks away to use the equity method or to forget to take only the group share of the joint venture. Part (a) is time consuming, but straightforward.

Easy marks. Easy marks are available for textbook knowledge of the equity method in Part (b).

Part (a)

	$'000
ASSETS	
Non-current assets	
Property, plant and equipment (322 + [25% x 280])	392
Goodwill (W2)	10
	402
Current assets	
Inventories (111 + [25% x 120] – 5 (W4))	136
Receivables (115 + [25% x 132] – 6 (W5))	142
Held for trading investment (35 + 7 (W6))	42
Cash and cash equivalents (21 + [25% x 40])	31
	351
Total assets	753
EQUITY AND LIABILITIES	
Equity attributable to owners of the parent	
Share capital	120
Revaluation reserve	18
Retained earnings (W3)	235
	373
Non-current liabilities	
Long term borrowings (90)	90
Current liabilities	
Payables (185 + [25% x 160] – 6 (W5))	219
Income tax payable (48 + [25% x 92])	71
	290
Total equity and liabilities	753

Workings

1   Group structure

BG

25%

JV PAR = $40,000

2   *Goodwill*

	$'000	$'000
Consideration transferred		70
Less: fair value of net assets at acquired		
Share capital	200	
Retained earnings (W1)	40	
	240	
Group share	X 25%	(60)
		10

3   *Retained earnings*

	BG	JV
	$'000	$'000
Per question	213	120
Provision for unrealised profit (W4)	(5)	
Revaluation gain on investment (W6)	7	
Pre-acquisition (W1)		(40)
		80
Share of JV post acquisition (25% x 80)	20	
	235	

4   *Provision for unrealised profit*

    JV ─────────➤ BG

Provision for unrealised profit = $200,000 x ½ in inventories x 20/100 margin x 25% group share = $5,000

Reduce retained earnings by $5,000 (in BG's column so don't multiply by our % twice)

Reduce inventories by $5,000

5   *Intra-group payables and receivables*

Balance at year end = $24,000

Cancel group share: $24,000 x 25% = $6,000

Reduce 'Receivables' and 'Payables' by $6,000

6   *Held for trading investment*

	$'000
Fair value at 31 March 2011	42
Carrying value	(35)
Revaluation gain (post to P/L and therefore retained earnings and add to investment)	7

Part (b)

Alternative accounting treatment

The alternative accounting treatment permitted by IAS 31 *Interests in Joint Ventures* is equity accounting which is the accounting treatment also used for associates in the group accounts.

How this policy would change BG group's statement of financial position

Instead of adding the group share (25%) of JV's assets and liabilities line by line, there would **just be one line for JV** ie 'investment in joint venture'. The amount would be calculated as follows:

	$'000
Cost of joint venture	X
Share of joint venture's post acquisition reserves	X
Impairment loss on investment in joint venture	(X)
	X

There would be **no separate goodwill in 'non-current assets'** – effectively goodwill will be included in the 'investment in joint venture' above.

Consolidated retained earnings would remain at $235,000.

The adjustment for unrealised profit would be the same but the group share of intra-group payables and receivables would not be cancelled because these lines would not have been added across in the first place.

Overall, under the equity method, the **amounts in the individual asset and liability lines would be lower** as they would only comprise the parent's figures rather than the parent and the group share of the joint venture.

Question 2

Text reference. Substance over form is covered in Chapter 1 of the Study Text.

Top tips. Part (a) required discussion of a sale and repurchase of land which has been incorrectly treated. You are steered towards applying IAS 18 and the *Framework,* although IAS 18 applies more to inventory. Part (b) asked for the treatment of a company's relationship with another entity.

Easy marks. There are no obvious easy marks here. However, in Part (b), the question, by saying that the directors wish to avoid consolidating the entity, are giving a strong hint that it ought to be consolidated.

Part (a)

Explanation

DRT have treated the disposal of the land as a true sale by derecognising it and recording a gain on disposal of $290,000 (i.e. $1,600,000 - $1,310,000) in profit or loss.

This treatment follows the legal form but **in substance, this is not a true sale but a loan (secured on the land).** For a sale to be recognised, *IAS 18 Revenue* requires a sale to be recognised when the risks and rewards of ownership have been transferred. Furthermore, the *Framework for Preparation and Presentation of Financial Statements* requires financial statements to be reliable which encompasses the concept of substance over form – in substance, an asset should be recognised in an entity's statement of financial position when the entity has substantially all the risks and benefits of ownership.

In this scenario, a sale should not have been recorded because **DRT keeps the risks and benefits of ownership of the land.** This is indicated by the following terms of the agreement:

- The repurchase price is for more than the sales price increases depending on the date of repurchase – in substance, this increase represents interest.

- Although DRT only has the *option* to repurchase the land over the next four years, there is an *obligation* to repurchase it at the end of the fourth year if the option has not been exercise. This means that DRT retains the key risks (fall in value) and benefits (increase in value) of the land.

The **adjustment required is to reinstate the land in DRT's statement of financial position, reverse the profit on disposal and record the sales proceeds as a liability**. No interest needs to be recorded in the year ended 31 May 2011 as the sale took place on the last day of the year.

Accounting entries

DEBIT Land $1,310,000
DEBIT Profit or loss – profit on disposal $290,000
CREDIT Loan liability $1,600,000

Being reversal of the disposal of the land and recording of the loan liability.

Part (b)

IAS 27 *Consolidated and separate financial statements* defines a **subsidiary** as **an entity that is controlled by another entity.** Control is defined as 'the power to govern operating and financial policies of an entity so to gain benefit from its activities'. Whilst control is presumed to exist when the parent owns more than half of the voting power, **control may exist when a parent owns less than half the voting power but has the power to govern the operating and financial policies of the entity** under a statute or agreement.

Here, on the face of it, GHJ does not look like a subsidiary of DRT because DRT does not own any of the shares (it is 100% owned by GHJ's sales director). However, **the board of DRT control the operating and financial policies of GHJ under a contractual agreement.** Furthermore, DRT retain the risks (GHJ makes losses) and benefits (GHJ makes profits) of GHJ because profits and losses of GHJ (after deducting the sales director's salary) revert to DRT. Finally, there is one further indication that DRT takes on the risks of GHJ - DRT acts as guarantor to GHJ's loan and would become liable for repayment on default of the loan.

Essentially **GHJ is a special purpose entity of DRT** under SIC 12: *Consolidation – special purpose entities.* **DRT should consolidate 100% of GHT's assets of $300,000 and loan liability of $1m.** Non-consolidation just to avoid increasing gearing would result in non-compliance with IAS 27 and SIC 12 and therefore is not permitted.

Question 3

Text reference. Earnings per share is covered in Chapter 15 of your Study Text.

Top tips. This is a standard EPS question, similar to one set a few sittings ago, requiring calculation of basic earnings per share and diluted earnings per share and an explanation of why diluted earnings per share is useful.

Easy marks. The explanation of why diluted EPS is useful is a good source of easy marks.

Part (a)

Basic EPS for year ended 30 June 2011 = $\dfrac{\$3.8m}{8.75m \text{ (W1)}}$ = 43.4 cents

Restated basic EPS for year ended 30 June 2010 = 48.2 cents x 2/3 = 32.1 cents

(W1) *Shares*

Date	Narrative	No of shares	Time	Bonus fraction	Weighted average
1.7.10	B/f	5,000,000	2/12	3/2	1,250,000
1.9.10	Bonus issue (1 for 2)	2,500,000			
		7,500,000	5/12		3,125,000
1.2.11	FMP issues	3,000,000			
		10,500,000	5/12		4,375,000
					8,750,000

Part (b)

Diluted EPS for year ended 30 June 2011 = $\dfrac{\$3.8m}{8.75m \text{ (W1)} + 225,000 \text{ (W2)}}$ = 42.3 cents

(W2) *No of shares for nil consideration*

No of shares under option	1,000,000
No that would have been issued at average market price	(775,000)
[(1,000,000 x $3.10)/$4.00]	
No of shares for nil consideration	225,000

Part (c)

It is important for users to have **diluted earnings per share** presented in the financial statements as it acts as a **warning to current shareholders of the potential adverse impact** of instruments in existence now which could become shares in the future.

It assumes the worse possible scenario ie that all the options will be exercised and will become ordinary shares so that the existing ordinary shareholders are prepared for all potential eventualities.

The presentation at the foot of the statement of comprehensive income emphasises the importance of this very useful investor ratio to users of the financial statements.

Question 4

Text reference. Financial instruments are covered in Chapter 2 of your Study Text. Employee benefits are covered in Chapter 3.

Top tips. Part (a) was very typical of the examiner's requirements and style for examining this topic. The key was to know that financial liabilities are initially measured at fair value less transaction costs and this debt instrument should subsequently be measured at amortised cost. In Part (b), potential errors would be to do full disclosures when only SOCI notes were required; to forget to do asset/liability working to find actuarial gain/loss for year or to accidentally do 10% corridor calculations.

Easy marks. In part (b) you can get some easy marks by copying figures from the question into the right column.

(a)   Financial instrument

    (i)   Initial and subsequent measurement

        The redeemable debt is a **financial liability** as QWS has an obligation to pay the annual interest of 6% and to repay the capital and premium on redemption totalling $6.02m.

        It is **initially measured at its fair value ie the cash paid** of $6m. Transaction costs of $200,000 should be deducting resulting in an initial financial liability of $5.8m (i.e. $6m - $200,000).

        For the purposes of subsequent measurement, IAS 39 *Financial instruments: recognition and measurement* breaks financial liabilities into two categories:

        •   At **fair value through profit or loss** (held for trading or unfavourable derivatives)
        •   **Amortised cost** (most financial liabilities)

        This debt is not in the category of 'at fair value through profit or loss' as it is not held for trading ie it was not issued with the intention of making a short-term profit, nor is it a derivative. **Therefore, at the year end of 30 June 2011, it should be held at amortised cost.**

        The effect of amortised cost spreads the finance costs (ie issue costs, interest and premium on redemption) over the life of the debt (4 years) by applying the effective interest rate of 7.06% to the brought forward balance and gradually builds the financial liability up to its redemption value.

    (ii)   Carrying value of liability at 30 June 2011

	$'000
1.7.09 Financial liability	5,800
Finance cost (7.06% x 5,800)	409
Coupon paid (6% x 6,000)	(360)
30.6.10 Financial liability	5,849
Finance cost (7.06% x 5,849)	413
Coupon paid (6% x 6,000)	(360)
30.6.11 Financial liability	5,902

(b)   Pension plan

Expense recognised in profit or loss for the year ended 30 June 2011

	$'000
Current service cost	300
Interest cost (W1)	98
Expected return on plan assets (W1)	(48)
Net expense	350

Amount recognised in other comprehensive income for the year ended 30 June 2011

	$'000
Actuarial loss on plan assets in the year (W1)	(28)
Actuarial loss on plan liabilities in the year (W1)	(22)
	(50)

(W1) *Changes in FV of plan assets and PV of plan liabilities*

	Assets $'000	Liabilities $'000
Balance at 1 July 2010	1,200	1,400
Interest cost (7% x 1,400)		98
Expected return (4% x 1,200)	48	
Current service cost		300
Contributions	400	
Benefits paid	(220)	(220)
	1,428	1,578
Actuarial loss on assets (balancing figure)	(28)	
Actuarial loss on liabilities (balancing figure)		22
Balance at 30 June 2011	1,400	1,600

Question 5

Part (a)

Progress towards convergence

The US has traditionally adopted a **rules-based approach** to financial reporting standard setting, whereas the **IASB's** financial reporting standards are **principles-based**. The **US** has, in light of a number of major corporate scandals, **now accepted that a principles-based reporting framework is more appropriate** to current corporate reporting need.

In October 2002, the IASB reached an agreement with the USs FASB (Financial Accounting Standards Board) (the '**Norwalk agreement**') to undertake a short-term convergence project aimed at removing a variety of individual differences between US GAAP and IFRS. The agreement **committed the two parties to making their existing standards fully compatible** as soon as possible and to co-ordinate their future work programs to avoid future differences in approach.

A short-term project was undertaken to **remove some of the differences between existing standards** in order to achieve the first objective of the Norwalk agreement. In order to meet the second, the two bodies have **collaborated on the development of new and revised standards**, and continue to do so.

A 'Memorandum of Understanding' between the FASB and IASB then set out a 'roadmap' of convergence between IFRS and US GAAP from 2006 – 2008. This was aimed at removing by 2009 the need for entities having prepared their financial statements under IFRS to prepare reconciliation to US GAAP in order to be listed on a US exchange. The requirement for this reconciliation was subsequently removed ahead of schedule in November 2007.

In February 2010, the **SEC published a statement of continued support for a single set of high quality global standards and acknowledged that IFRS is best positioned to serve in that role**. The SEC intends to make a decision in 2011 as to if, how and when to further incorporate IFRS into the US public markets.

How this has been achieved

Projects undertaken jointly between the FASB and the IASB have produced the following:

- The issue of IFRS 5 *Non-current assets held for sale and discontinued operations*

- The issue of IFRS 8 *Operating segments*

- Revision of IAS 23 *Borrowing costs to bring it into line with US GAAP*

- Revision of IAS 1 *Presentation of financial statements and an agreement on common wording to be used in accounting standards*

- Revision of IFRS 3 *Business combinations and IAS 27 Consolidated and separate financial statements*

- The issue of IFRS 9 *Financial instruments*

  More recent developments include the issue of the 'pack of five' new or revised financial reporting standards in May 2011 addressing the joint project on consolidation agreed in the 2006 Memorandum of Understanding:

- IFRS 10 *Consolidated financial statements*

- IFRS 11 *Joint arrangements*

- IFRS12 *Disclosure of interests in other entities*

- IAS 27 (revised) *Separate financial statements*

- IAS 29 (revised) *Investments in associated and joint ventures*

Part (b)

Benefits of convergence to investors

- In times of increasing globalisation, once US GAAP and IFRS are fully converged, it will enable investors to compare different entities in US and elsewhere in the world (where IFRS is adopted). This will enable easier investment decisions.

- IFRS are seen to be of high quality so preparation of financial statements under IFRS acts as a form of quality control giving investors greater confidence in the financial statements.

Benefits of convergence to accounting students

- Once fully converged, accounting students will only have to learn one set of accounting standards

- It will enable students to work anywhere around the world (where IFRS is adopted) giving them greater flexibility in their career

- At work, preparing consolidated financial statements for a global group will become easier as there will be no need to convert from local GAAP to IFRS if all group companies prepare their accounts under IFRS.

Question 6

BH GROUP
CONSOLIDATED STATEMENT OF COMPREHENSIVE INCOME
FOR THE YEAR ENDED 31 MARCH 2011

	$'000
Revenue (3,360 + [3/12 x 3,240] – 200 (W5))	3,970
Cost of sales (1,800 + [3/12 x 1,860] – 200 (W5) + 20 (W5))	(2,085)
Gross profit	1,885
Administration expenses (380 + [3/12 x 340] + 16 (W3))	(481)
Distribution costs (400 + [3/12 x 300])	(475)
Investment income (80 – 32 (W6))	48
Finance costs (180 + [3/12 x 140])	(215)
Profit on derecognition of financial asset (W3)	125
Share of profit of associate [(350 x 6/12 x 40%) – 38 (W4)]	32
Profit before tax	919
Income tax expense (200 + [3/12 x 160])	(240)
Profit for the year	679
Other comprehensive income	
Revaluation of property, plant and equipment (70 + [3/12 x 40])	80
Available for sale reclassification adjustment (W3)	(100)
Tax effect of OCI (50 + [3/12 x 16])	(54)
Share of other comprehensive income of associate (20 x 6/12 x 40%)	4
Other comprehensive income for the year, net of tax	(70)
Total comprehensive income for the year	609

Profit attributable to:	
Owners of the parent	654
Non-controlling interests (W2)	25
	679

Total comprehensive income attributable to:	
Owners of the parent	581
Non-controlling interests (W2)	28
	609

Workings

1   *Group structure and timeline*

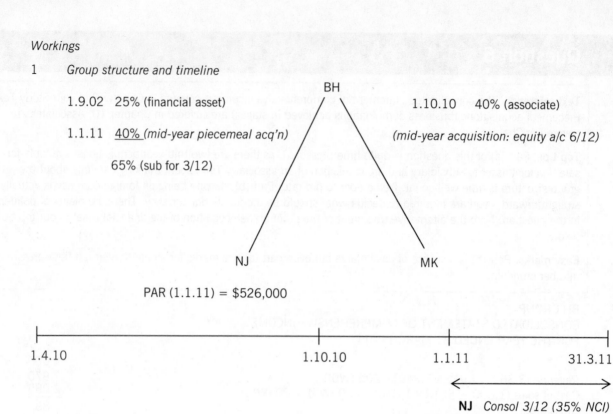

1.9.02   25% (financial asset)

1.1.11   <u>40%</u> *(mid-year piecemeal acq'n)*

65% (sub for 3/12)

1.10.10   40% (associate)

(mid-year acquisition: equity a/c 6/12)

BH

NJ   MK

PAR (1.1.11) = $526,000

1.4.10	1.10.10	1.1.11	31.3.11

NJ   *Consol 3/12 (35% NCI)*

MK   *Equity account 6/12*

2   *Non-controlling interest (NJ)*

	Profit for year $'000	*Total comprehensive income* $'000
Per question		
(440 x 3/12)	110	
(464 x 3/12)		116
Impairment of goodwill (W3)	(16)	(16)
Provision for unrealised profit (W5)	(20)	(20)
	74	80
NCI share	X 35%	X 35%
	= 26*	= 28*

* Rounded to nearest $'000

3   *Goodwill (NJ)*

	$'000	$'000
Consideration transferred (for 40% on 1.1.11)		680
Non-controlling interests (at fair value)		581
Fair value of previously held equity interest		425*
Fair value of net assets at acquisition:		
Share capital	1,000	
Retained earnings (per question)	526	
		(1,526)
		160
Impairment (10% x 160) *(add to 'admin expenses')*		(16)
		144

Profit on derecognition of financial asset*:

	$'000
Fair value at 1.1.11	425
Carrying value at 1.1.11 (assume not revalued since 31 March 2010 i.e. only revalued at year end)	400)
	25
Reclassification of previous revaluation gains (400 – 300) *(remove from OCI)*	100
Total profit to be recognised in P/L *(separate line of face of SOCI)*	125

> **Top tip.** An alternative presentation would be to assume that the financial asset had been revalued to its fair value of $425,000 at the date of derecognition i.e. 1.1.11. If that had been the case, the revaluation gain from the start of the year to the date of derecognition of $425,000 - $400,000 = $25,000 would have been recognised in OCI in the consolidated SOCI for the current year. And the full revaluation gain from acquisition on 1.9.02 to derecognition on 1.1.11 of $425,000 - $300,000 = $125,000 would be reclassified out of OCI. The gain on derecognition in P/L would still be $125,000 (i.e. Fair value at 1.1.11 $425,000 – carrying value at 1.1.11 $425,000 + reclassification of previous revaluation gains $125,000). The overall answer would be the same but there would just be 2 lines in OCI rather than one (i.e. revaluation gain in year of $25,000 less reclassification of previous revaluation gains of $125,000 resulting in same net effect of $100,000 shown above).

4 *Investment in associate*

	$'000
Cost of associate	334
Share of post-acquisition reserves [(370 x 6/12) – 80] x 40%	42
	376
Impairment loss (10% x 376) *(deduct from share of associate's profit)* *(rounded to nearest $'000)*	(38)
	338

5 *Intragroup trading*

NJ (in Jan 2011 i.e. when NJ was a 65% subsidiary) → BH (parent)

(a) Cancel intra-group revenue and cost of sales of $200,000 (all in post-acquisition period so no need to pro-rate)

(b) Provision for unrealised profit = $200,000 x ½ in inventories x 20/100 margin = $20,000
    [Increase NJ's cost of sales (and as subsidiary is seller, need to adjust NCI)]

6 *Intra-group dividend income*

On 31.3.11, MK (associate) pays BH a dividend of $80,000 x 40% = $32,000. This amount must be cancelled from 'investment income' as in the group accounts; the group share of MK's profit is included instead.

Functional currency of NJ

IAS 21 *The effects of changes in foreign exchange rates* defines the **functional currency** as the **currency of the primary economic environment in which the entity operates**. This is the currency used to measure the results and financial position of the entity.

IAS 21 lists **factors to consider** in determining the functional currency of an entity. The following factors indicate that should NJ be moved overseas, the functional currency of NJ would become the KRON:

(a) The country whose competitive forces and regulations mainly determine the sales prices of goods or services . As NJ would be subject to local corporate regulations; this appears to be the overseas country, indicating the functional currency would be the KRON.

(b) The currency that **mainly influences labour, material and other costs**. Given that NJ would source all material locally, recruit a local workforce and be subject to local taxes, this currency would be the **KRON**

(c) Whether the activities of the foreign operation are carried out as an **extension of the reporting entity or with a degree of autonomy.** Given that NJ has operating relatively autonomously since acquisition and this is expected to continue, this appears to be another indication that the functional currency would be the KRON

(d)   Whether **transactions with the reporting entity are a high or low proportion of the foreign operation's activities**. In the year ended 31 March 2011, NJ sold $200,000 of goods to its parent BH, representing 6% of NJ's total revenue. This is a **relatively low proportion of NJ's revenue** although if NJ had been a subsidiary for a full year it might have been higher. This relatively low level of intra-group trading is **another indication that NJ would operate independently** and the functional currency would become the KRON.

Only one of the factors is less clear:

The currency that mainly influences sales price for goods and services. It is not clear if NJ is moved overseas whether the sales price would still be denominated in dollars or the overseas currency of KRON.

On balance, it would appear that if NJ were to move overseas, **the functional currency of NJ would change from the dollar to the KRON**. This would mean that for the purposes of consolidation, **NJ's year end financial statements would need to be translated from the KRON into the presentation currency of the group accounts ie the dollar**. The closing rate would be used to translate the assets and liabilities and the actual rate (or average rate as a close approximation) to translate income and expenses – any resulting exchange difference would be recognised in other comprehensive income.

Question 7

Part (a)

REPORT

To: Mr X

From: Member of Mr X's management team

Date: 31 August 2011

Subject: Financial performance and position of ABC

Introduction

The aim of this report is to analyse the financial performance and position of ABC and determining whether or not it would make a good investment.

Financial performance

Growth

Revenue has increased by an impressive 62% in the year. This is largely due to the newly appointed sales director's actions of:

(a)   Setting up a new online store which has been trading for the last 14 months – even though this is a new venture, it generated 18% of ABC's total revenue in the year ended 30 June 2011

(b)   Securing a lucrative deal with a boutique hotel chain to manufacture products for the hotel – this new contract generated 15% of the revenue in the year ended 30 June 2011 and with the sales director's contacts, other such deals could be won with other hotels in the future, generating further growth in revenue.

Profitability

Gross margin has improved slightly from 30% in the year ended 30 June 2010 to 32% in the year ended 30 June 2011. An analysis of the margins of the three different business areas reveals that the improvement is largely due to the strong margin of 43% on the new hotel contract, perhaps due to a mark-up on the sales price for the right of the hotel chain to use its own name and logo on ABC's products. ABC needs to ensure that it does not lose its own brand strength by allowing others to put their name to ABC products.

Net margin has also improved from 8.3% to 9% despite the increase in finance costs due to reliance on an overdraft in the current year. This is largely due to the online store generating the strongest margin of 12.6%. This is likely to be due to the store not having to pay the overheads associated with the retail sites.

The online store and new hotel contracts have been successful initiatives in terms of growing revenue and increasing both absolute profit and margins.

ABC could improve their overheads cost control though as administration expenses have increased by 111% in the year.

Efficiency

ABC's efficiency in using its assets to generate both revenue and profit has **improved** as illustrated by asset turnover increasing from 1.91 to 2.84 and return on capital employed from 21.8% to 33.3%. This can be attributed to **improved margins** (see above) and **stronger working capital management** (see below).

Financial position

Liquidity

The **current ratio has declined slightly** from 4.05 to 3.98 – this is largely due to reliance on an overdraft in the current year and reduced receivable and inventory days.

However, the **quick ratio has improved** from 0.93 to 1.06 largely due to paying suppliers more quickly (32 days compared to 53 days).

Overall though, ABC can easily afford to pay its current liabilities out of its current assets. However, **long-term reliance on an overdraft** is both **risky** as the overdraft facility could be withdrawn at any time (especially in light of the bank's has recent rejection of ABC's request for additional funds) **and expensive.**

Working capital management

Inventory days have decreased from 166 days to 113 days indicating that ABC is selling their inventories more quickly. This is presumably to meet the increased demand from the new online store and the new hotel contract.

Inventory days remain high though – presumably this is due to the nature of the products (perfumes, lotions and candles, having a long shelf-life. If the development costs result in new improved products, there is a **risk of obsolescence** amongst the existing products.

Receivable days are low as expected when the majority of the sales are from retail stores where the customers pay in cash. ABC is now only taking 28 days on average to collect cash from its credit customers as opposed to 31 days in the prior year. It may be that favourable credit terms have been negotiated with the hotel chain.

Interestingly, **ABC is paying its suppliers more quickly** in 2011 i.e. taking on average 32 days as opposed to 53 days in 2010. This seems **inadvisable** given that a significant overdraft has arisen in the current year. ABC should take full advantage of the credit period offered by their suppliers. It may be that they are sourcing from a new supplier with stricter credit terms to fulfil the hotel contract.

Solvency

Even though the bank is refusing further funding, ABC's gearing, despite a small increase in the year, remains at a manageable level (38% in the current year). Furthermore, ABC can easily afford to pay the interest on its debt as illustrated by an interest cover of 13.6 in the current year.

Conclusion

On initial analysis, there seems to be a **strong case for investing in ABC.** The business is **growing and innovative** having just expanded into 2 new areas with the online store and new hotel contract due to the skills of the new sales director. It also **profitable** and the profitability is improving year on year. Perhaps the **only concern** is **reliance on the overdraft** but this can be resolved by **improving working capital management** and ensuring that the **full credit period of suppliers is taken advantage of**. With further new initiatives from the sales director such as new contracts with other hotel chains and further growth of online sales, there is potential for even more growth in the future.

Appendix

	2011	*2010*
Return on capital employed = PBIT/(Debt + Equity)	$\dfrac{540+43}{412+68+1{,}272}=33.3\%$	$\dfrac{307+34}{404+1{,}160}=21.8\%$
Asset turnover = Revenue/total assets	$\dfrac{6{,}000}{2{,}115}=2.84$	$\dfrac{3{,}700}{1{,}942}=1.91$
Gross margin = Gross profit/revenue	$\dfrac{1{,}917}{6{,}000}=32.0\%$	$\dfrac{1{,}110}{3{,}700}=30\%$
Gross margin of retail operations	$\dfrac{1{,}200}{4{,}004}=30.0\%$	
Gross margin of online store	$\dfrac{330}{1{,}096}=30.1\%$	
Gross margin of hotel contract	$\dfrac{387}{900}=43\%$	
Operating profit margin = PBIT/revenue	$\dfrac{540+43}{6{,}000}=9.7\%$	$\dfrac{307+34}{3{,}700}=9.2\%$
Net margin = PBT/revenue	$\dfrac{540}{6{,}000}=9\%$	$\dfrac{307}{3{,}700}=8.3\%$
Net margin of retail operations	$\dfrac{320}{4{,}004}=8.0\%$	
Net margin of online store	$\dfrac{138}{1{,}096}=12.6\%$	
Net margin of hotel contract	$\dfrac{82}{900}=9.1\%$	
Current ratio = Current assets/current liabilities	$\dfrac{1{,}715}{431}=3.98$	$\dfrac{1{,}532}{378}=4.05$
Quick ratio = (Current assets – inventories)/current liabilities	$\dfrac{1{,}715-1{,}260}{431}=1.06$	$\dfrac{1{,}532-1{,}180}{378}=0.93$
Inventory days = (Inventories/cost of sales) x 365	$\dfrac{1{,}260}{4{,}083}$ x 365 = 113 days	$\dfrac{1{,}180}{2{,}590}$ x 365 = 166 days
Receivable days = (Receivables/revenue) x 365	$\dfrac{455}{6{,}000}$ x 365 = 28 days	$\dfrac{310}{3{,}700}$ x 365 = 31 days
Payable days = (Payables/cost of sales) x 365	$\dfrac{363}{4{,}083}$ x 365 = 32 days	$\dfrac{378}{2{,}590}$ x 365 = 53 days
Gearing = Debt/Equity	$\dfrac{412+68}{1{,}272}=38\%$	$\dfrac{404}{1{,}160}=35\%$
Interest cover = PBIT/interest expense	$\dfrac{540+43}{43}=13.6$	$\dfrac{307+34}{34}=10.0$

Part (b)

Benefits and limitations to Mr X of relying on traditional ratio analysis when deciding whether to invest in ABC

Benefits

(a)   Traditional ratio analysis is performed on published financial data which has therefore been **audited**. This is effectively an indication of strong quality control over the **reliability** of the underlying date

(b)   Ratio analysis will **allow Mr X to compare ABC with other entities** in the same industry as it is based on financial statements which are readily available

(c)   Traditional ratio analysis is **useful in analysing past trends** of an entity such as ABC and these past trends are often indicative as to what might happen in the future

(d)   **Notes to the accounts** which disaggregate information, such as the segment reporting note of ABC **allow detailed analysis** (although only publicly traded entities are required to make this disclosure)

Limitations

(a)   Traditional ratio analysis is **based on historic data** which is not necessarily indicative of what might happen in the future. In the case of ABC, as both the online store and hotel contract are new, there is **not much of a track record yet to assess these new ventures on.**

(b)   Traditional ratio analysis is **based on financial information**. Mr **X also needs to take into account non-financial information** in his investment decision. For example, what further opportunities would the sales director like to invest in? Is the sales director tied into a long contract as he seems key to the future success of ABC?

(c)   Financial statements are often **too aggregated for meaningful analysis** . For example, a breakdown of the development costs would be useful to ascertain which new products/processes are in the pipeline and how they might impact on the longevity of existing inventory.

(d)   Traditional ratio analysis is **based on year end figures** which **might not necessarily be representative of balances during the year.**

(e)   Traditional ratio analysis is **prepared on information produced by the directors** of the entity who are likely to be **subjective.** It is important not to just rely on this information and to seek third party independent opinion too, in the form of a credit rating for example.

MATHEMATICAL TABLES

Present value table

Present value of £1 = $(1+r)^{-n}$ where r = interest rate, n = number of periods until payment or receipt.

Periods					Discount rates (r)					
(n)	1%	2%	3%	4%	5%	6%	7%	8%	9%	10%
1	0.990	0.980	0.971	0.962	0.952	0.943	0.935	0.926	0.917	0.909
2	0.980	0.961	0.943	0.925	0.907	0.890	0.873	0.857	0.842	0.826
3	0.971	0.942	0.915	0.889	0.864	0.840	0.816	0.794	0.772	0.751
4	0.961	0.924	0.888	0.855	0.823	0.792	0.763	0.735	0.708	0.683
5	0.951	0.906	0.863	0.822	0.784	0.747	0.713	0.681	0.650	0.621
6	0.942	0.888	0.837	0.790	0.746	0.705	0.666	0.630	0.596	0.564
7	0.933	0.871	0.813	0.760	0.711	0.665	0.623	0.583	0.547	0.513
8	0.923	0.853	0.789	0.731	0.677	0.627	0.582	0.540	0.502	0.467
9	0.914	0.837	0.766	0.703	0.645	0.592	0.544	0.500	0.460	0.424
10	0.905	0.820	0.744	0.676	0.614	0.558	0.508	0.463	0.422	0.386
11	0.896	0.804	0.722	0.650	0.585	0.527	0.475	0.429	0.388	0.350
12	0.887	0.788	0.701	0.625	0.557	0.497	0.444	0.397	0.356	0.319
13	0.879	0.773	0.681	0.601	0.530	0.469	0.415	0.368	0.326	0.290
14	0.870	0.758	0.661	0.577	0.505	0.442	0.388	0.340	0.299	0.263
15	0.861	0.743	0.642	0.555	0.481	0.417	0.362	0.315	0.275	0.239
16	0.853	0.728	0.623	0.534	0.458	0.394	0.339	0.292	0.252	0.218
17	0.844	0.714	0.605	0.513	0.436	0.371	0.317	0.270	0.231	0.198
18	0.836	0.700	0.587	0.494	0.416	0.350	0.296	0.250	0.212	0.180
19	0.828	0.686	0.570	0.475	0.396	0.331	0.277	0.232	0.194	0.164
20	0.820	0.673	0.554	0.456	0.377	0.312	0.258	0.215	0.178	0.149

Periods					Discount rates (r)					
(n)	11%	12%	13%	14%	15%	16%	17%	18%	19%	20%
1	0.901	0.893	0.885	0.877	0.870	0.862	0.855	0.847	0.840	0.833
2	0.812	0.797	0.783	0.769	0.756	0.743	0.731	0.718	0.706	0.694
3	0.731	0.712	0.693	0.675	0.658	0.641	0.624	0.609	0.593	0.579
4	0.659	0.636	0.613	0.592	0.572	0.552	0.534	0.516	0.499	0.482
5	0.593	0.567	0.543	0.519	0.497	0.476	0.456	0.437	0.419	0.402
6	0.535	0.507	0.480	0.456	0.432	0.410	0.390	0.370	0.352	0.335
7	0.482	0.452	0.425	0.400	0.376	0.354	0.333	0.314	0.296	0.279
8	0.434	0.404	0.376	0.351	0.327	0.305	0.285	0.266	0.249	0.233
9	0.391	0.361	0.333	0.308	0.284	0.263	0.243	0.225	0.209	0.194
10	0.352	0.322	0.295	0.270	0.247	0.227	0.208	0.191	0.176	0.162
11	0.317	0.287	0.261	0.237	0.215	0.195	0.178	0.162	0.148	0.135
12	0.286	0.257	0.231	0.208	0.187	0.168	0.152	0.137	0.124	0.112
13	0.258	0.229	0.204	0.182	0.163	0.145	0.130	0.116	0.104	0.093
14	0.232	0.205	0.181	0.160	0.141	0.125	0.111	0.099	0.088	0.078
15	0.209	0.183	0.160	0.140	0.123	0.108	0.095	0.084	0.074	0.065
16	0.188	0.163	0.141	0.123	0.107	0.093	0.081	0.071	0.062	0.054
17	0.170	0.146	0.125	0.108	0.093	0.080	0.069	0.060	0.052	0.045
18	0.153	0.130	0.111	0.095	0.081	0.069	0.059	0.051	0.044	0.038
19	0.138	0.116	0.098	0.083	0.070	0.060	0.051	0.043	0.037	0.031
20	0.124	0.104	0.087	0.073	0.061	0.051	0.043	0.037	0.031	0.026

Cumulative present value table

This table shows the present value of £1 per annum, receivable or payable at the end of each year for *n* years.

Periods (n)	Discount rates (r)									
	1%	2%	3%	4%	5%	6%	7%	8%	9%	10%
1	0.990	0.980	0.971	0.962	0.952	0.943	0.935	0.926	0.917	0.909
2	1.970	1.942	1.913	1.886	1.859	1.833	1.808	1.783	1.759	1.736
3	2.941	2.884	2.829	2.775	2.723	2.673	2.624	2.577	2.531	2.487
4	3.902	3.808	3.717	3.630	3.546	3.465	3.387	3.312	3.240	3.170
5	4.853	4.713	4.580	4.452	4.329	4.212	4.100	3.993	3.890	3.791
6	5.795	5.601	5.417	5.242	5.076	4.917	4.767	4.623	4.486	4.355
7	6.728	6.472	6.230	6.002	5.786	5.582	5.389	5.206	5.033	4.868
8	7.652	7.325	7.020	6.733	6.463	6.210	5.971	5.747	5.535	5.335
9	8.566	8.162	7.786	7.435	7.108	6.802	6.515	6.247	5.995	5.759
10	9.471	8.983	8.530	8.111	7.722	7.360	7.024	6.710	6.418	6.145
11	10.37	9.787	9.253	8.760	8.306	7.887	7.499	7.139	6.805	6.495
12	11.26	10.58	9.954	9.385	8.863	8.384	7.943	7.536	7.161	6.814
13	12.13	11.35	10.63	9.986	9.394	8.853	8.358	7.904	7.487	7.103
14	13.00	12.11	11.30	10.56	9.899	9.295	8.745	8.244	7.786	7.367
15	13.87	12.85	11.94	11.12	10.38	9.712	9.108	8.559	8.061	7.606
16	14.718	13.578	12.561	11.652	10.838	10.106	9.447	8.851	8.313	7.824
17	15.562	14.292	13.166	12.166	11.274	10.477	9.763	9.122	8.544	8.022
18	16.398	14.992	13.754	12.659	11.690	10.828	10.059	9.372	8.756	8.201
19	17.226	15.678	14.324	13.134	12.085	11.158	10.336	9.604	8.950	8.365
20	18.046	16.351	14.877	13.590	12.462	11.470	10.594	9.818	9.129	8.514

Periods (n)	Discount rates (r)									
	11%	12%	13%	14%	15%	16%	17%	18%	19%	20%
1	0.901	0.893	0.885	0.877	0.870	0.862	0.855	0.847	0.840	0.833
2	1.713	1.690	1.668	1.647	1.626	1.605	1.585	1.566	1.547	1.528
3	2.444	2.402	2.361	2.322	2.283	2.246	2.210	2.174	2.140	2.106
4	3.102	3.037	2.974	2.914	2.855	2.798	2.743	2.690	2.639	2.589
5	3.696	3.605	3.517	3.433	3.352	3.274	3.199	3.127	3.058	2.991
6	4.231	4.111	3.998	3.889	3.784	3.685	3.589	3.498	3.410	3.326
7	4.712	4.564	4.423	4.288	4.160	4.039	3.922	3.812	3.706	3.605
8	5.146	4.968	4.799	4.639	4.487	4.344	4.207	4.078	3.954	3.837
9	5.537	5.328	5.132	4.946	4.772	4.607	4.451	4.303	4.163	4.031
10	5.889	5.650	5.426	5.216	5.019	4.833	4.659	4.494	4.339	4.192
11	6.207	5.938	5.687	5.453	5.234	5.029	4.836	4.656	4.486	4.327
12	6.492	6.194	5.918	5.660	5.421	5.197	4.988	4.793	4.611	4.439
13	6.750	6.424	6.122	5.842	5.583	5.342	5.118	4.910	4.715	4.533
14	6.982	6.628	6.302	6.002	5.724	5.468	5.229	5.008	4.802	4.611
15	7.191	6.811	6.462	6.142	5.847	5.575	5.324	5.092	4.876	4.675
16	7.379	6.974	6.604	6.265	5.954	5.668	5.405	5.162	4.938	4.730
17	7.549	7.120	6.729	6.373	6.047	5.749	5.475	5.222	4.990	4.775
18	7.702	7.250	6.840	6.467	6.128	5.818	5.534	5.273	5.033	4.812
19	7.839	7.366	6.938	6.550	6.198	5.877	5.584	5.316	5.070	4.843
20	7.963	7.469	7.025	6.623	6.259	5.929	5.628	5.353	5.101	4.870

Notes

Notes

Notes

Notes